1992

LIBERALISM AND
ITS CHALLENGERS

LIBERALISM AND ITS CHALLENGERS:

From F.D.R. to Bush

SECOND EDITION

Alonzo L. Hamby

New York   Oxford
OXFORD UNIVERSITY PRESS
1992

Oxford University Press

Oxford   New York   Toronto
Delhi   Bombay   Calcutta   Madras   Karachi
Petaling Jaya   Singapore   Hong Kong   Tokyo
Nairobi   Dar es Salaam   Cape Town
Melbourne   Auckland

and associated companies in
Berlin   Ibadan

Library of Congress Cataloging-in-Publication Data
Hamby, Alonzo L.
Liberalism and its challengers : from F.D.R. to Bush /
Alonzo L. Hamby. — 2nd ed.
p.   cm.   Includes bibliographical references and index.
ISBN 0-19-507029-1.
ISBN 0-19-507030-5 (pbk.)
1. United States—Politics and government—20th century.
2. Liberalism—United States—History—20th century.
3. Politicians—United States—Biography.
4. Presidents—United States—Biography.   I. Title.
E743.H237   1992
973.9—dc20   91-16469

2 4 6 8 9 7 5 3 1

Printed in the United States of America
on acid-free paper

For Three Who Taught Me:
John A. Garraty
Richard S. Kirkendall
William E. Leuchtenburg

Preface

I am gratified that the response to this book warrants a second edition. *Liberalism and Its Challengers* was originally completed in the early Reagan years when the challenge to the liberal tradition was at its peak and the eventual outcome still murky. With Ronald Reagan some two years out of the White House at the present writing, it is possible to deliver a full, if highly tentative, assessment of his years in office and their impact upon what remains the dominant outlook of American political culture—or at least of the elites who play so great a role in defining it.

Liberalism and Its Challengers employed biography as a vehicle for explaining the transformation of American politics over the past half-century. Its major themes, some of which may be clearer in retrospect than when I initially grappled with them, included the following propositions:

1. The presidential administration of Franklin D. Roosevelt established as the dominant theme of American politics a tradition of New Deal liberalism emphasizing welfare statism and government management of the economy; along with this came a commitment to large-scale international involvement built around the concept that American liberal values should be defended and extended in the larger world.

2. The new American purpose thus established derived its political support from the concomitant development of an opera-

tional political system of "pluralist liberalism" in which a political coalition was marshaled behind the liberal ideal through the distribution of benefits to a wide variety of groups.

3. In the 1960s, after about a generation of political dominance, the new liberalism found itself overloaded and disrupted because of an ambitious extension of its original themes, both domestic and international, and because of the addition of newer cultural objectives that transformed its meaning in ways unacceptable to key groups within the original pluralist liberal political coalition.

4. The original definition of the new liberalism, its changing content in the 1960s, and its eventual disruption all owed much to the growing political importance of the intelligentsia since 1933. Substantially enlarged in the years of postwar prosperity, given a vast constituency by the expansion of higher education that occurred after 1945, united by a substantial consensus critical of traditional cultural values and the capitalist ethic, the intellectual elite succeeded in establishing what might be called a "cultural hegemony" in American life by way of its dominance in education and communications.

5. Strong political leadership, whether charismatic or tactical, has been throughout American history critical in popularizing a political ideology and mobilizing support for it. It is this circumstance (I am tempted to say "fact") that justifies a biographical approach to the history of American politics, for leaders can rise and fall on the basis of individual personality characteristics unrelated to the substance of the issues they address.

6. The character of political leadership, moreover, has been transformed by the steadily increasing dominance of electronic communications in American politics since the 1930s. By fostering a sense of personal contact between candidate and voter, radio, then television, allowed politicians to bypass established political institutions that once had served crucial intermediating roles in American politics. The communications media gave the public something like a firsthand opportunity to evaluate its politicians, but it also established a certain degree of media mastery as a primary requisite of political leadership quite independent of the substantive issues that intellectuals like to see as the ultimate object of the political process.

7. Another development with its origins in the 1930s—the rise of scientific public opinion survey research—gave candi-

dates a surer sense than ever of the transient attitudes of their constituents on matters of wide concern. In the hands of a creative and sensitive leader, the polls could provide a sense of limits and define realistic parameters for action; to a more routine politician, they could fuel impulses to substitute pandering for leadership.

8. The personal confidence necessary for successful political leadership has in most cases come to an individual from sources outside politics, a notoriously insecure profession. In some cases, the sense of personal security that is a prerequisite to effective democratic leadership may be a matter of birthright, as with Franklin Roosevelt or John F. Kennedy; in others, it may be a product of career achievement before entering the political world, most spectacularly in the case of Dwight D. Eisenhower.

Seven years later, I see no reason to renounce any of these propositions; and in fact most are relatively commonplace. What gave the book some small claim to be a contribution to American political history was its effort to synthesize them. As I view my assertions neatly listed in near-Teutonic order, it is apparent that I was considerably more successful in dealing with some of them on a systematic basis than with others. Nevertheless, I have not been tempted to engage in a thoroughgoing revision of my text. For better or worse, the book has by now achieved an identity that should not be altered. I rather doubt, moreover, that it would be made more readable or otherwise improved by mechanical efforts at systematization.

There are, of course, some things I might do differently if I were starting with a clean slate. Above all, I would give fuller consideration to the transformation of liberalism in the 1960s. The Great Society seemed then in most ways a natural extension of the New Deal impulse; thanks to Barry Goldwater's candidacy in 1964, it escaped serious, thoughtful debate. The election that made it possible appeared little more than yet another mobilization of the pluralist liberal coalition that FDR had pulled together in the 1930s. My own caustic, albeit I believe fundamentally accurate, description of Lyndon Johnson's flawed personality appeared to imply to at least a couple of perceptive reviewers that when things began to go wrong, the cause was primarily rooted in LBJ rather than in the structure of a new style of liberalism that departed perceptibly from the New Deal–Fair Deal heritage in some of its guiding assumptions.

I did, it is true, point out the way in which what was left of the Socialist party had become a rather important part of the new liberalism; I called attention to the fashion in which the goal of equality of condition (social democracy) was beginning to displace the goal of equality of opportunity (liberal democracy); and I remarked on the unprecedentedly ambitious scale of the Great Society programs. Still if I were doing it over, I would discuss more thoroughly certain themes that I merely suggested. I would give greater attention to exploring the ways in which Great Society and post–Great Society liberalism came to represent the views of a newly empowered class of political intellectuals who combined a sense of moral mission with a rationalist faith in the social sciences. I also would lay greater emphasis on the ways in which the moral sense of the new liberalism on such issues as abortion, affirmative action, and America's mission in the world marked a departure from an old sensibility, tore liberalism loose from its political moorings in the blue-collar and lower-middle classes, and transformed the liberal political coalition into one precariously built on activist segments of the intelligentsia and demi-intelligentsia in alliance with various interest groups and minorities that have largely lost the sympathy of the wider public.

To some extent, I have attempted to fulfill that agenda in my discussion of Ronald Reagan, whose presidency may be seen in part as an effort to restore the earlier liberalism and in part as a revolution against more fundamental assumptions of the New Deal liberal tradition. I suggest that one reason the Reagan revolution never came to fruition was that neither Reagan nor most of his supporters had decided which of these objectives to pursue. Thus liberalism, however battered, retains its hegemony in American life, but at the expense of an increasing popular skepticism that does not bode well for its survival into our future.

I am indebted to Nancy Lane for her interest in a new edition of this work and even more for the supportive friendship that over the years has added so much to our professional relationship. As always, my wife, Joyce, facilitated this project in ways too numerous to mention. My colleagues at Ohio University, Charles Alexander, John Gaddis, Alfred Eckes, Lowell Gallaway, and Richard Vedder read the manuscript, as did Peri Arnold of the University of Notre Dame and John Kessel of Ohio State University. I appreciated their efforts, frequently took their advice, and am alone responsible for whatever dubious content remains.

I have retained the dedication that accompanied the first edition and welcome the opportunity to express my enduring gratitude to three mentors who taught me so much about writing history.

Athens, Ohio A. L. H.
June, 1991

Preface
to the First Edition

This book is an outgrowth of interests that long have engaged my attention: the ideological bases of American political conflict, political biography, and the techniques of political leadership. By focusing upon ten individuals of central importance in American politics from the Depression years to our own day, I have attempted to trace the development of all three themes in what might be called the contemporary period of American history. The effort was begun several years ago, and along the way I have found some of my own ideas in a state of development. If I seem to be writing primarily as a critic of the liberal tradition as it had evolved by the end of the 1960s, I hope it will be understood that I continue to admire its aspirations and its many accomplishments. I have, however, also come to believe that any ideological tradition, liberal or conservative, is prone to excesses and capable of losing contact with the realities of human nature that must in the end govern us all.

As this is primarily a work of synthesis, I must acknowledge first of all my indebtedness to the many fellow scholars whom I have cited in the bibliographical essay. I am grateful to Nancy Lane of the Oxford University Press, not simply for commissioning this book but even more for tolerating one delay after another with good humor and friendly support. Doris Dorr typed the manuscript with her customary efficiency. My wife, Joyce, has once

again given me invaluable help. My friends and colleagues
Charles C. Alexander and John L. Gaddis read the entire manuscript and improved it at more points than any of us care to
recall. Research for portions of this volume received generous
support from the Ohio University Research Committee and the
Harry S. Truman Library Institute.

Without meaning to burden them with any of its substance, I
have dedicated this book to three individuals who over the years
have provided me with knowledge, have given me unselfish
assistance and encouragement, have inspired me, and possibly
have even imparted to me a bit of their wisdom.

Athens, Ohio   A. L. H.
March, 1984

Contents

Contents

LIBERALISM AND
ITS CHALLENGERS

Introduction

This book rests on two convictions: that our history is profoundly affected by the style and character of our political leaders, and that they in turn must exercise their leadership inside the limits of a broad, deeply felt American consensus if they are to be effective. It attempts to examine through the medium of the biographical essay the development and maturation of a contemporary American political tradition and the accompanying rise of a new mode of political leadership within it. These processes, it seems to me, both effectively began with the presidency of Franklin D. Roosevelt, steadily gathered momentum in the quarter-century after World War II, and reached a culmination of sorts with the administration of Richard M. Nixon. To comprehend them is to understand a substantial portion of our national experience in the middle years of the twentieth century.

The era of Franklin D. Roosevelt was a turning point in American history. Exercising imaginative and charismatic leadership, Roosevelt changed popular conceptions about the purpose of American politics. His ultimate legacy was a political climate of opinion that would be sustained by the epoch of national power and affluence that followed his death. The new liberal tradition of social reform at home and energetic involvement overseas was consolidated by Harry S. Truman, elevated to the status of a national consensus by Dwight D. Eisenhower, expanded to a near breaking point by Lyndon Johnson, and largely accepted

3

by Richard Nixon as part of the synthesis of liberalism and conservativism that characterized his presidency.

Before FDR, the dominant American political tradition had been characterized by an overriding concern for property rights and entrepreneurial opportunity; it was individualistic in its assumptions about the nature of man and society and about the purposes of government. Its approach to foreign policy was nationalistic and, at least in the sense of avoiding diplomatic commitments outside the Western Hemisphere, isolationist. Within this broad framework, which had endured since the founding of the American Republic, there had existed room for vehement debate and harsh conflicts of interest, but there was virtually no leeway for argument about ideological basics.

The first major, if ultimately unsuccessful, challenge came with early twentieth-century progressivism. Numerous progressive reformers advocated social welfare legislation and asserted that the United States had become a world power with global interests and responsibilities. Yet many of them also looked toward the restoration of an atomistic, competitive society. A number of their leaders were isolationists. Progressivism undeniably faced in two directions; that it did not establish a distinct new tradition in American politics was in large measure the result of this fundamental ambivalence. With the election of Warren G. Harding in 1920, it was fragmented at the practical working level of American politics. It did, however, leave a substantial and enduring legacy to be drawn upon by the next challenge to the old order.

The New Deal made collectivist democratic liberalism the norm in American politics. Without explicitly repudiating the hallowed values of individualism and competition, it established a mixed, welfarist economy, accepted large-scale bureaucratic organization, and created an economic-political situation of countervailing powers. It emphasized the protection and promotion of civil liberties and civil rights even as it deemphasized property rights and entrepreneurial opportunity. Vastly enlarging the federal establishment, it created one new government agency after another, adding substantially to already established departments and making Washington the arbiter of major new areas of social and economic policy. Unavoidably, it brought into being a collection of bureaucracies that, however benign their purposes, however commendable the intentions of those who staffed them, exhibited the unpleasant tendencies of all bureaucracies—self-perpetuation, expansionism, impersonal routinization, the accumulation of power.

As World War II made relations with the rest of the world a central concern of American life, the New Deal tradition became internationalized. It envisioned a world role for the United States —active global leadership in the drive for a world community organized around liberal democratic values. From the Four Freedoms through the Truman and Eisenhower doctrines on into Vietnam, every American president would assert an urgent American mission that extended to every corner of the planet. Each would depict the United States as the world's foremost exponent of liberty and justice. Even Nixon, skeptical as he was about tender-minded univeralism, would feel compelled to cloak a realist frame of reference in the garb of liberal idealism.

The new liberal tradition won gradual, reluctant acceptance from a conservative opposition forced toward it by the imperatives of acquiring and keeping political power. The careers of Robert A. Taft and Joseph R. McCarthy demonstrated the futility —indeed the irrationality—of attacking the new consensus from the right; those of Eisenhower and Nixon displayed the tactical wisdom of accommodation. In consequence, from Roosevelt on, the momentum of American politics was in the direction of more liberalism. The New Deal and the Great Society were assuredly products of the same impulse, but Lyndon Johnson's agenda for America was far grander than FDR's. Martin Luther King, Jr., moreover, would show that it was possible for a determined, resourceful agitator-leader to operate on the fringes of the national consensus, so long as his purpose was to pull it to the left. As a result, the liberal tradition could find its limits only through the experience of excess, an experience that would come with startling rapidity in the 1960s when a remarkable confluence of unparalleled political victory and unequaled economic prosperity appeared to remove all barriers at home and abroad.

By the 1970s, after the disappointments of the Great Society and the Vietnam War, the process of expansion appeared for the foreseeable future to have run its course. A number of publicists and analysts who once had identified wholeheartedly with New

Deal-Great Society liberalism began to call themselves "neoconservatives" and to assume a stance as critics of hitherto-neglected negative aspects of a generation of reform: sentimentalism, bigbrotherism, excessive bureaucracy, waste, out-of-control budgets, endemic inflation, an economically debilitating tax structure, and the persistence—indeed, the seeming aggravation—of many social problems the Great Society liberals had promised to ameliorate.

The internationalist side of the liberal tradition had somehow degenerated into a ruinous adventure in Southeast Asia, leading to a widespread loss of confidence in the legitimacy of America's purpose in global politics and, on a smaller scale, a wave of neoisolationist sentiment that pointed toward withdrawal from the rest of the world. The election of Richard Nixon was largely a result of the confusion and fragmentation the liberals had inflicted upon themselves. It would signify not a wholesale repudiation but the beginning of an era of consolidation and reconsideration that would continue into the presidency of Ronald Reagan and mark the terminal point of a well-defined period in our political history.

II

Political leadership requires both the acquisition of power and the ability to wield it effectively once gained. While an individual's opportunities for political success are defined by the larger social-political situations in which he functions, it is ultimately within himself that he must find the resources to achieve power, exercise it constructively, and maintain it in the face of opposition.

The most crucial prerequisite is a sense of psychological security. Among the most successful American political figures of our time, one usually finds patterns of childhood and adolescence that contained little to breed insecurity. Their families were stable, and their parental relationships, especially those with their mothers, characterized by mutual fondness and maternal support. More often than not, incongruent though it is with the American success myth, they grew to maturity in financially solid families of upper-middle-class status or higher. Those who came from more modest homes usually managed to meet challenges and find success before making a career of politics. For the most part, their upbringing involved the systematic inculcation of a set of values that included personal honesty, hard work, and a sense of duty—the classic ideals of the inner-directed American. Yet most of them also developed the outlook of the other-directed man—a disposition toward tolerance, flexibility, and sensitivity to the needs of others. They reconciled within themselves both the traditional and the new in mid-twentieth-century American culture.

The political world that began with FDR imposed a crucial additional requirement—mastery of the newly dominant electronic communications media (first radio, then, after about 1960, television). Electronic communications went beyond the print media to transmit a direct, unfiltered sense of an individual's style and personality, thereby generating an instant emotional response from an audience whose needs, like those of all mankind, were for more than pure policy. Only the electronic media could bring to the American people a first-hand experience of FDR's jaunty optimism, Ike's fatherly reassurance, or JFK's cool glamour. Only they could establish a direct encounter with a leader's charisma; conversely, they alone could ruthlessly uncover intimations of self-doubt, uncertainty, or inarticulateness.

Radio and television allowed for more than the projection of an appealing personality. In the hands of a shrewd leader, they could be the vehicles for elemental, compelling political theater that dramatized issues in a direct, emotional way. The process matured with television, sometimes simply as slickly conceived commercials but more often as a vital yet shrewdly staged slice of real life featuring peaceful civil rights demonstrators confronting fascistic Southern police; youth and idealism, "neat and clean for Gene," mobilizing against war; or George C. Wallace "standing in the schoolhouse door" until forced aside by federal power, or later utilizing as evidence of the decadence of the liberal establishment long-haired hecklers at his campaign rallies. Such images exerted powerful influences upon individuals grappling to understand their society. Taken up by a mode of communications that sought drama as a way of holding viewer interest, they could have a politically transforming effect.

The rise of electronic communications coincided with and helped promote an important development in contemporary American social history—the growth in size and influence of the intellectual and professional groups, the intelligentsia. Idea people who functioned as writers, scholars, journalists, and, increasingly, as government administrators, they defined the American experience, imprinted their own vision of the country's needs upon the popular consciousness, and established themselves as the trend setters of American life. They could do so initially because the Great Depression effectively discredited the entrepreneurial-managerial ethic that had dominated American popular culture in the 1920s. They could prevail in the long run because the expansion of higher education after World War II created a vast "demi-intelligentsia" of middle-class professionals far more receptive to them than the noncollege, business-oriented middle classes of previous generations.

On matters of substantive public policy, the intelligentsia and its following tended to identify with the liberal tradition. Geographically mobile, independent-minded, and scornful of intense partisan attachments, they constituted a large new free-floating, quasi-alienated segment of American political society with few traditional institutional reference points. More than any other group, they were attuned to the more serious communications media, which they expected to reflect their styles and tastes and to which they looked for cues to their own behavior. The political leader who sought their allegiance would most likely gain it through effective use of the media.

Beyond this growing, special part of the population, there existed a larger public more established in its patterns of life and thought but also strongly affected by the power of electronic communications. For the first time in American history, the people as a whole could listen to, then see, political leaders on a day-to-day basis; increasingly, moreover, one could view them in situations that were not stage-managed and thus were apparently revelatory. Unavoidably, the result was to cut into the cueing processes once so nearly monopolized by the political party, the labor union, the business association, the religious affiliation, or the ethnic organization. People able to view the merchandise themselves necessarily would be more prone to make an independent choice.

Although radio began the process, the television age brought it to fruition and left the "old politics" suddenly more vulnerable than ever to assaults from outside the establishment. Stripped of almost every veil that once had separated them from the public, political leaders found that electronic media appearances, in every sense of the word, were crucial. Physical attractiveness helped, but even more important were such perceived qualities as idealism, emotional strength, and decisiveness. Those who were uneasy with television and unable to project their better qualities over it found their authority, and their careers, in jeopardy. Those who could employ it effectively might camouflage their weaknesses and move beyond their natural level. As in other aspects of American life, the medium verged on becoming the message it ostensibly had been created to deliver.

While mastery of the media might increasingly displace the more traditional means of gaining office, it was less likely to become a dependable basis for governing. Appeals to the unorganized masses tended to run counter to the web of allegiances and values required for viable day-to-day leadership. The ability to gain election was after all only the first test of political leadership; the ultimate tests involved the achievement of goals in the pursuit of the public welfare—the passage of legislation, the successful establishment and administration of new policies, the effective conduct of diplomacy in the national interest. Charisma and idealism, however vital as media qualities, could not substitute for the brokerage functions of political captaincy—the gathering of organized group support, the striking of compromises, the skepticism about political absolutes that stemmed from private bargaining with one's public enemies. The most durable and important political leaders of the contemporary era were those from Roosevelt on who managed to combine media mastery with brokerage skills and to reconcile with seeming effortlessness whatever contradictions existed between the two.

At bottom, however, the first essential of successful political leadership remained an ability to perceive the dominant needs of an era and to align oneself with them. Roosevelt achieved greatness because he understood, however imperfectly, that his country needed a change of direction. Of those who followed him, the least successful were those who dedicated themselves to halting the trends he set in motion; the most successful were those who accommodated in one fashion or another. In politics, as in other professions, a grasp of technique was in itself no substitute for substance as a basis for long-term success.

III

The writing of contemporary history is at best a difficult business. To their engagement with the issues of the past, historians as political beings inevitably bring their present-day commitments. The very recent past is too close to us to allow the easy development of a sense of dealing with a distinctively different period, possessing its peculiar values and priorities. The impression of sameness obscures important contrasts, blocks efforts at detachment, invites scholars to vent their political beliefs, and encourages a literature of praise or condemnation (more frequently the latter). A singularly unproductive dialogue of accusation versus defense has dominated the political historiography of the contemporary period. More often than not, a penchant for judgment has taken priority over a quest for understanding.

Historians assuredly should feel free to make moral evaluations; however, they need to do so with a greater sense of perspective than has been the case in the liberal-center versus left-radical argumentation that dominates American historical thinking on the post–World War II period. The channeling of historical inquiry into two rather narrow streams and a consequent typing of scholarship has led to a stultification of thought rather than illumination of the dynamics of the era.

Our efforts at understanding have also been hindered by our very human tendency to expect those about whom we write to be much as we imagine ourselves to be—intellectuals dedicated to principled consistency and to the pursuit of truth. Yet the practice of politics allows little time for contemplation and extensive reading, provides scant opportunity for the rigorous application of ideas to real-world situations, and places a premium upon action over thought. Politics demands flexibility, even backtracking; accommodation to conflicting interests and pressures requires movement, not fixed positioning. These demands in turn grow from a larger democratic political culture that expects leaders to be responsive to the wishes and needs of their followers.

Of course, we all know in the abstract that political leaders have different thought patterns and career imperatives, but we frequently fail to incorporate that knowledge into our writing. We have an instinctive aversion to the unprincipled, manipulative aspects of the politician's role; however justified that aversion may be, it gets in the way of our scholarship.

Understanding does not preclude disagreement or condemnation. It does require that we know how our subjects perceived themselves; it also requires that we know their world and accept it as it was, not as we would have preferred it to be. Scholars need not shrink from judgment, but it is among the least of their obligations. Their primary purpose is to explain the world they study and those who inhabit it. By almost any standard, the preeminent political figures of the contemporary era were extraordinary individuals—in their personalities, their talents, their achievements, and, in some instances, their flaws of character. Our task must be to explain their powers as well as to lament their deficiencies.

1

The Founding Father:
Franklin D. Roosevelt

Governor Roosevelt, wrote the eminent columnist Walter Lippmann in January 1932, was not to be taken seriously: "An amiable man with many philanthropic impulses, but . . . not the dangerous enemy of anything . . . no crusader . . . no tribune of the people . . . no enemy of entrenched privilege . . . a pleasant man who, without any important qualifications for the office, would very much like to be President." Lippmann's evaluation was to become the most frequently quoted example of the perils of punditry in the history of American journalism. But when it appeared it was just another expression of a widely held assessment of Franklin D. Roosevelt, written at a time when it was still possible to assume that his determined optimism and issue-straddling were the marks of a lightweight who by some accident had twice been elected governor of the nation's largest state.

By the time of FDR's death, four presidential election victories later, Lippmann's condescending dismissal was an object of ridicule. Roosevelt had become the focus of intense emotions, united in agreement only on his standing as a moving force in history. To his enemies, he represented evil incarnate—socialism and communism, dictatorship, war. To his admirers, he was an object of worship—the champion of the underprivileged, the symbol of the world struggle of democratic, humanist civilization against the darkness of fascism. Millions wept at his passing.

Roosevelt had in fact profoundly changed the nature of American politics. Although he failed to achieve many of his most important immediate objectives, although he was notoriously eclectic and nonsystematic in his approach to the enormous problems of his era, FDR was the founder of a distinctively new tradition which was to preempt the mainstream of American politics after his death.

Like all great departures in American politics, the Rooseveltian political tradition had deep roots in the past, specifically in the progressivism of Theodore Roosevelt and Woodrow Wilson, and generally in the optimism of a more innocent epoch. It was Roosevelt who achieved the actual implementation of what had been in many instances little more than abstract concepts formulated by earlier progressives, added to them—however unwittingly—Keynesian economics, and encased the whole package within a framework of "pluralist" or interest-group liberalism. And it was Roosevelt who fused the diplomatic realism of his cousin Theodore with the idealism of his old leader Woodrow Wilson in such a way that the American nation was irreversibly committed to active participation in a world it had largely shunned.

To all this, he added a new *style* of political leadership scarcely less important than the substantive changes he achieved. After Roosevelt, the most consistently successful American politicians were not those who relied upon the increasingly decrepit political machines or employed old-fashioned press agentry. They were those who mastered mid-twentieth-century mass communications to impart a sense of direct contact with the people. Like many political leaders of the highest historical rank, Roosevelt was great both because of what he did and how he did it.

The Man Behind the Masks

To be born and raised a Roosevelt in the penultimate decade of the nineteenth century was to discover the world in an environment of remarkable privilege and security. It was the quaint world of an American patrician aristocracy, a setting of Hudson River mansions, European vacations, private tutors, ponies, and loving, attentive parents. Moderately wealthy, possessing blood lines running back to the *Mayflower*, esteemed by the arbiters of society, still prominent in business and finance, the Roosevelts and the class they represented were on the whole free from the taints of greed, irresponsibility, vulgarity, and conspicuous consumption that the popular mind attributed to the *nouveaux riches* of the period.

Perhaps no other segment of American society so fully accepted and synthesized the dominant values and hopes of Western civilization at the high noon of the Victorian era. The young Franklin Roosevelt absorbed a climate of opinion characterized by belief in the near-inevitability of progress; the unquestioned superiority of Anglo-American liberalism; the imperative of duty to one's friends, family, church, and country; and the unimpeachable character of traditional moral standards. The Victorian world view imparted to those who accepted it an ebullient confidence and an unquenchable optimism.

The close, attentive world in which Roosevelt lived as a child provided little of the experience that one usually associates with the building of leadership. His vigorous, domineering mother both doted on him and attempted to make all his decisions up through the early years of his marriage. From a very young age, however, he managed to establish his individuality in a smothering atmosphere. He developed a calculating other-directedness based on an understanding that he could secure his own autonomy and achieve his own objectives only by seeming to be the type of person that others—his mother, his schoolmates, his political associates—wanted him to be.

At the exclusive Groton preparatory school, at Harvard, and at Columbia Law School, he was never more than a respectable scholar. He preferred instead to concentrate on the nonacademic activities that he knew would win him the recognition of his peers. He stayed on as a nominal graduate student at Harvard only to be eligible to assume the editorship of the *Crimson* and never bothered to complete his M.A. A marginal law student, he dropped out of Columbia after passing the state bar examinations although he was but a few months away from his degree. His intelligence was keen and his interests wide-ranging, but he felt a certain amiable contempt for the world of academic scholarship and indeed for almost any sustained, disciplined intellectual effort.

The appearance he presented to the world was that of a young man conventionally handsome, somewhat overeager for popularity, and determined to suppress the cerebral aspects of his personality. Girls who knew him as a college student called him "feather duster" and "the handkerchief-box young man." Many of his male acquaintances found him unimpressive. Indeed, Porcellian, the elite Harvard club of his father and of Theodore Roosevelt, rejected his candidacy for membership.

Largely because of his name and social position, young Roosevelt was taken into a prestigious Wall Street law firm. Establishing himself as a competent young attorney, he faced a secure, well-defined future in which he would move up from clerk to junior partner to senior partner, earning an increasingly lucrative income and spending his weekends as a country gentleman. Yet he possessed little interest in so confined and comfortable a life. In a rare moment of open introspection, he told some of his fellow clerks that he intended to go into politics and that he would follow precisely in the footsteps of his distant cousin, Theodore Roosevelt—from the state assembly to the assistant secretaryship of the navy to the governorship of New York to the presidency. It is hard to say how serious he was, and it is uncertain whether he actually had acquired the toughness and ambition that would eventually take him to the top. It is safe to say that he had been caught up in the idealism of early-twentieth-century reform.

The progressive movement that dominated American life in the first and second decades of the century was actually several reform movements representing different social groups, drawing upon diverse political philosophies, and pursuing divergent objectives. At its heart, however, was a rejection of the unfettered industrial capitalism of the late nineteenth century and a sense of concern for the victims of its abuses. As such, it had a special appeal to the somewhat displaced younger members of older socially prominent families such as the Roosevelts. Assuming that the American system would respond to pressures for gradual change, progressivism appealed to the Victorian optimism on which Roosevelt had been nurtured. It was made irresistible by the example of young FDR's Theodore Roosevelt, long hero, then his uncle-in-law when Franklin married Eleanor Roosevelt.

FDR's early political career followed a progression along the lines he had projected to his fellow law clerks; it moved also from a shallow amateurism to a deep professionalism. Nominated for the state assembly in 1910 by a local Democratic organization that did not take him seriously, he campaigned intensively, frequently speaking to small groups from an open touring car. His nervousness and inexperience displayed themselves in awkward pauses as he tried to remember his lines or groped for something to say to the farmers who came to hear him. Roosevelt's district was strongly Republican, but he capitalized on a national surge of discontent with the inept administration of William Howard Taft. He had the advantage of the Roosevelt name, and he employed incessant denunciations of "bossism" to identify himself with the GOP insurgent movement that looked to Theodore Roosevelt for inspiration. His victory was one of many Democratic upsets around the country.

In Albany, Roosevelt quickly made himself the leader of a small group of Democratic dissenters determined to block the election of a Tammany senatorial candidate. He held the quixotic movement together for two months, using his name and his already considerable talent for drawing attention to himself to garner national recognition. He made an ultimate defeat seem somehow a victory for political virtue, but he and his followers had exemplified only the shallow side of progressivism.

To many upper-middle-class Yankee reformers, Tammany Hall was simply a corrupt, Irish-Catholic political machine engaging in every manner of boodle and sustaining its power by buying the votes, one way or another, of illiterate immigrants. This attitude was true enough as far as it went, but incomplete and a shade bigoted. It showed little awareness of the social conditions to which the machine addressed itself through an informal but well-organized system of assistance to the poor and through increasing support of social welfare legislation. Moreover, Tammany produced men of substance (among them Roosevelt's legislative colleagues Robert F. Wagner and Alfred E. Smith)—honest, creative, and equipped by their own experience to understand the problems of the urban masses far more vividly than could an upstate neophyte. For the next two years, Roosevelt played the role of gadfly to Tammany, delighting his own district but needlessly making enemies of the powers within the Democratic party.

Had this been the sum of his politics, he doubtless would have gone the way of many a good government reformer of the time, enjoying a brief period of influence and attention followed by a long exile on the fringes of American public life. He was, however, capable of growth. Some of his "good government" causes, such as a bill to establish an honest, efficient state highway commission, were more soundly based. His progressivism gradually moved in other directions also: women's suffrage, conservation, public control of electrical power, workmen's compensation, and regulation of hours and working conditions in mines and factories. By the end of his second year in the legislature, Roosevelt had loosely identified himself with a style of progressivism that moved across the spectrum of reform causes. In doing so, he had paralleled the evolution of his revered kinsman, TR. Established as a noted, if not powerful, New York Democrat, he needed only the right bit of good fortune to move onto the national scene.

Remarkably, his advancement stemmed from the ostentatious insurgency that normally would have made him unelectable to any statewide office. Displaying sound instinct, he attached himself to a new national progressive figure destined to eclipse Theodore Roosevelt—Woodrow Wilson. Although he could deliver no votes, FDR served as an attractive spokesman for the New Jersey governor and became identified as one of his major New York supporters. Wilson's victory would bring the isolated young insurgent to Washington.

It was far from coincidental that he took the post of assistant secretary of the navy. He might have obtained other powerful positions—collector of the Port of New York or assistant secretary of the treasury, for example—but the navy position was yet another step along TR's old path. Moreover, it gave Roosevelt a chance to wield power and influence on a large scale. It was an extraordinary opportunity for a man who loved ships and the sea and who from his student days had been a disciple of the great advocate of naval power, Admiral Alfred Thayer Mahan.

As assistant secretary of the navy, young FDR functioned as the second-ranking official in the department and was primarily responsible for its day-to-day administration. Like his cousin before him, Roosevelt was the official who actually managed the navy: his chief, Josephus Daniels, was a small-town North Carolina progressive chosen for his devotion to the ideals of the New Freedom and for his influence with Southern congressmen rather than for any knowledge of military matters.

In most respects, Roosevelt's performance was excellent. The coming of World War I made his office even more important than he could have anticipated, and he contributed significantly to the American military victory. Possessing more knowledge of technical naval matters and better read in the strategy of sea power than perhaps any other high civilian official in Washington, he was also a strong and effective administrator, audacious in the exercise of his authority, receptive to new ideas, daring in his own strategic concepts. He delighted in cutting red tape to facilitate one procurement operation after another; almost single-handedly, he overcame the opposition of both the entire British Admiralty and many of his own officers to secure the laying of a massive anti-submarine mine barrage across the North Sea.

He learned much, too. He established relationships with the ranking naval officials of the Allied powers, with important business executives, and with labor union leaders in the shipyards. He gained a sense of the contours of international diplomacy and developed the art of dealing with powerful interest groups. A key figure in a federal bureaucracy attempting to manage a national crisis, he received firsthand training in the use of governmental power to create a feeling of national purpose.

He also absorbed lessons of another sort. Still playing the role of insurgent, he had allowed his name to be entered in the 1914 New York Democratic senatorial primary as the anti-Tammany candidate. The machine had countered masterfully, backing President Wilson's widely respected ambassador to Germany, James W. Gerard, who won by a margin approaching 3 to 1. FDR quickly moved toward a rapprochement; by 1917, he was the featured speaker at the Tammany Fourth of July celebration, posing amiably with Boss Murphy for the photographers. Soon the organization indicated its willingness to accept him as a unity candidate for governor.

Instead, he was an attractive vice-presidential candidate in 1920—young, able, nationally known, a resident of the largest state in the union. Among the Democratic rank and file, and especially among young intellectuals and activists, his nomination was popular. Handsome, vigorous, and by this time a skilled public speaker, he toured the country, delivering perhaps a thousand speeches. He attracted about as much attention as his running mate, James Cox, and made hundreds of personal contacts with the state and local leadership of the Democratic party from Massachusetts to California. When he and Cox went under in the Harding landslide, few would ever again tender Cox serious attention. But somehow Roosevelt seemed to speak for the future of the party. He alone had emerged from the debacle in a position of strength, possessing greater public recognition than ever and having obtained a first-hand knowledge of the structure of the Democratic party.

In such circumstances, it seemed especially tragic that in 1921, at the age of thirty-nine, he incurred a crippling attack of polio that promised to end his active political career. It is unquestionable that Roosevelt's suffering—both physical and psychological—was enormous. The ordeal may have deepened his character, giving him a greater sense of identification with the unfortunate of the world and strengthening his resolve. It was an existential challenge from which he emerged triumphant in spirit if not in body. Despite intensive physical therapy over a period of several years, he never regained the use of his legs. But he achieved a feat of self-definition against the will of his mother, who expected him to settle down under her wing to the life of an invalid country gentleman, and against that current of American political culture that expects political leaders to be specimens of perfect health. He quickly decided to stay in politics and to continue to pursue his ultimate goal, the presidency. From the perspective of that decision, his personal tragedy was political good fortune.

Polio removed Roosevelt from active political competition in an era in which the Democratic party was in a state of disintegration, effectively subdued by the economic successes of Republican normalcy and torn by bitter dissension between urban and rural factions led by Alfred E. Smith and William Gibbs McAdoo. Engaging instead in numerous charitable and civic activities, ostentatiously maintaining an interest in the future of his party, and carefully keeping lines open to both its wings, he remained a public figure and functioned, in Frank Freidel's phrase, as a "young elder statesman." The most elementary dictates of political loyalty required him to align himself with his fellow New

Yorker Smith, but he did so in a way that could have antagonized
only the most fanatical McAdoo supporter. His 1924 nominating
speech for Smith was an attention-getting formal return to politics
and the most universally praised event of an intensely bitter
Democratic convention. He steadfastly avoided name-calling and,
after the disastrous Democratic defeat in November, he sent out a
letter to every convention delegate asking for suggestions on the
regeneration of the party. In this and other ways, he reminded the
rank and file of his probable eventual availability as the man who
could unify them, and yet he could bide his time.

Roosevelt's paralysis was fortunate in another way. In common with the leaders of both wings of his party, he was unable to
offer compelling alternatives to Republican normalcy. Throughout the twenties, he attempted in a general way to identify himself
with the heritage of Wilsonian liberalism and internationalism; yet
his specific activities were much in tune with the conservative
Republican business ethos of the twenties. He was vice-president
of an important bonding firm, head of a construction trade association, and a speculative plunger in his private finances. He talked
of the need to construct a progressive platform for the party, but
he seldom got beyond fuzzy generalizations. Much of the political
criticism he fired off at the Republicans appeared carping and
nit-picking. He admitted as much when he declined in 1928 to
compose a political attack on his "old personal friend," Herbert
Hoover.

That same year, Roosevelt benefited from another stroke of
unlikely political luck—he was drafted for the Democratic gubernatorial nomination in what seemed certain to be a Republican
year. Pressed into the race by the presidential candidate, Al Smith,
who realized that Roosevelt's name on the ticket would be a great
help in upstate New York, he eked out a narrow victory. Smith,
nonetheless, lost the state badly to Hoover. Roosevelt had established himself as New York's senior Democrat, and his new office
was generally considered in those days to be the best jumping-off
position for a presidential nomination. At the end of his first year
as governor, with the national economy dropping sharply down-
ward, that jumping-off position began to look much more valuable
than either he or Smith could have imagined in mid-1928.

Roosevelt was a strong and effective governor, although his tenure, inhibited by constant political warfare with a Republican legislature, was more important for what it attempted than for what it accomplished. Under the pressures of political responsibility and economic distress, Roosevelt's vague progressivism began to take on a more definite shape. He pushed strongly for conservation, public development of hydroelectric facilities on the St. Lawrence River, rural electrification, help for the hard-pressed farmer, and work relief projects for the unemployed. He surrounded himself with able, liberal-minded aides—Samuel I. Rosenman, Harry Hopkins, Frances Perkins. He developed his strongest grasp yet of public relations. Press releases and news handouts spewed from his office and got his viewpoint into many Republican papers. He took highly visible inspection trips that carried him around the state from one institution or project to another. Most importantly, he made superb use of the newest and most important medium of mass communication since the invention of the printing press—the radio. Undertaking a series of "fireside chats," he established himself as one of the few public figures of the era who instinctively knew how to project his personality over the airwaves. Roosevelt swept to a resounding reelection victory in 1930, establishing himself as the dominant contender for the Democratic presidential nomination in 1932.

The nomination was nonetheless a near thing. Facing the then-hallowed rule of the Democratic party that a nominee required a two-thirds majority of the convention votes, he nearly fell to a "stop Roosevelt" alliance of candidates ranging from his former ally Smith to the one-time Wilsonian Newton D. Baker to the crusty old Southern conservative John Nance Garner of Texas. His opponents had only one thing in common: they all lacked the ideological flexibility to deal with the economic crisis America faced by 1932. Roosevelt went over the top, just as his support was on the verge of disintegration, by making a deal to give Garner the vice-presidency.

Victory in November was certain, and he took no chances in the campaign. He made it clear that his presidency would depart sharply from the policies of Herbert Hoover, that he had no respect for outmoded tradition, that he would, as he put it, give the nation "a New Deal." He ostentatiously put together a "Brains Trust" of advisers headed by three of the country's foremost political economists—Raymond Moley, Adolf A. Berle, Jr., and Rexford G. Tugwell. Still, he presented no coherent platform. His pronouncements hit both sides of some issues and approached others in the most general terms. Faced with two sharply opposing drafts of what was to be a major address on tariff policy, he was capable of telling his speechwriters to "weave the two together." He defeated Hoover by seven million votes.

The New Dealer

Like most politicians, Roosevelt had followed a path to success based upon an appealing style and a mastery of political techniques. Any effort to stake out a fixed, precise ideological position probably would have been politically counterproductive. But the American political and economic systems faced an unprecedented situation that seemed to demand rigorous analysis and reevaluation. The collapse of the economy during the Hoover years, the quantum increases in the unemployment rolls, the mortgage foreclosures that afflicted small-scale farmers and middle-class homeowners alike, the crops that went unharvested for lack of a market, the collapse of the banking system, the rapidly spreading misery and deprivation that attended the lack of any decent government aid for the unfortunate—all added up to the worst crisis of capitalism in American history.

Marxist solutions were unacceptable in America, even during the worst part of the Depression. The other reform alternative, the American progressive tradition to which Roosevelt loosely subscribed, had been forged during a time of general prosperity and was torn between conflicting economic visions of competition and concentration. Intellectually, progressives were almost as unprepared for the appalling disaster as Hoover had been. It is hardly surprising that Roosevelt and those around him met the challenge of depression with a curious blend of halfway measures, irrelevant reforms, and inconsistent attitudes.

Roosevelt sensed that the American people in 1933 wanted action above all, backed by displays of confidence and optimism. In his inaugural address, he exhorted America to fear nothing but fear itself. Invariably, he maintained a buoyant appearance, exemplified by his calculated cheerfulness or by the jaunty angle of his cigarette holder. Comparing himself to a quarterback who would call the next play only after the present one had been run, he made no pretense of working from a fixed design. Instead, he simply announced that his objectives would be relief, reform, and recovery. He pursued them with a bewildering cluster of programs that left no doubt of the government's concern for the plight of its citizens and of the administration's activism.

Relief was the easiest goal to pursue. By the time Roosevelt took office, poverty seemed on the way to becoming the normal condition of life for a majority of Americans. Facing a sea of human misery, untroubled by ideological inhibitions against federal aid to the needy, the Roosevelt administration swiftly instituted public works jobs, mortgage relief legislation, farm price supports, and federal insurance for bank deposits—programs aimed directly at the plight of the individual who had been hit in one way or another by the Depression.

By contemporary standards, it is true, these efforts were relatively modest. Moreover, Roosevelt fretted constantly about their cost, and, while accepting them as a necessity, he never allowed them to be expanded sufficiently to provide jobs for the majority of the unemployed. All the same, most people who received some sort of help—a WPA job, a refinanced mortgage, a AAA acreage allotment check—were grateful in a direct personal way.

Reform posed a more difficult problem. In his own experience as an admirer of TR's New Nationalism and a participant in Wilson's New Freedom, Roosevelt embodied the two conflicting main lines of progressive thought, neither of which had been formulated to address the problem of recovery from an economic depression. The debate at bottom was between the TR–Herbert Croly vision of a political economy that accepted the dominance of the large corporation and sought to regulate it in the public interest and the Wilson–Louis Brandeis faith in an atomistic, intensely competitive economic society. The New Deal's resolution of the argument would in the end amount to little more than an evasion of choice.

The most permanent and successful items of the New Deal reform agenda were not specifically directed at Depression-created problems but had some of the appearance of relief acts. During the progressive era, reformers had reached a substantial consensus on the need for social legislation to provide ongoing protection to the working classes and the disadvantaged. The Social Security Act of 1935 established a national system of old-age insurance and committed the federal government to extensive subsidies for state welfare programs. The act marked a revolution in federal responsibility for the welfare of the needy. It quickly became politically unassailable, and over the next generation its coverage and benefits grew steadily.

Much the same process occurred with regard to agriculture. With the immediate objective of fighting the Depression, the New Deal introduced an extensive and quasi-permanent system of benefits and subsidies for rural America. For the cash-crop farmer and the agrarian middle class, the administration produced a series of devices aimed at achieving profitable market prices (most important among them acreage allotments and federal purchase of surpluses). Roosevelt seems to have considered the price support program a temporary expedient, but his hopes that agriculture could become self-sufficient ran up against reality. By his second term, Secretary of Agriculture Henry A. Wallace was justifying long-term buying of surpluses by proclaiming the goal of an "ever-normal granary."

Price supports were only the centerpiece of the New Deal agricultural program. Other aspects, such as rural electrification and soil conservation, were largely successful attempts to enhance the quality of life on the land. Through the Resettlement Administration and the Farm Security Administration, the New Deal undertook the first important attack in American history on the structure of rural poverty. The agencies delivered assistance of one variety or another to the forgotten classes of the agricultural community—the impoverished dirt farmers, the sharecroppers, the migrant laborers. Their aid and rehabilitation programs sought to transform an agrarian *lumpenproletariat* into a self-sufficient yeomanry.

The results were mixed. Price support programs probably saved the average farmer from liquidation but failed to produce real prosperity; electrification and conservation brought firm gains to individuals and the land; the antipoverty efforts, underfunded stepchildren, were less successful. But in the guise of fighting the Depression, the New Deal had put the federal government into agriculture on a vast scale and a permanent basis.

The same was true of the labor programs. From the beginning, the New Deal endorsed the right of collective bargaining, and from 1933 on, union leaders told prospective recruits, "President Roosevelt wants you to join the union." Roosevelt actually had little personal enthusiasm for militant unionism. It was nonetheless a force that drew special sustenance from the New Deal's general endorsement of social change and fair play for the underdog. The Wagner Act of 1935 was not introduced at Roosevelt's behest, but it won his endorsement as it moved through Congress. The new law projected the federal government into labor-management relations in ways that would have been unimaginable just a few years earlier. It established procedures by which unions could win recognition from management, prohibited certain anti-union practices by employers, and set up a strong, permanent bureaucracy (the National Labor Relations Board) to provide continuing enforcement. For workers at the lowest, usually non-unionized levels of American business, the Fair Labor Standards Act of 1938 established nationwide wage and hour standards, prohibited child labor, and provided strict rules for the employment of teenagers.

In providing help to a blue-collar work force that had been hit hard by the Depression, the New Deal had effected long-term changes whose significance could barely be grasped as the thirties came to an end. Organized labor had emerged as a major force within the Democratic party, providing the campaign support Roosevelt and his followers needed to stay in power. The members of its unions would constitute the bulk of the additions to the post–World War II middle class.

Reform of the banking system, accompanied as it was by federal deposit insurance, was both relief for the "little people" who had lost their savings in bank failures and retribution against the bankers. Regulation of the securities markets, long overdue, was widely accepted as a form of discipline against the financiers who had encouraged irresponsible stock market practices during the twenties and thereby, it was widely (if erroneously) believed, brought on the Depression. An effort at establishing a more steeply graduated tax system, the so-called Wealth Tax Act of 1935, could achieve broad support as a way of striking at a class that had exhibited indifference to economic suffering.

The Tennessee Valley Authority, the most unique and in many ways the most radical of New Deal innovations, was an expression of Roosevelt's fullest progressive aspirations. Combining flood control, conservation, and public ownership of electrical power, it functioned in the short run as another work relief project but in the long run it was the most ambitious effort at regional economic planning ever undertaken in the United States. By almost any standard, the TVA was a resounding success. It tamed the destructive Tennessee River, encouraged sound land use practices, generated inexpensive power for homes and industries, and contributed greatly to the prosperity of the Tennessee Basin area. Yet it was never duplicated in any other region of the United States, nor did it become a model for the New Deal's approach to the American economy. These nonevents were indicative both of the American political system's resistance to sweeping change and of a split within the progressive mind over what may have been the central problem posed by the Great Depression—the organization of the American economy.

Roosevelt himself had always been primarily attracted to the New Nationalism of his kinsman, and the experience of World War I had reinforced this inclination. His natural impulse upon coming to power was to mobilize the nation in a great crusade against the Depression, much as the country had been mobilized against Germany in 1917. The economic corollary of such an effort was central management of the economy, and the New Deal's first mechanism for industrial recovery, the National Recovery Administration (NRA), was patterned closely upon the experience of the World War I War Industries Board. Quite in line with that experience, the NRA did much more than impose responsibilities upon the business community; it recognized business management as a legitimate and responsible sector of the American political economy and extended substantial benefits to it. NRA regulations, purposely mislabeled "codes of fair competition," actually stifled competition and in many instances sanctioned such cartel practices as production quotas, allocation of marketing territories, and price-fixing. The NRA represented in its way both the New Nationalism and a style of broker politics with which Roosevelt began his presidency. Had it been successful in overcoming the Depression, the words *New Deal* might today conjure up the image of a relatively moderate reform movement at war with no segment of American society.

The NRA failed for a host of reasons, some of them conceptual, some of them political. It failed to address what now appears to have been the central malady of the Depression, the liquidation of consumer spending power; in fact, its price-fixing approach actually made that problem worse. It was not sufficiently coordinated with the work relief programs, which could have injected much more money into the economy had they been managed less cautiously. It collapsed to some extent of its own weight as its frenetic head, Hugh Johnson, traveled about the country attempting to organize every mom-and-pop enterprise in sight and wildly overpromising what his agency could accomplish. By late 1934, Johnson had suffered a nervous breakdown, and the agency was washed up. Liberals decried its concessions to business; yet the business community displayed little support for it. In the spring of 1935, the Supreme Court ruled the NRA unconstitutional, dredging up a seldom-invoked sanction against excessive delegation of legislative authority by the Congress and reverting to a hyper-restrictive interpretation of the government's authority to regulate interstate commerce. Economically, politically, and constitutionally, the NRA had reached a dead end—and so had the idea of central management of the economy.

Roosevelt and those who now became the dominant economic thinkers of his administration turned to the other readymade alternative the progressive tradition had created for them—antitrustism. It was a natural move for an administration that had become bitter over persistent hostility from the business establishment. The Wheeler-Rayburn Public Utility Holding Company Act of 1935 struck an important blow at private consolidation in a key American industry. The Antitrust Division of the Department of Justice under Robert Jackson and then Thurman Arnold became larger and more active than ever. In Congress, administration supporters secured the establishment of a special Temporary

National Economic Committee (TNEC), which over several years undertook a massive study of the problem of consolidation and anticompetitive activities in the American economy.

Yet antitrustism, while it might be a valuable component of a program designed primarily to restore consumer purchasing power, did not directly address the urgent problem of the Depression. Moreover, it was not consistently applied. Here and there, in the railroad and coal industries, for example, centralized regulation continued dominant. And in order to protect small retailers, "fair trade laws" sanctioned price-fixing for many consumer items. The antitrust effort was directed more against specific abuses than against the fundamental structure of American big business. The TNEC became an academic enterprise that produced a shelf of scholarly monographs but no meaningful legislation. Far from resolving the conflict that existed in the progressive mind, the New Deal had simply acted it out. In part, this reflected Roosevelt's own uncertainty; but it also exemplified the mood of a nation that since the beginnings of modern American industrialism had feared the growth of the large corporation while lusting after its supposed economic benefits.

This ultimate inability to arrive at a coherent strategy for dealing with the structure of the American economy leads one finally to the most conspicuous failure of the New Deal—it never achieved a full economic recovery. It is easy today to pick out some of the reasons; any above-average undergraduate economics student can recite what might be called the Keynesian critique of Roosevelt's leadership. The fundamental task of the New Deal, so the argument runs, had to be the reconstruction of consumer purchasing power. The surest and most direct way of accomplishing this objective was through massive government spending. Because the unemployment problem was so horrendous, the amount of federal economic stimulus would have to be enormous and the federal budget deficits unprecedented. But once most Americans were back at work, paying off old debts and spending money on all manner of consumer goods, a prosperous economy would be able to maintain itself, federal tax revenues would roll in, and the budget deficits would become surpluses.

In addition to its economic merits, the Keynesian approach promised the political dividends that would accrue from even higher levels of relief spending. Yet Roosevelt disregarded the Keynesian argument. He did not fully understand it, and it was incompatible with his personality. "A Keynesian solution," James MacGregor Burns has written, "involved an almost absolute commitment, and Roosevelt was not one to commit himself absolutely to any political or economic method." The result was a halfway Keynesianism that failed to provide a full cure for a desperately sick economy and yet outraged conservative sentiment. And even this policy was inconsistent. In 1937, with economic recovery having reached at best an intermediate stage far short of prosperity, Roosevelt ordered cutbacks in government spending and attempted to balance the budget. A disastrous recession ensued; there were months of hesitation, then a return to the old halfway spending levels. Roosevelt, the Keynesian argument concludes, had failed as an economist, and his failure had prolonged the Depression.

Roosevelt's "failure," if it can be called such, becomes more understandable when one recalls that Keynesian doctrine was extraordinarily novel, that John Maynard Keynes was an Englishman heretofore known to liberal Democrats as an acidic critic of Woodrow Wilson and the Treaty of Versailles, and that his major theoretical writings were all but impenetrable to the layman until they began to be popularized near the end of the thirties. The Keynesian revolution in economics was similar in a sense to the Freudian revolution in psychology—an affront to conventional wisdom stoutly resisted by establishment thinkers. Roosevelt was flexible and experimental, but acceptance of Keynes required a reorientation of one's most fundamental views on the nature of economic society, just as acceptance of Freud required a totally new conception of the human psyche. The hectic political world of Depression Washington was hardly the place for such exercises.

The failure to achieve economic recovery may be more fairly traced to the nature of the American progressive experience. Theodore Roosevelt and Woodrow Wilson had faced only sporadic economic difficulties. Roosevelt had coped with the panic of 1907 by cooperating fully with the financial establishment, led by J. P. Morgan; Wilson had all but ignored the economic problems arising from World War I. The older Populist tradition had grown out of economic distress, but its inflationary panaceas could hardly be taken seriously. (Some New Deal monetary tinkering—abandonment of the gold standard, devaluation of the dollar, a lavish silver purchase program—exhilarated populist-style politicians but failed utterly to have a positive effect on the economy.) The mainstream of American reformism, having come out of an era of prosperity, sought humanitarian social programs, advocated a more equitable distribution of American abundance for all social groups, decried unregulated corporate power, and possessed some impulses toward social engineering. Proceeding from this frame of reference, the New Deal seized upon an opportunity to realize old reformist aspirations, doing so at times with little regard for their impact upon the economy.

The Social Security Act, for example, financed by a system of payroll taxes on employers and employees, sucked millions of dollars out of the private economy and constituted a drag on the drive for recovery. While Roosevelt fully understood this, he nonetheless insisted upon payroll contributions, which he saw as a way of guaranteeing the program's fiscal integrity and providing political insurance for it. "With those taxes in there," he remarked privately, "no damn politician can ever scrap my social security program." The NRA likewise had great appeal to Roosevelt, representing as it did a culmination of the New Nationalism and something of a recreation of the World War I effort at industrial mobilization. In practice, however, it probably had a contractionist effect on the economy, by sanctioning cartel practices based on assumptions of oversupply and depressed consumer demand.

In general, moreover, Roosevelt's increasingly vehement antibusiness attitude after 1935 probably did more to prolong the Depression than to solve it. Business confidence can be a critical determinant in investment decisions if the economy is unprosperous, and it was terribly unprosperous even at the peak of the partial recovery the New Deal did achieve. During the recession of 1937–38, Roosevelt fumed that business was deliberately refusing to help recovery along by investing in new facilities. However, in an economic environment characterized by unemployment levels of around 15 percent, only a business community that had achieved a sense of identification with the New Deal could have seriously contemplated expansion. Instead, of course, the leaders of American corporate enterprise were overwhelmingly irrational and unenlightened in their attitudes toward Roosevelt and the New Deal. Discredited by the Depression, they had been psychologically declassed. Yet although they were hard to deal with, although it was easy and politically profitable to return their hostility in kind, there were no economic benefits in doing so.

Throughout Roosevelt's public rhetoric, beginning with his inaugural address, one finds a steadily increasing hostility toward the business elite. The money changers, he declared after taking the oath of office in 1933, had been driven at last from the temple of government. (In fact, as Arthur Schlesinger, Jr., has observed, they were helping the New Dealers draw up the Emergency Banking Act of 1933.) By 1936, he had declared open warfare, characterizing his opponents as "economic royalists" and delighting in inflammatory rhetoric. "We had to struggle with the old enemies of peace—business and financial monopoly, speculation, reckless banking, class antagonism, sectionalism, war profiteering," he declared in his final big campaign speech. "They are unanimous in their *hate* for *me—and I welcome their hatred.*"

Roosevelt was, of course, responding to a campaign of abuse that was equally bitter from his opposition. He suffered routine denunciation in the clubs and corporate boardrooms of America in the most irrational and scurrilous fashion—as a Communist, as a sinister tool of some imagined Jewish conspiracy (his "real name," so the story went, was Rosenfeld), as a syphilitic (the "actual cause" of his crippling paralysis). He derived emotional satisfaction from striking back, but he might have been better advised to do what many other great political leaders have done from time to time—to absorb criticism like a sponge and seek to coopt his enemies.

Nevertheless, Roosevelt was essentially correct in responding to conservative critics with a famous story in which he depicted himself as having rescued an aged and wealthy capitalist from drowning only to be attacked for having failed to retrieve the old man's silk hat. Roosevelt indeed probably had saved American capitalism, even if he was not appreciated by the capitalists. Although the New Deal never solved the Depression, it did bring forth some moderate reform legislation that strengthened the structure of the capitalist system. In particular, banking and securities legislation brought a new degree of responsibility and safety to the American financial world.

In a broad sense also, the New Deal strengthened American capitalism by changing its structure in a largely unplanned way. Throughout the 1930s, Roosevelt and his associates sought to balance conflicting groups within the American political economy. The New Deal farm programs had the effect of organizing agriculture; the Wagner Act permitted the self-organization of labor with federal encouragement; the once-dominant position of business was whittled down to some extent; and big government functioned as an arbiter between these forces. Half-consciously, Roosevelt created a political economy of countervailing powers.

Despite an economic record that might be charitably described as spotty, Roosevelt was remarkably successful in making himself the nation's dominant political figure and in rebuilding the structure of American politics. The intellectual and moral bankruptcy of his opposition obscured the shortcomings of the New Deal. His own charisma and his well-developed skills in the art of politics enabled him to take maximum advantage of his opportunities. Better than any other personality of his time, Roosevelt combined the two major techniques of democratic political leadership: the achievement of a sense of direct identification with the people and the construction of formidable organizational support. Neither objective required a total victory over the Depression, nor was it necessary to have a coherent vision of economic reorganization. (Here, Roosevelt's confusion may even have been politically profitable, reflecting as it did that of so many Americans.) What was required, and what Roosevelt delivered, was some progress combined with, above all, the *appearance* of caring about and attempting to alleviate the plight of the unfortunate.

Roosevelt provided the appearance with his expert use of the communications media. He regularly brought the White House reporters into the Oval Office twice a week for press conferences; a dramatic departure from past presidential aloofness, the practice won him the sympathy of most working journalists and assured his views a prominent place even in implacably Republican newspapers. His radio talks demonstrated a technical skill in the use of the medium, an ability to transmit a sense of warm concern over the airwaves, and a talent for explaining complex social-economic policies in simple but not condescending language. His entire demeanor, most fully captured by the newsreels (then shown in every movie house in America), was that of an optimistic, energetic chief executive with a sense of concern for the unfortunate.

To this, Roosevelt added the dispensing of real benefits of one sort or another to millions of people, who more often than not responded naturally enough with the feeling that he had given them a job or saved their homes or preserved their farms or secured their bank deposits. The New Deal relief programs were not evaluated by a populace employing today's expectations; rather, they were received by people who were desperate for any assistance and who could contrast FDR only with the seemingly cold and indifferent Herbert Hoover. Roosevelt encouraged the contrast and doubtless believed it valid. "Better the occasional faults of a Government that lives in a spirit of charity than the consistent omissions of a Government frozen in the ice of its own indifference," he declared in his acceptance speech at the 1936 Democratic convention. He won the uniquely personal allegiance of many individuals who had been helped in some way by the New Deal or who simply felt touched by his manifestations of sympathy with their difficulties.

At the same time, Roosevelt built organizational support broader and stronger than that of any previous Democratic leader. He was successful in bringing behind him both the traditional Democratic machines and the trade unions, the most natural representatives of the working classes and the underprivileged. He secured the support of key leaders of almost every ethnic or religious minority in the nation, ranging from such figures as Robert Vann, the most influential black newspaper editor in the country, to Joseph P. Kennedy, perhaps the wealthiest and most powerful layman in the Irish-Catholic community. The minorities were most likely to be among the underprivileged that the New Deal attempted to help, but the Roosevelt administration also took pains to give them symbolic recognition in the form of visible appointments to office.

Finally, as a fitting capstone to his coalition, Roosevelt pre-empted the progressive impulse for himself and his party like no

Democrat before him. He actively sought and gained the backing of reformers who ran the gamut of American politics from heartland Republican mavericks to New York social democrats. Treating them almost as a minority group, he gave them important and prominent places in his administration. His secretary of the interior, Harold Ickes, and his secretary of agriculture, Henry A. Wallace, were eminent former progressive Republicans. Both embraced the Democratic party as well as the New Deal and in some respects became the rhetorical and ideological point men of the administration.

The grand old man of twentieth-century Republican progressive politics, George W. Norris of Nebraska, nominally a political independent, became one of Roosevelt's firmest supporters; in 1936, Roosevelt returned the compliment with an ostentatious endorsement of Norris's candidacy for reelection to the Senate over a Democratic opponent. For various left-oriented groups—the End Poverty in California (EPIC) movement, the Washington Commonwealth Federation, the Minnesota Farmer-Labor party, the New York American Labor party, the League for Independent Political Action—the pull of the New Deal was irresistible. Reform-oriented journalists and intellectuals, individuals who were playing an increasingly important role in defining the nature of American politics, found FDR's appeal overwhelming. Small in numbers, these independent progressives were important beyond their count as swing voters, as braintrusters who created programs and issues, and as committed activists skilled in the art of controversy. They were the vanguard of the intelligentsia that a generation hence would acquire a mass following, provide the dominant voices of the national communications media, and serve as the critical arbiters of the nature of American liberalism.

Roosevelt's first reelection victory in 1936 was a landslide in which he won support from all groups. But from the beginning, his most fervent and devoted support came from the independent progressives and from those groups that might loosely be described as "working class" in the larger cities of America. (Roosevelt was not the first Democratic candidate to win over the urban working and lower classes—Alfred E. Smith had done so in 1928—but his appeal was broader and deeper.) The liberals, the unionists, the ethnic-religious minorities, the blacks, and the urban lower classes would stay with FDR to the end.

Roosevelt and those around him interpreted the 1936 results as a mandate for an extension of the New Deal. In his second inaugural address, the president declared, "I see one third of a nation ill-housed, ill-clad, ill-nourished." He made it clear that more help for the underprivileged was his first priority. Armed with an overwhelming popular endorsement, given a Congress with Democratic majorities of 331-89 in the House of Representatives and 76-16 in the Senate, Roosevelt appeared all but invincible. Actually, his program faced serious institutional and popular obstacles. By the end of 1938, the New Deal was dead.

The immediate precipitant was Roosevelt's push for legislation to pack a Supreme Court that had demonstrated unqualified hostility to the New Deal. He handled the effort clumsily and somewhat dishonestly (he argued that he was simply trying to invigorate an excessively aged court), and he ran squarely up against popular reverence for the judicial system and the constitutional concept of separation of powers. Any chance of success evaporated when the two "swing justices," Charles Evans Hughes and Owen Roberts, began to vote with the liberal bloc and thereby converted a pro–New Deal minority into a majority. The Court bill was killed in the Senate after a debate that split the Democratic party. Roosevelt bravely insisted that he had lost a battle but had won the war. Perhaps so, but he had sustained serious wounds. The demonstration that he could be beaten on an issue of vital importance encouraged many potential opponents who had been intimidated by his popularity.

Other events drained FDR's political strength. His identification with organized labor became something of a liability as militance increased during his second term, manifesting itself in sit-down strikes that outraged millions of property-owning Americans. The severe recession of 1937–38 graphically exposed the New Deal's failure to achieve economic recovery. Roosevelt attempted to "purge" several opponents within his own party in the 1938 Democratic primaries. Poorly conceived and executed, the purge was a near-total failure—and yet another exhibition of the limitations inherent in the president's ad hoc approach to public policy problems.

From the Court-packing battle on, Roosevelt faced an increasingly strong opposition bloc in Congress. Made up of Republicans and anti–New Deal Democrats, the conservative coalition was composed largely of congressmen who represented safe, rural constituencies. It subscribed to the individualistic ethic of an older America shocked by the changes the New Deal had inflicted upon the nation. It benefited also from a rather general congressional resentment against FDR's "dictatorial" tactics in his dealings with Capitol Hill. Heartened by Roosevelt's post-1936 setbacks, convinced by the failure of the purge that he could not oust them from office, augmented by sizable Republican gains in the 1938 elections, the congressional conservatives became the strongest political force in Washington. From 1939 on, it would be FDR who was on the defensive, unable to enlarge the New Deal and at times forced to accept cuts in some of its peripheral programs.

Thus ended a remarkable story of success and failure in domestic reform. Roosevelt had changed American life in many ways, but he had not overcome the Depression. He had drastically altered the pattern of American politics only to create a domestic stalemate that would endure long after his death. He had made the Democratic party the country's dominant political vehicle, yet he could not control it. The new shape of American politics included a reform-oriented presidential Democratic party able to control presidential nominations and a moderate-to-conservative congressional Democratic party. Seldom in tune with the White House on domestic issues, the congressional party represented local and regional interests, was generally removed from the pressures of close electoral competition, and often willing to cooperate with the Republicans. These contours would endure for a quarter-century—until reshaped by one of FDR's most devoted followers, Lyndon B. Johnson.

The Diplomatist

At the time he was elected president, Franklin Roosevelt's attitudes toward America's role in the world were no more well defined than were his ideas about domestic reform. In fact, they were fuzzier; they were the product not just of Roosevelt's intuitive eclecticism but also of political pressures that he could not ignore so long as the Depression was America's most immediate problem and so long as his personal objective was the establishment of an all-inclusive progressive coalition. The first diplomatic period of the Roosevelt presidency, extending from 1933 through 1938, can only be described as an attempt to escape from diplomacy. It would in turn establish the basis for a second period, 1939–41, in which FDR would have to lead a nation unprepared for the grim realities of international power down a twisting and often devious path to war. Not until after Pearl Harbor was Roosevelt able to conduct a foreign policy in line with his own impulses—and these were by then mortgaged to a goal that defied full achievement, the establishment of a new world of total peace, justice, and democracy.

Roosevelt's personal views on U.S. foreign policy were, as was the case with his domestic liberalism, a rather inconsistent amalgam derived from the two dominant strains of twentieth-century American liberalism personified by Theodore Roosevelt and Woodrow Wilson. From his cousin and boyhood hero, FDR had obtained some sense of the need for national strength, the importance of national self-interest, and the imperative of a forceful American role in the larger world. He had supplemented these perceptions with his reading of Mahan and his own role as a military organizer and strategist during World War I. But from Woodrow Wilson he had received a different vision of the purpose of diplomacy—the objective of a pacific world community, united in adherence to a supranational body and striving to meet the needs of all mankind rather than engaging in petty struggles for national advantage. It was a vision FDR had pursued in his own support of Wilson's League of Nations. At bottom, the two world views were even more inconsistent than the conflicting varieties of domestic liberalism; yet, as with the New Deal, Roosevelt's ability to embody the conflicts of his creed would ultimately enhance his appeal to the liberal community.

During the 1930s, however, he had to contend with the fact that large segments of the progressive movement and an even larger segment of the American public as a whole wanted to avoid international involvement of any sort. Reflecting disillusionment with the failure of the Wilsonian crusade, the isolationist impulse peaked during the 1930s. It was especially strong among many progressives predominantly from the Midwest and the Far West; products of an older, quasi-populist tradition that had fought involvement in the world war, men such as Borah, Johnson, Wheeler, Nye, Shipstead, and La Follette constituted an honor role of the recent progressive past. Roosevelt felt little sympathy for their isolationism, but he needed their support badly for the New Deal and for the grand reform coalition he was trying to build. Thus, during the thirties his public policies exemplified little of the interplay of TR's nationalism and Wilson's internationalism that preoccupied his own mind.

Even before he was elected to the presidency, Roosevelt reversed his hitherto fervent advocacy of United States entry into the League of Nations in order to gain the editorial endorsement of William Randolph Hearst. One of his first important acts in foreign policy was to wreck the London Economic Conference, a last-ditch attempt to stabilize the major currencies of the Western world. The decision may well have been in the best short-term interests of the United States, but it set a more general pattern of economic nationalism and isolationism that probably was not good for the nation. (FDR's secretary of state, Cordell Hull, was a believer in free trade and did negotiate several reciprocal trade agreements; however, these had little impact upon the American economy.) When the administration made a gesture toward the Wilsonian legacy by advocating U.S. adherence to the World Court, the Senate vetoed the recommendation after an emotional debate over the dangers of foreign domination. Such events were representative of a larger pattern Roosevelt faced during the thirties: rejection of international involvement usually won acclaim and promoted his domestic political goals; espousal of involvement created intense strife and tended to be counterproductive.

The pattern was strongest in that area of diplomacy that had given rise to the American isolationist tradition: the problems of neutrality in a warring world. As Europe moved toward war, America met one crisis after another—the Italian invasion of Ethiopia, the Spanish Civil War, the German occupation of the Rhineland, the Japanese invasion of China, the German annexation of Austria, the Sudeten problem, the eradication of Czechoslovakia —with a determination to avoid involvement. Congress, probably reflecting popular sentiment rather accurately, passed a series of neutrality acts designed to avert any of the circumstances that had brought America into World War I. The legislation forsook any claims to protection for Americans traveling on passenger liners or merchant ships under the flag of a belligerent nation, prohibited loans or the sale of weapons to belligerents, and banned American vessels from trade with them.

Presidential gestures in the other direction either went unheeded or drew stiff criticism. Roosevelt's advocacy of a moral embargo on the sale of strategic materials to Italy during the Ethiopian war was futile. His declaration in favor of quarantining the aggressor in 1937 brought forth an angry outcry. At the end of 1938, after Japanese planes had bombed the American gunboat *Panay*, the president responded with intimations of military retaliation only to find the House of Representatives nearly passing a proposed constitutional amendment for a national referendum on declarations of war. It was far easier and more politically rewarding to play the role of peacemaker and hail, as FDR did, the Munich agreement. With World War I a bad memory and the European democracies committed to appeasement, few Americans were concerned about faraway conflicts. Roosevelt, concerned with domestic priorities as well as foreign dangers, had little choice but to follow the course of least resistance, make foreign policy a secondary consideration, and wait upon events that might shape a new public consciousness.

The German invasion of Poland, the effective beginning of World War II, changed the focus of public attention and gave Roosevelt an opportunity to assist in the building of the new awareness he felt was necessary. Opinion polls, which the president followed carefully, demonstrated both vast sympathy for Great Britain and France and an equally widespread determination to stay out of the war. From September 1939 to December 1941, Roosevelt's leadership consisted of constant interaction with an inconsistent, self-deceptive public mood. Attempting to lead the nation toward ever greater aid to the Allies without getting too far out in front, Roosevelt fashioned a diplomacy that reflected the contradictions of the country's mood even while trying to shape it. Partly because of Roosevelt's leadership, partly because of the pressure of real events, the nation would in fact increasingly perceive a serious threat from the Axis powers, but the process would be slow, erratic, and characterized by deep emotional divisions. Roosevelt's efforts involved back-pedaling, obfuscation, impossible promises, and, occasionally, outright deception. There can be little doubt that at some point he realized war was unavoidable, but he could not, and would not, say so. Whether or not he behaved in the best interests of the country, he assuredly laid himself open to charges of duplicity.

His first step evoked only a minor controversy and indicated how remote and "phony" the early stages of the war appeared. He requested and rather easily obtained a revision of the Neutrality Acts to allow the sale of weapons to belligerent nations on a "cash and carry" basis, despite some bitter opposition from isolationists already convinced of the president's bad intentions. Its ultimate passage by wide majorities in Congress represented the national impulse to aid the Allies and a national feeling that no further steps would be necessary.

The Nazi offensives of 1940 destroyed this illusion. As Denmark, Norway, the Netherlands, Belgium, and France went under, as the English hastily extricated their defeated army from Dunkirk, the American people experienced a terrible shock. In retrospect, it is easy to see that Hitler's early victories made American participation in the war inevitable. At the time, the Nazi sweep created overwhelming support for a drastic military preparedness program and a somewhat less unanimous consensus that the country would have to extend some aid to Great Britain. However, most Americans remained unwilling to face the prospect of full-scale United States participation. Throughout 1940 and 1941, public opinion polls were remarkably consistent in their findings: about a quarter of the people wanted to stay out of war whatever the costs; about a quarter were prepared for total participation in the fighting; and about half wanted to aid Great Britain by all means short of war. The ambiguity of the public mood was apparent to all, underscored in mid-1940 by the imminence of a presidential campaign.

From the fall of France on, Roosevelt cautiously steered the country toward war. He all but emptied military supply depots to provide war materiel for sale to Britain. He gave the British navy four dozen destroyers to secure the English Channel. He got selective service legislation through Congress. Invariably, he let others, including his Republican campaign opponent, Wendell Willkie, get out in front on the issues, waited for public opinion to swing toward them, then seized leadership. Always, he handled matters with a keen sense of public relations—the destroyer transfer, for example, was a "deal," a good trade for British military bases. When Willkie, desperate for an issue in the closing days of the 1940 campaign, accused Roosevelt of warmongering and Caesaristic ambitions, FDR responded effectively—and with equal demagoguery: "I have said this before, but I shall say it again and again and again: Your boys are not going to be sent into any foreign wars." He won the election with 55 percent of the popular vote.

The next step was Lend-Lease, an effective repudiation of the Neutrality Act prohibition of loans to belligerents. It was smoothly packaged as yet another way of keeping the country out of war and preserving national independence. Wouldn't anyone, Roosevelt asked, lend his neighbor a water hose if the neighbor's house were on fire and the fire threatened to spread? And of course the neighbor would return the hose once the fire was out. Lend-Lease passed Congress with heavy public support. What followed was a logical path toward war with Germany: "patrol operations" which amounted to an ill-disguised escort service for British convoys; American occupation of Greenland and Iceland; incidents between U.S. naval vessels and German submarines; the emergence of an undeclared naval war with the Third Reich. By August 1941, Roosevelt and Churchill could meet at Argentia, Newfoundland, release "a joint declaration of war aims"—the Atlantic Charter—and occasion little controversy. In October, Congress assented to the inclusion of the Soviet Union in Lend-Lease; in November, it authorized the employment of armed U.S. merchant ships to carry supplies to Britain. Still, by December 1941, the national mood remained stalemated. Americans were willing to take all steps short of war but determined to avoid a final commitment. Hitler, for his part, was equally wary of an incident that might push the United States over the edge. War, when it came, would come from the Far East.

Throughout the 1930s, Japan had played an increasingly prominent role in American popular demonology. As initiators of a war of conquest against China, a nation traditionally regarded with missionary benevolence, the Japanese came to be perceived as ruthless militarists. They seemed the Oriental counterpart of the Nazis, but even more menacing as they stirred up half-submerged feelings of racial hostility. Inevitably, the Japanese empire became in the minds of many Americans part of a worldwide threat to liberal democracy, and the early events of World War II served only to confirm the linkage. After the Nazi victories in Europe, Japan occupied northern French Indochina (North Vietnam), demanded shipments of petroleum from the Dutch East Indies (Indonesia), and threatened the dominance of all Southeast Asia, including the colonial possessions of Germany's enemies. In September 1940, Japan joined Germany and Italy in a mutual defense treaty directed against the United States.

Popular indignation against Japan had expressed itself in a vocal movement for an embargo on the shipment of strategic materials. Through the first half of 1940, Roosevelt appears to have felt that such strong measures could only draw resources and attention away from his fundamental objective of assisting the anti-Nazi Allies. During this period, the United States placed only relatively inconsequential restrictions upon trade with Japan; every move could be explained as necessary to the United States military program, and even the Japanese protests were rather half-hearted. However, when Japan allied with European fascists and turned its ambitions toward Southeast Asia, the Nazi problem and the Japanese problem began to merge.

As Roosevelt became more militant toward Germany, his Far Eastern policy followed a parallel course. In July 1941, with the undeclared war of the Atlantic in its early phase, Japan moved into southern French Indochina (South Vietnam), and the administration responded by cutting off shipments of the one commodity vital to the Empire's war effort—oil. In subsequent negotiations, American diplomatists asserted that normal trade could be resumed only if Japan gave up every military gain since its invasion of Manchuria in 1931. The demand, if serious, was inconceivable; Japan preemptorily rejected it. Pearl Harbor came in less than two weeks.

Pearl Harbor brought the United States into the war at last, but it raised doubts about the quality of Roosevelt's leadership.

His most extreme enemies charged that he himself had all but planned the surprise attack. The accusation could convince only those who had already come to hate FDR with a passion beyond reason, and it obscured far more sober and legitimate questions. In retrospect, it appears certain that he more or less intentionally moved the nation toward war even as he presented each step as the latest method of averting all-out conflict. Perhaps serving the best interests of the United States, he nonetheless did so with a notable lack of candor. Even so sympathetic a historian as Arthur Schlesinger, Jr., writing against the backdrop of Vietnam, has found in FDR's behavior early traces of "the imperial presidency."

Yet Roosevelt's leadership may well have been the best the country could have hoped for in the situation. It is unlikely that a people so divided in their impulses would have responded to frankness, whether in advocacy of war or of isolation. The majority of Americans—anxious to prevent an Axis victory, equally anxious to stay out of the war—followed Roosevelt because in his inconsistencies he reflected their conflicting concerns with great consistency.

Whether consciously or otherwise, Roosevelt managed American diplomacy during the war in much the same manner. When the national impulse was strong, he embodied it unequivocally, as he did in constantly reiterating the themes of "unconditional surrender" and total victory. When presented with conflicting impulses, he drew them as always into himself. At times, very much in line with one side of the American mood, he rejected idealism and called the war a "survival war" forced upon America by an enemy that had to be beaten simply as a matter of preserving the national safety. More frequently, however, his rhetoric expressed the other side of his country's aspirations—the millennial side that envisioned America as the savior of a benighted world. In his conduct of World War II diplomacy, FDR sought a feasible way of combining the two impulses. The imposition of a design of such complexity and magnitude upon a world in flames was a task too awesome to be carried through to complete success.

Roosevelt's wartime management and objectives may be summed up by three phrases: Total War, Total Victory, Total Peace. The practice of total war for total victory required enormous sacrifices of lives, resources, and property; for most Americans, such sacrifices could be justified only by the objective of a peace that would establish justice and democracy throughout the world. Total peace was a goal derived directly from the American impulse to make the world over. In one form, expressed by the publisher and opinion shaper Henry Luce, total peace could be the achievement of an "American Century" in which a benign United States would bring the blessings of its values to the rest of the globe. In another form, as stated by Vice-President Henry Wallace, total peace could mean the fulfillment of a "People's Revolution" and the establishment of a "Century of the Common Man," a worldwide social reform movement. It was Roosevelt, however, who gave total peace its most universally appealing formulation when, nearly a year before Pearl Harbor, he defined the aims of American diplomacy as the establishment of Four Freedoms: freedom of speech, freedom to worship, freedom from want, freedom from fear—everywhere in the world for everyone in the world.

The Four Freedoms provided a splendid inspirational banner, but they could only interfere with realistic diplomacy, which was obliged to deal with the world as it was, not as America would have preferred it. Privately, Roosevelt appears to have understood that the Four Freedoms possessed merit mainly as an expression of America's ultimate hopes for the world but that it was impossible to achieve them simply by defeating the Axis. He was, moreover, still too much the cousin of Theodore Roosevelt and the disciple of Mahan to believe that for the foreseeable future the world could be organized by means other than power relationships. Thus he aimed his diplomacy toward the establishment of a concert of power in which the four major Allied Nations—the United States, the Soviet Union, Great Britain, and China—would act as Four Policemen maintaining the peace, each exercising primary jurisdiction in his own part of the globe. It was this design, not the more grandiose United Nations organization, that motivated his behavior. Despite its apparent realism, however, it was all but impossible from the start.

Roosevelt himself did nothing to prepare the nation for reality. War requires a rhetoric of grand aims and idealistic objectives, not of grubby compromise. One searches FDR's wartime declarations in vain for any warnings of the limits of idealism or the difficulties of negotiating with allies. Instead, he attempted to plaster over serious problems with a thick layer of optimism. He failed wholly to foresee the international power structure that would emerge from the war. His concept of the Four Policemen assumed that Nationalist China would become a viable power rather than a fragmented nation and that Great Britain would be able and willing to maintain its imperial position. He even told Stalin that American troops would not be kept in Europe after the war because the American people would not stand for it.

Reality intruded with equal persistence upon FDR's hopes of a successful relationship with the Soviet Union. The British-American relationship, although difficult at times, was solidly grounded in common political and cultural traditions. The Soviet-American relationship possessed no common basis other than a mutual interest in the defeat of Nazi Germany, an interest that would evaporate with the conclusion of the war. Politically, the United States was a liberal, capitalist democracy while Russia was a totalitarian, Communist state. The ideological gulf was so broad and so deep as to be unbridgeable. Leaders on both sides worked from deeply ingrained sets of incompatible assumptions which in turn dictated quite different meanings for such key concepts as "security," "freedom," and "democracy."

To all these conditions for mutual misunderstanding, one must add the divergent personalities of Roosevelt and Stalin. Open, confident, always optimistic, Roosevelt was perhaps least equipped of all the Allied leaders to deal with Stalin. The Soviet dictator was utterly ruthless, pathologically suspicious of his own associates as well as of his foreign allies, opportunistic enough to have concluded an alliance with Hitler, consummately skilled in the use of terror as a means of rule, convinced that the Western capitalist world always would seek the destruction of the USSR. He combined in his world view and in his psychological makeup the worst qualities of Ivan the Terrible and Lenin.

There can be little doubt that Stalin envisioned the Anglo-American alliance as a matter of transitory convenience for both sides, to be followed by a reversion to the more natural hostility that had characterized relations between Russia and the West after World War I. Where Roosevelt in his rhetoric and assumptions depicted the war as a culmination of history, Stalin saw it

merely as another episode in a long process of historical development. Where Roosevelt sought security through alliances and
through the establishment of what a later generation would call
favorable atmospherics, Stalin sought security through the grab-
bing of territory and the imposition of Soviet Communist dominance upon alien peoples.

Roosevelt might have abandoned the objective of preserving
the alliance once the war was ended, but such a course would
have run against the grain of American expectations. The alliance
might theoretically have been maintained by a candid acceptance
of power politics and the negotiation of an unambiguous division
of captured territory with Stalin. Yet such a solution was equally
unacceptable to the American mind. There remained, it seemed,
only one alternative—the establishment of an atmosphere of trust
and goodwill that might somehow eclipse vast ideological and
cultural differences. It is easy to see with hindsight that such an
effort had little chance of success; historical understanding, a
rather different type of vision, tells us that the war and all its
sacrifices required that the effort be made.

Roosevelt's attempt to secure the peace through atmospherics
involved overpromise, the employment of personal charm, and
the postponement of differences. Early Lend-Lease commitments
to the USSR were ludicrously optimistic in terms of both America's
productive capacity and Anglo-American shipping capabilities.
In the spring of 1942, FDR actually promised visiting Soviet
foreign minister Molotov that the United States would establish a
major second front in Western Europe before the end of the year;
instead, the USSR had to content itself with comparatively minor
sideshows in North Africa and Italy until 1944.

In his personal meetings with Stalin, Roosevelt made determined efforts to win the Russian dictator's liking and trust. He
seized occasions to disagree with Winston Churchill, a militant
opponent of Bolshevism. Privately, he assured the Soviet leader
of his distaste for British imperialism, only to find Stalin more
interested in enlarging his own empire than in dismantling the
British domain. Finally, as part of the policy of friendship, Roosevelt never pursued a disagreement far. He preferred instead to
engage in a policy of postponement of the most critical issues of
the war—the futures of Eastern Europe and of Germany. He did
so at least partly in the hope that victory and the growth of trust

would make it easier to resolve such issues in the future, that with the winning of the war, somehow things would work out.

But extravagant, unkept promises probably fed Soviet suspicions and surely gave the USSR greater leverage in demanding concessions as the war went on. Nor could good personal relations solve much. Roosevelt and Stalin communicated daily, but they actually met face to face at only two conferences. The rather scant available evidence provides us with no certain answer to the question of whether Stalin developed a deep trust in Roosevelt. It seems reasonable to assume, however, that he entertained the same skepticism toward the American leader that he harbored toward other mortals. From the Russian victory at Stalingrad on, he managed his military campaigns not only to defeat the Nazis but also to bring all of Eastern Europe under his dominance. In the end, the American policy of postponement facilitated this effort; in effect, it enabled Stalin to take what he wanted without meaningful American protests as the Soviet armies moved westward.

As the war moved into its final months, Soviet policy became increasingly obvious and increasingly an outrage to the millennial American rhetoric that had sustained the total war effort. Although Stalin agreed that the liberated nations of Eastern Europe would be permitted to hold free elections and engage in self-determination, he took no steps to translate these vague affirmations into reality. American attention focused upon Poland, the most intractable situation in the region. Ignoring the claims of the Polish government-in-exile and the intermittent protests of Roosevelt and Churchill, the Russians installed a puppet regime and unilaterally restructured the country's boundaries. Such moves outraged Polish-Americans and other Eastern European ethnic groups from whom Roosevelt had received strong electoral support. By laying bare the gap between the reality of the war and his rhetoric about it, the Russian actions exposed the president to attack from a political opposition that demanded full delivery of the promises he had made. Soviet behavior had begun to disillusion a warweary people that had dared to hope for a new era of human history.

The course of the war at home was no easier for Roosevelt. The conservative coalition consolidated its strength in Congress, and the New Deal began to take on the appearance of a ragged, beaten military force attempting a difficult retreat. As the New Deal techniques of big government and manipulation of the economy became identified with a panoply of wartime controls and restrictions, popular discontent or indifference with Rooseveltian liberalism grew apace. A few agencies from the Depression era—the Works Progress Administration, the National Youth Administration, the National Resources Planning Board, the Farm Security Administration—suffered emasculation or outright abolition at the hands of an angry Congress. In the most symbolic manifestation of the new mood, Roosevelt found himself forced to dump his militantly liberal protégé, Vice-President Henry A. Wallace, from the party ticket in 1944.

Yet the war only put Roosevelt and his coalition on the defensive. It neither destroyed nor defeated them. In some respects, it created new directions for a liberalism that had reached a dead end. With the government spending whatever was necessary to train and equip the U.S. and Allied armies, the economy quickly reached full employment. Thereby it provided economic policy makers an example of the way in which a massive fiscal stimulus relentlessly applied might create prosperity. Faced with increasing black militance, Roosevelt established the Fair Employment Practices Committee (FEPC) to work for an end to discrimination in civilian employment. Set up by executive order, funded in a roundabout manner, and lacking majority support in Congress, the FEPC was an anemic educational and conciliatory agency with no real powers of compulsion. Still, its very existence constituted a significant administration recognition of discrimination and moved the issue of civil rights to the center of American liberalism. Nor did Roosevelt give up on New Deal welfarism. To the very end of his administration, he and his advisers appear to have nourished the belief that domestic reform would return as a potent issue once the war was over and the nation faced the uncertainties of a future that might include a new economic depression.

Roosevelt's final campaign provided a fair measure of support for this faith. With the end of the war in sight, he devoted a substantial portion of his rhetoric to the resumption of the New Deal—the establishment of an Economic Bill of Rights, the creation of sixty million jobs, the continuance of the FEPC, the enlargement of the welfare state for which the Social Security Act had provided a small basis, and active government management of the economy. Amid all the distractions of the war, his political support still held up well. The labor unions, more politically involved than ever, gave the president organizational support that supplanted or excelled that of the old Democratic machines in many urban areas.

Roosevelt himself remained a brilliant campaigner still capable of expressing his lofty objectives in ways that inspired his followers, of deflating his opposition with sarcastic thrusts, of showing himself to the public in exhausting campaign trips. Having come to embody the spirit of American liberalism in both its domestic and diplomatic manifestations, he was perhaps the only Democrat who could have been elected. Nonetheless, he faced all the obstacles that would confront any politician with twelve bitterly disputed years of power behind him. His haggard physical appearance betrayed his precarious health and provided the Republicans with an underground issue. Under the circumstances, his victory over Thomas E. Dewey (although the smallest of his four presidential margins) was a remarkable triumph.

The agenda that Roosevelt had set for his fourth term was staggering to contemplate. It involved no less than the restructuring of American life and the creation of a new world order. Yet the president had the means to achieve neither goal. The conservative coalition, weakened only a bit by the election, hung onto power, many of its members personally alienated from FDR and determined to make no concessions whatever. Despite the president's grueling journey to Yalta in February 1945 and the maintenace of the facade of Allied unity, Soviet-American relations reached a near-crisis in March and early April; the Russians imposed their will upon Poland in spite of Anglo-American protests, and Stalin hysterically charged that the West was negotiating a separate peace with Hitler. Still, FDR retained his fundamental confidence. On April 11, 1945, he remarked in a message to Winston Churchill that problems always arose with the Russians and usually got straightened out. The next afternoon, working at his desk at the vacation White House in Warm Springs, Georgia, he suddenly remarked, "I have a terrible headache," slumped over, and died.

The Accomplishment

Roosevelt left a deep imprint upon his era. At his death, he was fiercely hated by his opponents and all but worshipped by his followers. As emotions subsided over the next generation, however, the most frequent criticism of him came from liberal and radical scholars in sympathy with his aims and disenchanted by his inability to achieve all of them. In some instances, they appeared to speak little more than a lament that the New Deal failed to establish some variety of democratic socialism or to resolve all the problems of American life. Others, evaluating him by the criteria of the seminar rather than the real world of the political leader, voiced unhappiness at his lack of a systematic social and political philosophy. Some leveled the charge that after 1937 he had failed as a party leader, and there could be no arguing that mass Democratic defections had made the conservative coalition possible. They have, however, been less convincing in demonstrating the means by which FDR or any president could have whipped well-entrenched congressmen and independent local party leaders into line. His undeniable tactical mistakes seem relatively insignificant when placed against such formidable constitutional barriers to presidential control as federalism and the separation of powers.

It is legitimate to observe that Roosevelt's New Deal failed to restore the prosperity of 1929 and that his diplomacy failed to erect the structure of total peace he had encouraged the American people to expect. But from almost any vantage point, the nation was stronger and more secure at his death than at the time he took office. If the New Deal did not restore prosperity, it did in a number of ways lay a strong groundwork for the maintenance of prosperity after World War II. By restructuring the American political economy into a system of countervailing powers, by establishing a minimal welfare state, the New Deal smoothed out the business cycle and laid the basis for a postwar political consensus based on a widely distributed affluence. Roosevelt's role in engineering the defeat of fascism removed the most serious challenge the nation had ever faced to its security. He brought America no utopia, but he took his country through difficult times and left it able to face the future with strength and confidence.

The way in which Roosevelt gained political power and support was in some respects as important as what he did. He won the backing of established organizations actively involved in the game of political power—the machines, the unions, the various organized interests—and he achieved a sense of direct communication and empathy with the ordinary people. He employed radio as a supplement to organizational support, not as a substitute for it, and by bringing the average American into direct involvement with his personality, he called forth the intensity with which his admirers loved him and his enemies hated him.

Roosevelt created a new era in the history of American politics. His moderate liberalism, fumbling though it might seem to later critics, and his charismatic optimism, whether realistic or not, drew millions to the Democratic party and made it a vehicle of majority sentiment for the first time since the Civil War. He created a new consensus to which that majority subscribed—one that defined the objectives of American politics as pluralist and liberal and the national interests of the United States as worldwide. FDR's final legacy to the nation was no less than a new political tradition.

2

The Commoner:
Harry S. Truman

Few presidents have experienced fluctuations in their public and scholarly reputations as great as those connected with Harry S. Truman. Shortly after Truman assumed the presidency, a Gallup poll revealed an astounding 87-percent approval level for him. At Truman's nadir, during the Korean conflict, Gallup came up with only a 23-percent rating, lower than anything Richard Nixon would experience during the worst days of the Watergate crisis. Between these extremes, Truman's public approval tended to bob up and down in the manner of an out-of-control yo-yo.

The majority of academic historians (mainstream liberal intellectuals for the most part) retain a favorable impression of him. Those who have done active research on his administration, however, have engaged in an academic debate that provides a curious reverse image of the controversies of the Truman presidency. Characteristically attacked largely from the right during his administration, Truman the historical figure has most frequently encountered scholarly criticism from the left. In both cases, his major defenders—reluctant ones at times—have come from the liberal center with which he identified himself. Few situations demonstrate so neatly the wide gap that separates the intellectual elite from the rest of American society.

Among the general public, Truman's standing rose perceptibly soon after he left the White House and moved sharply upward during the administrations of Lyndon Johnson and Richard Nixon.

Disenchanted with presidential leadership that seemed devious and synthetic, the American people made Truman into a folk hero. Although widely regarded as something of a bumbler too small for his job when he went into retirement, Truman has more recently won acclaim as a rough-hewn, profane, latter-day Mark Twain, a man of honesty and cracker-barrel wisdom, frank, feisty, and decisive, a modern Cincinnatus who exemplified the virtues of American democracy. Not since William Jennings Bryan had the Democratic party produced a leader who seemed so much the apotheosis of the common man.

This was about the way Truman wanted to be remembered, but the image bears only a shaky relation to reality. Truman actually was, as William V. Shannon has remarked, "a closet intellectual," fascinated by history and biography; he was a devoted lover of classical music, doomed by his political career to spend much of his life suffering through one rendition after another of "The Missouri Waltz." Reputedly prone to snap decisions, he actually weighed most important issues carefully before acting. Famous for his salty language, he ordinarily used profanity sparingly and never in the presence of women. In his day-to-day working career and in his remarkably unruffled family life, he was more the neat, efficient businessman than the impulsive, sharp-tongued politician he usually is made out to be.

Nonetheless, almost all observers have agreed that whatever Truman was, he was enormously different from his awesome predecessor, Franklin D. Roosevelt. Yet when one goes beyond some readily apparent differences in style—many of them quite superficial but a few representing important qualities of leadership—the contrasts seem to disappear. Truman lacked Roosevelt's appeal to the popular imagination, but in fundamental attributes of thought and character, the two were far more similar than different.

Both men were products of the Victorian culture of the late nineteenth and early twentieth centuries. Both absorbed a determinedly optimistic faith in human progress. Both were political moderates who began as cautious reformers and became leaders of liberal democratic movements. Both were condemned by more conservative opponents as dangerous radicals or socialists, although of course they were neither. Both identified themselves with the ideal of American leadership of the world. Finally, both possessed fundamentally positive images of their own personalities and thereby developed the confidence and sense of security essential to creative political leadership.

Of the two, Roosevelt was by far the strongest presence in almost every way—more charismatic, more creative, more subtle— and Truman's reputation has tended to suffer by contrast. Roosevelt had begun a revolution in American politics and diplomacy; Truman consolidated and institutionalized it beyond recall. His historical role, like that of any consolidator, was inevitably less innovative, and it rested in the end upon the political climate of opinion. Still, the task required a considerable amount of personal skill and a shrewd understanding of American politics.

The Liberal Democrat

As an old man, Truman liked to remember his childhood as if it were a chapter from *Tom Sawyer*. There were some similarities. Young Harry Truman did spend his formative years in the little Missouri town of Independence, a few miles from Kansas City. Still, his childhood was hardly a Tom Sawyer experience. The thick glasses he had to wear from an early age made him a sissy to his boyhood friends. His mother protected him, encouraged him to read, and arranged piano lessons. He was not close to his father, an ambitious, hot-tempered livestock dealer and speculator. Nevertheless, his father provided a definition of masculine identity toward which he aspired. The boy was an avid reader, and his interests centered not on the lives of concert pianists but upon those of great soldiers and political leaders. He set his sights on a life as an army officer.

The ambition was of course aborted by his weak eyesight, which foreclosed an appointment to the U.S. Military Academy and relegated him to part-time soldiering in the National Guard. He found himself unable to go to college at all because the family had incurred serious financial reverses. Instead, he held some odd jobs, worked as a bank clerk for a few years, helped his father manage the family farm, and ultimately took over the enterprise himself after his father's death. The first decade or so of his adulthood appears in retrospect a bit aimless. The personal confidence that was so natural to Roosevelt came to Truman slowly and with difficulty.

His farm experience was important. He was a prosperous farmer, not just because he could plow a straight furrow, but because he was a good manager. The favorable market conditions of the early twentieth century provided him with financial rewards and the experience of his first success. He worked closely with his father, and the two men seem to have achieved the closest relationship of their lives. At no time, however, did he plan to spend his life as a country gentleman. He joined the Masons, was an officer in the local Farm Bureau, and held political appointments as a county road overseer, and—very briefly—as postmaster of nearby Grandview, Missouri. He made speculative investments in zinc-mining and oil-drilling, but these failed to pay off.

World War I was a decisive turning point. As the commander of an artillery battery, Truman was an effective administrator and a courageous combat officer. He showed others—but perhaps most importantly, he showed himself—that he could lead men and win their loyalty. He also discovered that he had no taste for the professional military life. By the time he returned from France, he had plans to move ahead in the world as a civilian.

He married Bess Wallace, left the farm, and established a haberdashery business in downtown Kansas City in partnership with a close army comrade, Eddie Jacobson. The business failed during the brief but intense economic depression that marked the first two years of the Harding presidency. The event solidified two traditional rural Democratic convictions that Truman doubtless had been taught by his parents: that the Republican party could not manage the national economy and that tight money policies were economically and morally unjustifiable. Thirty-eight years old and broke, he refused to file for bankruptcy, which he considered a disgrace. He would remain in debt for twenty years. For a time, according to some stories, he could not even establish a bank account for fear that his creditors might try to attach it.

He turned to politics naturally. His family was fervently devoted to the Democratic party, and his father had been passionately interested in Democratic politics. The Trumans were of the old Democratic party—white, Anglo-Saxon, Protestant, rural,

conservative in race relations, populistic on economic issues, un-
easy and embarrassed by its urban, rum-drinking, Romanist
Northern city machines. Their heroes were Andrew Jackson,
Jefferson Davis, William Jennings Bryan, and Jesse James.

Truman moved away from his early provincialism. He associated easily with men of different backgrounds. His artillery
battery had been primarily Irish-Catholic, his business partner
Jewish. He aligned himself with the Kansas City machine of Boss
Tom Pendergast, whose power and personal fortune derived
from almost every unsavory source the rural Protestant mind
could imagine—corrupt rake-offs, saloons, gambling establishments, and bawdy houses. In 1922, Truman won election as
county judge from the eastern, rural half of Jackson County, but
was narrowly defeated for reelection in 1924 because of a party
split and because of the hostility of the Ku Klux Klan. He dabbled
in various business ventures—a savings association, the fledgling
Automobile Club—but he had determined that politics was his
life.

In 1926, Truman was elected presiding judge of the Jackson
County Court and would hold the office until 1934. Maintaining
his close affiliation with the Pendergast organization, he functioned
after a time as the leader of its rural county wing. He saw to it that
county jobs went to deserving Pendergast men, but he also ran
the county with a scrupulous honesty and efficiency that won
praise from many of Pendergast's enemies. Presiding over the
building of an extensive road system, he let contracts with strict
fairness and denied the machine multiple opportunities for graft.
Instinctively understanding the virtues of a bipartisan appeal, he
involved prominent Republicans in his county projects and won
over the opposition *Kansas City Star*. In the process, he established
himself as an important asset to an organization that, after all, had
many other sources of corruption to tap. "In any election I could
deliver eleven thousand votes and not steal a one," he told
Jonathan Daniels in 1949. "It was not necessary. I looked out for
the people, and they understood my leadership."

Like many politicians, Truman was a pragmatist willing to
associate with a corrupt organization if such was the price of
success. But he was also a respectable showpiece for the machine

and a leader capable of delivering votes from actual living, breathing constituents. It is a bit surprising that Truman was eternally grateful for Pendergast's favors. In fact, he received few; in the early thirties, he was unable to obtain organization backing for governor, for the House of Representatives, for county collector. Pendergast moved behind him for senator in 1934 only after two other possibilities had declined to run.

Harry Truman entered the U.S. Senate in 1935 as just another of the many Democrats who had ridden to victory on a wave of popular approval for the New Deal. Progressives looked down upon him as the flunky of an increasingly notorious urban machine; the administration tendered him little recognition. Although he was a supporter of the New Deal, his main associations were with the moderate and conservative Democrats who constituted the core of the Senate establishment. Adhering to the traditional values of the leadership, he devoted his first term to quiet, serious work and established himself as an authority on transportation policy, an important but dull area.

Chairing a subcommittee of the Senate Interstate Commerce Committee and encouraged by the maverick Montana Democrat Burton K. Wheeler and by Supreme Court Justice Louis Brandeis, Truman conducted a scathing investigation of railroad financing. He created a brief sensation by alleging gross mismanagement and widespread manipulation by the nation's financial establishment. His major legislative accomplishments, however, were the Civil Aeronautics Act of 1938 and the Transportation Act of 1940, both of them stunningly unspectacular.

As his first term expired, Truman faced an uphill fight for reelection. The Pendergast machine, which he had loyally supported to the end, was in shreds. Two of its major enemies opposed him in the Democratic senatorial primary: Governor Lloyd Stark of Missouri and U.S. Attorney Maurice Milligan. President Roosevelt offered Truman an appointment to the Interstate Commerce Commission as a graceful exit. After considerable hesitation, he resolved to fight out the election. Waging a badly financed campaign, he barnstormed the state, made especially strong appeals to labor unions and blacks, pulled together the remnants of the Kansas City organization, and secured the last-minute backing of the St. Louis machine. His two rivals split the anti-Pendergast majority. He won by a few thousand votes and went on to a comfortable general election victory.

Truman became a national figure for the first time as the chairman of a special Senate investigating committee that probed World War II mobilization, ferreted out graft and inefficiency, argued for postwar economic planning, and won wide praise. The committee's origins and the way Truman managed it are revealing. It was a product of the senator's concern for the way in which the military procurement agencies were passing over small businesses, especially those based in Missouri. It represented not only his genuine interest in efficiency and honesty but also his determination to do something in the struggle against corporate bigness. The committee was established because he promised to conduct it as a good Democrat. It frequently criticized the administration but almost always in a constructive, nonsensational way; the White House accepted it in that spirit, cooperated with it, and gave its chairman extensive recognition. Finally, Truman demonstrated remarkable political skill in achieving a committee consensus on most matters and in keeping the proceedings reasonably bipartisan.

The investigations made him a big man in Washington. Capitol Hill correspondents voted him the nation's most effective senator, and Roosevelt asked him to be chairman of the Democratic National Committee. When he declined, FDR accepted his recommendation of Robert Hannegan, the St. Louis leader who had shifted away from Governor Stark in 1940. Truman's name became prominent in the movement for postwar internationalism and in the drive for extension of the New Deal at home. On the Hill, he appears to have become a respected member of the Senate establishment. Yet his personality had left little impression on the nation, and his nomination for the vice-presidency in 1944 was a surprise to the general public.

The vice-presidential nomination came to Truman in 1944 because he was acceptable to all factions of his party. The conservatives viewed him as more moderate and level-headed than Henry Wallace; the liberals could accept him as a politician with a New Deal voting record. The political bosses knew he was a man with whom they could do business. The White House hoped he could improve the bad relationship between Roosevelt and the Congress. More than any other potential candidate, he had lived the experience of the twentieth-century Democratic party, moving from the country to the city, from the little county-courthouse world of the rural white Anglo-Saxon Protestant democracy to the urban political world of big city machines, ethnic minorities, blacks, and labor unions. Always a Bryan-Wilson progressive, he had become a New Dealer. He layered his new experience and outlook on top of his old, retaining both within himself.

At times, Truman could appear diffident to the point of ineffectuality; few who heard him speak to large gatherings could muster praise for his oratorical skills or his powers of persuasion. In other situations, especially those involving one-on-one contacts, he could indulge in sharp, opinionated thrusts. Above all, he valued his independence and saw himself as an ordinary man representing the needs of other ordinary people, beholden to no interest group or narrow point of view, speaking out as he wished.

Corresponding with constituents in the 1940s, he excoriated big business, condemned wartime strikes as akin to treason, expressed disgust with the federal bureaucracy, heatedly criticized the Roosevelt administration's political tactics, and lectured a pacifist minister on the realities of human nature. Few who corresponded with him on any issue were left with much doubt about where he stood or, at times, how he felt about them. One hapless individual who wrote him a contentious letter was told: "From my past correspondence with you I am very sure it is pretty hard for you to understand a common sense proposition."

Tolerant of diversity, Truman wanted to keep the Democratic party open to all viewpoints. Like most people who achieve high public office, he was at bottom a professional politician devoted above all to his party; and he had little use for dogmatists of either the Right or the Left who had not faced the difficulties of practical politics. Beyond that, he saw the purpose of American politics as the creation of opportunity for the common man—the blue-collar worker who wanted a job without having to buy a union card or pay off a labor leader in advance, the small businessman threatened by monopolistic practices, the minorities attempting to make their way against discrimination. The business of representative government, he told a constituent in 1941, was "to see that every

one has a fair deal." At bottom, he was, like Roosevelt, an instinctive advocate of what would soon be called the liberalism of "the
vital center." Within that framework, he and his White House
advisers formulated a coherent attempt to institutionalize and
extend the political tradition that Roosevelt had created.

The Fair Dealer

Although Truman was disposed to follow in Roosevelt's footsteps,
the political realities he faced nearly compelled such a course. To
secure his own future and that of his party, he had to hold
together the coalition FDR had assembled. Lacking Roosevelt's
charismatic appeal, he was under even more pressure to deliver
substantial results. As the war came to an end, he faced three
important responsibilities: (1) the maintenance of economic stability and prosperity, (2) the preservation of the rudimentary
welfare state the New Deal had established and perhaps a modest
enlargement of it, (3) progress toward equal justice and equal
opportunity for an awakening black minority.

The economic problems were at once the most fundamental
and the most complex. New Deal reformism had accepted responsibility for economic prosperity and had failed grievously to
achieve it. World War II had brought the nation out of the
Depression, but the prosperity it engendered was feverish and
unsatisfactory. The end of the war presented two equally frightening possibilities: runaway inflation caused by the release of
pent-up consumer purchasing power, or a reversion to the Depression, perhaps as a result of the boom-and-bust cycle that un-
controlled inflation would set off. The Truman administration
had to formulate policies that would keep the economy from
overheating while maintaining current employment levels and
also providing jobs for millions of returning servicemen.

It is hardly surprising that the task was imperfectly performed;
that it was performed at all may have been a considerable achievement. The dominant economic policy voices in the administration
believed, probably rightly, that the maintenance of wartime
economic controls was essential to a smooth reconversion. For the
most part, these were holdovers from the Roosevelt administration who had run the control apparatus during the war. Others,

mostly Truman appointees, argued that controls tended to clog the economic mechanism and should be lifted as quickly as possible; to the extent that it is possible to generalize about this group, one can say that it represented the viewpoint of the harried small businessman, who had experienced great difficulties with wartime controls. When the president at a press conference both stated his support of economic controls and characterized them as "police state" methods, he demonstrated a divided mind that mirrored the conflict in Washington.

Historians have concentrated upon this debate because it nicely fits the progressive preconceptions of the academic establishment. Liberal intellectuals drawing upon the political support of urban consumer and labor groups argued for a planned economy; conservatives, decidedly nonintellectual in their social orientation and backed by business and farm organizations, argued for a Hoover-like laissez-faire. The administration zigged and zagged, alienated about every important voting bloc in the country, and was overwhelmingly repudiated in the 1946 elections.

The account is valid enough as far as it goes, but it rather quickly passes over what may be a more important reality of the reconversion period—the revolt of *every* group in American society against those controls that directly affected its interests. The conservatives who argued against controls in general could at least lay claim to the virtue of ideological consistency. The labor unions, on the other hand, demanded, and obtained, the lifting of wage controls and the retention of price controls. Consumer-oriented spokesmen adamantly defended controls, especially price controls, even as consumers, frustrated by the shortages that controls caused, eagerly patronized black markets. Truman faced a no-win situation.

The Democratic political disaster of 1946 has obscured the more fundamental fact that the much-anticipated postwar economic disaster never materialized. Aside from the sharp but brief economic recession of 1949, aside from the price spurts set off by the removal of World War II controls and by the outbreak of the Korean War, the economic history of the Truman period was characterized by full employment, economic growth, and a relatively acceptable rate of inflation. In part, this record stemmed from the fact that Truman operated within favorable circumstances—wartime prosperity had created a solid base for the postwar era in many ways. Still, one cannot pass lightly over the fact that almost every responsible economist appeared more impressed by economic dangers at the end of the war. The Truman administration fostered postwar prosperity by transcending the economic limitations of the New Deal.

The New Deal had been far better at social reform than at solving the unemployment problem, and it might have been fatally discredited on this count had not the war heated up the economy. Its most important economic achievement was long-run. Its agricultural and labor policies and its determination to curb the power and prestige of large corporations created a political economy more characterized than before by a situation of countervailing powers. In its dealings with business, labor, and agriculture, the Truman administration tried to preserve this balance. But it also made both structural and conceptual advances in liberal economic policy.

On the structural side, until 1946, the executive branch of the U.S. government possessed no central mechanism for formulating an economic policy with a truly national perspective. Neither the Treasury Department nor the Bureau of the Budget had an institutional mandate to handle the job, although a vigorous and talented person at the head of either could become a chief economic policy maker. The debates over fiscal policy in the late thirties involved many cabinet officers and brain trusters who were only marginally conversant with economic theory. The establishment of the Council of Economic Advisers by the Employment Act of 1946 gave the president for the first time a unit charged with surveying the economy from the viewpoint of the general public welfare and making recommendations accordingly. There was no assurance that the council would be used or staffed intelligently, but Truman, with his passion for administrative neatness, was anxious to establish it as a policy-making center. His appointees possessed the talent to make it something more than another obscure niche in the bureaucracy.

The conceptual problem is well known—neither Roosevelt nor many of the New Dealers had developed a grasp of Keynesian economics by the time World War II began. However, the war forced massive government spending, produced prosperity, and demonstrated the strength of the American economy. A number of publicists spread the new economic gospel in a coherent, readily understandable manner; and an imposing phalanx of liberal congressmen introduced the full employment bill, the original version of the Employment Act of 1946. Democratic liberalism, having groped unsuccessfully for an economic program during the Depression, had come out of the war with a well-developed set of proposals for maintaining prosperity. Within the administration, the Council of Economic Advisers would provide a forum for these new ideas.

The most important member of the council and the chief economic thinker of the Fair Deal, Leon Keyserling, was not in any precise sense a "Keynesian," nor, most assuredly, was Truman. On the surface, moreover, Keyserling—Jewish, a product of elite Eastern universities, a protégé of Robert F. Wagner, a veteran of social welfare politics—was about as different from Truman as he could be. But both were economic progressives in the broad sense—advocates of growth, comfortable with social welfare programs, sympathetic to the principle of graduated taxation. Truman himself knew little of economic theory, but his impulses served him well in the postwar era. His very lack of training in economics reinforced his flexible, nondoctrinaire approach to public policy. For example, he instinctively believed in a balanced budget and in reduction of the national debt, and this was a belief appropriate to containment of the inflationary tendencies that dominated most of his years in office. But during the 1949 recession, he readily accepted a budget deficit rather than take a chance on damaging the economy by calling for higher taxes.

Truman's early life as a businessman, civic booster, and county administrator had made him what one might call an entrepreneurial liberal. His was the classic experience of the small businessman from the provinces, suspicious of the business and financial establishment, hopeful of rapid economic growth and development, looking at times to the federal government for help but resentful of bureaucratic regulations and controls. His economic policies reflected this experience, and on the whole they served the nation well.

The social welfare agenda that Truman came to call the Fair Deal reflected the heritage of its predecessor. Its most successful efforts involved the updating and extension of programs that Roosevelt had initiated. The Social Security Act of 1950, for example, has drawn scant attention from historians because it at first appears to be simply an addition to an ongoing program. Yet when one considers the state of the Social Security system at the time, the act takes on far greater significance. Social Security was still pegged to the deflated dollar and low expectations of the 1930s; the last significant amendments to the original legislation had been enacted in 1939. As Arthur J. Altmeyer has commented, "An entire decade had passed during which the only change had been to reduce its coverage." The 1950 legislation extended old age and survivors' insurance coverage to an additional ten and a half million people, raised the level of benefits an average of 80 percent, and considerably liberalized many federal-state public assistance programs. Not simply a routine addition to existing law, it got through Congress only after a year and a half of effort and may fairly be described as a milestone in the history of American social welfare legislation.

Truman's efforts to move beyond the New Deal in social reform were less successful and are more familiar to historians. They merit examination because they demonstrate both the moderate postwar political consensus against which the Fair Deal struggled and the conceptual limitations of the liberalism that the Truman administration adopted. Two issues are especially illustrative: Truman's proposal for national health insurance, a bill that never had a chance of passage, and his advocacy of public housing, which did clear Congress only to prove a disappointment.

Roosevelt had intended to make national health insurance a part of his postwar attempt to revive the New Deal. Truman picked up the proposal without hesitation and seems to have deeply believed in it—although the nature of postwar politics and diplomacy was such that it could never be his highest priority. Congressional enactment was never a serious possibility. The opposition was much better financed and organized than the tiny liberal lobbies that tried to drum up support for the bill. A majority of Americans were receptive to the charge that it was an attempt to establish "socialized medicine" and alien to the American tradition.

Most fundamentally, there was no widely felt public need for major changes in the existing medical care system. Private health insurance plans more than doubled their coverage during Truman's presidency and largely met the needs of the politically articulate. Public opinion polls taken in 1949 displayed widespread public ignorance and apathy about the proposal.[1] Truman had, nonetheless, succeeded in floating an idea that could be modified in later years to help one increasingly larger group of people that had difficulty with the existing system—the elderly.

On the surface, Truman seemed much more successful in rallying support for major public housing legislation and pushing it through Congress after four years of unceasing effort. Here he spoke to a widely felt sense of deprivation. With the exception of inflation, no problem was more broadly experienced during the Truman years than inadequate housing. Young working families, nominally of middle-class status but forced to double up with parents or pay exorbitant rents for substandard accommodations, could identify to some extent with poverty-stricken slum dwellers. A substantial majority of Americans, according to the opinion polls, favored not only subsidies for middle-class home-building but also slum clearance and public housing.[2] Even Robert A. Taft climbed aboard the bandwagon.

It is revelatory of the strongly antireformist structure of the Truman Congresses that an omnibus housing bill was not passed until 1949, its public housing provisions squeezing through the House of Representatives by only five votes. In practice, the new legislation provided substantial help for the middle-class home buyer but did little to improve the lot of the slum dweller. Its public housing authorization was weakly administered, blocked by local interests in many cities, and financially drained by the competing demands of the Korean War after 1950. Moreover, most of the public housing projects that were built turned out badly. In their high-rise form especially, the projects tended to

---

[1] In the first poll, 44 percent of the respondents were unfamiliar with the administration health plan; 14 percent were aware of it but had no opinion; and the remaining 42 percent was evenly divided. The second poll explained both the administration proposal and the AMA alternative of encouraging private health insurance. It drew an opinion from 80 percent, of whom 47 percent backed the AMA and 33 percent the administration.

[2] In January 1949, Mr. Gallup's pollsters found 69 percent of their interviewees in favor of the concept.

exaggerate all the bad features of urban poverty—crime, vice, vandalism—and to become instant slums themselves. The Fair Deal reformers had assumed that slum housing was a major cause rather than an incidental consequence of urban crime and poverty. One can say with some confidence that they were wrong, but it would be fatuous to pretend that recent thinkers have been more perceptive.

Perhaps the most revealing aspect of the Fair Deal, both for what it tells us about Truman and for what it has to say about the evolution of the modern Democratic party, is the way in which it approached the movement for black civil rights. By the time Truman reached the presidency, blacks had become a key part of the Roosevelt coalition. They were attracted primarily through the New Deal relief programs and secondarily through token recognition of black aspirations. During World War II, the establishment of the Fair Employment Practices Committee had cemented the alliance. With Roosevelt's death, however, the relationship, based mainly upon a sense of personal allegiance to FDR, was thrown into doubt. Some black political tacticians began to stress the importance of independent voting.

Truman's background implied little commitment to the cause of black advancement. His grandparents had been slaveowners; Missouri mandated school segregation in its constitution; he himself had often made it clear that he did not believe in "social equality." Yet from the days that his political ambitions moved beyond rural Jackson County, Truman had displayed sympathy for black aspirations. The Pendergast machine had been probably the first Democratic urban organization to solicit black support, partly because the European immigrant population of Kansas City was relatively small. As a senator, Truman had been a reliable and increasingly prominent supporter of civil rights causes but hardly a leader. His mixed attitude was well symbolized by the contrast between his public support of an antilynching bill and his private belief that it was an unconstitutional invasion of states' rights.

No historian can precisely define Truman's motivation on so complex and emotional an issue; it was probably not entirely clear even to Truman. It seems fair to say that he really believed in the principles of equal rights and equal opportunity. But it is also just to observe that he was well aware of the importance of the black vote. It is reasonable to assume that he acted in part out of a sense of self-interest but more important that he interpreted his self-interest in a fashion both astute and morally enlightened.

Truman's commitment to civil rights was not unswerving: he wanted to keep the South within the Democratic party and was willing to make gestures to Southern sensibilities. Still, it was about as consistent as most political commitments tend to be. During his years in office, he identified himself more strongly with the aspirations of black Americans than had any president before him. His special committee on civil rights, a body packed with liberal activists, issued findings and recommendations that established an agenda for two decades of attacks against segregation. His Justice Department began a practice of filing *amicus curiae* briefs in important civil rights cases, including the first argument of the *Brown* case near the end of 1952. As early as 1950, these friend-of-the-court briefs had thrown the considerable moral and political weight of the executive branch behind the assertion that the old "separate but equal" doctrine should be overruled. Presidential executive orders created some additional opportunity in the federal civil service and ended segregation in the armed forces. With these actions, Truman appealed to the black vote and fed the beginnings of what a later generation would call the black revolution.

Truman's central success as a political leader was the maintenance of the polyglot, unstable political coalition that made first the New Deal and then the Fair Deal possible. In the process of becoming the nation's majority party in the 1930s, the Democratic party had functioned, to use Samuel Lubell's terminology, as the sun in the political heavens, exerting a gravitational pull that attracted groups diverse in their cultures and at times irreconcilable in their political interests. Under the pressures of the Depression, Roosevelt had for a time been successful in making this conglomerate a powerful force for liberal reform. By the end of the thirties, however, it had begun a process of disintegration that brought the New Deal to a halt and initiated an era of political stalemate.

The squabbling within the party has been described in various ways—North versus South, urban constituencies versus rural ones, labor versus agriculture, minority groups versus WASPs, liberals versus conservatives. All these descriptions possess a measure of accuracy, and the conflicts they encompass all worsened during World War II. Roosevelt's death left observers wondering whether the coalition he had fashioned would soon follow him to the grave. Truman's first two years in office, culminating in the Republican capture of Congress in the 1946 elections, seemed to provide little but confirmation for the pessimists.

Truman ultimately held the Roosevelt coalition together by means of his struggle with the Eightieth Congress and his 1948 reelection campaign. It is tempting to see him as a plucky underdog fighting the interests, winning the sympathy of the people, and emerging triumphant against the odds; but while he may have picked up some support this way, his 1948 victory was not a personal triumph, and the Truman cult of personality was not a phenomenon of the presidential years.

Whatever his virtues, Truman had never been mistaken for a magnetic mass leader. His career had developed in the plodding commonplace fashion of American politics; he had built it upon personal friendship and loyalties, allegiance to a larger organization, and intensive campaigning among small, usually amicable groups of constituents. Handicapped by his poor eyesight, he found it difficult to follow a prepared speech text, and he never mastered the art of speaking to large audiences. His radio addresses, haltingly delivered with a Midwestern twang, were as dull and conventional as Roosevelt's had been inspirational.

Eventually, Truman developed some appeal by reverting to the political techniques of his earlier years, speaking in a natural off-the-cuff manner to small crowds, recalling real or fancied family ties to the town or area in which he found himself, introducing his family, invoking partisan loyalties, and in general presenting himself, much as in his Jackson County days, as an ordinary, hard-working person running for office. It was an approach that might strike a responsive chord from time to time but was hardly suited to the development of enduring personal loyalty. The American common man, like common men all over the world, would respond to the heroic, to the larger-than-life, more consistently and fervently than to a leader who seemed very much like himself. Unable to overawe the electorate in the manner of Roosevelt, Truman could never muster more than a fragile popularity.

He appears to have understood his limitations. From Jackson County on, he had consistently attempted to identify himself with *issues*. His 1947-48 battles, with all the dramatic vetoes and give-'em-hell rhetoric, were meant to define issues in a way consciously calculated to rally the Roosevelt coalition. If one reads through his three hundred or so rear-platform speeches in the 1948 campaign, one finds them packed with references to issues that vary a bit according to location—inflation, the housing crisis, the progressive income tax structure, the Taft-Hartley Act and its restrictions upon labor, the maintenance of high farm income, Social Security, federal electrical power projects and resource development.

Again and again, he charged that the Republicans were engaged in the first stages of an offensive against the New Deal—the Eightieth Congress became an embarrassment that Thomas E. Dewey could never shake off. He urged the voters to cast their ballots after rationally calculating their own interests. "All I ask you to do is vote for yourself, vote for your family," he declared at one stop. He knew that if the electorate accepted his definition of the issues, it would vote for preservation of the New Deal.

Truman's victory held the Roosevelt coalition together, but it could not reconcile the conflicts and contradictions within it. The president and many liberals chose to believe that the 1948 election represented a mandate for a new age of reform. They enthusiastically moved to create a farm-labor political alliance intellectually based on the concept of economic abundance, politically based on the Brannan farm program, which would combine low consumer prices with high farm income. The result, they hoped, would be an unbeatable political coalition that would secure the passage of the Brannan Plan, Taft-Hartley repeal, aid to education, a new FEPC, federal health insurance, and public housing. The effort was a failure; exciting in theory, the goal of farmer-labor unity had little foundation in the real world.

The Fair Dealers had misread the meaning of the election. Truman's 1948 speeches had not been pitched to the need for brave new worlds; they had emphasized dangers to the accomplishments of the New Deal. He had appealed to a new and insecure middle class, determined to protect its gains but feeling no urgency about a new wave of liberal reform. Public opinion polls taken in 1949 displayed little enthusiasm for most of the components of the Fair Deal (housing was a conspicuous exception). The polls did, however, display vast concern about another issue that would increasingly consume both the Truman administration and the cause of liberal reform—Communism.

Thus, Truman scored no liberal breakthroughs but he was able to build in important ways upon existing New Deal programs. These included not only Social Security but also public power, the wage and hour statutes, conservation, resource development, rural electrification, and even the antitrust laws. Moreover, his administration had established a conceptual and structural basis for future liberal reform.

After the outbreak of the Korean War, the unfulfilled portions of the Fair Deal stood no real chance of passage. The president soft-pedaled them for the sake of party unity in dealing with the challenges presented by McCarthy and MacArthur. In 1952, however, he was waving the banner of the Fair Deal again, this time not out of any electoral cause of his own but out of a determination that the liberalism with which he had identified himself should remain at the center of national political debate. He systematically set about making a series of public addresses which, as he told Eleanor Roosevelt, were designed to cover "nearly every phase of the program of the Democratic party for the last twenty years." That fall, although he was a sixty-eight-year-old noncandidate, he stormed across the country on a series of tours more extensive than in 1948. "How odd that a Pendergast alumnus should be so wise and bold," remarked the *New Republic*, "but what a tribute to the American system."

The Cold Warrior

"Diplomacy has always been too much for me—especially diplomacy as it is practiced by the great powers," Senator Harry S. Truman wrote to a constituent in 1943. "They always have some deep, dark ulterior motive for everything they do." The declaration reflected at least in part the provincial, common-man affectation so central to Truman's political style, but it equally bespoke a lack of preparation and sense of insecurity that he never wholly surmounted in dealing with international politics. Nonetheless, it is fair to say that his diplomacy, considered as a whole, was a sizable success story.

No American before Truman had assumed the presidency at a time of such rapid change and deep U.S. involvement in world affairs. Few of his predecessors had been so lacking in the training and experience generally deemed necessary for success in the world of high-pressure diplomacy. The new president had traveled to Europe only as a soldier in World War I and had displayed practically no interest in foreign policy before World War II. During his short tenure as vice-president, the Roosevelt White House failed to give him even the most elementary briefings.

When Truman moved into the Oval Office, he had no direct knowledge of the several areas of dispute that had developed between the United States and the USSR, of the project to develop an atomic bomb, or of Roosevelt's private attitudes and expectations. He slowly overcame a deep inner insecurity that from time to time in the early years of his administration he attempted to mask with ostentatious displays of decisiveness. Like Roosevelt, he interpreted foreign policy in terms of his domestic political experience; but where Roosevelt was cosmopolitan, Truman was provincial; where Roosevelt had tended toward indirection, ambiguity, and postponement, Truman came down on the side of bluntness, clarity, and quick decision-making.

No aspect of Truman's attitude and experience was more fundamental in defining his approach to foreign policy than his intuitive embrace of vital center liberalism. Just as he disdained the extremism of both the Left and the Right in American politics, he drew no moral distinctions between the totalitarianism of the Left and the Right in foreign affairs, an attitude deeply rooted in his own Midwestern, egalitarian background. "Really there is no difference between the government which Mr. Molotov represents and the one the Czar represented—or the one Hitler spoke for," he wrote to his mother and sister in November 1946.

To this, he added a wide-ranging and rather naive idealism loosely derived from Protestant millennialism and Victorian optimism. Not a devout man, he was enough a product of his culture to accept unquestioningly the assumption that the American national mission was divine in its origins and purpose. God, he told audiences from time to time, had given America the task of world leadership. In 1949, the State Department had to talk him out of an effort to organize all the religious leaders of the world in opposition to Stalinist Communism and in support of a drive for peace.

The more secular side of his outlook came directly from the Victorian idealism in which he, no less than Roosevelt, had been reared. It was represented most vividly in a passage from Tennyson's "Locksley Hall," a poem that had so deeply affected him as a boy of sixteen that he copied several stanzas and kept them with him for the rest of his life:

For I dipt into the future, far as human eye could see,
Saw the Vision of the world, and all the wonders that would be;

Saw the heavens fill with commerce, argosies of magic sails,
Pilots of the purple twilight, dropping down with costly bails;

Heard the heavens fill with shouting, and there rained a ghastly dew
From the nations' airy navies grappling in the central blue;

Far along the world-wide whisper of the south-wind rushing warm,
With the standards of the people plunging thro' the thunder-storm;

Till the war-drum throbbed no longer, and the battle-flags were furl'd
In the Parliament of Man, the Federation of the World.

There the common sense of most shall hold a fretful realm in awe,
And the kindly earth shall slumber, lapt in universal law.

It was, he told John Hersey, a remarkable prophecy, and not just in its forecast of air warfare: "Notice also that part about universal law. We're going to have that someday, just as sure as we have air war now. That's what I'm working for. I guess that's what I've really been working for ever since I first put that poetry in my pocket."

Truman was capable of genuine eloquence when he spoke of the need for U.S. leadership in aid for the impoverished and underdeveloped areas of the world. "I have been dreaming of TVAs in the Euphrates Valley to restore that country to the fertility and beauty of ancient times, of a TVA in the Yangtze

Valley and the Danube," he once told David Lilienthal. "These things can be done and don't let anybody tell you different. When they happen, when millions and millions of people are no longer hungry and pushed and harassed, then the causes of wars will be less by that much." His vision found a bit of fulfillment in various programs of economic assistance to underdeveloped nations, collectively known as Point Four of his foreign policy. But his dreams ran far beyond the possibilities of the real world along the Euphrates, the Yangtze, or the Danube.

In addition to his idealism and his centrist liberalism, Truman, very much like Roosevelt, possessed a tendency to personalize foreign policy and conceptualize it in terms of his political experiences. He was, however, even less sophisticated about it. Stalin impressed him quite favorably at the Potsdam conference, their only face-to-face meeting; affected by the Soviet dictator's apparent candor and by the blunt strength of his personality, Truman remarked that the Russian reminded him of Tom Pendergast. From time to time throughout his presidency, he returned to his belief that the Cold War had developed only because Stalin was the prisoner of sinister forces in the Politburo.

In discussions with friends and visitors, he frequently passed similar personal and occasionally misinformed judgments on important foreign leaders and their regimes. He appears to have hated the Spanish *caudillo* Francisco Franco not simply or even primarily for his fascism but because Franco persecuted Truman's fellow Baptists and Masons. He dismissed Chiang Kai-shek and Chiang's entire Nationalist government as just a failed group of crooked political operators. Irritated by Jawaharlal Nehru's Third World neutralism, he privately characterized the Indian leader as a Communist. He invariably focused upon the personal and the specific rather than the abstract and the complex.

From this emphasis, he moved easily into a highly legalistic view of foreign relations. Men with whom one could do business, whether political bosses or foreign leaders, had to be honest, if not in their personal financial conduct then at least in the fundamental matter of keeping their word. Honest leaders therefore scrupulously observed the agreements they had made with other nations. Truman rarely interpreted diplomatic agreements as ambiguous. In his mind, the wartime agreements reached between the United States and the Soviet Union at Teheran, Yalta, and Potsdam were crystal-clear, admitting of no room for different interpretations of their reciprocal obligations. The Russians, he told C. L. Sulzberger in 1947, had broken forty-seven treaties in the past twenty-five years. "How can you negotiate an understanding with people who have no moral responsibility?" Sulzberger was nonplussed; the president, he confided to his diary, had "a rather rural knowledge of the world."

Anti–Cold War liberals at the time and since have possessed a gut conviction that if only FDR had lived he would have managed a suitable arrangement with Stalin and would have led the world into the new era he had so eloquently promised. Two related fallacies dominate their thinking: the belief that relations between great powers are largely a matter of personal relations between their leaders rather than the interplay of divergent national interests and aspirations and the following premise that diplomacy is solely the function of the president. These are attractive assumptions. Taken together, they simplify the real world, thus making it superficially more comprehensible; and they allow one to believe that things could so easily have been different and better. Little wonder that they have possessed appeal even to highly educated and supposedly sophisticated scholars.

Even under Roosevelt, American diplomacy had not been a one-man show. Truman had a surer sense of his own limitations and an almost fervent dedication to the administrative principle of line responsibility. Embracing the role of chief diplomat and determined to reserve major decisions for himself, he nevertheless wanted the day-to-day conduct and conceptualization of foreign policy to reside in the State Department. He largely returned diplomacy to professionals and semiprofessionals more knowledgeable and experienced than he.

Especially after Gen. George C. Marshall became secretary of state, it was the State Department that did the basic thinking about American foreign policy, gave the president most of his information, and presented him with alternatives. From time to time, as with the Point Four program or the decision to recognize the state of Israel, the White House staff might add touches of its own, but it never had the resources to compete with State on a sustained, across-the-board basis. Marshall and his successor, Dean Acheson, kept Truman fully informed and paid him the deference due his position; moreover, they functioned as intermediaries and interpreters between the president and the foreign service professionals, whom Truman was wont to describe contemptuously as "the striped pants boys." This method of operation ensured that Truman would make few, if any, significant decisions resting primarily upon personal prejudice or misinformation; yet it allowed ample play for the expression of his *temperament* as a basic force in American foreign policy. The result—a fairly harmonious reconciliation of the president's aspirations with international reality—served the nation well.

Truman's most important foreign policy contribution may have been his success in obtaining Republican support for his course. Among the most partisan of political leaders, usually at war with the opposition over domestic issues, he nevertheless proved adept at establishing and maintaining what he called a "bipartisan foreign policy," actually little more than wide Republican assent to the administration's decisions. He was able to manage this in the first instance because his foreign policy possessed considerable merit but also because in soliciting diplomatic support, he was much more able than in managing domestic issues to revert to his old role as a centrist legislator, positioned neatly between extremes of Right and Left, seeking friendship and political support from the moderates of both parties.

He and his chief aides were especially good at appealing to key GOP congressmen, foremost among them Senator Arthur Vandenberg of Michigan. The administration courted him and lesser Republicans assiduously, briefing them, giving them extensive recognition, yet largely excluding them from any active policy-making responsibility and leaving them with at most an implicit veto. As a result, the basic legislation providing for the containment of Soviet Communism and the reconstruction of Europe sailed through a GOP Congress in 1947 and 1948 even as Truman was tearing into its leadership on one domestic issue after another. There was in the end, however, one indispensable prerequisite for the maintenance of a bipartisan foreign policy—it had to be successful. Truman's European policy provided a glow in which all concerned could bask contentedly; his efforts to define the American interest in Asia would be less satisfactory.

Despite the various charges that it was Truman who in one way or another started the Cold War, it is more accurate to say that his administration originated no truly new major policies during the first year or so of his presidency. Rather, he and his aides groped for the meaning of the policies they had inherited, attempted to adapt them to new situations, and eventually discovered that they had a Cold War on their hands. Truman himself possessed conflicting impulses toward the Soviet Union in the closing months of World War II. He had little use for the Soviet dictatorship but apparently felt that it had the support of the Russian people. Above all, he wanted to preserve the Big Three alliance, an objective very much in line with his desire to carry out Roosevelt's policies and with his vision of a world of peace and unity.

He felt especially bound to observe the agreements FDR had made and to exact compliance with the pledges he had received. His foreign policy advisers were to a man individuals who had been associated with FDR; yet their outlooks ran the gamut from the emotional pro-Sovietism of Joseph Davies to the hard-eyed suspicions of W. Averell Harriman. They were able to provide no consensus because they reflected in the aggregate all the contradictions and ambiguities of Roosevelt's diplomacy, and Truman had become president just as these were being exposed by events. There could be little doubt that the USSR was violating the spirit, and probably the letter, of the Yalta agreements as it vigorously moved forward with the establishment of supremacy in several Eastern European countries. In such circumstances, some sort of American protest was unavoidable.

Truman's own temperament impelled him to react stiffly. The impulse was reinforced by the advice of Averell Harriman, who had been wartime ambassador to the USSR. Harriman possessed more recent first-hand experience with the Soviet leadership than any other American policy shaper of the first rank. Oppressed by Stalinist totalitarianism and by the truculent hostility he customarily encountered in dealing with Soviet officials, he knew that friendship between the two great powers would not come easily and was convinced that the USSR was embarking on an expansionist program that could lead to dominance of all of Europe. Persuaded that Roosevelt had been unable to cement an alliance with gestures of goodwill, he advised negotiation from a stance of firmness; the Russians, he believed, would be more likely to respect frank language, demands for quid pro quos, and policies more surely based upon American interests and values.

Truman adopted the advice perhaps a bit too enthusiastically, underscoring his determination with a sharp lecture to Soviet foreign minister Molotov less than two weeks after becoming president. Yet for every example of "toughness" in dealing with the Russians during the first year of Truman's administration, one finds an example of softness. The degree of American economic and strategic interest in Eastern Europe was quite small, and it was inconceivable that expressions of moral indignation would be carried beyond rhetoric. Truman, bound as he was to Roosevelt's objectives, intermittently behaved much as had Roosevelt—he hoped for the best. Between sporadic protests over various Soviet barbarities in the Eastern European countries, the United States tendered de facto recognition to a Russian sphere of influence. Postponement, no longer possible, gave way to ineffective rhetoric.

A month after his meeting with Molotov, for example, Truman sent Harry Hopkins to Moscow to negotiate an agreement with Stalin that in effect recognized Soviet control in Poland. A Big Three foreign ministers' conference in Moscow in December 1945 recognized other Soviet-influenced Eastern European regimes. At Potsdam, in the meantime, Truman had formed a good impression of Stalin. As late as September 1945, it was still possible for the president and his cabinet to discuss the possibility of sharing atomic technology with the USSR as a grand goodwill gesture. Of course, Truman decided against it, and, throughout 1945, U.S.–Russian relations suffered from displays of rhetorical ill will. Still, one can easily believe that no Cold War would have emerged as it did if Russian ambitions had been clearly and strictly limited to dominance of Eastern Europe, the Eastern zone of Germany, and the Manchuria–North Korea sector of the Far East.

The instability that the war had wrought would have made a limitation of this sort difficult, although probably not impossible. The suspicions of Truman and those around him were fed less by the understandable Soviet determination to control nations on the borders of the USSR than by the fear that Russian ambitions were almost without limit and thereby directed toward areas of great importance to the United States and its close ally, Great Britain. These suspicions stemmed not simply from Truman's provincialism nor even the sophisticated amateurism of Harriman. They rested most surely upon the formulations of George F. Kennan.

One of the most learned and respected members of the professional foreign service, Kennan possessed an expertise in Russian history and culture that few Americans could match. As counselor at the U.S. embassy in Moscow during and immediately after the war, he decided that Stalinist Communism was incapable of coexisting with the Western world in a friendly alliance; it was too suspicious and too much in need of external hostility to justify its totalitarian rule. The only way to deal with the USSR, Kennan concluded, was to assume its aggressiveness as a matter of course and to frustrate its expansionism through a policy of constructive containment. Kennan's major exposition of this thesis, a long dispatch from Moscow in February 1946, won wide attention in Washington, led to his appointment as the State Department's chief of policy planning, and served as a more or less definitive text of the administration's changing foreign policy course.

Kennan's theorizing would have possessed little significance, however, if Soviet policy had not seemed to confirm it. For a time in late 1945 and 1946, the USSR refused to withdraw military forces from northern Iran and actually established a secessionist puppet state there. The policy infuriated Truman, who saw it as mistreatment of a wartime ally that had served as the primary conduit for Lend-Lease shipments to Russia. Moreover, Iran, rich in oil and strategically placed at the head of the Persian Gulf, was a country of considerable importance to the United States. Under American pressure, the Russians withdrew in the spring of 1946. But their activities elsewhere indicated that they had not foresworn the extension of Soviet power. It was this situation that would launch containment as a coherent policy and lead to its greatest successes.

It was not until the beginning of 1947 that the Truman administration was ready to move vigorously against the increasingly felt threat of Soviet expansionism. It was finally ready to engage in more than words because it perceived Soviet efforts at hegemony in the eastern Mediterranean, the Middle East, and, most crucial of all, Western Europe. Unlike Eastern Europe, these areas were of vital strategic and economic significance, and all were extraordinarily vulnerable. The administration's short-term solution was military aid to Greece and Turkey, thereby bolstering Turkey's resistance to Russian demands for control of the straits between the Black Sea and the Mediterranean and enabling Greece to fight off a Communist-controlled insurgency. The long-range solution was the Marshall Plan, a vast program of economic aid for all of non-Communist Europe based on the premise that the surest mode of containment was the erection of strong, non-Communist economies. Only after the Marshall Plan cleared Congress did the administration move forward with a comprehensive military containment plan, the North Atlantic Treaty Organization, an alliance committing the United States to defend Western Europe against outside attack.

In all, these were a remarkable set of departures. Yet despite the enormity of their military and economic pledges, they moved through Congress rather easily. The opposition, consisting mainly of elements from the far Right and the far Left, provided eloquent testimony of Truman's success in preempting the middle of the political-diplomatic spectrum.

One may duly credit Truman and Marshall with considerable political skill while still granting that the Russians themselves were in the last analysis the most convincing promoters of containment. The needless Soviet-promoted coup in Czechoslovakia at the beginning of 1948, followed by the senseless and reckless blockade of the Western sectors of Berlin, gave the Soviet Union the appearance of an irrational, militarily aggressive nation, bent on stamping out every vestige of independence. Against this backdrop of menace, Truman and his diplomats could easily unite non-Communist Europe behind whatever they proposed and with a minimum amount of skill push those programs through a Congress disposed to regard them as an unwelcome necessity.

By the end of 1949, containment had been accomplished in

Europe. The Continent's economies were reviving, NATO provided an assurance of military protection and assistance from the United States, and Communist parties had been excluded from positions of influence. The Russians had given up on their demands for the Turkish straits, the insurgency in Greece was crushed, and the Berlin blockade had been lifted. These successes brought with them new questions: How long would containment last? How could it be brought to an end? What would follow it?

Neither Truman nor those around him could produce wholly satisfactory answers; perhaps indeed there were none. Implicit in the concept of containment was the assumption that Soviet expansionism represented a long-term challenge that would require equally persistent economic and military countermeasures. The entire record of Soviet behavior since 1945 presented almost no basis for optimism. It was not surprising therefore that Truman and his new secretary of state, Dean Acheson, talked of the need to negotiate from strength and engage in "total diplomacy." The administration, enjoying wide public approval, dismissed Soviet overtures for a broad negotiation of East-West differences in mid-1949. It considered the Russian move simply a ploy to undercut the rearmament of Western Europe and the establishment of a West German state. Then and now, the analysis was speculative; the precise nature of Soviet intentions in 1949 is unverifiable. What we do know is that Truman and Acheson never considered a serious effort to explore them. Having taken a year and a half to settle on containment and another two and one half years to implement it, they were hardly in a position to reverse the momentum the policy had achieved. Moreover, their reading of the situation appeared so plausible to their contemporaries that historians must hesitate to question it in the absence of tangible evidence that it was wrong.

Truman faced one more serious inhibition in imagining that the USSR might be ready to talk in earnest about a general settlement: the course of the Communist revolution in Asia. Given a measure of American will, containment was a policy almost guaranteed to succeed in Western Europe, a region favored with abundant economic resources, requiring only a temporary stimulus to be self-sustaining, and intensely fearful of Soviet domination.

In the United States, it was rather easy to build broad bipartisan support for a course so relatively painless. Asia presented a situation so different as to defy comparison from almost every perspective. Culturally alien, economically impoverished, more ambiguous in its relationship to American self-interest, Asia presented American diplomacy with a set of challenges for which the Truman administration was unprepared. Neither Truman nor his colleagues appear to have reached a consistent determination about whether containment even actually applied to Asia. Whatever their private attitudes, however, the public believed that it did, and it was in Asian policy that the administration's diplomacy suffered its worst reverses, both at home and abroad.

At the center of all Truman's problems in Asia was China. Just as FDR had been unable to make China a great power by fiat, Truman was unable to make it pro-American with a policy of good intentions. It is difficult to see how American diplomacy could have changed the course of Chinese history; it is nevertheless fair to judge China the great failure of Truman's diplomacy because neither he nor his State Department achieved a full and mature understanding of the situation there nor did they prepare the American people for the inevitable. Correctly judging that Europe presented both a more important goal and a more manageable situation, the president, his secretaries of state, and his diplomatic service never fashioned a global diplomacy in which the fate of Asia was clearly outlined. As a result, the American people would tend to see only failure in U.S. Asian policy instead of a mixture of success, stalemate, and failure. The Republican party would find a policy of limited retreat considerably less palatable than the European successes of containment.

The Truman administration's initial failure in dealing with China was its inability to perceive the depths of the division between the Nationalists of Chiang Kai-shek and the Communists of Mao Tse-tung. Chiang was not, as some right-wingers have argued, "sold out" by American diplomats; he seems to have been defeated largely because his government was corrupt and ineffective. It is nonetheless true that U.S. diplomats in China tended to depict the Communists as more a reformist than a revolutionary faction. This view had a basis in the moderation that Mao actually practiced in Communist-controlled areas during World War II, but it was hardly the careful, incisive analysis that one expects of a good foreign service.

The administration first attempted to deal with the problem by negotiating a peace between the two factions and establishing a coalition government. The undertaking, headed up by General Marshall in 1946, seemed to assume that the differences between Chiang and Mao were as relatively modest and resolvable as those between the Republicans and Democrats in the United States and that the political culture of China was attuned to a practice of compromise and accommodation that actually was peculiar to a few Western democracies. The Marshall negotiations quickly became an arena within which the two warring sides maneuvered for advantage. At their collapse, the Communists were well positioned to begin a final series of campaigns against the disintegrating Nationalist government.

The administration decided to cut its losses; yet it did not prepare the American people for the certain denouement. It was too preoccupied with containment in Europe and the struggle for the Marshall Plan. In addition, the need to build support for European containment among the Republicans precluded a frank explanation of the Chinese situation. Simply stated, although the vast majority of the Republican party felt that the containment of Communism in Asia was every bit as important as in Europe, few were willing to face the question of cost.

One could make a substantial strategic argument for Asia's importance, but its appeal was primarily emotional. Among the middle-class white Anglo-Saxon Protestants who made up the core of the Republican party, there existed a deeply felt "missionary attitude" toward the Chinese dating back to the mid-nineteenth century. Originally expressed as an attempt to spread Christianity, the missionary impulse had developed into a broader secular impulse to spread the blessings of Western economic development and democracy. Years of Japanese aggression had deepened this popular sympathy for China. Chiang Kai-shek himself, like the other Allied leaders of World War II, had been publicized as a great democrat.

In such circumstances, it was a normal enough impulse for the administration to downplay China. It was equally normal for the Republicans to insist upon aid for Chiang without ever attempting to present a precise measurement of the enormous cost. In order to get Marshall Plan appropriations through Congress, Truman had to maintain a formal commitment to Chiang and agree to a Chinese aid amendment large enough to satisfy the Republicans but too small to make a perceptible difference in his situation. The administration quietly awaited his defeat and hoped for an accommodation with the new Communist government, which it expected to be substantially independent of Soviet control.

When it came, the Nationalist collapse occurred with stunning rapidity. Possessing nominal control of most of the country outside of Manchuria at the beginning of 1949, the Nationalists were forced to flee to Taiwan by the end of the summer. The administration hastily compiled a thousand-page "white paper" that attempted to vindicate its China policy, but the effort was too late to make much of an impression. Moreover, the authors of the white paper felt compelled to defer to Republican sensibilities and popular myths. A letter of transmittal to the president, signed by Dean Acheson, depicted the Chinese Communist victory as a triumph for foreign domination although the State Department had earlier rejected that thesis. The Chinese Communists, for their part, behaved as if they were bent on vindicating the State Department reversal; from the beginning, they engaged in a harsh anti-Americanism and proclaimed their solidarity with the USSR. To almost any observer, it had to appear that the United States had suffered a setback. To the defenders of Chiang, the Truman administration had "lost China."

The situation was complicated all the more by Chiang's position on the strategically important island of Taiwan. In an episode that neatly illustrated the way in which Asia had become the afterthought of the Cold War, State Department planners considered the possibility of Taiwanese independence in early 1949—only after it was too late to prevent Chiang from establishing himself there. The administration instead announced that it would not defend the island against Chinese Communist attack, a policy that enraged Republican critics while winning no demonstration of friendship from the Chinese Communists. Through the first half of 1950, Chiang consolidated his authority in Taiwan unmolested by his Communist enemies; his friends in the United States mounted a campaign depicting him as a victim of Truman, Acheson, and pro-Communist diplomats in the State Department.

The outbreak of war in Korea near the end of June 1950 deepened the American sense of failure in Asia and immeasurably strengthened Truman's critics. The North Korean attack upon the South was, of course, the outgrowth of a bitter civil rivalry, but it may have come when it did because of the failure of Truman's diplomats and military strategists to define the American relationship to South Korea in terms clear both to themselves and to the rest of the world. In a major, yet poorly thought out speech in January 1950, Secretary Acheson did not place Korea within the American defense perimeter in the Far East and left the American commitment to it extremely vague. Congressional Republicans added to the uncertainty by defeating a Korean aid bill, although they subsequently supported it when it was broadened to include assistance to what remained of Nationalist China. The North Korean leadership may have interpreted these "signals" to mean that the United States would not resist a Communist effort to unify the peninsula.

Yet when faced with an actual attack, Truman and Acheson quickly decided that intervention was the only possible course. Had the Korean incursion been part of a worldwide Communist attack, they would have made their stand elsewhere; instead, they faced the bleak choices of throwing in troops to save a country they had come close to abandoning or of doing nothing and thus giving in to an act of aggression that was much clearer than any situation posed by the Chinese civil war. To a generation convinced that World War II had been caused by a failure to stop fascist aggression at Munich or some earlier point, there was only one thing to do, and the conclusion meshed well with Truman's combative temperament. He took nearly a week to decide on the commitment of ground troops, but there is a poetic truth to his later claim that when Acheson called him to tell him of the invasion, he replied, "Dean, we've got to stop the sons of bitches right here and now."

Even then, neither he nor Acheson was able to translate that resolve into sound and effective policy planning. Somehow, stopping the North Koreans entailed a decision to employ the U.S.

Seventh Fleet to neutralize the straits between Taiwan and mainland China, a move that provided protection for the Nationalists
and enraged the Communists.[3] The administration failed equally
to arrive at a solid, viable definition of just what it would mean to
stop the aggression. After General MacArthur's troops scored a
remarkable success at Inchon and effectively destroyed the North
Korean army, Washington could not resist the temptation to unify
the Korean peninsula; American and South Korean troops undertook a general advance designed to end only at the Yalu River, the
boundary between Korea and China. Remarkably, Truman and
Acheson assumed that the Chinese would give credence to U.S.
professions of peaceful intent. Instead, Mao and his associates
were so disturbed by the prospect of the eradication of North
Korea and an American presence on the Manchurian frontier that
they were willing to go to war.

The result was a disaster: military, diplomatic, political. The
military setbacks, grievous and unnecessary though they were,
could be most easily retrieved. By the spring of 1951, the United
States was in firm control of prewar South Korea and entrenched
in positions from which it could inflict heavy punishment upon
the Chinese. The diplomatic losses were, in the short run, irreversible. Far from establishing a working relationship with Communist China, the administration was at war with it; the conflict
would drag on into 1953, leaving relations between the two
countries among the most venomous in world diplomacy. Far
from encouraging Chinese independence from Soviet control, the
Korean War had driven China closer to the USSR.

One must not attribute this wretched turn of events to bad
luck, the wrongheadedness of General MacArthur, or Republican

---

[3]The neutralization of the straits has never been explained in a wholly
satisfactory manner. It once was widely assumed that the move was largely a matter
of domestic politics, designed to appease the Republican supporters of Chiang and
protect the administration from the potential embarrassment of a Communist
triumph in Taiwan while American troops were fighting other Oriental Communists in Korea. Some administration figures appear to have felt that the emplace-
ment of the fleet in the straits would reassure Mao that the United States was not
planning to assist Chiang in an attack upon the mainland. A third possibility is that
the neutralization was designed to ward off not just the Chinese Communist
subjugation of Taiwan but the long-feared establishment of a major Russian
military base there.

obstructionism, even if all these played a part. In the end, the failure of Truman's Asian policy must be laid to the administration's inability to meet the admittedly more difficult problems of Asia with the same perception and foresight that had marked its handling of Europe. The Asian failures, coming as they did *after* the European successes, led to another unhappy development. They severely damaged Truman politically and buried both rational domestic politics and rational diplomacy under a bitter anti-Communism.

The Challenge of McCarthyism

The Cold War posed a serious challenge to American civil liberties. It cast widespread suspicion upon Communists and fellow travelers as disloyal and, by extension, made almost any sort of radicalism suspect. Yet wholesale suppression of Communists and quasi-Communists who were not engaging in criminal acts could only harm the quality of American life—not because genuinely committed Stalinists had a moral claim to tolerance from a culture they were trying to destroy but because a wholesale violation of the civil liberties of any group would jeopardize the rights of all. The American tradition and the best interests of the Republic required a toleration of any legal form of expression, but the national hostility toward Communism and the fear of subversion generated a powerful impulse toward persecution. The Truman administration's behavior mirrored these conflicting impulses, although it was more solicitous of civil liberties than its conservative opposition.

The first serious blot on Truman's civil liberties record was his decision to establish a federal loyalty program in March 1947. It is true that he authorized the move to head off the imposition of a loyalty program by the Republican Eightieth Congress, fearing that the Congress would sanction wholesale violations of civil liberties. It is also true that no president could or should have ignored the very real problems of security that the presence of Communists might imply in some areas of government service. Nonetheless, the Truman program was ill conceived and insufficiently protective of individual liberties. Instead of focusing upon areas where the national security was paramount, it extended to every government worker. It investigated whether individuals were loyal to the United States rather than the theoretically more precise problem of whether they might be security risks.

Inevitably, a program of such vast coverage and imprecise objectives generated injustices, but they were not large in number. Fewer than four hundred federal workers were dismissed as a result of the loyalty program, and no doubt a good security case existed for firing many of them. Some, however, appear to have been demonstrably wronged. A conservative bias hostile to any form of dissent or liberal ideas crept into the administration of the program, injuring some innocent individuals and casting a pall of conformity over the government.

Even more questionable was the administration decision to prosecute the top leadership of the American Communist party under the Smith Act. In effect, the administration decided to jail the Communists for the crime of having planned to engage in verbal denunciation of the government, not for acts of violence or espionage. It secured convictions, which were upheld by the Supreme Court in what amounted to an abandonment of the hallowed "clear and present danger" test.

With a record of this sort, Truman could not claim to be an unequivocal defender of civil liberties, but it is excessive to charge, as have some historians, that he actually created the anti-Communist hysteria that came to be known as McCarthyism. Such interpretations usually assume that the entire Cold War was needless, and that all varieties of anti-Communism were essentially alike. The first assumption implies that an inactive foreign policy with an accompanying rise in Soviet influence on the European continent would have been met in the United States with less anti-Communist sentiment than the course Truman actually took. The second assumption passes over the difference between denouncing Communists as such and making false accusations against non-Communists. As spotty as was Truman's civil liberties record, he nonetheless was more likely to discount charges of Communism than to hurl them; in general, the same was true of his administration. It would have seemed inconceivable to contemporaries that a president who had dismissed the charges against Alger Hiss as a "red herring" could later be called the creator of McCarthyism.

Loose charges of Communism against Democratic administrations by conservative Republicans were nothing new when
Truman became president. They were in fact a routine feature of
right-wing GOP rhetoric, but they were of little importance until
the public began to perceive a real threat emanating from the
USSR. In 1946, as the Soviet Union tightened its control in several
Eastern European nations, Republican charges of Red penetra-
tion of the Democratic party became a prominent and effective
theme in the congressional elections. In 1948, however, the Communist issue was relatively unimportant. Truman was riding the
crest of a foreign policy that had successfully contained Communism in Europe, and liberal Democratic elements still relatively friendly toward the USSR had been largely pushed out of
the party or had left it to back Henry Wallace's Progressive
insurgency.

The Communist issue staged a potent resurgence in the latter
part of 1949 and early 1950 for a number of reasons that historians
have frequently noted—the Hiss case, the Soviet atomic bomb,
the Rosenberg arrests, and the fall of China. Taken together, all
these events indicated that Communism was again on the advance; the "loss" of China was a special shock to many moderate
Republicans, who for the first time found themselves willing to
give some credence to charges of Communist influence or softness toward Communism within the administration. Far from
creating McCarthyism, containment had been the first line of
defense against it; a postwar Red Scare emerged only as a full-
blown powerful political movement when containment proved
unsuccessful in China.

McCarthyism was above all a politics of revenge engaged in
by groups that coupled resentment against Communism with
indignation at the works of the Roosevelt and Truman administrations—the welfare state, restrictions upon business, intervention in World War II, the Europe-centeredness of Truman's Cold
War policies, the sheer success of the Democrats in holding onto
power. The combination was all the more explosive because it
was fundamentally irrational, an expression of rage on the part of
various elements unable to accommodate themselves to the drift
of post–New Deal American politics and diplomacy. It was also a
convenient partisan bludgeon for the party out of power. The

McCarthyite impulse could be contained as long as it seemed Communism was being contained around the world. Any apparent breach of Cold War containment, however unavoidable, fueled the anger and frustration that McCarthyism embodied, and any chance of cooling those emotions was engulfed by the Korean stalemate and the dismissal of General MacArthur.

Truman's own instinctive anti-Communism was offset by his reading of history, his personal experience, and the civil libertarian advisers with whom he surrounded himself. As a student of history, he unquestioningly accepted the partisan interpretation of the politics of the early Republic produced by such Democratic historians as Claude Bowers; he felt a natural sense of identification with Jefferson the defender of civil liberties against Hamilton, the High Federalists, and the Alien and Sedition Acts. As an ally of Tom Pendergast, Truman had suffered investigation into his finances and personal life that left him wary of police invasions of privacy. Although he felt compelled to praise the FBI in public, he privately distrusted the agency and detested its head, J. Edgar Hoover. His chief advisers on matters of civil liberties and national security—Clark Clifford, Charles Murphy, Stephen Spingarn, and Max Lowenthal—consistently displayed more concern for civil liberties than fear for Communist subversion.

While some historians have asserted that Truman exaggerated the dangers of domestic subversion, they actually have produced little evidence for the charge. In fact, he consistently argued that the Communist threat was primarily external and consistently minimized the dangers of domestic subversion. It is safe to say that this was his sincere and considered opinion, but he expressed it with special vehemence because the charges of the McCarthyites aroused deep-rooted partisan and personal instincts. As the administration came under increasingly effective fire from Senator McCarthy and his allies, Truman compared the situation to that of the 1790s and saw himself as a defender of American liberties. As the McCarran Act moved through Congress in the months after the beginning of the Korean War, he resisted pressure from normally liberal Democratic congressmen to come out for it and privately told his advisers he would not sign "a sedition bill." His veto, which he surely understood to be a futile gesture, must rank among the most libertarian presidential documents in American

history. Throughout the remainder of his administration, he denounced McCarthyism and Senator McCarthy himself more
strongly and regularly than almost any other active American
politician.

But neither the president nor his allies were very effective.
With the Korean War dragging on, McCarthyism gained strength.
The McCarran Act veto was all but shouted down when presented to the Congress. When Truman attempted to establish a
special committee to review the abuses of the administration
loyalty program, congressional McCarthyites blocked usually
routine legislation that would have allowed it to function. Truman
could produce evidence to show that McCarthy's specific charges
were invariably mendacious, and he could demonstrate that his
administration had been forceful and determined in its opposition
to Communism. Yet McCarthyism prospered because as a movement of rage and frustration it was immune to rational argument.

McCarthyism in fact was most remarkable for the way its
leader levied charges not simply against left-wing professors such
as Owen Lattimore or China hands who had been mistaken about
the character of Maoist Communism but against the very pillars
of American resistance to Communist expansionism. Aside from
Truman himself, McCarthy's most prominent targets were General
George Marshall, who as secretary of state had overseen and
abetted the development of containment, and Dean Acheson,
whom a later generation would remember as among the hardest
of hard-liners in negotiations with the Soviet Union.

Attacks such as these touched off the final impulse that
led Truman into the vehemence with which he responded to
McCarthyism—his loyalty to his associates. When Alger Hiss
was convicted of perjury, Acheson promptly declared to the
press that he would not turn his back upon his old friend. He then
went to the White House to offer Truman his resignation. A more
detached chief executive might well have accepted it; Truman
not only refused it but recalled to Acheson the criticism he had
suffered for failing to repudiate Tom Pendergast. Truman liked
and respected Acheson; he revered General Marshall and carried
his indignation at the smearing of Marshall to anyone who con-
doned Joe McCarthy, including the 1952 Republican candidate
for president. A major speech in Boston condemning McCarthy-

ism, the slander of Marshall, and Dwight Eisenhower's acquiescence in both revealed not simply the depths of Truman's indignation but the bottom line of his motivation: "Most of us, I think, believe a man ought to be loyal to his friends when they are unjustly attacked; that he ought to stand up for them, even if it costs him some votes. At any rate, that is a rule of my life. I stand by my friends." Combining both principle and the rules of politics, Truman's declaration was a fitting epitaph for his career.

The Accomplishment

It has been Truman's fate—partly a fate of his own making—to be misperceived in both the memories of the public and the scholarship of large segments of the academic community. He was not in reality simply a feisty, salty-tongued epitome of the common man, although the myth probably pleased him. Nor was he the cranky, inept reactionary of revisionist historiography. As a product of the Victorian Midwest, as an archetypical inner-directed man, he frequently appeared more conservative than he was. Rather, he was a liberal of the center. Seeing himself as Roosevelt's heir, he followed the course of many heirs to important positions, that of continuing the work of his predecessor while establishing his own claims to history. His achievement was mixed, but when one considers his own resources and the unpromising situation he faced, it is remarkable that he realized so many of the goals he set for himself.

Although Truman's attempt to bring about a post–New Deal wave of reform failed, he was successful in preserving and institutionalizing Roosevelt's works almost in toto. His victory in 1948 and his subsequent ability to focus political debate upon post–New Deal reform proposals largely removed the fundamental structure of the New Deal from the realm of political controversy. Even after a reaction began to set in against the administration in 1951, the ideologists of the Right remained hopelessly isolated on domestic issues, if not diplomatic ones.

Truman, moreover, had laid out the agenda for the extension of the New Deal. His advocacy of national health insurance, aid to education, and, above all, civil rights largely defined the unfinished business of the Democratic party and American liberalism for the next decade and a half. It would be fallacious to believe that liberal Democrats would have ignored these issues in the face of White House indifference, but it seems undeniable that presidential leadership helped them attain prominence and sharpness. This was perhaps the ultimate measure of Truman's fundamental commitment to progressive government. Faced with tension in his party between stand-patters and movers for change, he had little hesitation in siding with the forces of change. In part, the decision reflected a shrewd sense of his own political needs and of the future of the Democratic party, but it equally reflected personal preferences that he would continue to promote after he had left the White House.[4]

Truman left the United States irrevocably committed to a strong role in world politics. He moved within the broad outlines Roosevelt had drawn, but the result almost certainly was not what Roosevelt had expected. In part, Truman and those around him had taken Roosevelt's ideals more seriously than had Roosevelt. In part, they were simply locked into those ideals by the legacy of World War II itself and the grand objectives that had been so incessantly proclaimed to mobilize the American people. But most fundamentally, they were forced to move by reality, by the probability of a Soviet threat to the democratic West and to the interests of the United States. They achieved much in Europe; in Asia, they grappled less successfully with the same intractabilities as did previous and future administrations and displayed the same failures of comprehension of Eastern cultures and politics. The European experience was a relatively painless victory for American interests and ideals. The Asian experience tested the limits of the nation's commitment to the Cold War and cost Truman a dear political price. In the aggregate, however, his diplomacy served the nation well.

[4]During the 1950s, Truman was a prominent member of the Democratic Advisory Council. This group of liberal Democratic politicians and intellectuals attached to the Democratic National Committee was determined to steer a liberal course for the party despite the moderate congressional leadership of Lyndon Johnson and Sam Rayburn. Truman's adherence to the DAC is rather revealing. On a personal level, he felt a much greater identification with the Rayburn-Johnson group and was clearly uncomfortable with many of the DAC liberals. This appears to have been less important with him, however, than the need to pursue the ideals and objectives he had laid down as president.

However one feels about the nature of Truman's achievement, perhaps it is most remarkable that a politician possessing so fragile a personal appeal could leave behind a record of such substance. That he did so was in some measure a tribute to the strength of provincial America and the "common man," but it resulted more from the effort, intelligence, and determination which enabled him to move beyond his limitations and establish himself as one of the most effective of American presidents.

3

The Crisis and Regeneration of Republican Conservatism: Dwight D. Eisenhower, Robert A. Taft, and Joseph R. McCarthy

Dwight D. Eisenhower was the last of the twentieth-century American presidents to be nurtured in the Victorian climate of opinion that had produced Roosevelt and Truman. He was also the only twentieth-century president, other than Theodore Roosevelt, to have experienced public celebration as a military hero, and he possessed a more tangible democratic touch than any of his predecessors save Truman. These attributes coalesced to make his administration an oasis of placidity between eras of extraordinary turbulence in American politics. Eisenhower's espousal of the values of a cherished past provided Americans with a sense of continuity in a troubled, changing time. His status as a hero blended with his image as a democrat to secure him a combination of reverence and trust that made him all but invulnerable to political sniping.

Eisenhower's career as a politician, even more than his career as a soldier, was one of almost storybook individual success, as measured by landslide election victories and remarkable popularity ratings. His larger goals, however, were much more elusive. He sought the presidency because he felt a duty to save his party and his country from forces of irrational extremism. Ultimately, he gave the nation a badly needed breathing spell and time of adjustment to the realities of the post–New Deal, post-atomic, postcolonial world, and he made a modest beginning in his more ambitious objective of establishing a moderate-to-conservative

94

political tradition and a cadre of political leaders who could carry on after him. If less than creative, his leadership may have served a useful purpose in times that did not demand creativity.

The Democrat as Hero

Eisenhower's early life was in many respects similar to Truman's. He grew up in a small-town Midwestern environment; his father had business ambitions that turned sour; his mother was a steady source of stability and comfort; he entertained dreams of a military career. There were, of course, differences. Abilene, Kansas, unlike Independence, Missouri, was far removed from any semblance of cosmopolitan life. The Eisenhowers lived in real poverty; the Trumans were a middle-class family that had suffered financial reverses. Young Dwight Eisenhower, in contrast to young Harry Truman, was an excellent athlete and a fighter ready to take on any snob or bully who attempted to humiliate him. The religious atmosphere in his home appears to have been much more pietistic than in Truman's; his parents were Mennonites, then Jehovah's Witnesses. Still, the similarities appear overriding. Both men grew up in a white, Anglo-Saxon, Protestant cultural milieu at the turn of the century, and both absorbed its inner-directed values of discipline, hard work, and self-help. Truman became a man of broader vistas because he was unable to realize his military ambitions. Eisenhower stepped from one narrow little world into another of similar outlook; throughout his life he personified both the strengths and the shortcomings of his constricted experience.

All the Eisenhower children acquired the will and drive to move up in the world, and all were successful in varying degrees. From adolescence, however, young Dwight demonstrated the sort of will and endurance that the poor must possess to advance in life. At the age of fourteen, he came near death because he refused to let a doctor amputate a badly infected leg, a procedure that would have destroyed him as an athlete and handicapped him in the larger competition of life. Yet he was uncertain of his own goals in that race. Although his parents were pacifists, he decided to seek an appointment to one of the military academies as a means of obtaining a free education. His first choice, he indicated after passing the preliminary examinations, was Annapolis. He took West Point only after learning he was overage for the Naval Academy.

Life at the Point in the early twentieth century was almost monastic. Sealed off from civilian society, the academy was characterized by rigid discipline and constant immersion in the secular theology of Duty, Honor, Country. From the beginning, Eisenhower took to it well. He possessed the right combination of intelligence, toughness, and individuality to establish himself as an above-average cadet with considerable leadership potential. Until a knee injury at the end of his second year put an end to his football participation, he was a star halfback. He took over the plebe team from an unsuccessful coach and ran it capably for two years, a turn of events that foreshadowed much of his early army career as an organizer and a trainer of men. He graduated in 1915, sixty-first in a class of 164.

Embarking upon his career at the time of the greatest American military expansion since the Civil War, he quickly won repute as a rising young officer capable of handling soldiers well, popular with his comrades, and increasingly noticed by his seniors. When America entered World War I, he aggressively sought a combat assignment in Europe, impelled by his sense of duty and no doubt by the widespread conviction that leadership in fighting was crucial to moving ahead in his profession. Instead, he shuttled from one training post to another, spending most of 1918 as commander of the Army Tank Training Center at Camp Colt near Gettysburg. Lacking facilities and equipment of every variety (including tanks), he somehow built a respectable post out of the mud. Finally, he received orders to report to Camp Dix for assignment to Europe on November 18, 1918. The war ended on November 11.

By the end of 1920, just five years out of West Point, he held the permanent rank of major, but by then the U.S. Army had become one of the last areas of American life to which an ambitious young man might look for rapid advancement. Cut back as quickly as it had been expanded, it amounted to little more than a skeleton force of professionals scattered about the country, largely segregated from the pursuits of civilian life, engaging in their own factional infighting, and sooner or later getting to know almost everyone else of consequence at their level. The pay was mediocre, living conditions often difficult, public esteem minimal, and chances for promotion very scarce.

Throughout the 1920s, the real action for a man of executive ability was in the bustling universe of commerce. Eisenhower's wartime experience had given him impressive managerial credentials, and his well-to-do father-in-law doubtless could have helped him move into the business world rather painlessly. Instead he stayed with the army, finally achieving the rank of lieutenant colonel in 1936 after holding a number of positions that would command one or two stars as a matter of course today. Despite the frustrations, he never wavered in his devotion to a military life. Counseling his son John on a career choice in 1939, he emphasized the limited prospects. He would, he surmised, never advance beyond the rank of full colonel, but the army had brought him into association with men of ability, honor, and a sense of dedication to their country, thereby giving him satisfaction and fulfillment.

Within the limits of this constricted environment, Eisenhower built an enviable record that demonstrated both raw ability and a sense of the politic. Warm and gregarious, he and his wife developed a large circle of friends among their junior-grade peers. He won the affection and respect of senior officers on both sides of the basic factional conflict in the army, the disciples of Pershing versus those of MacArthur. Throughout the interwar period, one finds him close to the centers of military power and influence.

As a Tank Corps officer at Camp Meade after the war, Eisenhower attracted the attention of General Fox Connor, one of the most learned and respected generals in the army and a favorite of Pershing. Connor was taken by the young major's advocacy of mobile armor as an important new force in warfare. Influenced by his friend and colleague George Patton, Eisenhower had written an article calling for the development of fast, medium-weight tanks and for a reorganization of the infantry to make room for one armored company in each division. For this farsighted suggestion, his superiors, persuaded that his ideas were subversive of sound, established military doctrine, promptly reprimanded and silenced him. Connor, himself a probing and original thinker, seems to have been intrigued by the young man's audacity.

Commander of American troops in the Panama Canal Zone, Connor secured Eisenhower for a three-year stint as his chief of staff, adopted him as a protégé, and administered what the junior officer later recalled as an informal but nonetheless intensive postgraduate curriculum in the humanities and in military history and tactics. When his aide was sent back to the United States, Connor saw to it that he received a prized appointment to the Command and General Staff School at Fort Leavenworth, Kansas. Thanks to Connor's tutelage and his own intelligence and shrewd study habits, Eisenhower graduated first in a class of two hundred seventy-five and thereby put himself high on the list for whatever opportunities existed in the peacetime army.

From this point on, he worked near the highest command levels. For two and a half years, he was a senior staff officer of the Battle Monuments Commission, an agency of the War Department charged with building and beautifying the cemeteries of American war dead in Europe and with preparing guides to their battle areas. Eisenhower, a fluent writer by military standards, composed an acceptable draft of a guidebook in a few months and left the commission for a year at the Army War College. He returned to it for a year in France during which he visited the old battlegrounds himself and wrote the final draft on the basis of his first-hand observation. It was a relaxed, satisfying, and honorable tour. The commission was headed by General Pershing himself; appointment to it was a signal honor; and the ease with which Eisenhower could come back to it after his year at the War College was an indication of the reputation he had carved out for himself.

Upon his return to the United States in the fall of 1929, he was appointed to the office of the assistant secretary of war, the second-ranking civilian in the department. His work on contingency plans for wartime industrial mobilization brought him into contact with Bernard Baruch and other leaders of American business and finance. After 1930, the new army chief of staff, General Douglas MacArthur, encouraged the establishment of an Industrial College in the War Department. Eisenhower participated as a member of a team, but he was the most active member and the draftsman of the final documents. In January 1933, General MacArthur, impressed with the major's work, made the younger man his administrative assistant. For the next six years, in Washington and in the Philippines, he served MacArthur faithfully, although with a deepening sense of frustration at the general's political machinations and exaggerated sense of his own grandeur. In 1939, with the outbreak of war in Europe, he arranged for duty in the United States, at first hoping only for a regimental armored command under his old friend, George Patton.

Moving rapidly through a series of staff and command positions, Eisenhower was instead appointed chief of staff of the Third Army in August 1941, just in time to manage his troops in the largest peacetime war games in army history. The result, for which he received most of the credit, was a stunning success. Engaging in mock battles in Louisiana swamps, his Third Army routed the "enemy" Second Army, thereby winning him national notice and a promotion to brigadier general. Operating in a subtropical climate and enduring a brush with a hurricane, he proved not just that he was capable of practical war-gaming, but that he had the endurance to manage large-scale operations in exhausting circumstances, use staff effectively, and—no small matter—maintain the best of relations with journalists. On December 12, five days after Pearl Harbor, he received urgent orders to report for duty in Washington as a planner for army chief of staff General George Marshall. Momentarily resentful that he had been removed from a potential combat command position, he did not sense the glory that lay just beyond the horizon.

As it turned out, he stayed in Washington only long enough to win Marshall's trust and confidence, an important accomplishment because he had spent six years in MacArthur's orbit while Marshall had moved up with Pershing's enthusiastic backing. As Marshall's primary aide, Eisenhower demonstrated both that he could handle difficult assignments of war-planning and organization and that he could transfer his loyalties from one man to another with the utmost goodwill and with a sense of dedication to the common cause. Within a few months, he had established himself as too valuable to remain in Washington, even in a key secondary role. At the end of June 1942, he was off to England to take command of the planned Allied invasion of North Africa, then to become supreme commander of the attack upon the European continent itself. A soldier who had never commanded troops in combat, he was about to take control of the mightiest war effort in American history and become one of the authentic heroes of Western civilization. The way in which he did so tells us much about the nature of twentieth-century warfare and perhaps more about the values of twentieth-century Western society.

Eisenhower's contribution to victory was primarily that of a planner, a conciliator, a compromiser, and a public relations figure. His involvement in determining the grand strategy of the war was rather peripheral, and his strategic sense has been justly questioned—he had once thought it possible to invade the Continent in 1942, and his decision for a broad front advance into Germany in the fall of 1944 appears dubious in retrospect. Unlike his field commanders, he was not deeply involved in tactical decisions, and he had little of the flair of a Montgomery or a Patton or of lesser figures among the general officers such as Lightning Joe Collins or Matthew B. Ridgway. Nor—perhaps fortunately—did he possess the quick decisiveness that popular mythology attributes to great military leaders; faced with reverses at the Kasserine Pass, at Arnhem, in the Ardennes Forest, he displayed hesitation and, some observers believed, self-doubt. In all cases, however, he proved capable of measuring a situation and taking the action necessary to retrieve it.

His military greatness stemmed in the end from his managerial ability. He held together a vast corporate war effort, placated civilian leaders, made effective use of difficult military prima donnas, and established himself as an engaging and popular symbol of the fight. In contrast to the regal MacArthur, he built an image as a plain-living, plain-speaking democrat. Like a number of the American and British generals of World War II, he dressed in public almost as if he were a private, lived in relative simplicity for his rank, foreswore unnecessary pomp, and freely expressed his concern for the enlisted man; to this, he added a simple American charm and an engaging smile that transformed him from a high-level manager to a public figure of mass popularity— Ike. He emerged over more brilliant generals as the great hero of World War II because his achievement and his style so perfectly blended and exemplified the two central tendencies of mid-twentieth-century society—bureaucratic organization and democracy—in a way that seemed both effective and benign.

Men become heroes of durable appeal not just because of great accomplishments but because they somehow have established themselves as representatives of the values of their cultures. John William Ward has written incisively of the way in which Andrew Jackson embodied the classic nineteenth-century values of Nature, Providence, and Will: he seemed a product of the frontier, favored by the Almighty, leading the nation toward its God-given destiny, a self-made man who had elevated himself from obscurity through indomitable strength and perseverance, thereby demonstrating the special power of American democracy. Much the same analysis is applicable to the two other superheroes of that century, Lincoln and Grant. As far as it goes, it applies in large measure to Eisenhower. Shaped by the previous century, he accepted its values without question; he merely layered the requirements of the present century over them and thus combined the reassurance of old tradition with the needs of the contemporary world.

At the time of victory in Europe, Eisenhower was in his mid-fifties. He was too young for retirement but past the better part of most men's productive adult life. Most observers sensed at the time that his career might move in either of two directions: into an appropriately distinguished anticlimax or toward national political leadership. As events developed, it did both. First he undertook a tour of duty as army chief of staff, presiding with scant enthusiasm over the rapid demobilization of the army while his old superiors engaged in other, more consequential pursuits—Marshall as a high-level diplomat, MacArthur as a twentieth-century proconsul in Japan. In mid-1947, he accepted the presidency of Columbia University, a position in which he seemed ludicrously miscast.

The appointment was a matter of symbolism both for the trustees and for Eisenhower. It gave the university a leader of international renown, capable of attracting substantial publicity and badly needed funds. It gave Eisenhower the kind of position he had come to consider appropriate for a person of his stature and role, a dignified, noncommercial mode of public duty that could serve either as a relatively satisfying quasi-retirement or a place at which he remained in touch with most of the leaders and opinion shapers of American life, able to speak out on the issues, able, if he wished, to enter the political world. Backers from both major parties did in fact attempt to draft him for the presidency in 1948. Unwilling to oppose Thomas E. Dewey, whom he probably could not have stopped, and Harry S. Truman, whom he might well have deposed, he turned away Republicans and Democrats, settled into the presidency of Columbia, and, for all his lack of interest in intellectual life, probably did the school more good than harm.

It was the persistence of the Cold War and the creation of the North Atlantic Treaty Organization that propelled Eisenhower back into the center of American public life. NATO had been an extraordinary development in the history of the twentieth-century Western world. Largely a product of the frightening specter of Communist aggression that had emerged out of the Czech coup and the Berlin blockade, it had impelled the European democracies to an unaccustomed display of cooperation and had led the United States to repudiate its ancient tradition against entangling peacetime alliances. The Korean War gave NATO even more urgency and almost guaranteed that its military commander would be the great hero of the European war. The call came from Truman in the fall of 1950; by February 1951, Eisenhower was presiding over the organization in Paris. He performed magnificently as the symbol of strength and unity he was supposed to be. He did not of course make NATO into a mighty conventional military force, but to Western Europeans no less than Americans he was an inspirational figure. His command underscored the importance that the United States government attached to NATO and served as a convincing guarantee of American determination. Truman and Acheson were heartened by his work.

In different circumstances, Eisenhower's Paris command might have been an honorable and fitting conclusion to his career; instead, it was an interim position. The Cold War had brought him back to the center of world affairs; now it was to take him from Paris to the presidency. It had created not just the policy of containment that he sought to personify but also a politics of irrationality that was coming to dominate his Republican party. He would let himself be persuaded to run for the White House in order to save America from Robert A. Taft and Joseph R. McCarthy.

Taft, McCarthy, and the Crisis of Republican Conservatism

By 1952, Robert Taft long had been known as "Mr. Republican." Few politicians so personified the causes they represented. Taft's receding hairline, his vested business suits, his rimless glasses, and his austere manner all suggested a solid citizen of the WASP upper middle classes, perhaps a Midwestern banker to whom people unhesitatingly would trust their savings, but surely an unlikely political leader in a democratic society. Born in 1889 into one of the first families of Cincinnati, Ohio, educated at elite schools, the son of a president, Taft gravitated toward politics because of an interest in public policy and a family tradition of public service and clearly not because of an intense ambition for popular acclaim. His scarcely concealed distaste for handshaking, baby-kissing, and all the varieties of American campaign hoopla was in fact most likely an indication of inner qualms about democratic politics.

Taft's life was of one piece. He never questioned the Social Darwinist conservatism of his father, William Howard Taft. His first significant public position was as an aide to Herbert Hoover during World War I, and he revered Hoover ever after. His early forays into elective politics were as a regular Republican; his attachment to his party and the cause of conservatism became the single fierce emotional commitment of his life, belying the cool rationalism that normally guided his conduct. From the time he was first elected to the Ohio legislature in 1921, he envisioned himself as a spokesman for sound, businesslike government and functioned as a conservative tax reformer. He also won the respect of his colleagues for his industry, tenacity, and—on most matters—intelligence and moderation.

On one set of issues, however, he displayed little moderation. Throughout the 1930s and 1940s, he was a vehement critic of the New and Fair Deals and the welfare state whose coming they portended. Time and again during the Depression, he assailed the New Deal as mistaken, wasteful, arbitrary, excessively bureaucratic, alien, and dictatorial. Outraged by New Deal monetary policies, he even undertook a highly publicized and quixotic legal struggle to force the payment of federal obligations in gold. "If Mr. Roosevelt is not a Communist today," Taft declared in 1936, "he is bound to become one." By the time of his election to the U.S. Senate in 1938, he was already a nationally known foe of Rooseveltian liberalism.

He immediately won recognition as his party's leader on Capitol Hill, gaining respect on both sides of the Senate chamber for his raw intellectual ability and his seemingly endless capacity for hard work. By the beginning of his second year in Washington, he was generally perceived as a serious presidential possibility. He also was an oppositionist who slashed away at the Roosevelt-Truman tradition of welfare liberalism with no quarter. Speaking to partisan gatherings, he easily and naturally indulged in a rhetorical extremism that delighted those who already were converted but made him seem a crass reactionary to those he needed to persuade if he ever were to reach the White House. From his early attacks on Roosevelt on up through the Truman administration, he threw out one emotional line after another that all came to the same ultimate message: whatever their intentions, the leaders of the new liberalism were taking America down an irreversible road from welfarism to socialism to totalitarian Communism.

Taft's fears, exaggerated to be sure by his vehement partisanship, were natural products of the creed he had learned from his father. "The whole history of America," he declared in 1939, "reveals a system based on individual opportunity, individual initiative, individual freedom to earn one's living in one's own way . . . on rugged individualism, if you please, which it has become so fashionable to deride." Taft was a civil libertarian, but he assumed that at bottom all personal liberty rested on economic liberty, that activist presidents and the bureaucratic regulatory state represented the most serious threats conceivable to the American tradition, that the handout state inevitably would undermine the work ethic and cripple the entrepreneurial spirit that had made America great. Such was not simply the creed he had learned from his father; it was also a value system common to many Ohio businessmen whom he had represented as a corporate attorney and who were even more suspicious of and more vulnerable to the New Deal political economy than the Wall Street establishment.

Yet while Taft seemed a primitive, partisan reactionary when he spoke out on conservative generalities, he could be surprisingly moderate when he examined specific issues. Had he been a man of greater political calculation and more balanced emotions, he might have won recognition as a moderate conservative, a Tory liberal, attempting to accommodate to his times rather than to fight them. Instead, he forfeited an opportunity to become the founder of a New Republicanism and quite possibly gave up with it the presidency itself. Nonetheless, his efforts to come to grips with the welfare state merit attention as the first stirrings of a reformulation of American conservatism.

As early as 1939, he engaged in a critique of the Social Security system that now seems perceptive. He diagnosed a financing system that was getting in the way of economic recovery for the sake of building a trust fund that would be at first grotesquely overblown but ultimately inadequate. His remedy? A national-federal-state old-age pension system financed on a pay-as-you-go basis by a national sales tax, the benefits to be held to "subsistence" levels.

In the postwar years, he staked out interesting positions in some of the most important areas of national concern. In the process of giving his name to the Taft-Hartley labor relations act, he led the drive to moderate a harsh, restrictive bill that his party had produced in the House of Representatives. Emotionally denounced as a "slave labor act" by union leaders, the law had little effect on the labor movement where it already was established; its most significant provision simply affirmed the powers of the states to prohibit union shop arrangements if they wished to do so. Accepting minimal welfare functions as part of the responsibility of the federal government, Taft formulated modest programs for medical care for the indigent, aid to primary and secondary education, urban slum clearance, and public housing.

His alternatives to Democratic liberalism all tended toward smallness in size, soundness in financing, enhancement of the role of the states in administration, stringent safeguards against dispensing benefits to those not in need, and concern for the preservation and encouragement of individual and local initiative as a cornerstone of good social policy. It was true that they usually were responses to proposals brought forth by his opponents and thus easily typed, as one liberal leader put it, as "a mask for a reactionary policy." Yet Taft offered them, so far as one can tell, in good faith; and to a good many of his fellow partisans they were a flirtation with radical heresy.

Responding to charges from the far right wing of his party that these initiatives were socialistic, he asserted that they neither preempted private enterprise nor sought to bring a deadening equality to American life; rather, they were designed to foster an equal opportunity based on "a minimum standard floor under subsistence, education, medical care, and housing." Taft's cautious reformism may have a special relevance to a generation increasingly skeptical of the problem-solving capabilities of the state and increasingly aware of the limits of welfare liberalism. But he could neither establish himself as a moderate to the public nor bring along most of his party. In the end, his partisanship and ideological extremism were more vivid than his pragmatism on specifics. His propensity to identify Democratic liberalism with the Communist threat to the American way ultimately became the most salient feature of his world view, bringing him and his party to their greatest failure of the post–World War II era.

As did many other Republicans of his generation, Taft found foreign policy an unwelcome interruption from the domestic issues that preoccupied him. His opinions nevertheless were vehement and intensely partisan. From the time he entered the Senate, he felt a deep revulsion against European politics and diplomacy, believed that the vital interests of the United States were confined to the Western Hemisphere, and rejected any assertion of a national mission to spread American ideals abroad. He was from the first convinced that the Soviet Union and international Communism were the most intolerable evils on the world scene. Yet as an antistatist conservative, he feared the expansion of government that an activist foreign policy and possible war would likely produce; and he was prone to see the internationalist-interventionist activities of the Roosevelt and Truman administrations as excuses for the expansion of the liberal-bureaucratic state. At times he made shrewd points about the nature of international politics, but the majority of his contemporaries rightly found him unable to cope with internal inconsistencies in his thinking and out of touch with the real world.

Taft's reaction to World War II provided the first manifestation of his difficulties in coping with the dilemmas of power in the contemporary world. Before Pearl Harbor, he consistently opposed aid of any consequence to the opponents of European fascism. Help for England, he declared, would bring the United States into a war "to save the British Empire." Help for the Soviet Union after it was attacked by Hitler would be counter to American interests: "The victory of communism in the world would be far more dangerous to the United States than the victory of fascism." He spoke out against all the domestic implications of involvement in the war—deficit spending, economic controls, conscription, the growth of the bureaucratic state. "I am very pessimistic about the future of the country," he wrote to his wife in the summer of 1940, "we are certainly being dragged towards war and bankruptcy and socialism all at once." On the floor of the Senate, he declared, "War is worse even than a German victory."

Yet the alternative to which he always was emotionally attracted presented no easy escape from the consequences he feared so deeply. Throughout his career, Taft argued that in the last analysis America should be prepared to go it alone, protecting the Western Hemisphere as the last bastion of its ideals. But his hemispheric defense outlook necessarily presumed a Fortress America strong enough to repel any invader, capable of defending a twelve-thousand-mile defense perimeter stretching down from the Arctic Circle across both the Atlantic and Pacific oceans. In an unfriendly world, it would mean a garrison state, expensive, bureaucratic, imposing controls on economic activity, conscripting its young men into big military forces. Taft's attempts to cope with the world that had been forced on him neither then nor later could find solid grounding.

He learned little or nothing from World War II. It and the events of the postwar years only deepened the keen frustrations that he and many conservative Republicans felt. Big government and the welfare state remained ascendant at home, ratified by the electorate in the presidential election of 1948. Inflation cruelly penalized those who had faithfully practiced traditional values of thrift and hard work. The United States involved itself to an unprecedented degree in a turbulent international scene marked by revolutions around the globe, the spread of Communism into Eastern Europe and China, an increasingly frightening escalation of tensions between the United States and Russia, and, ultimately, the stalemated "police action" in Korea. Taft's responses to these developments exemplified the diverse reactions of the Republicans—at their best and at their worst. He forcefully criticized the welfare state but also made cautious attempts at accommodation with it. He would fashion a strong, principled critique of the American role in the world; but he also would immerse himself in a mean-spirited search for political scapegoats.

His objections to Truman's foreign policy possessed some merit; a few would seem farsighted to a later generation of liberal intellectuals burned by the experience of Vietnam, and a few would appear to anticipate the New Left critique of modern American diplomacy. He was an early and vociferous critic of what would come to be called the imperial presidency, asserting the need for Congress as an institution to be fully consulted and have a strong voice in major foreign policy decisions. His angry denunciation of Truman for sending troops to Korea without congressional approval was graceless and partisan, but hardly without foundation. He was a constant critic of military spending and the entire military establishment, arguing that defense expenditures were wasteful, unproductive, and inflationary. Persuaded that the Soviet Union planned no military action against the West, he declared that any competition with it had to be ideological, based on the creation of a better society. By stationing troops in far-off nations and extending large amounts of foreign aid to client states and by attempting to intermesh the American economy with those of other countries, U.S. policy makers were undertaking imperial endeavors, likely to foster resentment rather than appreciation among foreign peoples. The Truman administration was inventing new economic and security interests around the globe, and these ultimately would be damaging rather than beneficial to the United States.

Clearly, Taft's foreign policy criticisms were not without substance. Still, they hardly amounted to a balanced assessment of America's position in the world. Just as in the days before World War II, he advocated what amounted to a write-off of democratic Western Europe and, in consequence, a Fortress America. As in those days, he produced no credible alternative to the garrison state his proposals would require. His foreign policy declarations always developed as reactions to events that occurred under Democratic administrations; and his criticisms invariably were partisan, harsh, and carping. His alternatives were frequently shifting and contradictory; they at no point rested on a well-formulated, comprehensive view of American diplomacy but instead reflected his prejudices.

Initially, he was against Truman Doctrine assistance to Greece and Turkey, the Marshall Plan, and other forms of assistance to Europe; then his opposition softened to advocacy of less aid; ultimately, he cast a grudging vote for the final legislation. He was unremitting in his opposition to the North Atlantic Treaty; yet with apparent seriousness, he proposed that the United States might issue a unilateral commitment to defend Western Europe against Soviet attack even as he continued to oppose increased military spending!

His attitude toward the Cold War in Asia was even more self-contradictory. Taft's fundamental distaste for Europe was obvious, but he was powerfully attracted to intervention across the Pacific. Like many Republican "New Isolationists," he was an increasingly emotional supporter of Chiang Kai-shek's Nationalist struggle against the Maoist insurgency in China. Chiang's fight held a powerful appeal to many traditional Republicans, for it fused two deeply rooted feelings: an angry anti-Communism and a benevolent "missionary impulse" toward the Chinese. When the Nationalists fled to Taiwan, Taft demanded a naval commitment to the island's defense. At least partly in response to Republican pressure, Truman sent the Sixth Fleet to neutralize the Taiwan straits at the onset of the Korean War. Taft in turn supported intervention in Korea but deplored Truman's failure to ask for congressional assent and blamed the North Korean aggression on "the bungling and inconsistent foreign policy of the administration." As the war progressed, he at one point or another supported crossing the Thirty-eighth Parallel after Inchon, advocated withdrawal from the peninsula after the Communist Chinese intervened, endorsed MacArthur's call for an air war against the Chinese, and argued in favor of using Chiang's troops for an attack upon mainland China.

Behind all these surface contradictions was one controlling contradiction. A dedicated enemy of Communism, Taft was also a partisan hater of an administration that had proclaimed a global anti-Communist commitment and a conservative repelled by the means that a total offensive against Communism would require— expensive foreign aid programs, heavy military spending, big government. He dealt with this predicament by engaging in an increasingly obsessive search for scapegoats among the Democrats. The Cold War had hardly begun before he had in his own mind largely internalized it and made it a problem best approached simply by getting rid of a few wrong people in the government.

Having long accused New Deal Democrats of moving toward Communism at home, he and many Republicans found it natural enough to condemn them for "softness on Communism" abroad. Taft's early postwar political rhetoric routinely condemned the "giveaways" at Yalta and Potsdam. After the Chinese Nationalists retreated to Taiwan, he asserted that State Department China policy had been "guided by a left-wing group who have obviously wanted to get rid of Chiang and were willing at least to turn China over to the Communists for that purpose." With these and similar charges, he and many like-minded Republicans helped lay the groundwork for the ultimate anti-Communist flight from reality—McCarthyism.

Senator Joe McCarthy was an unlikely ally for a legislator of Taft's stature and patrician background. Reared on the margins of poverty in rural Wisconsin, he had achieved a measure of prominence and political success only through determined effort and a flouting of political ethics. A man who almost congenitally misrepresented his opponents, lied about his military career, and cut serious ethical corners in his relationship with interest groups, McCarthy had been elected to the Senate in the Republican year of 1946, the beneficiary of fluke circumstances that allowed him a narrow primary victory over the esteemed progressive Robert La Follette, Jr. Never very highly regarded by his colleagues, his questionable finances under investigation by journalistic enemies at home, and known to the public primarily for taking up the cause of Nazi SS troops convicted of murdering American prisoners, he seemed at the beginning of 1950 to have all the makings of a one-term senator.

Like many Republicans, he turned naturally to the issue of Communism. It had been a routine feature of Republican rhetoric to engage in accusations of Communism against the Roosevelt and Truman administrations, at times in the rather general fashion of Taft, at other times with charges against specific individuals. McCarthy already had used the issue in both fashions, but before the beginning of 1950 neither he nor any other Republican had stirred the general public. By that February, however, the Communists had taken control of mainland China; the Soviet Union had exploded its first atomic bomb; and Alger Hiss had been found guilty of perjury. It was natural enough then for the young senator to pound the theme of subversion in government as he flew around the country on a speaking tour in February 1950. In Wheeling, West Virginia, he told the Republican Women's Club that he possessed a list of 205 Communists employed by the Department of State; two days later in Reno, Nevada, he made the same speech, but the number had fallen to 57.

There was little that was new in McCarthy's rhetoric, but he clung to his charges tenaciously and became a serious force in American politics. He never produced his list, never uncovered a single Communist, and made charges so ludicrous that they defy belief. (He asserted, for example, that Owen Lattimore, a prominent left-wingish scholar of Asian history and politics, was a "top Russian spy.") In July, a select Senate committee headed by the impeccably conservative Democrat Millard Tydings issued a majority report characterizing McCarthy's campaign as "a fraud and a hoax . . . perhaps the most nefarious campaign of half-truths and untruth in the history of this Republic."

By the end of the year, Tydings and other critics of McCarthy had been defeated for reelection, and the Wisconsin senator, for all the emptiness of his allegations, had emerged as a major political power. Baffling and irrational, his achievement possessed three bases: his extensive newly discovered skills as a demagogue; the continuing pressure of events that created a political climate of near-hysterical anti-Communism; and, most crucially, the tolerance, then the active encouragement of most of the Republican establishment.

McCarthy's talents for media manipulation, for political bobbing and weaving, and for rhetorical counterpunching confounded his supporters and enemies alike. He maintained a good personal relationship with many reporters and knew the daily deadlines of almost every major paper in the United States. He released sensational charges too late for a follow-up, and they tended to receive headline plays even if distinguished columnists and editorialists denounced him on the inside pages. He employed what Richard Rovere has called "the multiple untruth"—throwing out so many accusations that neither the press nor the public could keep track of them, offering up reams of "documentation" that actually provided little evidence for his claims but were not susceptible to a quick, thorough examination. Before one allegation could be refuted definitively, two more would take its place, leaving the first half-forgotten. Those who attempted to follow his charges detail by detail sooner or later threw up their hands in despair, and many average citizens assumed that there must be some substance to them.

World and national events helped McCarthy also. The arrests of Julius and Ethel Rosenberg for espionage occurred the same day the Tydings committee released its report. The invasion of South Korea underscored the Communist menace. Truman's decision to fight a frustrating limited war and his veto of the McCarran Internal Security Act on civil libertarian grounds enraged those who believed that the United States was duty-bound to strive for the utter eradication of world Communism.

But McCarthy in the last analysis was successful because of the support of the Republican establishment. His charges hurt a vulnerable administration and appealed to a substantial following of traditionally Democratic Catholic ethnics. Anti-Communism had emerged as a common denominator of a politics of revenge that united all the groups nursing grudges against the Roosevelt and Truman administrations, and McCarthy was well on the way to becoming its most prominent practitioner. Acting out of a combination of cynicism and conviction, the Republican leadership saw no need to repudiate him. His few Republican critics were mostly New Englanders on the fringes of the party, and even they all sooner or later succumbed to pressure to mute their complaints. The party leadership—predominantly Midwestern, conservative, and neoisolationist—found in McCarthy an unlikely champion.

Taft played a key role in making McCarthy an acceptable partisan figure. His backing rested in part on rational calculation, but at bottom it was an emotional choice. McCarthy vented a bitterness that Taft and many other GOP loyalists had long felt against both the liberal Democrats and the bipartisan Northeastern establishment; McCarthy's rhetoric was just a bit more extreme. Taft already believed that Communist and pro-Communist sentiment was strong among major columnists and radio commentators, important in the publishing world, and influential in the State Department. In both his public pronouncements and his private correspondence, he tended to use as synonyms such words and phrases as *Communist, left-winger,* and *New Dealer.* His whole way of thinking left him fundamentally receptive to McCarthyism. Aware of its moral and intellectual shoddiness, he was nevertheless drawn to it, as Richard Rovere observed, like an alcoholic to the bottle.

A month and a half after the Wheeling speech, Taft admitted that McCarthy had yet to make a credible charge against anyone but declared that he "should keep talking and if one case doesn't work out, he should proceed with another one." Shortly afterward, he commented, "Whether Senator McCarthy has legal evidence, whether he has overstated or understated his case is of lesser importance. The question is whether the Communist influence in the State Department still exists." In May 1950, he actually forwarded to McCarthy what he himself described as a vague charge against a minor State Department official.

Having become a partisan symbol, McCarthy was virtually unstoppable through the rest of the Truman presidency. Maintaining the tactic of shotgun accusations, he became perhaps the most discussed politician in America. The orgy of public frustration that accompanied the dismissal of General Douglas MacArthur gave McCarthyism another boost and McCarthy a chance to take a particularly nasty swipe at Truman—"the son-of-a-bitch must have been drunk on bourbon and benedictine." He took indiscriminate potshots at presidential associates with impeccable anti-Communist credentials. Engaging in a bitter feud with Drew Pearson—the famous muckraking radio commentator and newspaper columnist—he managed to pressure Pearson's sponsor into dropping his radio broadcasts. In mid-1951, he launched an attack on George Catlett Marshall—secretary of defense, former secretary of state, general of the army, and the most venerated nonpartisan figure in American public life—charging that Marshall had aided and abetted the Communist conspiracy, "a conspiracy on a scale so immense as to dwarf any previous such venture in the history of man." In 1952, he was a featured speaker at the Republican national convention and a sought-after campaigner in the fall. His most visible effort, a nationally broadcast address, purported to expose the Communist affiliations of the Democratic presidential candidate, "Alger—I mean Adlai."

Taft's career during the same period was a somewhat sanitized version of the same course. Ambitious for the presidency, more genteel than McCarthy, driven as always by a need to systematize and intellectualize his world view, Taft avoided the worst excesses of his Red-hunting colleague. Still, he could not resist McCarthy-like swipes at the administration, nor could he reconcile his militant anti-Communism with the limited means he was willing to employ in opposition to world Communism. In the end, his failure was political as well as intellectual.

Taft's last try for the presidency in 1951–52 stressed foreign policy more heavily than ever in the candidate's career. The Korean War and the fight against Communism had become the American public's primary concern. The death of Arthur Vandenberg had removed from the scene the major party spokesman on international relations and the most important Republican supporter of the Truman foreign policies. Taft surely had the intellectual ability to establish himself as an authority on foreign affairs, but his emotional partisanship left him open to charges of political opportunism.

Taft's criticisms were not wholly lacking in merit. It was possible to make a strong argument against the large-scale dispatch of combat troops by the president alone and to do so both on the grounds of constitutional theory and practical politics. Moreover, there was room for a reasoned criticism of the administration's entire Far Eastern policy. Nonetheless, Taft's military comments invariably laid bare a strategic and tactical amateurism reminiscent of his pre–World War II pronouncements. And whatever well-founded points he might put forth were obscured by the grating partisan harshness of his rhetoric: "This Korean War is a Truman war."

He remained emotionally opposed to any commitment in Europe. He argued that it was unnecessary to station American troops there because the Soviet Union (which he had charged with instigating the Korean War) had no aggressive designs on the Continent. The placement of U.S. soldiers could only provoke the Russians; any defense pledge could be fulfilled by air power. Nevertheless, he ultimately supported the sending of four divisions, thereby confounding both sides in the foreign policy debate.

Taft attempted to bring some sense of system to his foreign policy positions with the publication of *A Foreign Policy for Americans* in 1951. A slim, widely read volume, it was intended to serve as the programmatic flagship of his presidential quest, but it did little more than exemplify his difficulties. At one point, he seemed to advocate a sweeping and costly anti-Communist economic and military program. Characteristically, however, he began to impose limits on his means but not on his objectives. The U.S. military establishment should emphasize sea and air power; America should station only token numbers of troops on foreign continents. By the end of the volume, his recommendations were reduced to a propaganda effort; subversion in some manner of the Soviet empire; a general but not very tangible posture of support for anti-Communist governments; and the elimination from the U.S. government of "all those who are directly or indirectly connected with the Communist organization." The definitive statement of a man who had learned nothing and forgotten nothing, the book displayed Taft at his shallowest and probably contributed to his defeat by Eisenhower.

Holding the Line

In 1952, Eisenhower acquiesced to the political draft he had rebuffed in 1948, primarily because he was determined to stop a takeover of the Republican party by Taft and McCarthy. He succeeded Willkie and Dewey as the candidate of the party's "Northeastern establishment"—leaders of the world of finance, corporate business, and communications, moderate to conservative in their domestic outlooks, internationalist in diplomacy, and supported by a broad constituency that perceived far greater cultural and ethnic ties to Europe than did the American heartland. He was the last but also the best hope of a group that had lost three consecutive presidential elections and had no other viable candidate to offer against Taft.

More was involved in the establishment's choice than a sense of political expediency; its leaders must have instinctively seen in the Old Hero a man of kindred sentiments. Eisenhower's outlook, which Robert Griffith has labeled "the corporate commonwealth," was markedly similar to that of the executive elite of the country. He had respect for efficiency and organization, a generally concealed contempt for politics and politicians, a well-hidden distrust of popular democracy and mass emotions, and a commitment to duty and disinterested public service. To this he added a highly developed talent for compromise and conciliation, an intuitive skill in public relations, and a remarkable capacity for dealing with the press. He represented the idea of the organization man at the highest point of its development.

Eisenhower's campaign for the nomination, undertaken in the beginning without his assent, demonstrated both the smooth efficiency of the group with which he had aligned himself and the enduring depth of his own appeal. Throwing together a drive at the last moment without an active candidate, the Eisenhower Republicans scored victories in some key primaries and ran strongly in most others. Polls demonstrated that Ike was the overwhelming choice of the independent voters, whom the Republicans needed in order to win an election. Impressed by the primary results, convinced that the call of duty was genuine, warned by his backers that he had to work actively for the Republican nomination, Eisenhower resigned his NATO post and his army commission and returned to America.

By the time Ike opened his campaign on June 4, Taft, although ahead in committed delegates, was on the defensive; he was, the general and his forces charged, attempting to steamroll the convention. The final weeks before the Republican meeting amounted to a political blitz worthy of a Patton. Having thoroughly intimidated undecided delegates, Eisenhower successfully challenged the credentials of Taft delegations from three Southern states and took the Republican nomination on the first ballot. He was almost sixty-two years old, still loved by the country, still vigorous, and more capable than ever of simultaneously projecting auras of fatherly warmth and stern authority. Upon meeting him for the first time, Emmet John Hughes was impressed by the strength of his presence and by one feature especially: "the blue eyes of a force and intensity singularly deep, almost disturbing, above all commanding."

Although he had been nominated as an alternative to Taftism and McCarthyism, Eisenhower found himself heading a campaign that demonstrated the inroads that McCarthyism had made among Republicans of all varieties. His vice-presidential candidate, Senator Richard Nixon, had built a national reputation as a militant anti-Communist conservative. Leading Republicans from the Eisenhower segment of the party routinely threw charges of Communist sympathies at their Democratic opponents. The general's advisers persuaded him to behave almost with deference toward McCarthy and to omit from an important speech words of praise for George Marshall, one of McCarthy's most prominent targets.

In part, such moves were a matter of political tactics. The most telling issue the Republicans had was frustration with the Korean War in particular and with what appeared to be a larger pattern of Cold War reverses in general. Neither the tepid inflation that had attended Korea nor the small-bore corruption that had marred the Truman administration constituted compelling reasons for voting against Adlai Stevenson. Politics aside, however, even moderate Republicans had found the fall of China stunning, demoralizing, and ultimately inexplicable. They tended to resent the Truman-Acheson effort to put the best possible face on such setbacks and to work for an accommodation with Maoist China. The unhappy course of the Korean War had confirmed all their worst fears, convincing them that U.S. foreign policy shapers were, if not quite traitors, at least blundering fools who deserved the attacks they had sustained and who should be purged from the State Department. From that perspective, it was easy to give

McCarthy some tolerance while deploring his ham-handedness, and even to engage in a little bit of McCarthyism. Without fully sharing such prejudices, Eisenhower allowed himself to be carried along with them. He was too inexperienced in politics to be able to form the sound judgment that McCarthyism was not necessary for victory; thus, he was willing to swallow hard and tolerate it. After all, to acquiesce in an occasional smear was distasteful but hardly as terrible as the duty of sending men to their deaths.

Still, the Republicans would have won without McCarthyite tactics. Against one of the most revered figures of the Western world, the Democrats had been able only to come up with Adlai Stevenson, a man of unusual competence and eloquence but lacking both a well-established national reputation and mass political appeal. He had no chance of defeating Eisenhower, especially after the general delivered the necessary reassurances about preserving the New Deal and all but promised to end the Korean War by visiting the battle zone himself. After the turmoil—domestic and foreign—of the Roosevelt and Truman administrations, the nation elected an Old Hero, perhaps in the hope of gaining a lost sense of stability and confidence.

Eisenhower's presidential objectives have been well summarized by the titles of two historical works on his administration: Charles C. Alexander's *Holding the Line* and Gary W. Reichard's *The Reaffirmation of Republicanism*. He and the people around him wanted to preserve the essence of traditional Republicanism and at the same time make it palatable to mid-twentieth-century America. They wanted to impart a fresh tone to old values, produce policies that would somehow reconcile the needs of the present with the outlook of the past, and eventually develop the new personalities that would carry their effort into the future. They hoped to use his administration as the springboard for a viable new conservative tradition that would assimilate much of the accomplishment of the New Deal–Fair Deal tradition while drawing a line against its extension.

Eisenhower's management of the presidency reflected this larger aspiration. Conditioned by Roosevelt and Truman—and before that by the earlier Roosevelt and Woodrow Wilson—both contemporary observers and scholars since have been most impressed by the weak, passive, negative character of the Eisenhower leadership. Generally liberal-Democratic in their orientation, they have assumed that activism in the pursuit of social change is a commendable norm and that words such as *weak, passive,* and *negative* may be used almost as synonyms. Whatever the merits of this outlook, it is useful more as a point of departure for criticism than in aiding understanding.

Eisenhower's handicaps as president are obvious. His political experience was severely limited, and he had little working knowledge of the civilian Washington bureaucracy. What he eventually gained in experience may have been more than countered by the deterioration of his health through a heart attack, a stroke, and a major abdominal operation; there can be little question that he had lost substantial vigor and capacity for work by the end of his second term. Moreover, his well-established distaste for detail no doubt served him less well in the White House than it had in the military. He handled the presidency in the role of a supreme commander, reserving only the larger issues for his personal attention and engaging in compromise and conciliation as the major tools of leadership. If one accepts him and his objectives on his own terms, however, it really is not meaningful to characterize him, as does James David Barber, as a "passive-negative" president. He moved with vigor against excessive social activism when the occasion demanded and worked hard to remake the Republican party. Ultimately more successful than Taft, he nevertheless fell short of establishing Republicanism as a credible alternative to New Deal–Fair Deal Democracy.

However much he rejected vigorous Roosevelt-Truman–style leadership in some areas, Eisenhower never doubted that the presidency was a post that called for vigorous moral leadership. By preachment and deed, he sought to bring America back to the values of his youth—pietistic religion and self-help. Although he never before had displayed signs of having absorbed the devout faith of his parents, he assuredly had absorbed their broader outlook. He presented his political campaign as a "crusade." He took formal membership in the Presbyterian church. He began his inaugural address with a prayer and opened cabinet meetings in the same way. The custom spread quickly throughout the conformist atmosphere of the executive branch. (Soon a joke was making the rounds to the effect that a high-level official had exclaimed in the midst of an important meeting: "Dammit! We forgot the prayer!")

The religion that Eisenhower projected was the religion of a conservative, the classical—if misnamed—"Protestant ethic" with its connection between piety and worldly success, its affirmation of individualism and self-help as keys to salvation as well as riches. It provided both a sense of continuity with the past and a moral alternative to liberal welfarism. It also had a heavy dose of nationalistic patriotism, stemming from the assumption that the United States was a nation favored by God and that the atheistic Soviet Union represented a force that God's Nation had to crusade against. From the mouths of vulgar, right-wing demagogues, such assumptions had appeared ludicrous. Expressed in a benign, fatherly way by a beloved hero, they took on respectability.

The Eisenhower years witnessed a superficial religious revival of impressive proportions. Its most representative leaders were moderately conservative ministers, such as Rev. Norman Vincent Peale or Bishop Fulton J. Sheen, who doubled as personal advice writers and connected religion to getting ahead in the world. The result—when compared to the high philosophy of the theologians or the intense quest for salvation that had once characterized American Protestantism—was little more than a bland affirmation of faith, a homogenized, bloodless American religion that perfectly suited the yearnings of Eisenhower and of much of the American middle class in the fifties. In the end, it was less a search for redemption than a form of national self-congratulation.

This reassuring vision was only a small part of the new political appeal that Eisenhower attempted to develop. He must have understood that his presidency was a national tribute to him as an individual, not to the appeal of his party. The Republicans had won control of Congress only by a hairsbreadth in 1952, lost it in 1954, and never regained it. The old values of individualism and self-help had been grievously discredited by Herbert Hoover and could never be resuscitated in their starkest form. Eisenhower seems instinctively to have realized that a public willing to pay homage to the old values was unwilling to accept them in undiluted form.

He never was foolish enough to advocate a return to the 1920s and was apt to be curt with those who did. A sharp, private reprimand to his right-wingish brother, Edgar, vividly illustrates his grasp of reality:

> Should any political party attempt to abolish social security and eliminate labor laws and farm programs, you would not hear of that party again in our political history. There is a tiny splinter group, of course, that believes that you can do those things. Among them are H. L. Hunt, . . . a few other Texas oil millionaires, and an occasional politician and businessman from other areas. Their number is negligible and they are stupid.

He was even careful about applying the term *conservative* to himself, more often using such words as *moderate* or *middle-of-the-road*, and at times adopting the phrase *dynamic conservatism*. Not a theoretician, he could do little more than grope for ways to express a new mood.

The most conspicuous administration intellectual was Arthur Larson, a presidential speechwriter and subcabinet official with an academic background. In his widely read book *A Republican Looks at His Party* (1956), Larson set forth the principles of a "New Republicanism." He described it as a mean between the political principles of 1896 (McKinley Republicanism) and those of 1936 (Rooseveltian Democracy), based upon the ideological and tactical premise that "in politics—as in chess—the man who holds the center holds a position of almost unbeatable strength." The New Republicanism aimed at the preservation of the federal-state balance in American federalism, encouraged business enterprise as a legitimate, progressive force in American life, extended the same tolerance to labor (whether organized or unorganized), and accepted broad government responsibility for the general welfare. It professed a belief in God and a divine order of things. It cited the special American historical and political experience of national development without revolution or intense class conflict. Larson's thinking appealed strongly to Eisenhower, but the task of translating it into political experience and a usable political tradition was more formidable than either could have realized at the euphoric midpoint of Ike's reign.

In his personal values and preferences on most specific domestic issues, Eisenhower was actually a bit more conservative than Taft (with whom he developed a cordial relationship before Taft's sudden death in 1953). Yet the political tradition that Roosevelt and Truman had built emerged from his administration largely unscathed, cut back a bit here and there perhaps, but also advanced in other areas. This occurred even though the administration openly aligned itself with the only group in American life that had opposed Roosevelt and Truman with near unanimity— the business community. The counterrevolution never came and was never even attempted.

One can find no single answer for the smooth emergence of the New Republicanism and the widespread GOP acceptance of the works of the party's political enemies. Several considerations appear important. The New and Fair Deals were too woven into the fabric of society to be torn out; moreover, it was obviously unwise to contemplate such a step. The dispensing of benefits throughout society, whether or not it was just and enlightened, had surely been politically popular; any effort to take them away would be doubly unpopular. It was in any case conservatism at its simplest and most elemental to accept social and political arrangements much as they existed and to assume that change in any direction had to be a slow process. The New Republicanism reflected Eisenhower's well-developed style of leadership with its emphasis upon realism, accommodation, and compromise. It also reflected the changed character of American business, at least at the level of elite leadership.

The corporate tone of the Eisenhower administration was never in doubt. The president surrounded himself with successful financiers, corporate lawyers, and high-level business executives; those of his advisers who did not fit those categories usually possessed the values of the people who did. There were, to be sure, some characters in this group. Secretary of Defense Charles Wilson, the former president of General Motors, compared advocates of social welfare spending to kennel dogs that bayed for food rather than hunting dogs that worked for it; he announced to the world that the interests of GM were those of the United States.[1] Secretary of the Treasury George M. Humphrey, a vehe-

[1]Wilson's remark was actually a statement that what was good for the country would be good for General Motors and vice versa. Critics of the administration rather misleadingly rephrased it as "What's good for General Motors is good for the country."

ment fiscal conservative, in a moment of dismay at a substantial Eisenhower budget deficit predicted in public that continued large-scale spending would lead to a "hair-curling" depression.

But whatever the occasional tendency of a Wilson or a Humphrey to sound like political primitives, the Eisenhower business executives actually tended to represent the values and aspirations of the mid-twentieth-century corporate executive suite. They were torn between the inner-directed, individualistic ethos of the entrepreneurial past and the other-directed, adaptive values of the managerial present, capable of feeling nostalgia for Herbert Hoover while making the compromises necessary to run an organization in the real world. The new corporate outlook and experience mirrored Eisenhower's to a remarkable degree, gave coherence to his politics, and more than anything else accounted for his choice of the Republican party and the importance of the "millionaires" in his administration.

Much like executives who had learned to live with labor unions and government regulations even while grumbling about them, the president and those around him resignedly adapted themselves to the social-political structure of a new America. They reflected the values of both the managerial subclass and much of the broader middle class by working hard to govern efficiently, control costs, and thereby contain inflation. Within these limits, they displayed little resistance to government activism, social welfarism, or the continuing prosperity of those who had reaped benefits from the New Deal.

No group had received more from Roosevelt and Truman than organized labor; union spokesmen were thus persistently critical of the Eisenhower administration, just as they were of individual managements from whom they nonetheless received recognition and with whom they engaged in negotiations. Yet Eisenhower never posed the slightest threat to the position that the trade unions had achieved; like the American corporate elite, he had no foolish hope of turning back the clock. It is inevitably recalled that his first secretary of labor, Martin Durkin, resigned in protest against the administration's failure to recommend major changes in the Taft-Hartley Act. It is often forgotten that Durkin's successor, James P. Mitchell, a former personnel executive with vast business and government experience, enjoyed the respect of the labor establishment and much of the liberal community. The

administration's only significant move in labor legislation, the
Landrum-Griffin Act, was a mild, barely effective regulatory
measure aimed primarily at mobster infiltration of unions. In
general, Eisenhower and his team dealt with labor much as the
management of a large, mature organization might deal with a
well-established bargaining agent.

Farmers, the beneficiaries of increasingly expensive and de-
creasingly effective price support programs, fared less well for
several reasons. They were a declining segment of the population,
lacked organizational solidarity, and had failed to establish a
home in either party. They never had achieved an ideological
consensus about their own identity, thinking of themselves at
times as the neglected, downtrodden yeoman backbone of
America, and at times as entrepreneurs engaged in a business
enterprise. Democratic liberalism, predominantly urban in its
orientation and offended by the general failure of the farm community to support trade union objectives, became ever cooler to
agricultural subsidies as the fifties progressed. The corporate
managerial outlook of the Eisenhower administration rather
naturally responded negatively to petty entrepreneurs who demanded government aid rather than practice self-help.

Eisenhower and his secretary of agriculture, Ezra Taft Benson,
were able to secure legislation establishing ever lower price support levels. Although the program remained horrendously expensive, its cost grew at a much lower rate than would have been the
case with the continuance of high supports. One result was the
liquidation of many marginal farmers and the augmentation of
urban social problems by a rural migration to the cities. Benson
expressed the hope that the federal government could extricate
itself entirely from agriculture, but neither he nor Eisenhower
actually proposed withdrawal as anything more than a long-term
objective. Instead they moved cautiously back from what they
considered an overextended position.

Social welfarism as such did not give the Eisenhower administration grave difficulties so long as it met the tests of efficiency
and reasonable costs. It was Eisenhower who obtained the creation of the Department of Health, Education and Welfare, an
objective Truman had failed to achieve. He went along with a
higher minimum wage (not a cost to the government), extensive

increases in Social Security (a self-funded program), a limited program of medical care for the indigent elderly (a vital social duty with carefully controlled costs), and the National Defense Education Act (a response to Sputnik wrapped in the protective cloak of national security). Such positions, of course, pleased neither liberal Democrats nor hard-core conservative Republicans, a fact that doubtless confirmed the administration's faith in the rightness of its course.

Governmental activism held few terrors for Eisenhower so long as it met the same tests. His administration, for example, acceded to the St. Lawrence Seaway project (self-funded) and the interstate highway system (underwritten by a trust fund financed by new taxes). Both were monumental public works projects that spendthrift New Dealers would have envied, but established in such a way that neither would put a drain on the budget. When pressed to state some sort of philosophical principle, the president and most of his associates would declare themselves states' righters and deplore the size of the federal bureaucracy. From time to time, as in the return of the Tidelands oil claims to the states, they acted upon this intuition; in other cases, when the need for federal action appeared established and the expense could be managed, they ignored it.

Eisenhower's moderation had a powerful appeal to a nation ready for a period of peace and tranquility after years of domestic change and bitterness. But it also was a style of leadership incapable almost by definition of dealing with extreme situations that required something more than bland, moderate treatment. Perhaps the two major failures of the domestic side of Ike's administration were his treatments of McCarthyism and the black revolution.

In McCarthy, Eisenhower faced a nihilist and verbal terrorist for whom immersion in the administration atmosphere of compromise and moderation would have been akin to political suffocation. Having achieved fame and a sizable following with charges of Communism in government, McCarthy had no intention of disappearing from public attention just because his own party had won the White House. Like all terrorists, he had to be handled forcefully; this Eisenhower was unwilling to do, in part because the president himself had sanctioned the continued use of the

Communist issue against the Democrats by high officials of his own administration, in part because a strong denunciation of McCarthy would have conflicted with his own concept of party and national leadership. He did not want to alienate McCarthy's disciples on the Republican Right, and he wanted to avoid an unseemly public fight with one of the most accomplished of bare-knuckle brawlers. Unopposed by the one public leader who could have discredited him, McCarthy ran amok for almost two years, harassing and embarrassing his own party while the Democrats looked on in mingled delight and dismay. Finally, the Senate disciplined him with covert encouragement from the White House, and he slipped into a well-deserved obscurity.

However grievous, the damage that McCarthy had been permitted to cause was not irreparable; but it is hard to make the same statement about Eisenhower's indifference to the black revolution. In order to understand his attitude toward the American Negro, one must recall the narrowness of his professional experience. He had spent almost his entire life as a career soldier, breathing an atmosphere in which blacks were universally considered inferior, segregated, and kept in their very low place. He rarely, if ever, dealt with blacks on his own level; and unlike the professional politician who must build coalitions, he never had to negotiate with black leaders and discuss their aspirations. Intellectually and socially, he was about as unprepared for the explosion of the civil rights movement as a president could have been.

As the Supreme Court pondered its decision in the school desegregation case in 1954, the president invited the new chief justice, Earl Warren, to dinner at the White House. He expressed his personal hope that the Court's decision would not result in any fundamental change. At no time after the Court had ruled against "separate but equal" educational facilities did Eisenhower speak out in support of the decision. He saw the presidency as a place of moral leadership, but he clearly did not conceive of segregation as a moral issue. Moreover, any strong advocacy of civil rights might have damaged growing Republican strength in the South. His support of black objectives was quite limited and resulted mostly from the urgings of his Department of Justice; its most tangible fruits were two civil rights bills universally recognized as ineffective as soon as they were passed. It is often remembered that Eisenhower sent federal troops to Little Rock to enforce a desegregation order, but it is also frequently forgotten that he took no action in other cases, such as the expulsion of black student Autherine Lucy from the University of Alabama, a situation in which defiance was more subtle and hence more capable of being ignored.

Eisenhower was of course hardly the first political leader to temporize on the position of blacks in American life—and scarcely the last. His inaction was consistent with the entire tenor of his presidency, and it is perhaps foolish to assume that any political leaders will grasp the banner of a social revolution unless they are forced to make a choice. One may nevertheless regret that finding himself at a turning point in American history, Eisenhower could do no more than retreat from positions staked out by his predecessor.

Eisenhower's greatest failure by his own lights was his inability to make the New Republicanism into a movement of the American majority. As a hero, he enjoyed immunity from political defeat, but his status as a hero also blinded the public to both his partisan affiliation and to the ideological perspective he sought to advance. Moreover, his presidency demonstrated anew the old, sound political axiom that popularity is very hard to transfer. Even during the headiest days of the Eisenhower ascendancy, the New Republicanism as a doctrine had to stand on its own merits. However interesting it might have been as a social-intellectual phenomenon, politically it was a flop, incapable of producing the numbers of legislators, governors, and congressmen it needed to establish itself as an enduring force. Neither Eisenhower nor his partisans could persuade the public that the New Republicanism really differed from the Old.

The central problem was the uninspiring performance of the economy in the 1950s—slow economic growth, periodic recession, creeping inflation. The nation never approached a disaster akin to that of the 1930s; most Americans, in fact, perceptibly bettered their lot. Still, the lackluster performance of the economy generated a substantial upward trend in unemployment and created considerable apprehension in a nation not that far from the trauma of the Depression. The persistence of inflation, albeit at a modest rate that would have been welcomed as a salvation two decades later, added both to public irritation and to the problems of the administration. From the perspective of Eisenhower and his aides, inflation was the worst danger; they fought it relentlessly with conservative fiscal and monetary policies that contributed to the prolonged economic slowdown of the fifties and cast doubt upon their argument that the Republicans could bring the country prosperity as well as peace.

This doubt received considerable reinforcement from the failure of the New Republicanism to produce fresh new moderate faces on a national basis. The Old Hero, like Roosevelt or Truman, could do little to speed up the slow pace of change at the state and local levels of party organization; consequently, whatever the desires of the White House, the GOP faces before the electorate usually appeared a bit more reminiscent of Herbert Hoover than Arthur Larson. Here and there, the administration achieved a breakthrough. In the Illinois of the late fifties, Charles Percy, a successful young corporate executive, emerged as the up-and-coming figure in the Republican party of the appropriately named Everett McKinley Dirksen; the White House saw to it that Percy achieved maximum visibility by making him chairman of the platform committee at the 1960 Republican convention. An achiever in business, moderate in ideology, articulate, and handsome, Percy was the New Republicanism personified.

Unfortunately, few like him had emerged by the end of Eisenhower's second term, and fewer still (Percy included) had won election to major offices. The face of Republicanism was more typically that of an Everett Dirksen, a John Bricker, a William Jenner, a Bourke Hickenlooper—visages scarcely calculated to assure a nervous electorate that the party as a whole had entered a new era. Gradually, of course, the old generation would give way to the inexorable certainties of death or defeat, thereby clearing the path for younger moderates. In the meantime, it could fairly be said that Eisenhower had most clearly succeeded in bringing to a position of fame and strength only a dynamic young Republican whose moderation was questionable and about whom he seems to have entertained periodic doubts—Richard M. Nixon.

Massive Containment

In their domestic policies, Eisenhower and his associates easily reconciled the themes of holding the line and standing at the head of a resurgent Republicanism. The effort had required only a mild reformulation of GOP dogma. However, it was not easily applied to foreign policy. There, to hold the line was to repress some of the most deeply felt emotions associated with the Republican resurgence. It implied acceptance of the main lines of the Truman-Acheson conduct of diplomacy and thereby constituted a special affront to the Taft-McCarthy wing of the party.

Yet the Northeastern-centered "internationalist" Republicans who had propelled Eisenhower into the presidency had been co-conspirators in Truman's diplomacy. It was true that they had never fully accepted its Asian dimension, especially its disdain of Chiang Kai-shek. Nevertheless, they had repeatedly supported Truman administration measures that flowed from the assumption that developments in Asia were relatively unimportant compared to those in Europe. The capstone of these, of course, was NATO, and as its supreme commander, Eisenhower had for a time been one of the primary symbols of the diplomatic aspirations of the Truman presidency. John Foster Dulles, the party's chief spokesman on foreign policy after the death of Arthur Vandenberg, had also been associated with the previous administration in a number of ways. In 1952, Eisenhower the candidate and Dulles the diplomatic brain truster had to find ways of differentiating their policy objectives from those of the Democrats while following the same main lines; as president and secretary of state, they had to continue the quest.

Their first tactic was the doctrine of liberation. As formulated by Dulles, it met all the needs of the 1952 campaign. It assailed the Democrats for real and alleged losses in the Cold War while giving them no credit for stopping Communist advances in Europe. It appealed to the Taft faction by advancing the prospect of a rollback of Soviet power. It countered charges of warmongering by declaring that liberation could come only through the efforts of peoples behind the Iron Curtain themselves, that the American role could be only one of encouragement. It was a safe way of playing to the crusading urges of the GOP faithful, and it seemed to possess a certain dynamism that contrasted nicely with the stalemate in which the Democrats found themselves by 1952. The doctrine of liberation was doubtless an asset to Eisenhower in his first presidential campaign, but it was also a bit of rhetorical camouflage that was to be stripped away once and for all by the Hungarian uprising of 1956.

From the beginning of his presidency, moreover, Eisenhower needed more than the facade of liberation for the conduct of a coherent foreign policy. His biggest problems came not from the Democrats, but from the Taft-McCarthy Republicans. At times, as with the McCarthy-led effort to reject Eisenhower's nomination of Charles Bohlen as U.S. ambassador to the USSR, their hatred of the previous administration's doings wandered past the line of rationality. More generally, however, they simply had developed a strong inclination toward the negative in foreign as well as in domestic policy. As a party leader attempting to unite the GOP behind him, Eisenhower had to find ways to bring his nay-saying right wing over to a rational policy.

One method was to manipulate the symbols of liberation in a way that would touch the emotions of the Republican Right. The administration not only extended the protection of containment to Chiang Kai-shek but announced that he was being "unleashed" in the struggle against Maoist China. Even after the end of the Korean War, it undertook a diplomatic crusade against Communist China, refusing to deal with it, barring its entry into the United Nations, treating it as an international leper. The policy involved some risks, primarily the Quemoy-Matsu crises of 1954–55 and 1958. It may have cost some lost opportunities for normal relations with China, although this is doubtful. In the longer run, it made normalization all but unthinkable for Democratic presidents in the 1960s.

On issues that were more immediately disruptive of a sound diplomacy, Eisenhower could react vigorously. When right-wingers of his own party introduced a congressional resolution repudiating the Yalta agreements, he understood that the proposal was a meaningless bit of symbolism that would worsen relations with both the Soviet Union and the Democratic party. Refusing to endorse it, he worked with internationalist Republicans and Democrats to water it down to meaninglessness and watched it expire from a general lack of substance that disgusted the Taftites. When Senator McCarthy launched his attack against Bohlen, the president made Bohlen's FBI files available to Taft, persuaded the Ohio senator that Bohlen was not a security risk, and obtained his leadership in the drive for confirmation.

His most difficult challenge from the Republican Right was the Bricker amendment, a proposed consitutional amendment that would have placed strict limits upon the authority of the president to negotiate treaties or to enter into executive agreements with foreign powers. It was the product of years of Republican discontent over the generous interpretation of presidential prerogative that had marked the diplomatic conduct of Roosevelt and Truman. The 1952 Republican platform had advocated some such measure; Eisenhower and his advisers, however, were against it from the beginning. They engaged in protracted negotiations over a compromise throughout 1953, thereby slowing down the amendment's momentum. On January 25, 1954, Eisenhower finally announced that he opposed the measure "unalterably." A week and a half later, two versions of the Bricker amendment were defeated in the Senate by margins of 42-50 for the strongest variant to 60-31, one vote short of the required two-thirds, for a considerably diluted compromise. The president's leadership was hardly overwhelming—a majority of the Senate Republicans voted against him—but it was a remarkable accomplishment to obtain the defeat of a party position without opening serious wounds. On other issues where the party was less committed, officially and emotionally, he brought a substantial majority of GOP congressmen behind his foreign policy.

Eisenhower "internationalized" his party by effecting a more or less formal Republican ratification of Democratic initiatives. The first Republican president to support extensive foreign aid programs and reciprocal trade, he obtained support from a majority of his congressional delegations. His versions of these programs were, it is true, compromises designed to ease the shock that a good many veteran Republicans felt in voting for them. But in the long run that was less important than the act of making them for once and for all part of a bipartisan consensus.

In all instances—Yalta, Bohlen, the Bricker amendment, foreign aid, reciprocal trade—the president adopted a low-key style of leadership that annoyed many critics who wanted him to speak out forcefully and lead aggressively in the style of both Roosevelts, Wilson, and Truman. But Eisenhower had never led in that fashion; just as in World War II, he acted as a conciliator and a compromiser, and as in the war, he was able to achieve the objectives he had set for himself.

The core of Eisenhower's attempt to reconcile internationalist diplomacy with traditional Republicanism was the defense strategy that came to be called the "New Look." The New Look assumed that defense spending had to reflect larger budgetary considerations; specifically, it had to be cut back in the name of fiscal conservatism. The Truman administration had begun an intensive across-the-board military expansion, impelled by the short-run challenge of Korea and the long-range belief that the Communist world presented an increasingly serious military threat. The Eisenhower administration rejected the assumption that any Soviet military threat was imminent and acted instead from the more traditional Republican fears of budget deficits, overtaxation, and inflation. From the beginning, it relied heavily upon nuclear deterrence and expected allies to provide more fully for their own defense.

Yet at the same time the administration not only accepted the Truman assumption that the Communist threat was worldwide; it also orchestrated a global network of containment more definite and extensive than the Truman administration had ever contemplated. It not only undertook a binding commitment to the Chinese Nationalists; it threw up new alliance structures around the world (SEATO, CENTO, the Baghdad Pact), rejected Third World neutralism, and in general undertook to hold the line against Communist expansion of any kind, anywhere. If the objective of liberation was little more than overblown rhetoric, the Eisenhower administration embraced the concept of containment more categorically than had the Truman administration. While committing itself to more sweeping ends, however, it pursued them with fewer, less flexible, and more uncertain means.

The changing nature of the world, moreover, made the assumptions behind global containment increasingly questionable—even if the adminstration had possessed the means to enforce it. Two developments stand out as changing the shape of international politics in the fifties: the emergence of a Third World, generally anti-Western, anticapitalist, and non–liberal democratic in outlook,and the death of Stalin and his succession by a shrewder and subtler Soviet leadership. The new Russian ruling group, soon dominated by Nikita Khrushchev, sought to extend Soviet influence and power no less than Stalin; indeed, this was a goal it pursued in many respects with more zeal. But at the same time, its members wanted to devote more attention to internal Russian development and to tone down the atmosphere of confrontation with the West that had grown during Stalin's lifetime. In dealing with the major powers, they engaged in protestations of friendship and peaceful coexistence. Seeking to penetrate key areas of the Third World, they supported "wars of liberation" against colonial powers and presented the Russian Revolution as a model for developing nations.

Khrushchev and his associates presented little hope for a general settlement of the Cold War, but they required a response more flexible and sophisticated than Stalin had merited. Instead, the administration conducted a foreign policy based on assumptions that had jelled when Stalinism was at its height: that the Communist world was a monolith controlled from Moscow; that the Russian challenge was primarily a military one that would be resisted by any right-thinking non-Communist nation; that it was therefore idle to look for signs of fragmentation within the Communist camp; that it was imperative to bring the Third World into the anti-Communist fold alongside the Western capitalist democracies.

Increasingly misplaced, these propositions received their most dogmatic formulation at the hands of Secretary of State Dulles. Possessing formidable intellectual powers and long experience in international affairs, Dulles nonetheless regarded Communism with an intense moralistic bitterness that, while merited by the harsh tyrannies of the Communist world, consistently got in the way of a constructive diplomacy. At times downright rude in his personal contacts with Communist leaders, prone to lecture allies and neutrals as well as foes, Dulles had a way of appearing as an American Vishinsky. Employing rhetoric as if it were a blunt instrument, he declared American readiness to go to the brink of war, threatened massive retaliation against aggression, warned the NATO allies of an agonizing reappraisal if they blocked German rearmament, and told the Third World that neutralism was immoral. Tireless in his pursuit of the national interest, this most-traveled secretary of state in American history more often succeeded in alienating those with whom he dealt than in converting them.

The result was a diplomacy accurate enough in its perception that the Cold War was not over but too unsophisticated in its handling of increasingly complex foreign entanglements to inspire confidence among allies, win over a skeptical Third World, or reduce the level of hostility with the USSR. When Eisenhower left office, the Western alliance was in disrepair, largely as a result of his stand against the French-British invasion of Suez. The Third World nations, save for those in which the old colonial powers still possessed significant influence, had rejected Dullesian anti-Communism as inimical to their own development. Even the Egyptian regime of Gamal Abdel Nasser displayed little gratitude for the way in which the American government had saved it from disaster in the 1956 Suez crisis. Relations with the Soviet Union, having alternated between confrontation and accommodation in near-bewildering fashion, were at a low point, partly because of the Soviet drive to oust the West from Berlin, partly because of the U-2 affair, the most unnecessary crisis of the Eisenhower presidency and perhaps the worst-handled incident of espionage in American history. Despite increasing signs of tension between the USSR and China, the idea of a dialogue with Maoist communism remained unthinkable. Through all this ran a vein of inflexible self-righteousness that was no more serviceable in the cause of anti-Communism than in numerous other endeavors.

By the late fifties, intellectuals and defense analysts believed that the United States had grown weaker during the Eisenhower presidency, both in its means of defense and its sense of purpose. The defense critiques had their origin partly in Sputnik, which had generated the wide—if erroneous—belief that the United States was on the wrong side of a "missile gap." They also rested upon the dissatisfaction with which advocates of a flexible, conventional military capability viewed the New Look. These alarms, we know now, were overwrought.

What can be less easily dismissed was a mounting *impression* of declining American energy and of aimlessness in the face of a vigorous Soviet challenge. The new mood had several sources. The Rockefeller Brothers Fund published a series of reports on foreign and domestic policies, designed to advance the political ambitions of Nelson Rockefeller and carrying the clear implication that the country lacked a sense of direction. Numerous opinion leaders attempted to draw up an agenda of "national goals." And while the real difficulties of a changing world would have bedeviled any administration, Dulles's death in 1959 and Eisenhower's own declining health contributed to a public image of a less-than-forceful national leadership. For all his skills and accomplishments, the president had been unable to impart a lasting sense of national purpose.

He had, of course, not failed at every turn. It would be unfair and inaccurate to depict the Eisenhower years as an unmitigated series of setbacks for American foreign policy. Indeed, Eisenhower's reputation has enjoyed something of a comeback in recent years, largely on the basis of his perceived accomplishments in diplomacy, usually stated as follows: he ended the Korean conflict on satisfactory, if not "liberationist" terms; he did not lead us into war in Indochina; he cut the defense budget; he was willing, intermittently, to engage in discussions with the Soviet Union.[2] In the main, however, these were negative accomplishments which expressed no larger design.

If Eisenhower gave the nation an era of peace and low defense spending, he also reaffirmed and extended its commitment to a crusade against Communism. The effort to curb the spread of Communism was in itself valid as opposition to the extension of any type of totalitarianism, but in the post-Stalin, postcolonial world, it required careful application based on a

---

[2]Few, if any, historians or journalists have added to this list the successful CIA-arranged coups in Iran and Guatemala, the facedown of Communist China over Quemoy and Matsu, or the military landing in Lebanon. The need for these operations, not to mention their morality, is quite simply unverifiable, and the academic community has tended to be quite skeptical of them. From the perspective of the administration, however, they were important accomplishments.

sober sense of the diversity of the globe and the limits of American power. Eisenhower did not achieve such an application; one must doubt in fact that his administration ever developed an overall view of what was going on in a revolutionary world. For example, while Eisenhower wisely avoided war in Indochina, he subsequently involved the United States deeply in both South Vietnam and Laos; his own memoirs testify to his lack of comprehension of the political dynamics of Southeast Asia. The failure of his Egyptian policy, illustrated by a growing Egyptian rapprochement with the USSR after Suez, tells us much the same about his grasp of the Middle East.

Although Eisenhower's administration was frequently criticized in its last years for lacking a sense of purpose, its foreign policy actually possessed a well-defined mission. This was a global confrontation with Communism on a scale that went well beyond the practice of the Truman administration, from Berlin to Beirut, from Quemoy to Vientiane. Eisenhower achieved neither a sense of the varieties of Communism and neutralism nor a coherent strategy in dealing with a group of challenges that were remarkably diverse in their tactics and in their importance to the interests of the United States. Herein lies the source of the sense of malaise that developed during the closing years of his presidency. His failure to produce means commensurate with the purpose he had proclaimed was crucial in giving rise to the dismay about the national direction. Ironically, many of his critics, while understanding this conceptual shortcoming, were unable to perceive its other side: the inability to differentiate among the nature and significance of Communist initiatives. Dedicated only to developing the means to respond, they would do so within the framework of his other assumptions and ultimately would carry American diplomacy into far greater disrepute than he ever had achieved.

The Hero's Legacy

Any evaluation of Eisenhower's presidency must be equivocal. While he was not a professional politician, neither was he a "captive hero," taken in tow by the professionals. Even after his health became a problem, he remained a man in control, working with a definite sense of purpose toward broad objectives. If his leadership seemed at times less than forceful, it was because his style had always been accommodationist rather than combative. Seeking in the main to hold the line, he did not go in quest of new vistas for social policy or government activity. He was a moderate conservative who accepted American society as it existed while encouraging the nurture of traditional values. This led him to give scant attention to important new currents, such as the black revolution, but it also gave the nation and the Republican party time to digest most of the New and Fair Deals and make them part of the national consensus. Neither Eisenhower nor any imaginable substitute could manage the activist side of his goal, the remaking of the Republican party in his own image. Hindered like Roosevelt by the fragmented nature of the American party system, he could do little more than begin a time-consuming process.

Oddly, his diplomacy was less effective. His leadership style, which had in many respects met the needs of the nation domestically, was not so well attuned to a rapidly changing world. American foreign policy in the fifties required a process of adjustment, not an institutionalization and rigidification of the concepts and impulses of the early Cold War. To hold the line in diplomacy was increasingly to ignore the nature of a new international environment. To adjust to a world in flux is of course never easy, and it would be folly to assume that any president could have handled the task without error or reverses. It is not too much, however, to expect one to recognize what is happening.

Eisenhower was assuredly successful in the one area of politics where it matters most, at the ballot box. The recipient of landslide victories in 1952 and 1956, he almost certainly could have been elected by another overwhelming margin had he been able to run in 1960. Whatever shortcomings critics may find in his administration, he possessed the trust and love of the American people in a way that transcended party politics. It was in many respects more impressive than the esteem FDR had enjoyed, for that was based heavily upon the wholesale dispensation of benefits to the needy. Eisenhower offered Americans not tangible help but rather a sense of reassurance emanating from the qualities he embodied. Most visible among them were the qualities of the hero—strength, authority, command, identification with the aspirations and tri-

umphs of the nation itself. Less visible but probably more fundamental were the qualities of the managerial conservative as this
type had evolved halfway through this century—organization,
adaptation, cooperation—coexisting uneasily with a nostalgia for
a simpler, more individualistic past. They were qualities that in
the aggregate made Eisenhower a father figure to a nation that
wanted a breathing spell from the relentless pace of twentieth-
century change.

4

The Politics of Prophecy:
Martin Luther King, Jr.

Roosevelt and the important leaders who followed him frequently engaged in vehement political combat, representing the interests and philosophies of competing groups in American life. Nevertheless, they generally functioned within a loose consensus that stressed political accommodation and a broad spectrum of white middle-class values and assumptions. It was a consensus that became strongly perceived and widely celebrated in the post–World War II atmosphere, deeply embedded as it was in the American historical experience and given a beneficient aura by economic prosperity. Even so, it could not provide satisfaction and justice for all. The greatest segment of the population it effectively excluded was black, largely impoverished, socially and economically segregated, and disfranchised in the Southern states. It is surprising that black protest stayed for so long within the boundaries established by the political and legal system and hardly amazing that it eventually moved in other directions.

Martin Luther King, Jr., was the type of leader who has frequently emerged when relatively powerless, ill-treated people turn to direct action to help themselves. Widely—and correctly—perceived as an agitator who attempted to alter the political system from the outside, he was also a religious leader standing in a long tradition of millenarian Protestantism that throughout the history of Western civilization has possessed a special appeal to the oppressed. A theological scholar of extensive learning, he was first and foremost a preacher who adopted the role of a moral-religious prophet determined to awaken the conscience of America by exposing its racial sins. His mastery of the techniques of political communication was as thorough as that of any public man of his generation. His values appealed to a large and influential portion of the white population as well as to American blacks. In the end, his reach, like that of all millennial prophets, exceeded his grasp, but he did more than any other individual to change the racial consciousness of America in the fifties and sixties. In doing so, he proved that the agitator with a just cause and a sure sense of the imperatives of his time could wield effective leadership from outside the political establishment.

Struggle by Litigation:
The Civil Rights Movement Before King

From its establishment in 1910, the National Association for the Advancement of Colored People was the primary voice in the drive for black advancement. In its tactics and makeup, it represented not simply the experience and outlook of blacks but those of a larger American liberalism. From the beginning, the NAACP was multiracial in its composition, gradualist in its approach, and legalist in its methods. Its founders were of two distinct types. Intellectuals such as W. E. B. Du Bois represented a young, angry Negro elite, and white reformers such as the social worker Mary White Ovington or the academic classicist Joel Spingarn were prone to regard the plight of the Negro as another social problem to be attacked, just as early-twentieth-century progressives had confronted such problems as child labor, the exploitation of women workers, or unsafe factory conditions. Generally successful in setting the approach of the new organization, the white reformers were not alienated from American society in the manner of the black intellectuals; on the whole, moreover, they were believers in the Victorian cult of progress.

The whites who established the tone of the NAACP in its early history were predominantly Jewish. Their general interest in reform and special interest in the condition of American Negro had grown to a substantial degree out of their collective ethnic experience. Especially empathetic toward blacks, an even more stigmatized group with a harsher recent history of oppression, Jewish activists tended to be disproportionately represented in movements for racial tolerance. At the same time, their relative economic success and upward social mobility disposed them toward moderation.

The institutional structure of discrimination, so the reasoning went, constituted the main barrier to the advancement of blacks. Once this structure was toppled, they could get ahead, just as had other groups in American society. From 1910 to 1956, the civil rights movement, largely the NAACP, concentrated on legislative lobbying and court action designed to give Negroes full enjoyment of the fundamental rights of citizenship. It struggled for antilynching laws, equal employment opportunity, abolition of segregation, and the outlawing of devices that restricted the right to vote. A relatively moderate course of action, it was also realistic and eventually productive; necessarily, however, it was activity carried on by the black elite and its white allies in distant courtrooms and legislative offices. Acting in behalf of the interests of all blacks, the NAACP appealed to their minds rather than to their emotions. Furthermore, its immediate objectives were most likely to benefit the small black middle class.

By 1940, alternatives were beginning to surface. A. Philip Randolph, the president of the Brotherhood of Sleeping Car Porters, threatened to mobilize the masses. Proclaiming the March on Washington Movement in 1940, he planned a demonstration of thousands of Negroes in the capital city as a means of obtaining a Fair Employment Practices Committee (FEPC). Randolph's action never occurred; reacting to the pressure, President Roosevelt established an FEPC. After the war, Randolph led efforts to end segregation and discrimination in the U.S. armed forces; he also began to lay the groundwork for a large-scale black draft resistance movement. Partly in response, President Truman established a policy of equal opportunity in the military.

By any standard, Randolph had been spectacularly successful. He had confronted two presidents, who in turn had granted major concessions to the black population. All the same, he never came close to displacing the NAACP as the most important voice of the civil rights movement. His civil rights organizations were unstable, underfunded ad hoc coalitions. The NAACP, which was winning important victories of its own in the courts and receiving more recognition than ever from white politicians, remained the major institutional voice of civil rights.

Randolph nevertheless had demonstrated an important alternative that might one day supplant the old movement. That development, however, would await several conditions: (1) a growing sense that the NAACP approach was reaching the point of diminishing returns; (2) a catalytic event, the school desegregation decision of 1954, which gave hope to blacks across the country; (3) a growing, independent black middle class, acutely sensitive to discrimination and capable of giving both material and moral support to direct action against it; and (4) most fundamental, a charismatic leader who could assume the role that the aging Randolph had pioneered, mobilize blacks of all classes, and appeal to the white reform community—especially to the liberal intelligentsia and the news media it was coming to dominate.

The Making of a Prophet

It tells us much about the quality of race relations in the mid-twentieth-century South that Martin Luther King, Jr., could remember the atmosphere of his childhood years as "tension-packed." By Southern black standards, King had been born into and had grown up in unusually secure surroundings, the black bourgeoisie of Atlanta in the thirties and forties. No Southern city possessed so large and prosperous a black middle class, and King's family, headed by well-to-do clergymen, was among its pillars. His maternal grandfather, Rev. A. D. Williams, had established the Ebenezer Baptist Church and developed it into one of the leading Negro congregations in the city. His father, a big rough-hewn man who had risen from the poverty of the Georgia countryside, had carried on the ministry of Ebenezer with great success. Respected within the black community and financially well-off, the King family gave its children an environment largely insulated from that inhabited by the average Southern black. In its externals, the life of the young Martin King seemed not much different from that of any youth, black or white, nurtured by a loving, upper-middle-class family.

The childhood and adolescence of his wife-to-be, Coretta Scott, was far closer to the experience of the ordinary Southern black. She spent her early years in rural Alabama watching a determined, hard-working father struggle for independence against a system that feared the independent Negro above almost everything else. The elder Scott's eventual success in becoming a self-sustaining small businessman came only after he had surmounted what seemed almost perpetual debt to a local white merchant, the burning of his home and of a lumber mill he briefly owned, and a general pattern of harassment from white competitors. For his daughter, life meant resisting discrimination, overcoming handicaps imposed by a scandalously inferior segregated education system, and struggling for a college education with the help of scholarships. In all, it was an existence that verged at times on the desperate with almost every white person a potential exploiter or menace. Unavoidably, it inflicted wounds that could never be entirely healed.

Martin King never experienced a continuing trauma akin to that of the Scott family, but even the black middle class of Atlanta could not escape discrimination. Young King discovered it in a number of ways: the loss of white childhood playmates; a slap from a white woman who claimed he had stepped on her toes in a crowded elevator; a request to move to the black section of a downtown shoe store; a traffic policeman addressing his father as "boy"; insults from a white supervisor on a summer job; being forced to stand on a bus for some ninety miles in order to make a seat available for a white passenger. Perhaps his most biting memory was of an event that occurred while he was a high school student returning to Atlanta by train after a trip to Connecticut. Entering the dining car, he found himself forced to eat in a segregated section behind a curtain. "I felt," he wrote some years later, "as if the curtain had been dropped on my selfhood."

Still, such episodes were sporadic, and the King family, unlike the Scott family, was not compelled to suffer in silence. His father took him out of the shoe store rather than buy in a segregated section, fired back a sharp comment at the traffic cop, encouraged him to quit the summer job with the racist foreman, and never rode a bus. Protest and activism were in fact family traditions. Grandfather Williams had organized the first Atlanta chapter of the NAACP and had led the movement that forced the white power structure to accede to the funding of a public Negro high school in the mid-1920s. "Daddy" King was a black community leader, as active politically as was possible for a Negro Republican and vocal in his hatred of racism. "I don't care how long I have to live with this system," he had told his son as they left the shoe store. "I will never accept it." From the time he was able to be conscious of such things, King absorbed his father's ministerial sense of responsibility for his people and the older man's determination to fight the system.

What we know of King's childhood leaves the impression that his upbringing was in the classic mold of the Protestant fundamentalist household. While loving and supportive, his parents also expected strict obedience, tended to be firm disciplinarians, placed a religious sanction upon proper behavior, and transmitted to their offspring the fear of God. The effects upon a sensitive, introspective boy are hardly surprising. Even as a pre-teen child, King seems at times to have been overwhelmed by a sense of obligation and guilt. On two occasions—the accidental near-death of his grandmother, Mrs. Williams, then her actual death—he made half-hearted attempts at suicide by throwing himself out the second-story window of his home. Perhaps, as David Lewis suggests, he was attempting to assume and expiate the suffering of others through atonement by injury or death. Perhaps it was significant that his favorite hymn was "I Want to Be More and More Like Jesus."

King's education was one of unusual quality for a Southern black. He skipped grades in elementary and secondary schools, won oratorical contests, and matriculated at Morehouse College in Atlanta under a special early admission program at the age of fifteen. Soon he was earning outstanding marks and participating extensively in campus activities, including the football team, which he quarterbacked. At first aspiring to a medical career, he switched to a sociology major, a choice that apparently mirrored an interest in social problems and an ambition to engage in a socially useful career. He wrote eloquently as a senior about the need for educators to instill a sense of purpose and commitment, for students to reject the assumption that their learning was designed merely to give them the means to exploit their less fortunate fellow men. By this time, he had decided to enter the ministry. A trial sermon, preached when he was eighteen, attracted a huge crowd. The audience had to move from a small worship area into the main auditorium of Ebenezer. Shortly thereafter, he was ordained a Baptist minister, ready, so his father believed, to become co-pastor of the family church.

That the son thought differently speaks volumes about his maturity, independence, and reflective character. Before entering the ministry on a full-time basis, he intended to enlarge his education and to do so at predominantly white institutions in the North —Crozer Theological Seminary (B.D., 1951) and Boston University (Ph.D., 1955). At both schools, as at Morehouse, he was an outstanding student and a figure of note in the local black communities, from whose Baptist pulpits he frequently preached guest sermons.

As a student, his intellectual quest appears to have been for a meaningful synthesis of the interests and influences that had engaged him in earlier years: sociology and social activism, Daddy King's fundamentalist ministry with its emphasis upon personal redemption and salvation, and the speculative philosophy and theology to which he had been introduced at Morehouse. The theologian who appealed to him most was Walter Rauschenbusch, the central figure of the early-twentieth-century social gospel. Rauschenbusch, he later admitted, had made some mistakes—he had been too much a believer in automatic progress, too optimistic about human nature, too close to identifying the Kingdom of God itself with earthly social justice. Nevertheless, Rauschenbusch had performed an important service by giving the Christian churches a theological basis for social concern; by demonstrating the relationship between spiritual well-being and material well-being, he had shown that the church must deal with the whole person, not just with the soul.

If Rauschenbusch provided a basis for social reform, Thoreau and Gandhi provided a technique. Thoreau had excited King ever since his freshman days at Morehouse. He became thoroughly acquainted with the ideas of Gandhi while a theological student, devoured his works, and developed a deep attraction to the Indian leader's concept of *Satyagraha*, which convinced him that nonviolent resistance to injustice could be undertaken in a strong, forceful manner. Gandhi, he later wrote, had been the first great historical figure "to lift the love ethic of Jesus above mere inter-action between individuals to a powerful and effective social force on a large scale."

Rauschenbusch and Gandhi were unquestionably the domi-nant intellectual forces in King's life; his allegiance to them was tempered only a bit by his reading of Reinhold Niebuhr. Like Rauschenbusch and Gandhi, Niebuhr combined theology with social thought and social reformism; unlike them, he was pro-foundly pessimistic about human nature and institutions. For Niebuhr, democracy and social justice were means of amelio-rating the human condition and of checking the power of sin in the world; but sin was too pervasive, too integral a part of human nature ever to be eliminated. Again and again, he criticized re-formers who overlooked the enduring presence of sin in man and pridefully believed that their efforts could lead to utopia or, in theological terms, the establishment of the Kingdom of God on earth.

Niebuhr's critique of pacifism, a response to the rise of aggressive totalitarianism in the 1930s, followed naturally and was even more disturbing to the young theological student, for it established a conflict that could not be papered over with a few qualifications. Pacifism, Niebuhr declared, was ultimately a form of utopianism, based on an optimistic view of man's nature and denying man's sinful qualities; its latent perfectionism was yet another demonstration of the errors of the radical social gospel, and its practitioners frequently exhibited a self-righteousness that seemed to assert that they somehow had transcended the sin that stained all persons. Tactically, pacifism could be successful only in a very special situation—when used to confront oppressors who themselves had a highly developed moral conscience. It was for that reason alone that Gandhi had enjoyed a measure of success against the British. But nonviolent resistance in other situations would be at best futile if it ended only in maintenance of the status quo, and at worst immoral if it facilitated the spread of evil and injustice.

King's response was to draw a distinction between *Satyagraha* —active, if nonviolent, resistance to evil—and the pacifism that

Niebuhr decried, passive nonresistance to evil. He refused to join pacifist organizations as such, but Gandhi's concepts continued to be compelling. His answer was, in truth, more an evasion than a resolution.

Niebuhr was nonetheless important to King. No modern Protestant theologian of equal stature came as close to the old-time fundamentalist Protestant faith in which King had been reared. The concept of God at which King arrived was similar to Niebuhr's: it was a personal God offering personal salvation, not a theological abstraction. Niebuhr's strictures about sin also stayed with King, preparing him for the determined resistance he was soon to meet leading the children of light against the children of darkness, whom he would find strong, determined, and convinced of their own righteousness. If nothing else, Niebuhr gave him the intellectual equipment to shed a mistaken optimism that might have broken an individual unprepared for the enormity of the forces arrayed against him.

King's years as a student of theology and philosophy were productive in other ways. In Boston, he met, courted, and married Coretta Scott, a remarkable woman whose aspirations, talent, family encouragement, and hard work had pulled her out of Alabama to Antioch College and then to graduate study at the New England Conservatory of Music. Their relationship exemplified King's determination and sense of independence. He decided at their first meeting that Coretta would be his bride. She had, he told her, character, intelligence, personality, and beauty, the four qualities he wanted in a wife. In a matter of months, he persuaded her to give up her career plans for marriage. Then he prevailed upon his father to abandon a conviction that he should marry the daughter of a long-time friend in Atlanta. "I am going to make my own decisions," he told his new fiancée. "I will choose my own wife."

He was equally set on having his own career rather than returning to Atlanta and Ebenezer. An articulate young Ph.D. with a compelling presence, he had numerous opportunities in the black religious and educational worlds. His choice was oddly tentative. He decided that he wanted to *begin* his career in the ministry and probably turn to teaching later. Faced with a decision between posts in the North and in the South, he decided that it was his duty to go back to the South with all its disadvantages—for at least a few years. In 1954, he accepted appointment as pastor of the Dexter Avenue Baptist Church in Montgomery, Alabama.

The Politics of Prophecy

The Dexter Avenue Church was one of the oldest black congregations in Montgomery, primarily middle class in membership and long known for the high intellectual standards it expected of its pastors. In common with most other black churches in the city, it had no tradition of civil rights activism or social concern. For a man of a different temperament, it could have formed the basis of a safe, rewarding, relatively undemanding life in which one could be busy and useful without challenging the times.

King was determined to change things. He attempted to attract low-income Negroes, established social-political action and social service committees, organized a scholarship fund for black college students, and began a cultural program for youngsters with artistic talent. Apparently, he had little difficulty in gaining the support of his congregation and church officers and even less in persuading them to pay for the new ventures. He became a prominent member of the local chapters of the NAACP and the Alabama Council on Human Relations, an interracial body that fought discimination. Soon he was an officer in both groups. He had demonstrated a take-charge personality, unusual powers of persuasion, and a resolve to engage in social reform. Still, as his first year in Montgomery neared its end, few could have imagined how fast and how far he was capable of moving.

King's emergence as a national figure came with accidental suddenness in December 1955, when a black seamstress on the way home from work refused to surrender her bus seat to a white passenger in accordance with Montgomery law. Although she was an antisegregation activist, Rosa Parks acted upon impulse with no grand design in mind; as she later put it, "I was just plain tired, and my feet hurt." Promptly arrested, she was convicted of violating the local segregation ordinances and fined $10. There in earlier days the episode would have ended and soon would have been forgotten, but coming a year and a half after the *Brown* decision and involving a woman of dignity and character, it ignited a will to resist within the Negro community.

The initiative came from the Women's Political Council and the local NAACP, two local black organizations that had been awaiting an opportunity to strike a blow against segregation. Primarily middle-class, they were especially sensitive to the social insult of segregation. But in choosing the transit system as the focus of protest, they had hit upon an issue that affected the daily lives of the disadvantaged bulk of the local black population in an especially grating way. Montgomery blacks not only had to sit at the rear of the bus; they were also obligated to give up even those seats to standing white passengers. Within the black community, one heard countless stories of abuse and physical violence by white bus drivers. Abundant latent mass support existed for a blow against the bus company; all that was needed was the right weapon and the right leadership.

The weapon was obvious—the boycott, a technique that blacks had occasionally employed in similar situations. One of King's friends, Rev. Theodore Jemison, had successfully led such an effort in Baton Rouge, Louisiana, two and a half years earlier. The boycott was perhaps the only way in which an impoverished, nonvoting black population could apply substantial leverage against the bus company; Negroes, after all, constituted 75 percent of the ridership.

The question of leadership was trickier. The two instigators of the campaign were both unable to serve: Jo Ann Robinson of the Women's Political Council was apparently deemed ineligible because of her sex; and E. D. Nixon, the head of the local NAACP, was a working Pullman porter frequently absent from the city. The movement, which took the name Montgomery Improvement Association (MIA), made King its president for the most mundane reasons. As a minister, he was a prominent young member of the black leadership class; and, unlike many of his colleagues, he had involved himself in movements for social change. As a relatively new person on the Montgomery scene, he was acceptable to all factions of the organized Negro community. Finally, his youth and lack of roots in Montgomery would make it easy for him to pull up stakes if the movement was crushed; older, established black leaders understood better than he the wrath a spokesman would face from the white population.

If King's leadership was accidental, his swift rise to national prominence was not. No other American black in public life possessed so superb a combination of gifts for the leadership of a mass movement. Working eighteen to twenty hours a day, he was at first involved in excessive organizational detail. He later recalled: "The phone would start ringing as early as five o'clock in the morning and seldom stopped before midnight."

At the same time, he had to present his case in a credible and appealing manner to the public, both black and white, across the country. As a minister, he had customarily spent fifteen hours a week polishing his sermons. Now he proved himself a gifted extemporaneous speaker, capable of the grandiose in his rhetoric and objectives, yet without a trace of the ridiculous in his speech or bearing. Almost immediately, he became a deeply inspirational figure to the black community and to white liberals throughout the country.

The flavor of the movement and of King's leadership was established with his first address to Montgomery blacks after being named president of the MIA. With no time for preparation, knowing only that somehow he wanted to combine in his exhortation militance and moderation, he found himself facing an enthusiastic overflow crowd of some five thousand at the Holt Street Baptist Church, a large structure located in the heart of the black community.

> There comes a time when people get tired. We are here this evening to say to those who have mistreated us so long, that we are tired. Tired of being segregated and humiliated; tired of being kicked about by the brutal feet of oppression.
>
> We have no alternative but to protest. . . . our actions must be guided by the deepest principles of our Christian faith. Love must be our regulating ideal. Once again we must hear the words of Jesus echoing across the centuries: "Love your enemies, bless them that curse you, and pray for them that despitefully use you." If we fail to do this our protest will end up as a meaningless drama on the stage of history, and its memory will be shrouded with the ugly garments of shame. In spite of

the mistreatment that we have confronted we must not become bitter and end up by hating our white brothers. As Booker T. Washington said, "Let no man pull you so low as to make you hate him."

If you will protest courageously, and yet with dignity and Christian love, when the history books are written in future generations, the historians will have to pause and say, "There lived a great people—a black people—who injected new meaning and dignity into the veins of civilization." This is our challenge and our overwhelming responsibility.

The ovation was thunderous and prolonged. The oration, King realized, had evoked more response than any speech or sermon he had ever delivered. With astuteness and passion, he had spoken both to the pride and anger of his own people and to the conscience of a broader national and international public.

The black community of Montgomery did not have the financial resources to sustain the MIA over the long haul; it was kept afloat by outside donations—from blacks and black organizations across the country, from liberal Northern whites, from foreigners as far away as Switzerland and Singapore. By his faith and his eloquence, King had created a movement that extended far beyond Alabama.

In Montgomery, however, he met only resistance so bitter that it is scarcely possible to comprehend from the perspective of three decades. The initial demands of the MIA were modest: (1) courteous treatment by bus drivers; (2) passengers to be seated on a first-come, first-served basis, *Negroes sitting from the back of the bus toward the front, whites from the front toward the back*; and (3) the eventual employment of black drivers for predominantly black routes. The entire package amounted to little more than a request for a more polite form of segregation; its suggested seating arrangements were already in effect in some other Southern cities, including Nashville, Atlanta, and Mobile. (But the MIA was also appealing the conviction of Rosa Parks to the federal courts in the hope of obtaining a ruling that would outlaw segregated seating.)

The bus company, city officials, and the white population of Montgomery were unyielding. As the hard-line attorney for the bus company put it, "If we granted the Negroes these demands, they would go about boasting of a victory they had won over the white people; and this we will not stand for." Every member of the city commission soon took up membership in the local White Citizens' Council.

King, who had expected a quick settlement, despondently chided himself for his foolish optimism. He had learned, he later wrote, two important lessons. First, those who were privileged were unlikely to surrender their privileges—no matter how reasonable and moderate the requests of the other side—without strong resistance. Second, the real purpose of segregation was not simply to separate the races but to oppress and exploit the segregated; thus justice and equality for the Negro could come only with the elimination of segregation.

In placing himself at the head of the MIA, King, without entirely realizing what he was getting into, had placed himself in a position of confrontation with the entire structure of white society in Montgomery. In this confrontation, all the power was on the other side. During the next twelve months, he and his more visible associates faced the unmitigated hostility of the official institutions of local and state law and the even more ominous threat of white vigilantism. He was twice arrested, once for a minor traffic violation, temporarily jailed, and ultimately convicted of conspiracy under an Alabama statute. He and his wife were subjected to incessant anonymous threats and obscene telephone calls. The front of their home was demolished by a bomb. To endure such a situation took enormous courage and faith.

King's determination to adhere to nonviolent tactics was a natural enough outcome of his theological education, but he actually refined the concept of nonviolent resistance intellectually during a year of intense pressure. His primary motivation was primitive Christianity, as exemplified by the Sermon on the Mount and the quest for sacrifice and atonement that had characterized Jesus' early disciples. His intellectual rationale came substantially from Gandhi, who had taught him the difference between nonviolent *resistance* and passive acceptance. His guiding principle was the ancient Greek concept of *agape*, a general, disinterested love for all people, a recognition of the fundamental brotherhood of man. *Agape* was both personally enobling and a potential means of establishing a sense of community between black and white.

Following the concept of *agape*, nonviolent resisters sought the friendship and understanding of the oppressor, not his defeat or humiliation. Resistance would be directed against the forces of evil, not against evildoers as individuals. The resister, moreover, would accept suffering without retaliation, for unearned suffering was redemptive, both for the sufferer and the oppressor. Non-violence, finally, avoided not simply external physical acts of violence but also violence of the spirit; practicing *agape*, the resister refused to hate his oppressor and sought only to love him as a member of the brotherhood of man. All of this, King admitted, was "based on the conviction that the universe is on the side of justice," that the resisters would ultimately prevail because God was with them. "There is a creative force in this universe that works to bring the disconnected aspects of reality into a harmonious whole," he wrote in 1958.

King's employment of nonviolent resistance was a brilliant tactic. It avoided bloodshed that surely would have caused death and injury to many more blacks than whites. It united the black community as never before; "big Negroes," who owned Cadillacs and Buicks, arose with the sun to provide rides for black maids and laborers whom they previously had scorned. Segregation embittered blacks of all classes; King's methods drew the entire community together and gave every person in it a chance to become actively involved in a way that would not have been possible if the battle had been exclusively a courtroom affair. The result was to bring black pride and morale to their highest point in Montgomery since Reconstruction. Moreover, King had captured the imagination of white liberals across the country. From the beginning, it appears that the majority of his contributions came from white sources. His entire philosophy invited white participation, and while the number of whites active in the Montgomery effort was relatively small, the total would grow with each new crusade.

No one could doubt the depth and sincerity of King's personal commitment to nonviolence. After his own home was bombed with his wife and infant child narrowly escaping injury, his intervention prevented an angry, armed black crowd from lynching white policemen, city officials, and reporters who had come to the scene. Realizing from then on that his own life was in danger, he was determined to continue, no matter what the outcome. At a mass meeting, he declared, "If one day you find me sprawled out dead, I do not want you to retaliate with a single act of violence." In the first days of bus desegregation, after a rash of violent incidents and nighttime bombings, he addressed another rally: "Lord, I hope no one will have to die. . . . Certainly I don't want to die. But if anyone has to die, let it be me."

King's assault against segregation and his devotion to nonviolence captured the imagination of secular humanists, but neither he nor almost any mortal could have sustained himself in such impossible circumstances without the reassurance of a mystical, millennial commitment. There was always more of Rauschenbusch than of Niebuhr in King's makeup, and in the bitter environment of the Deep South it was nearly inevitable that a nonviolent crusade against segregation would have a touch of the utopian about it. It was also nearly inevitable that a religious leader under the pressure that King endured could find the will to go on only by coming to believe that he was a prophet of the Lord.

Several weeks into the boycott, his nerves strained to the breaking point by countless threats and obscene phone calls, King had been on the verge of quitting. Late one night, in a state of exhaustion after receiving a telephoned death threat, he prayed for guidance:

> At that moment I experienced the presence of the Divine as I never had experienced Him before. It seemed as though I could hear the quiet assurance of an inner voice saying: 'Stand up for righteousness, stand up for truth; and God will be at your side forever.' Almost at once my fears began to go. My uncertainty disappeared. I was ready to face anything.

King was henceforth convinced that he was a prophet of God, speaking the words of the Lord in the manner of an Isaiah or an Amos. He fully expected the persecution that came to all prophets who spoke unpalatable truths. It was a commitment that reflected not some messianic impulse but a combination of religious faith and leadership duty. He had given much thought to the nature and obligations of prophecy. Not every Christian minister could be a prophet, he wrote, but "some must be prepared for the ordeals of this high calling and be willing to suffer courageously for righteousness." To this burden he was now intellectually and emotionally reconciled.

The eventual victory of the MIA movement seemed to vindicate its tactics. The denouement in fact verged on the miraculous. Just as King and his fellow leaders were facing a state court injunction against their car pool operation, the U.S. Supreme Court sustained a lower federal ruling that the Alabama bus segregation laws were unconstitutional. "God Almighty has spoken from Washington," declared an excited black man.

A sober observer might also have taken the events as defining the limitations of direct action. Although the MIA had endured for a year, lifted the spirits of the black community, and brought the bus company to the verge of bankruptcy, it had failed to win a single concession and was on the brink of a court-ordered dissolution when it was saved by legal tactics handled by the NAACP. Far from converting or redeeming white sinners, it had demonstrated their recalcitrance; most successful in awakening blacks and white sympathizers, it nevertheless had to rely ultimately upon traditional approaches.

All the same, Montgomery unleashed a surge of militance, idealism, and great expectations, especially among young reform-minded intellectuals of both races. By employing nonviolent means and articulating his rationale so compellingly, King had laid the basis for an era of protest all over the South, conducted by zealous idealists to whom compromise was anathema. Few activists fully possessed King's theological outlook or religious mentality, but most of those who actually put their bodies on the line were more prone than he to believe they could achieve millennial results. Consequently, the new civil rights movement contained a considerable built-in potential for disillusionment.

King's public adulation carried the movement along. In the wake of Montgomery, he had become a world figure, admired and hated with great passion. In 1957, he took his first trip overseas, primarily as an honored guest at the independence celebration of the new African state of Ghana. The NAACP made him the youngest recipient ever of its esteemed Spingarn Medal. He was one of the featured speakers at a largely forgotten but nonetheless important Prayer Pilgrimage, a thirty-seven-thousand-strong demonstration held in Washington in May 1957 at the Lincoln Memorial to support the token civil rights bill that Lyndon Johnson was moving through Congress. In many respects, the pilgrimage anticipated the far larger demonstration of 1963, not least in the way that King's speech, his first national address, captured the enthusiasm of the crowd and overshadowed the efforts of the older Negro luminaries.

By this time also, King had taken the lead in founding the Southern Christian Leadership Conference (SCLC), whose head he became. Primarily an embodiment of King's personal philosophy in its assumptions and tactics, the SCLC existed in an increasingly uneasy relationship with the NAACP. The establishment of its headquarters in Atlanta eventually required King to leave Montgomery in 1960 and take up his father's standing offer to become co-pastor of the Ebenezer Church.

He also had become the object of intense hatreds. In Montgomery, while he was waiting for an associate in the lobby of the courthouse, policemen roughed him up and charged him with disobeying an officer. The state of Alabama prosecuted him for tax fraud, asserting that he had misappropriated MIA contributions and had failed to report them as income. The results were ironic. The Montgomery police commissioner felt compelled to pay King's fine on the first charge rather than undergo the embarrassment of jailing him; an all-white jury acquitted him on the second charge.

Other episodes were ominous. In 1958, a demented black woman stabbed him as he was autographing copies of his first book in a Harlem department store. The physician who removed the knife from his chest told him later that a sneeze could have severed his aorta. In 1960, he was arrested in Georgia for driving with an out-of-state driver's license, put on probation, rearrested for breaking probation after participating in a civil rights demonstration, and sentenced to six months in the state penitentiary. He was released pending an eventually successful appeal only after the personal intervention of John and Robert Kennedy. Such incidents increased King's standing as a civil rights leader by making him, more than any other figure, the focus of the passions the movement aroused. They also, as his writings make clear, constituted successive steps in his own psychological preparation for martyrdom.

In the meantime, the new era of civil rights protest, much of it not a result of King's initiative, demanded his support and frequently his physical presence. By the time King moved to Atlanta, a wave of activism was underway throughout the South in the form of mass demonstrations, sit-ins, and freedom rides, spearheaded less by the SCLC than by the Student Non-Violent Coordinating Committee (SNCC), an offshoot of the SCLC, and the Congress of Racial Equality (CORE). These developments reflected in turn a great upsurge of idealism among both black and white reformers, who felt impelled as never before to bear witness and risk suffering in the struggle against injustice. Convinced that they stood for a higher law than the earthly segregation statutes, believing that they could effect a radical change in Southern social mores, they were similar in assumptions and aspirations to the antebellum abolitionists with whom they were occasionally compared. Like the original abolitionists, who also had hoped to convert sinners by exhortation, they were even less prepared than King had been at the inception of the Montgomery boycott for the tenacity of the resistance they would face.

The freedom rides illustrated the dilemmas that faced both King and the movement as a whole. Initiated in 1961 by a CORE-SNCC coalition, they were efforts by biracial groups to ride through the South on chartered Greyhound and Trailways buses with the objective of integrating terminals. Although he had no effective control over the drive, King agreed to serve as chairman of its coordinating committee. The riders themselves did not meet violence at every stop, but their reception in Alabama was fully deserving of the adjective *explosive*—in Anniston, a mob burned one of the buses; in Birmingham and Montgomery, thugs savagely beat the passengers, including a Justice Department observer; when King went to Montgomery to address a rally in a black church, an angry white crowd surrounded the building, pelted it with missiles, and threatened to overwhelm a thin force of federal marshals that provided its only protection. Having once again become the target of the hatred of white segregationists, King now also took substantial criticism from those forces he supposedly led. When he counseled a cooling-off period and attempts at negotiation, he encountered open hostility from many younger activists, some of whom caustically denounced him for having failed to put his own body on the line as they had.

In the end, however, this division and discord was over-shadowed by some substantial success. By evoking a sense of national outrage, by appealing to the better instincts of a liberal president, by utilizing the visibility and moral prestige of King, the freedom riders achieved their immediate objectives, even if they did not change the predominant attitude of the white South. The Kennedy administration provided them federal protection and prodded the Interstate Commerce Commission into issuing strong antisegregation rules for interstate terminals. After pro-tracted negotiation and some litigation, desegregated bus stations became the rule in at least the large and medium-size cities of the South.

The year-and-a-half SNCC-led effort to desegregate Albany, Georgia, however, served only to demonstrate the limits of non-violent direct action. A bastion of segregationist traditionalism, Albany nevertheless had a white leadership determined to avoid open violence. Its chief of police, Laurie Prichett, refused to use brutality against demonstrators. He bowed his head in prayer along with them, politely requested a dispersal, and only then made peaceful arrests. By one subterfuge or another, the city resisted integration at every turn; its well-behaved policemen excited little indignation in the North and provided no excuse for federal intervention. Thoroughly covered by the news media, Albany developed into a national bore rather than a catalyst of change. King himself, despite an arrest and two-week jail term, became again an object of criticism from young activists, dis-gruntled by his preference for moderation and conciliation, by his inability to devote exclusive attention to the Albany situation, and by his decision to cease demonstrations when the city obtained a federal court injunction against them. Albany had demonstrated that direct action could be smothered to death.

David Garrow has argued that Albany marked a turning point in the development of King's tactics. He had begun his career as an activist dedicated to the concept of nonviolent persuasion, hoping to convert his bitterest enemies through moral example. Neither in Montgomery nor in Albany had he done so; in the former instance, the intervention of the federal courts had given him victory nonetheless; in the latter case, he had presided over a near-total failure. He and those around him, Garrow asserts, began to rethink nonviolence. They developed a theory of non-violent coercion, aimed not at converting the oppressor but at displaying his oppressions at their ugliest. They sought confrontations with some of the most vicious representatives of the white Southern establishment, hoping to use the national news media to dramatically display the fascistic qualities of segregationism. Albany and Laurie Prichett clearly were inappropriate targets for nonviolent coercion. King needed the opposition of violent political primitives; he turned to Birmingham.

High Tide: Birmingham, Washington, Oslo, Selma

Perhaps the most segregated and repressive urban center in the South, Birmingham, Alabama, had long been dominated by die-hard racist politicians led by Commissioner of Public Safety Eugene "Bull" Connor. A substantial portion of the black population was cowed or apathetic. Birmingham was also much more visible nationally than Albany. It thus provided a nearly ideal setting for a confrontation politics that would display suffering and oppression.

The SCLC's preparation for the Birmingham campaign took shape shortly after the Albany movement had sputtered to a close. For months, SCLC staffers familiarized themselves with legal questions, organized logistical support, raised money across the country, trained local volunteers in the philosophy and tactics of nonviolence, and mapped out demonstration areas with military precision. King and his associates vowed at the beginning to avoid what they had come to perceive as one major mistake of the Albany effort—an attempt to eliminate segregation everywhere in one swoop. They decided instead to concentrate upon segregation and discimination in Birmingham's major business establishments, especially the exclusion of Negroes from lunch counter service and their relegation to menial jobs. In focusing upon the business community, the SCLC singled out a white leadership group that was among the less resistant to change and the most vulnerable to an economic boycott. Demonstrations were scheduled to coincide with the Easter season of 1963 not just for symbolic reasons but because that time of the year was a peak retail buying period.

The Birmingham movement began on April 3, 1963, with a low-key series of sit-ins and peaceful arrests at downtown lunch counters. Although the SCLC had hoped to begin with a core of two hundred fifty local volunteers, it had been able to turn up only sixty-five. The numbers, however, were hardly true indicators of the depth of black discontent. Following the experience of Montgomery, King undertook a series of nightly mass meetings, moving from one church to another in the Negro community and harvesting recruits as other preachers harvested converts. Subjected to the rhetoric of freedom and inspired by the music of the movement, increasing numbers of blacks overcame their doubts, signed up for training in nonviolence, and, in effect, declared themselves rebels against the system that had subjugated them.

David Lewis has vividly captured the revivalistic atmosphere of one of these meetings—the interplay between King and his congregation, his Manichaean view of the issues, his underlying optimism, and, above all, his ability to move from the rhetoric and thought patterns of the sophisticated intellectual to the simpler emotional appeals of the Negro Baptist preacher:

> I got on my marching shoes!
> *Yes, Lord, me too.*
> I woke up this morning with my mind stayed on freedom!
> *Preach, doctor, preach!*
> I ain't going to let nobody turn me round!
> *Let's march, brother; we are with you!*
> If the road to freedom leads through the jailhouse, then, turnkey, swing wide the gates!
> *Amen, praise the Lord!*
> Some of you are afraid.
> *That's right; that's right.*
> Some of you are contented.
> *Speak, speak, speak!*
> But if you won't go don't hinder me! We shall march nonviolently. We shall force this nation, this city, this world,

to face its own conscience. We will make the God of
love in the white man triumphant over the Satan of
segregation that is in him. The struggle is not between
black and white!

No, no!

But between good and evil.

That's it, that's it.

And whenever good and evil have a confrontation, good will
win!

As his forces augmented, King stepped up the protest activities, moving from lunch counter demonstrations to kneel-ins at
segregated churches, sit-ins at Jim Crow libraries, and nonper-
mitted protest parades. At the end of the first week and a half,
four or five hundred demonstrators had been arrested; some
three hundred were still in jail. Surprisingly, Birmingham's police
carted away demonstrators with unexpected gentleness, and the
SCLC's pool of volunteers remained thin, despite the progress in
arousing enthusiasm. As a result, King found himself pushed
toward two important decisions.

The first and least difficult was to have himself arrested.
There can be little doubt that he sincerely felt a moral imperative
to share in the fate of those he had exhorted to disobedience. His
only cause for hesitation came from the belief that he might be
needed on the outside to raise bail money. The manner in which
he reached a decision was as revealing as the decision itself. In the
early morning hours of Good Friday, he withdrew from a room
filled with movement leaders to ponder the question in solitude.
Having made up his mind, he donned work clothes to lead the
next illegal demonstration, an act that led to his imprisonment
over the Easter weekend.

For more than a day, he was held incommunicado in solitary
confinement, a situation he compared to being in a dungeon. It
took the efforts of his sometime allies, the president and the
attorney general, to ameliorate the conditions of his confinement.
That his decision had been tactically wise seems beyond dispute.
The bail money took care of itself, its raising made easier by the
arrest. The jailing, moreover, gave King the time to prepare the
manifesto which stated the Birmingham movement's case in terms
so enduringly forceful that they became the text of the Negro
revolution.

The most significant aspect of "Letter from Birmingham Jail" was its prophetic quality; it expressed King's conviction that he was the trustee of a God-given mission to attack un-Christian institutions wherever they might exist. Responding to an "Appeal for Law and Order" issued by eight prominent white Birmingham clergymen, he began by rejecting the implication that he was an "outsider." Could not the same have been said of the prophets of the eighth century B.C. or of the Apostle Paul?

In the prophetic tradition, he challenged his critics to reach a higher state of moral awareness. They expressed concern about disorder, yet they displayed little interest in the conditions that had brought about and ultimately justified that disorder. He devoted most of his denunciation not to the Bull Connors of the South but to those more "respectable" elements that counseled order and patience. They preferred a negative peace, the absence of tension, to a positive peace, the presence of justice; they paternalistically believed they could set the timetable for the freedom of others. Perhaps most dismaying of all was the failure, with only a few exceptions, of Southern white clergymen to throw themselves into the struggle for justice. Some churchmen had been outright opponents; "all too many others have been more cautious than courageous and have remained silent behind the anesthetizing security of stained-glass windows." Like prophets throughout the ages, King employed denunciation as a tool to awaken those whom he considered not servants of the Antichrist, but morally insensitive. Like numerous prophets before him, he assailed the institutional church as corrupt and formalistic.

He sought a coupling of the quest for justice with the zeal and sense of dedication that had characterized primitive Christianity. "Whenever the early Christians entered a town, the people in power became disturbed and immediately sought to convict the Christians for being 'disturbers of the peace' and 'outside agitators,'" he wrote. "But the Christians pressed on, in the conviction that they were 'a colony of heaven,' called to obey God rather than man." Such, he made clear, was the brand of "extremism" he and his followers were practicing. They were creating tension, but it was a constructive, nonviolent tension designed to force a reexamination of existing arrangements and lead to the honest negotiations that the city's power structure had heretofore avoided. Birmingham had confirmed his reading of Reinhold

Niebuhr to the effect that "groups tend to be more immoral than individuals"; it had added to his "painful experience that freedom is never voluntarily given by the oppressor."

It was true enough, he conceded, that the SCLC demonstrations broke laws against trespass and parading without a permit. But there were two types of laws—those that were just and those that were unjust; moral man had a duty to obey the first and disobey the second. Man-made laws, in order to be legitimate, had to be in harmony with the law of God. Specifically, "Any law that uplifts human personality is just. Any law that degrades human personality is unjust." All segregation statutes hence were unjust; otherwise just laws, such as the trespass or parade statutes, could rightly be considered unjust when used to defend segregation. Civil disobedience, when undertaken to arouse the conscience of the community, amounted to respect for law, not contempt for it.

At first, he concluded, he had been disappointed at being called an extremist, but he had come to find the label satisfying. Jesus had been an extremist for love, Amos an extremist for justice, and Paul an extremist for the gospel. Martin Luther, John Bunyan, Abraham Lincoln, and Thomas Jefferson, uncompromising in their dedication to truth and justice, also had been extremists. As for him, "If I have said anything that understates the truth and indicates my having a patience that allows me to settle for anything less than brotherhood, I beg God to forgive me."

"Letter from Birmingham Jail" captured the spirit and motivation of the Southern Negro revolution of the early sixties. The movement had attracted many followers strictly on the humanistic merits of its objectives, and not all its adherents were devoted to nonviolence. Nevertheless, its driving force came from the religious commitment that King personified and articulated so well; the result was a sense of mission and an inspirational aura that secular rationalism alone never could have imparted. Along with this intense dedication, however, there also was inevitably a certain degree of inflexibility and self-righteousness; at times also, there was a tendency to assume that within limits the end justified the means.

It was this cast of mind that figured in King's second decision—the use of children ranging in age from six to sixteen as demonstrators. Apparently forced by the SCLC's inability to turn up reliable adult demonstrators in massive numbers, this move was morally ambiguous. King and other SCLC figures argued that the youngsters had a right to fight for their freedom, but critics might justly retort that few children of any race had minds mature enough to comprehend the commitment they were making or to assess the risks they faced.

Those risks became quickly and terribly apparent. By the time King emerged from jail, the tense weeks of demonstrations had worn away the veneer of civility that had characterized the beginning of the Birmingham campaign. On one or two occasions, black bystanders had pelted police with rocks and bottles; the police, in turn, had brought out attack dogs and fire hoses. As the campaign moved into its fifth week with a seemingly inexhaustible supply of young marchers, the authorities shed their restraint and created the intense crisis that King had sought. In full view of national television cameras, police sprayed marchers with fire hoses powerful enough to peel the bark off trees, released snarling, biting canines, and openly clubbed those whom they apprehended.

The outcome, of course, was more than the movement had dared hope for. By bringing business in downtown Birmingham to a near halt, by raising the specter of full-scale racial rioting even as the movement itself remained nonviolent, King managed to achieve a local settlement that resulted in substantial desegregation and enhanced job opportunities for blacks. The agreement itself, however, was less important than the sympathetic national attention King achieved. The federal government intervened, sending high Justice Department officials to act as mediators. Most importantly, the Kennedy administration rearranged its priorities drastically. Previously convinced that civil rights legislation was a losing proposition, the president made a dramatic call for a sweeping civil rights bill and threw all the strength of his office behind it. Kennedy's untimely death several months later deepened support for the legislation and paved the way for an even more effective effort by his successor, Lyndon Johnson. Before Birmingham, presidents had lent support to the cause of civil rights but never in so fervent a fashion. They did so now not simply out of a personal conversion but because King and the SCLC had created a broad non-Southern majority in favor of strong federal action.

The embodiment of that new consensus was the March on Washington on August 28, 1963. The realization of A. Philip Randolph's old dream, the march was sponsored by a dozen or so civil rights and liberal organizations and planned by Randolph's protégé, Bayard Rustin. It drew a quarter of a million participants, nearly one hundred thousand of whom were white; never before in American history had the integrationist ethic been demonstrated on so vast a scale. The meeting found its aspirations most powerfully expressed in King's address; the closing speech of the day, it reinvigorated a crowd drained by emotional music and oratory and captured the essence of the event so perfectly that it overshadowed every singer and speaker who had gone before. After it was over, the national memory of the March on Washington was of Martin Luther King standing in the shadow of the Lincoln Memorial and speaking for a new day in race relations.

He seems to have decided that his original talk, a tempered, carefully drafted demand for justice for the American Negro, was unequal to the spirit of the occasion. It was effective enough—Freedom now! Jobs now!—but the crowd wanted more, an even broader vision. He began to speak extemporaneously, drawing upon other recent addresses and upon all the skills of oratory he had nurtured over the years. "I have a dream . . ." that someday in the red hills of Georgia the offspring of slaves and slaveowners could sit together at the table of brotherhood . . . that even Mississippi could become an oasis of freedom and justice . . . that his four children might someday be judged on the basis of their character and not the color of their skin . . . that someday freedom would ring throughout America . . . that all of God's children, black and white, Jews and Gentiles, Protestants and Catholics could join together in the old Negro spiritual, "Free at last! Free at last! Great God A-mighty, we are free at last!"

That the speech was magnificent and inspired is beyond dispute; its larger influence, along with that of the entire event, is harder to pinpoint. Although many observers seemed to find it somehow remarkable and impressive that so many Negroes could hold an orderly demonstration, it is doubtful that the march contributed appreciably to the passage of the Kennedy civil rights bill in 1964. It did create a moment of national uplift that reminded the country of its best values. It also helped maintain the considerable momentum the movement had achieved and made indelible King's standing as the symbol of the aspirations of the American Negro. No other black leader had spoken so effectively to the sensibilities of both liberal white America and the liberal democratic cultures of Western Europe. *Time* magazine recognized his importance by naming him man of the year, but that notice was rendered trivial in October 1964 by the announcement that he had been named recipient of the Nobel Peace Prize.

In the tradition of such pronouncements, King's Nobel address was in the same vein of hope as the "I Have a Dream" speech. Affirming the ultimate potential of human nature and the efficacy of the nonviolent ideal, he proclaimed the optimism that always had undergirded his outlook:

> I accept this award today with an abiding faith in America and an audacious faith in the future of mankind. I refuse to accept the idea that the "isness" of man's present nature makes him morally incapable of reaching up for the eternal "oughtness" that forever confronts him. . . . I refuse to accept the view that mankind is so tragically bound to the starless midnight of racism and war that the bright daylight of peace and brotherhood can never become a reality.

Clearly, on that December day in 1964, the vision of the Kingdom of God on earth was at the front of his mind and the pessimism of Niebuhr all but expelled from his consciousness.

At home the kingdom remained far from realization, the struggle difficult and dangerous, but so long as the Negro revolution maintained its momentum, King's optimism could remain alive. Southern resistance and violence did much to sustain the broad national consensus in favor of black civil rights. Episodic bombings of homes and churches and assassinations of civil rights activists served only to deepen the commitment of the movement and to enhance the aura of martyrdom that enveloped it. By using nonviolent tactics to create a crisis, by urging his followers to accept suffering, King had achieved major civil rights legislation. Throughout the Deep South, however, blacks still faced insuperable barriers to voting. It was to meet this affront that at the start of 1965 King mounted a major crusade in the inhospitable northern counties of Alabama around the town of Selma.

Selma itself possessed a professional, relatively moderate police chief, Wilson Baker; but county and state authorities, personified by Sheriff Jim Clark and Highway Patrol Colonel Al Lingo, made even Bull Connor seem a bit pale by comparison. This seems to have been the reason for choosing Selma. Moreover, vigilantes were an even more constant danger than in Birmingham. King himself was momentarily attacked by a local racist while registering as the first black patron of the town's leading hotel, and a black demonstrator was shot and killed by state troopers in the nearby town of Marion. On March 7, 1965, after two months of parades, arrests, and sporadic brutality, troopers and a mounted sheriff's posse broke up a planned protest march from Selma to Montgomery. Before television cameras and newsmen from across the country, troopers immersed the demonstrators in thick clouds of tear gas; then the posse attacked with clubs, cattle prods, and bullwhips. Seen in millions of living rooms, the episode created a situation similar to that of Birmingham. Four days later, the national sense of outrage was deepened when racist thugs clubbed a white Unitarian minister to death.

The result was to bring swarms of white liberals to Selma and give an unstoppable impetus to a new civil rights bill with near-ironclad procedures to facilitate black voting. President Lyndon Johnson identified himself with the cause more emotionally and personally than had even Kennedy. The march itself finally took place under federal protection and produced another martyr, a white woman shot after its completion. Whatever its symbolic importance, the march was less important than the passage of the Voting Rights Act of 1965, a bill that in effect admitted Southern blacks to the most basic right of free citizenship, changed the character of the Southern electorate, and laid the basis for a quiet political revolution in several states. It also concluded most of the work that King could do to meet the special problems of the Southern Negro and encouraged him to broaden the scope of his mission.

The nature of King's rhetoric and the character of his concerns had evolved significantly since his emergence as a black leader less than a decade earlier. In his first book, *Stride Toward Freedom*, the story of the Montgomery movement, he had not hesitated to quote Booker T. Washington and had coupled his denunciations of white injustice with brisk exhortations for black improvement —less crime, less drink, less disorderly conduct, greater personal cleanliness, higher moral standards, better family life, a more developed sense of community obligation.

His second book, *Why We Can't Wait*, grew out of the Birmingham experience. Its tone was a product of the repression, brutality, bombings, and killings that had been employed against the Southern civil rights movement in the interval. Booker T. Washington merited notice only in a cursory, rather disapproving fashion that seemed to write him off as a representative of past, bad times. King castigated American white society more strongly than ever for its deeply ingrained racism and its tolerance of "genocide" against the American Indian and other nonwhites. More than before, he depicted black social problems as a result of disabilities inflicted by white society. Over three centuries, white society had not only deprived blacks of fundamental constitutional and human rights; it had also imprisoned them in a culture of poverty.

True freedom for the Negro would require more than integration, the right to vote, or the opportunity to compete on usually unequal terms for jobs. It necessitated an act of atonement more massive than most white liberals had faced. It would mean, King implied, preferential treatment for blacks, somewhat in the way that the Indian government of Prime Minister Nehru granted special preferences to long-oppressed untouchables. It should mean, above all, a Bill of Rights for the Disadvantaged, similar to the Marshall Plan in the scope of its objectives, patterned after the GI Bill of Rights in its benefits and preferences. Such a program could uplift the lives of many poor whites, but its major impact would be a dramatic alteration in black life. Change in human psychology might normally be a slow process, but Negroes were ready for change. They would respond with a "basic psychological and motivational transformation." The result would be a decline in the indicators of black social pathology—school dropouts, broken families, crime rates, welfare dependency—so large that it "would stagger the imagination."

With this program, King pursued the logical consequences of the hopeful theology that always had dominated his intellect. After Selma, the main focus of his attention would be upon black poverty, and his movement would become increasingly a national operation working actively in the North as well as the South. To King and his followers, the new developments simply amounted to a logical next step in the morally imperative struggle against racism and discrimination; for those outside the movement, the problem was more ambiguous.

The Other Side of the Mountain

After the triumph at Selma, King was faced with a new set of challenges for which his prophetic mode of thinking left him at best half-prepared. His successes had been primarily the result of his ability as a moral dramatist; in Montgomery, Birmingham, and Selma, he had staged a theater of confrontation that brought the most benign and sacred of human impulses into brutal conflict with the worst. The post-Selma situation presented only difficult, ambiguous problems with few easy answers; to attack them as a prophet took one into intellectual simplification and entailed considerable loss of credibility.

The most difficult of King's new challenges, both personally and tactically, was to define his relationship to the black militance that erupted in the mid-sixties. Occasionally violent in deed, always angry in rhetoric, usually vocally antiwhite, and frequently downright separatist, black militance threatened all the values King had preached and posed a serious danger to his moral leadership of the American Negro community. Because of the need to maintain a facade of black unity, it was necessary to downplay disagreements. Because of the need to understand the causes—both material and psychological—of the new mood, King had to reorient his thinking and move on to new issues. Yet his public persona was too sharply defined for him to abandon the prophetic role in which he had cast himself.

By Selma, the revolutionary spirit that King had done so much to awaken among blacks was overflowing the rather narrow channels of nonviolence and civil rights within which he had attempted to confine it. The black Muslims, a long-established but little-noticed sect, grew rapidly and won national attention in a white community at first stunned by their racial bitterness. By then also, urban ghetto riots were becoming an annual summer event. They arose from conditions and impulses that King grasped intellectually, but he never had experienced them himself, nor had he yet addressed his efforts to them. After the upheaval in Watts, he attempted to tour the slum and was taken aback by the number of blacks who did not recognize him and in some instances professed never to have heard of him.

Once considered an upstart by the older national black establishment, King now found himself upstaged by younger, more vehement figures such as Floyd McKissick of CORE and Stokely Carmichael, the new president of SNCC. All the latent tensions came out in 1966 when King, McKissick, and Carmichael led a march into Mississippi, a continuation of one begun by the enigmatic James Meredith, who had been shot and wounded by a white assailant. Carmichael and, at first, McKissick argued unsuccessfully for the exclusion of whites from the march; then Carmichael captured the attention of the nation by leading his followers in the chant "Black Power," a phrase that had a great many harmless meanings but that under the circumstances took on connotations of black racism.

The new militance shocked and angered some white liberals, especially those whose support of the movement had involved personal sacrifice. On the whole, however, the arresting thing about the new black militance was the way in which the white liberal intellectual community not only accepted it but fairly embraced it. The alienation of the militants appealed to the alienation of the intellectuals. The militant eagerness to deliver verbal floggings provided an easy release for white guilt feelings. The militant affectation of a hip ghetto style contrasted favorably in the minds of many white intellectuals with the uptight, bourgeois morality that King represented.

King's response was equivocal. Carmichael, McKissick, and other black militants said in their own way many of the same things he had been saying. On numerous occasions, most vividly in the Birmingham jail letter, King had lectured white liberals and moderates; moreover, he had consistently given his white support scant recognition in his own accounts of Montgomery and Birmingham. He always had been prone to appeal to black pride and self-help, just as did the militants. He also wanted to pull American blacks out of their state of relative powerlessness. He agreed that whites were collectively guilty of countless injustices and that some sort of compensatory action was long overdue.

His disagreements were equally important. He was convinced that black power militance was dangerous tactically—what good, he asked, could come of advocating black violence in rural Mississippi? Nor did he have any wish to indict whites in an angry, personal manner; his condemnations were those of the minister preaching to sinners he hoped to convert. Philosophically, he was repelled by racial separatism and violence, both of which violated Christian ideals of love and brotherhood.

Another diversion that increasingly occupied King's attention and sapped his national reputation was his impulse to extend his ministry to the realm of world politics. After Selma, he tended more and more to discuss the problems of the underdeveloped world and to denounce the Vietnam War. His wife had long been active in the international peace movement and appears to have approached it with a single-minded dedication that left her oblivious to the difference between genuine pacifists and Communists who attempted to manipulate peace organizations in the interests of the USSR. As a Christian minister who constantly preached the gospel of nonviolence, King maintained a categorical opposition to the use of war or force as an instrument of national policy. Moreover, he instinctively visualized the world scene as a projection of the American black struggle for equality. Tactically, the result was to divide the movement. Intellectually, it was to make the mistake of applying a one-dimensional prophetic analysis to a series of complex and ambiguous problems.

From his first trip outside the United States, King was convinced that Third World social and economic problems, as he observed them in Africa and India, were the consequence of white oppression and colonialism. Like most American blacks, he derived a substantial measure of emotional satisfaction from the way in which colored peoples were throwing off white rule and reestablishing their independence. The Ghanaian leader, Kwame Nkrumah, greatly impressed him; after Nkrumah established dictatorial rule and the nation foundered under his leadership, King attributed his troubles to the residue of British control and to continuing economic imperialism.

The Indian prime minister, Nehru, a far more significant

historical figure, made an even greater impact. King's visit to India was an inspirational experience that brought him close to the disciples of Gandhi. It also left him more confirmed than ever in his prejudices about the evils of colonialism, the fundamental virtue of the Third World, and the applicability of the civil rights analogy to the entire globe. One searches through King's pronouncements on peace, colonialism, and diplomacy in vain for any reference to social systems that had existed long before the white rulers and had been little changed by them. One looks unsuccessfully for some trace of the realism that he professed to have received from Niebuhr.

King's first public declaration of opposition to the growing American involvement in Vietnam came in mid-1965, but he spoke out only sporadically for the next two years. He was more concerned with domestic issues. He gave in from time to time to appeals from the Johnson administration, which protested privately that peace was its only objective and that it was, after all, responsible for the most important civil rights legislation of the twentieth century. And he was subjected to intense pressure from other black leaders who feared being labeled unpatriotic and wanted above all to avoid disruption of the single-minded quest for civil rights. Even the SCLC executive board refused to endorse his peace stance.

By early 1967, however, King's determination had hardened. Convinced that the peace movement was a matter of deep urgency, he committed himself to it with the same wholeheartedness as to domestic reform. His rationale was both practical and moral, both intellectual and deeply emotional. The war was drawing thirty billion dollars a year from the struggle against poverty. It was being fought largely by the poor, especially by poor blacks. America, King charged, was "taking black young men who had been crippled by our society and sending them eight thousand miles away to guarantee liberties in Southeast Asia which they had not found in southwest Georgia and East Harlem." Blacks and whites were integrated for destruction in the U.S. Army but still largely segregated in the peacetime society at home. Among the poor, moreover, the effect of the war was to spread a contagion of violence. The national use of military force as an instrument of policy had undermined his own effort to preach nonviolence to the militant black underclass. It had made him realize that he "could never again raise my voice against the violence of the oppressed in the ghettos without having first spoken clearly to the greatest purveyor of violence in the world today: my government."

His mission, he believed required him to come to grips with all major moral questions: "I have worked too long and hard now against segregated public accommodations to end up segregating my moral concerns." His new role was dictated by his position as a Nobel Peace Prize winner and a minister of Christ with a prophetic function. He had to strive for realization of the SCLC motto— "To save the soul of America." He had to be a spokesman "for the weak, for the voiceless, for the victims of our nation, and for those it calls enemy."

King also found motivation in his emotional identification with the struggles of the Third World. In his last published article, he castigated American foreign policy as racist in execution, run by white men who, without really understanding it, had been conditioned by their culture to discount the talents and aspirations of colored peoples. American diplomacy, he asserted, needed the involvement of more black men, men who had experienced discrimination, who were the products of a collective heritage of shared misery, who thereby were capable of a sensitive understanding of the legitimate concerns of the nonwhite populations of the world.

For King, Vietnam was a case study of the latent racism of American diplomacy. It was a product "of comfort, complacency, a morbid fear of Communism, and our proneness to adjust to injustice." The modern Western nations, once the spreaders of the revolutionary spirit, had become the archreactionaries of the world community. He made no effort to conceal his sympathy for the Vietcong insurgency, implying that it was akin to the American Revolution and citing Ho Chi Minh as a great national leader. In siding with Ngo Dinh Diem, the United States had supported "one of the most vicious modern dictators," an ally of extortionist landlords and a ruthless oppressor of the peasants. America was destroying Vietnamese society, both physically and morally, creating orphans, prostitutes, and hordes of uprooted refugees. "If we continue, there will be no doubt in my mind and in the mind of the world that we have no honorable intentions in Vietnam. It will become clear that our minimal expectation is to occupy it as an American colony, and men will not refrain from thinking that our maximum hope is to goad China into a war so that we may bomb her nuclear installations."

Ultimately, the most urgent problem that King perceived was still the condition of the American black. After Selma, however, effective leadership on the issue became more and more difficult. The Civil Rights Acts of 1964 and 1965 had outlawed the most blatant forms of discrimination and made them into federal legal problems that were tackled by a zealous bureaucracy increasingly eager to promote black advances. Black leaders might from time to time demand stronger enforcement, but they now could quarrel only with administrative decisions taken by officials who displayed none of the characteristics of overt racism. The easy, dramatic issues were gone; the victim of his own success, King now defined his mission as tackling the different ones.

During the last two years of his life, he was almost exclusively concerned on the domestic scene with economic deprivation. Like many white liberals and many other black leaders, he sought to spread the mantle of civil rights over the problem of poverty. On its surface, the move appeared timely, coming in a period of heightened national consciousness about the extent of poverty in the United States. Yet poverty was never amenable to the tactics and mood of the civil rights movement. If its existence was undeniable, its roots were obscure. To the extent that it was a result of discrimination, legal remedies had been established. To the extent that it stemmed from some inner deficiency within the poor, such as a lack of skills or motivation, self-improvement was the answer, perhaps with government help. To the extent that it was the fault of white society in some general sense, any remedy was vague.

King and most crusaders against poverty posited that white society was responsible for the plight of the poor and had a duty to help them through programs designed to increase their opportunities, develop their skills, relieve them of burdens, and better their material lot. By the time he focused his efforts in this direction, however, he was doing little more than joining a crusade that Lyndon B. Johnson had brought to national respectability.

From the beginning, he found himself in the position of berating a president who had devoted more attention than any chief executive before him to the problem of hard-core poverty and who had established scores of programs to deal with it. To most disinterested observers it was evident that the antipoverty effort required a time of testing in which its assumptions could be examined, costs measured against benefits, and ineffective components weeded out. But from King's perspective, the war against poverty was no more than tokenism; the only answer was a quantum increase in almost every experiment the administration was undertaking.

It was even more difficult to pursue poverty as a civil rights issue, and on this point King displayed considerable confusion. Manifestly, as he acknowledged, poverty was not just a black phenomenon; yet he advocated preferences in jobs and housing for blacks as a mode of national atonement. When pressed about the apparent contradiction, he might assert that the only real solution was the creation of adequate employment opportunity and good housing for all, but such answers were evasions rather than resolutions. Quite consciously, King was preaching a message of collective guilt to a liberal culture that traditionally had assumed guilt to be individual and specific. Few of his white admirers were fully prepared for what he had to say; that so many of them would go so far toward accepting it was a tribute to his eloquence.

The ambiguity of King's final crusade became clear when he led a drive to improve the conditions of blacks in Chicago, the Northern city with the second largest black population and some of the worst slums anywhere in the nation. He hoped to dramatize the wretched environment of the South Side and to negotiate specific concessions from the city's power structure—chiefly the Democratic machine and the business leaders—for open housing and more black jobs. Conducted during the first eight months of 1966, the operation developed into a long fizzle. It demonstrated that the tactics that had served so well in the implacably hostile South were not readily adaptable to the more ambivalent North. The theater of confrontation required easily identifiable adversaries, gullible enough to be willing accomplices; Chicago presented bad situations for which blame could not be easily attributed.

Even King's effort to share the experience of the slum dwellers, although sincere and commendable, came off badly. In mid-winter, he moved himself and his family into a foul, stinking tenement apartment; this gesture of concern and quest for more complete identification with the poor had considerable meaning for both himself and his wife. Nevertheless, it was largely negated by the fact that they customarily spent half of every week at their comfortable home in Atlanta while King attended to his pastoral duties. That summer, observers seemed more prone to note that he had ridden at the head of the demonstration in an air-conditioned limousine or had indulged in some other small luxury than that he had spent three or four days a week in a stifling set of rooms far beneath his status and income.

Tactically, Chicago was an even worse disaster than Albany. Neither King nor his evangelical organizers possessed the same visceral appeal as in the South, and the turnout for their meetings was disappointing. What was really damaging, however, was the absence of any highly visible, easily detested adversary. The King organization set up a rent strike against one of the worst buildings in the neighborhood only to discover that the slumlord was an impoverished old man barely able to care for himself. To dramatize the need for better housing for blacks, the movement undertook one march after another through white areas. Frequently greeted with obscenities, rocks, and bottles, the demonstrators invariably received highly professional protection from the local police, some of whom suffered minor injuries at the hands of white racists. Chicago authorities from Mayor Richard J. Daley on down remained cool, consistently expressed willingness to talk, and limited their complaints to expressions of concern about potential disorder and violence. When rioting did break out that summer, King inevitably drew accusations that he had promoted unrest. It was symbolic that one of King's major demonstrations, culminating with the nailing of a set of demands to the door of City Hall, took place on a Sunday afternoon, ignored by the city administration.

The Chicago campaign came to an end in August 1966 with the negotiation of a loose agreement in which business leaders and city authorities pledged to take several steps to upgrade employment and housing opportunities for blacks. In practice—if indeed it ever was put into practice—it had only a marginal effect on the daily lives of Chicago blacks.

King undoubtedly had raised the consciousness of many of them, and his campaign left in its wake Operation Breadbasket under the direction of the charismatic Jesse Jackson. Yet Chicago undeniably was more failure than success, and not simply because of the inadequacies of an agreement that was no worse than the one he had signed in Birmingham. King had done little to create a sense of national indignation over the problem he was dramatizing and had been utterly unsuccessful in establishing a national consensus on concrete steps to attack it. Chicago produced no federal housing act nor any new antipoverty effort; indeed, the campaign may even have hurt the prospects for such moves. After Chicago, King was increasingly isolated. His opposition to the war had drawn rebukes from some of the most prominent blacks in American life—Ralph Bunche, Roy Wilkins, Carl Rowan, Whitney Young. His nonviolence drew condemnation from a wide spectrum of "militants"—the young nihilists of the streets, embittered ideologists such as Stokely Carmichael, and bandwagon riders such as Adam Clayton Powell.

He continued his new course with few second thoughts. He had moved from attacking primarily the visible, indefensible, regionally isolated evils of segregation and disfranchisement to criticizing the American ethos itself. In the truest tradition of religious prophecy, he vehemently castigated the spiritual collapse of his country—its racism, its unconcern for the deprived, its propensity toward violence. His judgments, like those of most prophets, tended to be categorical; they made no references to mitigating circumstances or to the practices of other nations nor did they contain Niebuhrian allusions to the nature of man and human collectives. Instead, King declared America in the starkest terms an immoral nation facing divine retribution unless it could save itself by undertaking a conversion to peace and brotherhood. Without a trace of megalomania, he saw himself as the possible instrument of that conversion.

In the fall of 1967, after another series of the riots that had become predictable summer happenings in urban America, King seized upon the idea of a prolonged poor people's demonstration in Washington. He hoped to reorient the priorities of the nation by bringing thousands of the impoverished of all races to Washington, not just for a day, but for months; living in makeshift encampments, they could lobby congressmen and administrators, demand action, and dramatize the plight of the underprivileged. Creative and nonviolent rather than destructive and violent, the Poor People's campaign could be the salvation of America. If successful in diverting the government's enormous resources from the war in Vietnam to the war against poverty, it could be the first step in establishing an American concern for the needy of the entire world, thereby bringing the country the redemption that flows from love of one's fellow man.

King's sense of mission was intense. His speaking engagements, urging participation in the campaign and support of it, were as much exercises in evangelism as his antisegregation rallies. A talk to a black group in early 1968 was typical:

> We're gonna build our shanties right in Washington and live
>   right there!
> *Yes. That's it.*
> I'm not playin' about this thing. I've agonized over it, and I'm
>   tryin' to save America. And that's what you are tryin' to
>   do if you will join this movement. We're tryin' to save
>   this nation!
> *That's it!*
> We can't continue to live in a nation every summer goin' up
>   in flames, every day killin' our people in Vietnam like
>   we're killin'! We can't *continue* this way as a nation and
>   survive. You can believe it if you want to.
> *Yes, Amen.*
> And *some of us* (*Yes suh! Okay!*) . . . are gonna have to
>   take the burden of *saving* the soul of America."
> *All right!*

Beyond national salvation, the goal of the Poor People's Campaign remained a bit fuzzy. The major objectives that King proclaimed were a $12-billion economic bill of rights, federal legislation to end discrimination in housing, and strict enforcement of existing civil rights laws. But he and his supporters failed to produce specific draft legislation. According to David Lewis, "The demands were intentionally vague . . . in order to guard against the seductions of empty promises and legislative feints." Perhaps such tactical reasoning was sound, but more likely it was motivated by an impulse to stand in Christian witness that was incompatible with the sordid world of legislative compromise. If followed rigorously and uncompromisingly, it could only guarantee that the campaign would become an exercise in frustration. After Lyndon Johnson withdrew from contention for the presidency at the beginning of April, thereby creating the strong possibility that his successor would be an antiwar liberal Democrat, King apparently had doubts about going through with the project. (Perhaps this was an indirect admission of the impracticality of the whole plan.)

The Campaign underscored a shift in King's social vision away from an emphasis upon integration and toward a more class-oriented critique of the American social structure. The elements of the new approach, however, were solidly rooted in King's theology. Far from undergoing a conversion from bourgeois liberalism to Marxian radicalism, he was expressing more clearly than ever—in his calls for massive aid to the poor, for a new spirit of Christian brotherhood, for the salvation of American society—the Christian socialism of Walter Rauschenbusch that had so long captured his imagination. While he appears to have increasingly valued his black identity and understood his special role as a leader of his people, the wider reformism of the social gospel, integrationist by definition, remained his deepest inspiration. It carried him into courses that went beyond the more immediate and tangible needs of American blacks and that were consequently more difficult to navigate.

The last cause of his life was representative of the new ambiguities. He took time off from the final planning of the Poor People's Campaign to assume the leadership of striking Memphis garbage workers, mostly black but including a few whites, with major white unions and their leaders supporting the stoppage. To King, it was a simple issue of the oppressed striving for justice, and few impartial observers could deny that the Memphis city administration had treated its employees poorly. Yet it was equally true that the strike was illegal and a potential health hazard.

Perhaps most discouraging was the discovery that the major threat of violence came not from Memphis officials, hard-line antiunionist though they were, but from within the black community. King's advance staff failed entirely to establish control over young gang members and militants. When King stepped off a plane direct from a speaking engagement in New York to lead a protest demonstration in Memphis on March 28, 1968, he was wholly unprepared for what developed. Although most of the marchers remained nonviolent, the demonstration had scarcely proceeded three blocks before a less-restrained minority began to engage in rock-throwing and looting. The rioting that followed was comparatively minor and was quickly put down by over- whelming police and National Guard force. Still, coming without visible provocation, it seemed to reveal that the ethic of nonvio- lence was on the decline, that even King had lost the power to maintain it. The city of Memphis requested and obtained a federal injunction prohibiting further demonstrations.

Patently shaken, King nevertheless prepared for a new, more carefully organized march on April 8 and determined to ignore the federal injunction if necessary. On Wednesday, April 3, he spoke extemporaneously to a black mass meeting, moving as his talk went along from his endorsement of the audience's struggle to the multiple threats that he had received. He came finally to the premonition of personal disaster that had gripped him from time to time since Montgomery. He didn't know what would happen. He didn't know God's plans. But he had been to the mountaintop; he had seen the promised land. He might not get there, but he knew his people would. He was not worried, not afraid. His eyes had seen the glory.

The next afternoon, he was shot and killed from ambush. No one was surprised that the death of the world's leading advocate of Christian nonviolence touched off a national upheaval unlike anything in American history. In the arson and looting of the next few days, most observers saw only raw rage but, especially in those areas where guilt-stricken authorities made no real effort to interfere, some reporters detected a celebratory atmosphere, an instinctive sense among the ghetto dwellers that this latest atrocity had set them free from all the restraints and inhibitions that white society had imposed upon them.

The Prophet in Retrospect

King's death had contradictory results for the movement he had led. In the short run, it delivered a substantial gain: the Civil Rights Act of 1968 was a gesture of expiation designed to facilitate minority access to better housing. In the long run, however, it was a severe blow to a drive that had lost its most effective spokesman. No one remotely approaching his stature emerged to take King's place. The fate of the Poor People's Campaign demonstrated the depth of the loss. Its prospects had been dubious during King's life; they became hopeless with his death. Carried on by the SCLC, it attracted little sympathetic attention. Its shanties, regarded as disruptive eyesores rather than symbols of conscience, eventually were battered down by federal bulldozers.

Yet the same events might have occurred under King's leadership. At the time of his death, he was clearly on the decline, and there is no reason to assume that his eclipse was only temporary. Martyrdom may have ensured his historical reputation just as it enhanced the memory of Lincoln or FDR. Death, which overtook all three men close to the point of their supreme achievements, made it possible to believe that they would have gone on to even more impressive heights and obscured serious obstacles that lay ahead of them.

King had taken the helm of what had been the civil rights movement and had made it into a Negro revolution by utilizing the tools of leadership more effectively than any other leader of his generation. Using all the communications media, he projected an inspirational personality and set of values to a wide constituency, ranging from unlettered evangelical blacks to sophisticated white liberal intellectuals. More importantly, he aligned himself with an urgent social issue whose time had come. Among political figures of the middle third of the twentieth century, only Franklin D. Roosevelt had so thoroughly mastered the imperatives of public leadership.

The difficulties that King encountered after Selma were manifold, but they stemmed heavily from the limitations of his self-defined role as a prophet. Having won the simple moral issues, he brought the prophetic style to more difficult and ambiguous causes. The various struggles against segregation and disfranchisement in Alabama from Montgomery to Selma, with their jailings, bombings, killings, and meanspirited segregationist white officials, lent themselves to a politics of moral prophecy at the most elemental level. The struggle against poverty presented no such easily dramatizable situation and led to a dissipation of King's moral authority.

This difficulty was compounded by King's inability to deal with the rising tide of black militance and separatism as what had been called the Negro revolution began to be designated the black revolution. Anxious to lift black pride, King was nevertheless unprepared for the antiwhite sentiment that developed along with the so-called black power movement. It was to his credit that he refused to swim with the tide. But while he never abandoned the integrationist ethic, neither did he find convincing means of dealing with separatism nor with the growing trend toward violent protest. Increasingly, observers noted a tendency among King's own black followers to drop the phrase "black and white together" from renditions of "We Shall Overcome." The disintegration of the last march he headed in Memphis was a sad revelation of the problems he and his staff faced in maintaining control even of an effort they had put together.

It is hard to imagine that King's standing and authority would have been enhanced had he lived to witness the next phase of the black political experience—the movement from militance to affirmative action. One suspects that like the black leaders who survived him, he would have supported affirmative action efforts. His fundamentalist upbringing and biblical training disposed him to accept the concept of collective guilt and the requirement that the current generation atone for the sins of those that preceded it. At the same time, one may speculate that his support of the program would have been as ambiguous and self-contradictory as his support of the theory during his life.

If events had indeed passed King at the time of his death, that in no way should diminish his historical reputation. In a dozen years, he established himself as the greatest figure in American black history, as the American Gandhi, and as the most profound moral leader of his time. Any fair evaluation must consider him within the limits of the role to which he felt he had been called, that of the religious prophet attempting to save his nation, not that of the politician unable to afford the luxury of pure morality and cognizant that good and evil often coexist uneasily in man and his institutions. To engage in prophecy is to state simple, elemental truths, not to negotiate complex solutions for social evils. In the end, King's lasting greatness arose not from what he prescribed but from what he was.

5

From the Old Politics to the New: John and Robert Kennedy

John and Robert Kennedy were the most magnetic national political leaders of the 1960s. No major politician since has so captured the American imagination. There was more to this achievement than a triumph of style over substance and the legend-making effects of premature death. They possessed personalities uniquely suited to leadership. They acquired and cultivated the skills requisite to electoral success in their own time. They not only identified themselves with the dominant political tradition but also placed themselves at its cutting edge. Alone among their contemporaries, they appealed strongly to both the forces of old and new that threatened to fragment the Democratic coalition.

The Brothers

The Kennedy brothers came from a background unique among leaders of the contemporary era. Wealthy but hardly members of the patrician world in the mode of the Roosevelts or the Tafts, they grew to manhood on the fringes of an establishment of which they were not quite a part but from which they were not alienated. Having been taught a fierce competitive ethic that centered not on the acquisition of money but on the achievement of public office, they reveled in the exercise of power and sought recognition with intense determination and calculation.

The dominating figure in the Kennedy household—even during his protracted absences on business ventures—was their father, Joseph P. Kennedy, a self-made man who accumulated hundreds of millions of dollars from activities as diverse as banking, securities speculation, motion picture production, liquor, and real-estate. Neither likeable nor notably generous to his associates, openly unconventional in his personal life, and an Irish-American Catholic to boot, he won scant acceptance from the genteel Protestant social elite. He secured important appointive positions —chairman of the Securities and Exchange Commission, ambassador to Great Britain—but never had a chance of winning elective office. His break with Franklin D. Roosevelt over the question of World War II made him a maverick in politics as in business. He expected his children to achieve his frustrated ambitions for social acceptance and political recognition and deliberately guided them along that path.

Under the father's sway, the Kennedy household had much of the atmosphere of a Vince Lombardi training camp with its vigorous physical activity, emphasis on winning at casual family recreations, and team spirit. To its athletic character, the elder Kennedy added an education in public affairs, quizzing his sons relentlessly in the manner of a tough seminar instructor. Domineering to a degree that verged on the brutal, a stern disciplinarian whose angry stare seemed to penetrate an offender, and a believer in the school of hard knocks. Joseph Kennedy never coddled his children, never broke up their fights, and always exhorted them to do their best. In the manner of the best football coaches, he added a sense of loyalty and encouragement that must have gone far toward making the pressure tolerable. When he was absent, his offspring could count on the more gentle affection of a supportive mother, devoted to family and church.

To grow up in such a household must have been difficult. To grow up as the frail younger brother to a cherished eldest son must have been doubly hard. Joe Kennedy, Jr., occupied a position in the family akin to that of an heir apparent. Expected to be a model for the other children, he filled the role all too well. Robust, athletic, intelligent, charming, he appeared singularly equipped to realize his father's ambitions for him—to become the first Catholic president of the United States. His death in World War II traumatized his family.

John Kennedy, two years his junior, had to develop a sense of identity in this shadow. The sibling rivalry seems to have been intense. Whether in fisticuffs as children or in girl-chasing as young men, Joe usually won. Apparently born with an unstable spine, afflicted from childhood with some persistent digestive problem, and prone to a variety of illnesses, young Jack was neither a physical match for the older boy nor as good a student. It is remarkable that he neither withdrew into himself nor quit trying. At Harvard, he insisted on playing football and injured his back; during the war, he actively sought military service when he probably could have obtained an entirely justifiable medical deferment. Despite the physical and emotional difficulties of his early life, he developed a positive sense of his own identity even before he was called on to assume his brother's position.

Part of the reason for this achievement was a family élan. The Kennedys were winners who supported each other against the outside world. The family spirit was sustained by the vast range of material comforts and experience wealth guaranteed. Money was a matter of such indifference that John Kennedy seems never to have carried any; one encounters numerous stories of girlfriends paying for taxis, of employees, friends, or even strangers being asked for loans to pay small tabs. Wealth allowed the Kennedys to attend the best schools, associate with and compete against the nation's social and intellectual elite, travel extensively, and secure interesting jobs.

By the time John F. Kennedy was thirty, he had seen most of Europe and much of the United States; graduated cum laude from Harvard; written a best-selling book; been a noted young figure in cafe society, dating glamorous debutantes, models, and actresses; skippered a PT boat in the South Pacific and won minor acclaim as a war hero; covered the San Francisco United Nations conference and the 1945 British elections as a special correspondent for the Hearst newspapers; and been elected to the U.S. House of Representatives. Within his circle of acquaintances were the preeminent economist of British socialism, Harold Laski, and prominent young figures in the British establishment, including

Hugh Fraser, David Ormsby-Gore, and the ill-fated Marquess of Hartington, who married Kennedy's sister. At home, his father had made him acquainted with such eminences of the world of American journalism as William Randolph Hearst, Jr., and Arthur Krock; figures of the Washington political scene, among them James M. Landis, James V. Forrestal, and William O. Douglas; and many of the heroes and heroines of Hollywood, Gary Cooper, Gene Tierney, and Sonja Henie. At the same age, Franklin D. Roosevelt—himself a man with considerable resources and contacts—had been an isolated Democratic backbencher in the New York Assembly, facing a chancy political future; Harry S. Truman an unknown Missouri farmer; and Dwight D. Eisenhower an obscure major in a shrinking military bureaucracy.

Amid all the glitter, one can find patches of tarnish. Kennedy's war exploits appear upon close examination to have been the result of a botched mission in which he displayed bad judgment. It was largely through Joseph Kennedy's effort and largesse that an article on the PT-109 episode, written by another remarkable Kennedy friend, John Hersey, was published in America's largest circulation magazine, *Reader's Digest*. By emphasizing Kennedy's courage, Hersey created a small legend.

On a more personal level, the young Kennedy strikes one as self-centered and emotionally shallow. At times inconsiderate of male friends, he appears to have approached women on the level of a competitive sport. Although he dated, and occasionally avidly pursued, dozens of beautiful women, his emotional relationships with them appear to have been almost always superficial. He sought the excitement of the chase and the satisfaction of conquest rather than a lasting partnership. His marriage at the age of thirty-six seems as much a political decision as a romantic one.

Withal, he still emerges as a man of talent and substance. Not quite a contemplative intellectual, he was bright, quick-minded, and relatively thoughtful. He made friends easily and assumed leadership roles naturally; all who knew him speak of a charm that more than compensated for his shortcomings. His first book, *Why England Slept*, published in mid-1940, was a first-class piece of analytical journalism for a twenty-three-year-old just out of college. His war service, if less glorious than heroic legend would

have us believe, was nevertheless marked by courage and determination.

Even his shallow relations with others were part of a larger
detachment about the world and himself that was, on the whole,
healthy. The war and his numerous physical problems must have
given him a sense of his own mortality; his survival and relative
success in the world must have strengthened his confidence. It
is one of his most attractive features that he easily and naturally
formulated ironic jests about himself and his family. Detachment
provided the sense of perspective essential to rational leadership.

Finally, more than any other president in American history,
he had grown up as a celebrity of sorts, the son of a powerful
ambassador and financier, a participant in the social life of the
wealthy, a writer, a war hero. He found the spotlight easier to
manage than did most politicians and effortlessly assumed the
"star quality" that characterized his role in American culture during the final years of his life.

John Kennedy's first campaign for Congress in 1946 set the
stage in many respects for his subsequent political career. An
outsider, he had to establish residence in a Boston district where
he had never lived. A loner, he used an organization independent
of any Massachusetts political faction. A Kennedy, he relied
heavily upon his family. Determined to be a winner, he campaigned tirelessly. Cognizant of his personal appeal, he exploited
it to the utmost.

The family involvement was total. His father quietly built an
efficient organization of men experienced in the ways of Boston
politics; they operated behind a facade of students, volunteers,
and amateurs who were most visible at campaign headquarters.
Cash was available in abundance, and Kennedy's sisters campaigned at uncounted small teas. His college-age brother, Robert,
worked three wards in East Cambridge.

One of the most impressive aspects of the Kennedy campaign
was its calculated use of imagery on a level of sophistication that
was still unusual in American politics. Kennedy said very little
about the issues, which were of paramount interest only to the
small Harvard University element in the district. He sold himself
in a variety of shrewd ways. A handsome young veteran from a

famous family running for public office was certain to attract the news media, and the Kennedy organization got its candidate maximum attention. The campaign employed an advertising agency that handled publicity, advised on speeches, and engaged in a public relations drive that all but monopolized local newspaper space. The ambassador's influence with national news media landed a feature spot in Pathé newsreels and a photo story in *Look* magazine just before the balloting.

Yet more was involved than money and organization. Kennedy was a strong candidate on the basis of his personal qualities. He spoke at several functions a day and climbed flight after flight of stairs in tenement buildings. The day before the election, after marching five miles in the Bunker Hill Day parade, he collapsed at the home of a friend. A veteran, he benefited from a widespread feeling of patriotic gratitude toward former fighting men. Young, good-looking, and visibly underweight, he appealed to the motherly instincts of older women and the romantic fantasies of younger ones. A mediocre speechmaker, he was nevertheless a clever one. Once, speaking to a group of women who had lost sons in the war, he began to stumble, then recovered and ended the speech in a way that won every lady in the audience: "I think I know how you feel, because my mother is a Gold Star Mother too." On June 18, 1946, John F. Kennedy won the Democratic nomination for the House of Representatives in the Eleventh Congressional District of Massachusetts, capturing 42 percent of the total vote and piling up a nearly 2–1 margin over his closest opponent.

As a congressman, Kennedy was a mildly independent liberal Democrat. He routinely adopted the urban "bread-and-butter liberalism" of the New Deal coalition, a position that reflected the interests of his city, Catholic constituency. He took an especially strong interest in housing legislation and a higher minimum wage. Coming from a background of privilege, he was periodically appalled to discover that others lived in need and sincerely believed that government should provide them some help. Yet he was neither an unquestioning supporter of the Truman administration nor a follower of any political line. Although he voted against the Taft-Hartley bill, he favored some regulation of labor unions. On administration programs of little interest to the Massachusetts working class—agricultural subsidies, increased appropriations for the Department of the Interior—his vote was likely to be negative.

He supported the major foreign policy initiatives of the Truman administration but did not hesitate to express vocal reservations about reductions in the defense budget and policy toward China. Occasionally he favored cuts in some foreign aid programs. Once, he proposed to tie the stationing of U.S. troops in Europe to a formula that would require the Europeans to spend more on their own defense.

Kennedy did not develop into an important congressman. He put together a first-rate staff, financed in part from his own funds, and it handled routine constituent services with maximum effectiveness. He managed in a variety of ways to make himself highly visible, first in Massachusetts and eventually throughout the country. But he neither established himself as a hard-working young legislator respected by his peers nor as a leader of the younger liberal Democrats.

Like many Northeastern congressmen, Kennedy seems to have spent a great deal of time out of Washington on four-day weekends, leaving the Congress to be run by the Southerners and Border-Staters who long had dominated it. He was not a wheeler-dealer who prided himself on hammering out compromises and getting bills passed, nor was he prone to go along with the establishment. He was the only Massachusetts Democrat in the House who refused to sign a petition urging President Truman to pardon the Boston political legend James Michael Curley, an old family enemy, who was serving a federal prison term. He scathingly criticized the American Legion and voted against its pet project, a veterans' bonus. A lone wolf, he displayed little interest in the "get along, go along" game and took pride in his independence.

His personal life also limited his influence. Often described as a "playboy," Kennedy unquestionably had an active social life that may have distracted him from his work. Much more important, however, was the state of his health. His back continued to be a serious problem; by 1954, as a young senator, he was on crutches and suffering constant pain so intense that he decided to risk dangerous spinal surgery. At other times, he came down with feverish attacks that he described as a recurrence of malaria that he had contracted in the South Pacific. The affliction, however, may actually have been connected with the onset of a form of Addison's disease, atrophy of the adrenal glands. For the rest of his life, he controlled this condition, once invariably fatal, by taking regular doses of the recently developed drugs cortisone and DOCA, much as diabetics control their disease with insulin. Even so, any infection presented a threat; on at least two occasions —a trip to the Far East in 1951 and after his first back operation in 1954—Kennedy came close to death. It was not until the last half of the fifties that with his back partially repaired and his Addison's disease well under control, he became a truly vigorous man. Until then, he demonstrated a capacity for spurts of activity but not the day-to-day hard work that congressional leadership demands.

Ultimately, however, one must conclude that the explanation lay in Kennedy's temperament. Neither a legislative type nor an administrator, he saw himself as a public leader, concerned with campaigning, getting elected, educating the people on the issues, and exercising his informed, independent judgment on important policy matters. By 1952, he was anxious to move into the Senate and confident enough to make the race during a Republican year, in what was still a normally Republican state, against one of the great names of Massachusetts politics, Henry Cabot Lodge, Jr.

Kennedy possessed an appeal that transcended the ordinary Irish-Catholic Democratic base in the state. Without alienating liberal, labor, or ethnic forces in the Democratic party, he had defined himself as a moderate willing to criticize the excesses of the labor unions and the mistakes of the Truman administration. In his style and personality, he was, as Governor Paul Dever perceptively observed, "the first Irish Brahmin," an identity that probably deepened his appeal to the Irish while making him acceptable to many normally Republican Yankees.

The 1952 senatorial campaign was in many respects a replay of 1946 with its arduous campaigning, its intense family involvement (Bobby was now campaign manager), its ready cash, its smart advertising and public relations—and its lack of sharp distinctions between the candidates. Defections from bitter Taft Republicans who hated Lodge for leading the draft-Eisenhower movement and for his coolness toward Joe McCarthy helped also. On election day, Kennedy polled 53 percent of the vote while the rest of the Democratic state ticket collapsed before the Eisenhower juggernaut.

More than an aggressive, good-looking campaigner, Kennedy soon established himself as something of an intellectual in politics. The author of two books, the second a Pulitzer Prize winner, he sought and achieved recognition as a man of letters. In the process, he formulated a theory of democracy and political leadership that was more fully developed and more clearly expressed than that of any of his rivals, including Adlai Stevenson.

Kennedy's first two books, *Why England Slept* (1940), a revision of his college honors thesis, and *Profiles in Courage* (1956), a group of biographical essays about politicians willing to defy the clear sentiment of their constituents, both addressed themselves to the relationship between the leader and the people in a democratic society. This problem was central to his process of self-definition as a political man. Both works express what might be called a Whig view of popular government, not in the narrow sense of believing in a strong legislative and weak executive branch but in the broader sense of possessing liberal principles while harboring doubts about the ability of the masses to make wise choices.

Why England Slept was a respectable but not overly distinguished piece of contemporary history. It was remarkable primarily for its rejection of the prevailing attitude that British unpreparedness was largely the fault of a group of appeasers who had run the government and had vaguely reflected the pro-fascist sentiments of the upper classes. Appeasement actually had enjoyed wide popular support and had been all but dictated by the structure of English society and politics. To have matched the rapid, expensive military buildup of Nazi Germany, Britain would have been forced to abandon many of the essentials of free market capitalism and to place serious restrictions upon political dissent—prospects that were unthinkable. Totalitarian nations could mobilize public opinion and quell opposition through dominance of the media and the use of force. Democratic nations invariably resisted defense preparations until the need was unmistakable. In a world of modern military technology, such delays could mean disaster.

It was especially difficult for a British prime minister to defy opinion, for the parliamentary system gave him not even the security of a fixed term in which the wisdom of unpopular policies might be demonstrated. It was true, Kennedy admitted, that Stanley Baldwin and Neville Chamberlain had been notably lacking in strength and vision, but they had been caught in the system and ultimately had fallen prey to one of democracy's failings, its tendency to seek scapegoats for its own weaknesses. Still, Kennedy implied, good leadership might have made a difference. After all, if democracy as a system had any advantage in a contest with totalitarianism, it was that leadership of a totalitarian society rested upon the command of brute force while, ideally, leadership in a democracy rested upon ability. The task of a democracy therefore was to produce and follow the able leaders upon whom its survival might depend.

Profiles in Courage carried the examination to the American scene. Some of its subjects won vindication at the polls, but others experienced only defeat and oblivion. America, it seemed, provided only marginally greater opportunities for those politicians who disagreed with the majority. Yet Kennedy insisted that they should disagree if an issue were great enough to be a matter of conscience. He rejected the view that the function of the representative was "to serve merely as a seismograph to record shifts in popular opinion." At points of crisis, the democratic process required independent leaders willing to take chances. What mattered was the act itself, not ideology; *Profiles in Courage* contained chapters praising both George W. Norris and Robert A. Taft.

Widely praised, *Profiles in Courage* gave Kennedy a reputation as something of a young statesman. It also drew attention to what was probably his greatest failure as a senator: his equivocal position on the most searing issue of the early 1950s—McCarthyism. Because of conflicting constituency pressures and because of Joe McCarthy's close relationship to his family (he was a friend of the ambassador and recipient of his campaign contributions), Kennedy quite plainly waffled. There can be little doubt that he found McCarthyism distasteful, but he did not want to alienate large numbers of his ethnic supporters. His solution, such as it was, was to minimize the importance of McCarthy's escapades and to strike a pose of concern with the more fundamental issues of the day. His back operation in the fall of 1954 relieved him of the obligation of voting on McCarthy's censure, and he refrained from announcing a position. Four years later, he finally showed James MacGregor Burns a speech that he had prepared endorsing censure on narrow grounds. To both the McCarthyites, who had expected Kennedy to support his fellow Irish-Catholic, and to the liberals, who had become obsessed with McCarthy's behavior, it was a sorry performance.

On the whole, however, *Profiles in Courage* considerably heightened Kennedy's visibility and stature. Reviewers praised it, and it became a best seller. In August 1956, it received the Christophers Award, a prize of some distinction among Catholic intellectuals; and in May 1957, it won the Pulitzer Prize for biography. The effect was to make its author a figure of special note within a large literary-journalistic community highly attentive to liberal Democratic politics.

In the meantime, Kennedy had decided to support Adlai Stevenson for the Democratic presidential nomination in 1956 as a matter of both political calculation and personal preference. He respected Stevenson's moderation and cerebral approach to politics; he also viewed the Illinoisan as the presidential contender to whom he was most suited as a running mate. After a bruising, distasteful political battle, he managed to gain control of the state Democratic committee and deliver its national convention delegates to Stevenson. Aside from near-total control of the Massachusetts Democratic organization, he obtained maximum exposure at the national convention and laid the foundation for his drive for the presidency. First, he was narrator of the party campaign film, a coveted assignment itself. Then, he was given the job of making the nominating speech for Stevenson, a duty that would place him on coast-to-coast television at one of the most-watched times of the gathering. As he rode in a taxi to the convention hall in Chicago, determined to impress the nation, he clenched his fists and murmured to himself, "Go! Go!"

The speech made a good impression. When Stevenson decided to throw open the vice-presidential nomination, Kennedy ran a close second to Estes Kefauver. The young senator had established himself as one of the rising stars of his party. He was fortunate even in his ultimate defeat; he would receive none of the blame for Stevenson's crushing loss in November. It was as an important supporting actor in the campaign of 1956 that he began in earnest his final drive for the presidency.

More in demand as a Democratic speaker than anyone save Stevenson and Kefauver, he traveled across the country, making contacts, winning friends, and leaving favorable impressions with state and local party leaders, as had Franklin Roosevelt a generation earlier. For the next three years, he flew around the country making speeches at almost the same pace. By mid-1959, a few months before he formally announced for the presidency, his schedule was so frenetic that it was necessary for him to buy a forty-passenger airplane and hire a full-time crew to man it.

He also became a media figure of the first rank. Young, handsome, married to a beautiful wife, a prize-winning writer, a U.S. senator with presidential possibilities, he embodied a combination of glamour and substance that made him natural copy for every type of publication from the Sunday supplements to the small-circulation intellectual periodicals. Kennedy welcomed the attention and sought it out, preparing articles for and granting interviews to almost any paper or magazine that asked. He also requested and easily obtained access to the pages of prestigious journals such as *Foreign Affairs*. He cemented his popular reputation as a scholar by heading a select Senate committee to choose the five greatest senators in U.S. history. (The committee conducted its highly publicized survey for the purpose of commissioning five portraits to be hung in the Senate reception room.) Playing the media game with more savvy and deliberateness than almost any other twentieth-century leader, Kennedy placed himself among the most widely known and favorably regarded political personalities in America. He won reelection to the Senate in 1958 by a record margin of 875,000, demonstrating that in his home state at least, he was an awesome vote getter.

Kennedy realized the importance of establishing himself as more than an attractive personality and a popular politician. A presidential contender, he knew, had to possess some claim to statesmanlike qualities, and in post–World War II America the preferable credentials were those of the authority on foreign policy. His interest in foreign affairs was, in any case, deep and genuine. Foreign travel had been a routine part of Kennedy's life from his youth, and knowledge of world affairs had been required by his father. During his years in Congress, he continued to make trips to remote parts of the earth; few, if any, of his peers spent so much time in so many different places abroad. In 1957, he sought and received assignment to the Senate Foreign Relations Committee. In 1960, he published as the literary centerpiece of his presidential campaign a collection of addresses on foreign policy, *The Strategy of Peace.*

Addressing itself to a multitude of foreign and domestic issues, frequently more negative than constructive in its criticisms of the Eisenhower administration, and fuzzy in its approach to a good many difficult problems, *Strategy of Peace* possessed many of the self-interested, tendentious qualities of a lawyer's brief. Still, it amounted to the fullest and most coherent synthesis of two main Democratic themes put out by any of the major presidential candidates: these were the need to rebuild American power and the need to conduct American foreign policy according to liberal values.

Almost as if he were comparing the military position of the United States in the late 1950s to that of England in the late 1930s, Kennedy advocated a strong program of nuclear weapons development, a major upgrading of U.S. conventional forces to allow for intervention "effectively and swiftly in any limited war anywhere in the world," and the "rebuilding" of NATO into an effective alliance. He also demanded idealism in American foreign relations. America had to repudiate the old, discredited colonialism of the European powers and devote a substantial proportion of its foreign aid resources to constructive economic development in what people were beginning to call the Third World. Kennedy indicted the Eisenhower administration for being "unwilling to plan for disarmament, and unable to offer creative proposals of our own, always leaving the initiative in the hands of the Russians." He called for efforts to negotiate arms agreements with the Soviet Union and Red China and to "move toward the eventual rule of world law by working to strengthen the United Nations."

Kennedy's formula of strength plus idealism was not a bad general approach to foreign policy during the volatile Khrushchev era. Yet it also was facile and deceptive. Intentionally or otherwise, its "hard side" overstated American military vulnerability. Its "soft side" assumed too easily that the new, uncommitted states of the world could be won over by economic aid accompanied by protestations of friendship and understanding. On some matters he offered generalities that were vague but farsighted. He deplored the administration policy of "liberation" (abandoned anyway after 1956) and advocated efforts to forge more modest and realistic relationships with the Russian-dominated nations of Eastern Europe. Affirming the U.S. commitment to Taiwan, he favored attempts to engage in a dialogue with Communist China. As one of the first important American public figures to call for French negotiation with the Algerian insurgents, he foresaw the all but inevitable culmination of the national rebellion in French North Africa.

In other areas, he was less prescient. Determined to condemn Eisenhower's "failures" in such flash points as Berlin, the Middle East, and the Quemoy-Matsu crises, he nonetheless offered no coherent alternatives. In 1954, he had opposed U.S. involvement in Indochina; by 1956, he had become a strong backer of the American-supported South Vietnamese government of Ngo Dinh Diem, which he considered an expression of indigenous, patriotic, non-Communist nationalism. The force of his foreign policy critique came not from his specific positions but from his youth, vigor, and receptivity to new approaches; to a large extent, his style was as important as his substance.

Kennedy also worked to establish a reputation for himself on a domestic issue—labor union reform—in his effort to develop an image as a moderate statesman with appeal throughout the Democratic party. In this quest, he found himself working closely with his brother, Robert.

Eight years younger, Robert was superficially similar in appearance, mannerisms, and voice. His approach to political issues was the same as his brother's. His youth and education bore an equally strong resemblance—the best schools, including Harvard and the University of Virginia Law School, extensive travel, a bit of amateur journalism, preparation for public service, and the instillation of a determination to excel. Still, one perceived differences in temperament. In the older brother, there was evident a certain detachment, wit, and cynicism, demonstrated politically in an aversion to ideological absolutes and personally in a somewhat skeptical and formalistic approach to his religion. The younger brother, more pietistic in religion, more passionate in his engagement with political issues, was prone to displays of outrage and aggressiveness. Taught that he should support the ambitions of his older siblings in every way possible and willing to subordinate his own career to John's, he was a natural political chief of staff, confidential adviser, and, when the occasion arose, hatchet man.

After a brief stint as a junior criminal lawyer in the Department of Justice, Robert managed his brother's 1952 senatorial campaign, then found employment with Joe McCarthy. Kennedy investigated trade between Communist China and America's NATO allies and discovered a degree of economic intercourse that was not in the interests of the United States. McCarthy used the finding as the basis for some of his usual hyperbolic rhetoric and embarrassed the State Department by negotiating on his own an embargo of the China trade with a group of Greek shipping magnates. It was the only job Kennedy did for the Wisconsin senator. Apparently uneasy about the directions in which McCarthy was headed, he resigned after six months and worked for a time as assistant to his father on the second Hoover Commission. At the beginning of 1954, he returned to the McCarthy Committee as counsel to the Democratic minority, trading especially bitter charges with Roy Cohn as McCarthyism sank into the quicksand of the Army-McCarthy hearings.

At no time had Robert Kennedy engaged in malicious or indiscriminate mudslinging. Still, he had been drawn to McCarthy and liked him personally. As was the case with his older brother, he had been caught up in the anti-Communism of the period, and he was even less reluctant to criticize the sachems of his party. In 1954, he published a letter in the *New York Times* criticizing the Yalta agreements and provoking a sharp response in defense of Franklin Roosevelt from the Harvard historian Arthur Schlesinger, Jr. His own relationship with McCarthy, whom he never publicly denounced, continued to be friendly. A month after McCarthy's censure, he conspicuously got up and left a banquet hall at the beginning of an address by McCarthy's most celebrated journalistic antagonist, Edward R. Murrow.

After the Democratic congressional victory in 1954, Robert Kennedy became chief counsel to the old McCarthy Committee, now the Permanent Subcommittee on Investigations. Under its new chairman, Democrat John McClellan of Arkansas, it turned to the matters for which it originally had been created, waste and corruption in government. In 1956, Kennedy was instrumental in forcing the resignation of Secretary of the Air Force Harold Talbott, who had solicited business for his private firm from the Pentagon.

In 1957, he became immersed in the cause that consumed him for the better part of two years, an investigation of labor racketeering. The subject was politically touchy within the Democratic party, but it engaged every iota of Kennedy's crusading passion with its revelations of looted pension funds, gangster control of key union locals, brutal tactics against honest opponents, under-the-table deals with employers, and the robber-baron lifestyles of crooked labor leaders. Focusing upon the most corrupt of major labor unions, the Teamsters, he exposed the dishonesty of its president, Dave Beck, laying the groundwork for Beck's subsequent conviction for income tax evasion. Then he became embroiled in what was to become a vendetta of near-epic proportions against Beck's successor, Jimmy Hoffa.

After resigning from the committee in 1959, Kennedy wrote *The Enemy Within*, a widely read indictment of corruption in labor unions and in American society as a whole. News coverage of the labor investigations, then the book, made him a major public figure in his own right, although at times he was confused with his brother. The labor committee effort had illustrated important aspects of Kennedy's character—a crusading temperament, an instinctive attachment to the underdog, an emotional involvement in the causes he chose, an easily touched sense of outrage at injustice, and, in the case of Hoffa, a deep capacity for personal hatred. It also had demonstrated a talent for hard work and organization that he now was prepared to turn to his brother's presidential campaign.

John Kennedy's own approach to labor legislation meshed well with his presidential aspirations. Advocating regulations to curb dishonesty in union leadership and financial affairs, he could demonstrate to the public that he was an independent Democrat not in big labor's pocket. Opposing efforts to tighten collective bargaining restrictions on unions, he could present himself as a friend of the worker and the honest labor leader. He teamed up with moderate New York Republican senator Irving Ives to put together a middle-of-the-road labor reform package designed to prevent racketeering and protect the rights of rank-and-file members. Assuming the burden of the struggle for passage himself, he worked as never before on a piece of legislation, compromised a bit, and got the bill through the Senate.

In the House of Representatives, however, a coalition led by Michigan Republican Robert Griffin and Georgia Democrat Phil Landrum added a number of restrictive provisions. While these did little real damage to the labor movement, they impinged upon collective bargaining in a way that Kennedy had sought to avoid. Unable to bring the bill back to its original form in conference committee, Kennedy and Ives dropped their names from it. The Landrum-Griffin Act of 1959 foreshadowed future difficulties he would face as president in his dealings with the congressional establishment. But at the time, the public conception of the senator —and his younger brother—striving to protect the worker was immensely valuable to a campaign that was already well underway.

As a candidate for president, Kennedy possessed almost every asset prized in the world of mid-twentieth-century American politics. His wealth allowed him to secure every need. His organization was more formidable than that of any of his rivals; his father negotiated behind the scenes with old-line Democratic leaders, his energetic family spearheaded his campaign in more visible positions, and his large, highly competent staff handled the day-to-day problems with managerial efficiency. He was more nationally visible than any of his opponents save Adlai Stevenson, and he was clearly attractive to a broader spectrum of American society than was Stevenson.

Kennedy enjoyed the benefit of a telegenic personality. Not a speaker of high technical quality, as Roosevelt had been, he would have found the road to national leadership more difficult in the radio age. Television, suddenly America's dominant communications medium, projected not simply his voice but his total mood and physical presence. It emphasized his youth and good looks; it conveyed more fully than radio both his cool wit and his personal intensity. Against this attractive television charisma, his rivals all seemed limited men. Adlai Stevenson was twice defeated and too conspicuously a darling of the intelligentsia; Stuart Symington was a stodgy corporate executive; and Hubert Humphrey and Lyndon Johnson were both curiously old-fashioned in their hot, impassioned personal styles—Humphrey a prairie populist, Johnson foolish enough to believe that his skill as a legislative manipulator and his stem-winding Texas oratory counted for something in national electoral politics. In themselves, they presented easily vanquished obstacles; the most important thing Kennedy had to overcome was his religious affiliation.

While not the most deeply felt American prejudice, anti-Catholicism was probably the most widespread. Its roots in the Anglo-American libertarian traditions of the seventeenth and eighteenth centuries gave it a certain cachet even among liberals, although few of them were disturbed about Kennedy himself. In the fundamentalist Protestant areas of rural, small-town America, anti-Catholicism still thrived, living off symbols and impulses that dated back to the Reformation. Actually, Kennedy was among the most secular of men, accepting the practice of his faith as a casual obligation. Nonetheless, after the defeat of Al Smith in 1928, it had become a commonplace of American political commentary that Catholicism in effect disqualified one from the presidency. Consequently, Kennedy faced the skepticism of political pros who were concerned above all with finding a winning candidate.

Kennedy satisfied the pros and clinched the nomination by taking key presidential primaries, the most important of them in West Virginia, a state almost entirely Protestant and heavily fundamentalist. When the issue resurfaced in the presidential campaign and foretold serious losses in normally Democratic rural areas, Kennedy moved to turn a liability of serious proportions into an asset. Making a regionally televised address to an assembly of Baptist ministers in Houston, Texas, then taking questions from them, he declared his dedication to the principle of separation of church and state, decried religious bigotry, reminded his audience of the way in which he and his brother had served in World War II, and implied that the religious opposition to him impugned the patriotism of American Catholics. Filmed for rebroadcast, the event was most prominently played in the larger cities of the North, the centers of American Catholicism. Here it served as a powerful appeal to the assertive impulses of ethnic-religious minorities of all descriptions. Kennedy probably persuaded few of those Protestants who opposed him on religious grounds, but he aroused non-Protestants and made himself their candidate with an emotional finality that would pay heavy dividends on election day.

Kennedy also faced the task of proving to the larger American public that he possessed the experience and personal qualities needed to govern a nation effectively. On this critical point, his youth and glamour raised questions, which television gave him the means to answer. The four "debates" staged between himself and Richard Nixon would have been notable in any era, but had they been reported only in print or carried only by radio, their impact probably would have been much different. In print, Kennedy appeared less articulate than Nixon. Radio listeners, according to public opinion surveys, tended to pronounce Nixon the winner of the encounters. Most people, however, received the debates via the medium that was Kennedy's best showcase.

Kennedy *looked* better than Nixon on television, an accident of complexion but a fortunate one nevertheless. More importantly, television enabled him to display his entire personality, not just his mediocre speaking voice. In debate with the vice-president of the United States, he demonstrated poise and humor under pressure; to most observers, he seemed more calm and confident than his older, presumably more experienced adversary. In addition, he was able to display wide-ranging, solid knowledge of the major issues, thereby refuting contentions that he still had a lot to learn. Finally, to a much greater extent than Nixon, he stayed on the offensive, speaking primarily to his national audience rather than to his opponent or to the panel of questioners. Nixon was the better technical debater, but Kennedy was the one who sensed most fully that he was speaking to a broad public, not a group of debate judges. His performance assuaged the doubts of many Democratic officials, excited rank-and-file party workers, and swayed skeptical independents.

Kennedy also capitalized upon a mood that he had not created —a fear that the country was adrift without adequate direction in either its domestic affairs or its diplomacy. A product of many situations and events—Eisenhower's age and illnesses, weak eco-

nomic growth, Sputnik, the U-2 episode, sporadic demonstrations
of hostility to the United States in such supposedly friendly areas
as Latin America and Japan—the theme had been developed by
intellectuals and opinion leaders, by such Republican critics of
the administration as Nelson Rockefeller, and by numerous Democrats. By 1960, it had become almost a commonplace to declare
that America needed to recover a sense of purpose, renew its
strength, and refresh its idealism. Kennedy was the perfect candidate to spread the message.

As in any close election, many things contributed to Kennedy's
hairsbreadth victory, but his triumph was surely less an ideological
matter than one of symbol and style. It symbolized the ultimate
coming of age of the ethnic-religious minorities, the ascendancy
of youth and all the attractive qualities associated with it, the
nation's sense that he was a man of substance and self-possession.
Whether all this was a sufficient mandate for a presidential administration in the workaday world remained to be seen.

The Administration:
The Reassertion of Liberalism

The Kennedy brothers saw themselves as bearers of the New
Deal–internationalist tradition. They consciously identified themselves with it and pursued a political strategy designed to
strengthen and extend it. Nonetheless, theirs was a uniquely
personal presidential administration. John F. Kennedy did more
than appoint his younger brother attorney general of the United
States; increasingly, he employed him as a confidential adviser on
every policy issue of consequence from civil rights to foreign
affairs. Totally loyal to the president, eager to run interference for
him, moralistic and emotional by nature, Bobby Kennedy made
himself JFK's alter ego; he won a reputation as the hard-driving,
"ruthless" force in the administration, bent, one might conclude,
on making his brother look benign by comparison.

The president, by contrast, consciously pursued the images
of youth, vigor, determination, idealism. His inaugural address,
with its affirmation of the American purpose, its calls for progress
at home, and its balance between military strength and diplomatic negotiation, set a tone he never abandoned. He was the

first president to schedule live televised press conferences, which served as ideal vehicles for the image he wanted to project. In assembling his team of policy makers, he gave due recognition to various factional leaders within the Democratic party, but he sought above all men whose tough, pragmatic liberalism mirrored what he perceived as his own. Foremost among them was Secretary of Defense Robert McNamara, who combined a social conscience with strong executive skills and a passion for efficiency.

The Democratic liberalism of which Kennedy had made himself the standard bearer was a refined and systematized version of the tradition of Roosevelt and Truman. The product of eight years of opposition, it proceeded from a pent-up frustration with the domestic "do-nothingism" of the Eisenhower administration and a passionate conviction that the constructive potentialities of government had scarcely been tapped. Publicized and developed during the 1950s by the Democratic Advisory Council, a "government-in-exile" of liberal intellectuals, friendly but relatively powerless legislators, and out-of-office politicians, it elicited no enthusiasm from the moderate Democratic congressional leadership of the Ike Age. Its proposals inevitably were the agenda of any activist liberal Democratic candidate for president.

The liberal political tradition that the Kennedy administration adopted as its own had developed a new concern with the *quality* of American life. The quantitative problems of income distribution, so the reasoning went, had been largely solved by the New and Fair Deals. In advocating medical insurance for the elderly and federal aid to education, Kennedy picked up themes carried over from the Truman administration's initial grapplings with the problems and possibilities of postwar affluence. In other ways, however, he directly tendered recognition to the sensibilities and new status of the intelligentsia.

No doubt he perceived that the intellectuals had become a powerful new force in American politics; but beyond that, he identified with them himself. He catered to their interests because he thought it something a president should do and because he enjoyed doing so. He invited Robert Frost to recite poetry at the inauguration; he gave White House dinners to honor American Nobel Prize winners, and initiated a new award, the Presidential Medal of Freedom, primarily to honor renowned artists and thinkers. His wife undertook to refurbish and restore the White House. Such activities did not earn Kennedy unqualified support from the intellectual community, but they did much to soften what criticism he received. Moreover, they broke down the alienation and hostility that had characterized relations between the intelligentsia and the presidency during the Eisenhower administration.

Paradoxically, another concern of the new liberalism was the persistence of poverty. Some liberal thinkers had never subscribed to the rather glib assertion that problems of income distribution were a thing of the past; others had rejected the spurious dichotomy between quantitative and qualitative social problems, arguing, for example, that the enhancement of educational opportunity was among the more effective means of coping with economic deprivation. During the 1950s, reform-minded politicians and intellectuals had developed an awareness of the problems of "chronically depressed areas" and had begun to give special attention to the endemic poverty of "Appalachia." By the time Kennedy became president, he had a set of ready-made programs to propose for the most identifiable islands of economic distress in an affluent society.

Michael Harrington, the leading thinker of the American Socialist party, carried the process a step farther with a widely read book, *The Other America* (1962).[1] He argued that poverty was widespread, if relatively invisible, in the sea of prosperity that had been presumed to envelop most of the nation. Within the administration, Bobby Kennedy, ever the amateur social worker, developed a deep interest in the causes of juvenile delinquency and the plight of ghetto youth. Responding in part to the need to find outlets for agricultural surpluses, the administration revived

---

[1]Harrington's own influence tells us much about the nature of postwar American politics. The Socialist party had become an educational organization whose efforts were directed at the liberal intellectual community rather than at any mass electorate. Harrington was able to enjoy such influence without even shedding his party label, as had a great many other Socialists and would-be Socialists after World War II. To all intents and purposes, American socialism was by 1960 a small caucus of intellectuals and activists on the left wing of the Democratic party. The process disturbed only a small band of reactionaries prone to confuse the socialism of Norman Thomas with Stalinist Communism. It was accepted in the rest of the public—by those who noticed it—with little comment.

on a small scale the old New Deal food stamp program. By 1963, the president was ready to incorporate a full-scale offensive against poverty into his domestic program and make it a keystone of his reelection effort.

Kennedy became the bearer of yet another systematization of the Roosevelt-Truman tradition—the "New Economics." Combining Keynesian assumptions with post-Keynesian advances in the study of economic growth and the projection of statistical data, the New Economics represented in many respects the culmination of a revolution in economic thought that had won full acceptance from neither Roosevelt nor Truman. In Kennedy, it found a national leader at once skeptical yet receptive, divided between an instinctively cautious approach to economic policy that he had inherited from his father and an activist impulse to "get the economy moving again." Eventually, the second urge would prevail.

The formulators of the New Economics, foremost among them Walter Heller, chairman of the Council of Economic Advisers, proceeded from all the usual assumptions of liberal economics since the 1930s. They favored a strong federal role in stimulating and managing the economy. Their primary goal was the achievement of full employment, the firmest basis in their estimation for a democratic society. They rejected the argument that much of the nation's unemployment was structural in nature —rooted in depressed areas or in the persistence of large numbers of unskilled workers in an increasingly automated and sophisticated economy. Where the structuralists argued that unemployment had to be treated with specially focused programs such as area redevelopment or vocational education, the New Economists advocated broadly based economic growth generated by fiscal and monetary stimuli.

Moreover, they dismissed the old Keynesian notion that the federal budget needed to be balanced over the ups and downs of the business cycle. Most Keynesians, in theory at least, had favored budget deficits in times of economic distress and compensating surpluses in periods of prosperity. The New Economists argued that budget surpluses, while justifiable to cool down an overheated, inflationary economy, could constitute an unwarranted "fiscal drag" on a recovery from recession and could lead to another downturn before the achievement of full employment. Economic policy makers needed to concentrate single-mindedly on full employment and be prepared to incur substantial deficits well into an economic recovery.

But what if the country raced into both full employment and serious inflation? The New Economists, equipped with elaborate and precise tools of economic measurement and prediction, responded that it had become possible to "fine-tune" the economy to the optimum point and maintain it there with relatively slight deviations. All that was needed would be a president capable of responding decisively to events and engineering the necessary shifts in policy. The last requirement was indeed a large one; that it could be stated with optimism says much about the hopeful glow of the New Frontier era.

Kennedy probably opted for the Heller approach, despite strong initial misgivings, because it appealed to his innovative impulses. Piecemeal programs to attack the structural aspects of unemployment were unexciting, and they failed to address the need for an economic expansion to provide jobs for the coming surge of postwar babies rapidly approaching employment age. Beginning in 1962, Kennedy became an eloquent and effective advocate of the New Economics. To encourage business expansion, he proposed and obtained an investment tax credit for new plants and equipment. In 1963, with the nation enjoying a substantial recovery from the recession of 1960–61, he requested a major tax cut and an accompanying sizable budget deficit as the way to urgently needed economic growth and a plateau of long-term prosperity. Despite the political attractiveness of a tax cut, reaction in Congress was predominantly negative, and public opinion surveys indicated a general lack of enthusiasm and comprehension. Passage, while probable, remained uncertain at John Kennedy's death.

Another approach to economic growth was the expansion of foreign trade. Here the Roosevelt-Truman politics and, indeed, the ancient tradition of the Democratic party, were solidly on the side of free trade. The New Deal's reciprocal trade program, expanded and extended by both the Truman and Eisenhower administrations, provided a solid basis for an ambitious new effort at lowering trade barriers. Moreover, to the extent that expanded trade might bring the non-Communist world closer together, it could provide new strength for the North Atlantic alliance. Kennedy made the Trade Expansion Bill of 1962 his top legislative priority. He fought off the protests of both business groups and labor unions that would have been adversely affected, won the support of those who stood to benefit, and assiduously lobbied key congressmen. The bill passed Congress without major alterations and set the stage for what developed into four years of exhaustive negotiations with the European Common Market nations. The end result in 1967 was an average 35-percent reduction of tariffs on some sixty-three hundred items. Excruciatingly slow in coming to fruition, and less stimulative to the American economy than its formulators had hoped, trade expansion nevertheless was a constructive diplomatic and economic achievement.

Ultimately, the management of the economy was as much a political problem as an intellectual one, involving as it did a complex set of relationships with well-organized business and labor groups. Given the slack though far from desperate economic situation that existed when he took office and the widespread sense of dissatisfaction among liberal Democrats with the lackluster economic performance of the Eisenhower administration, Kennedy possessed room for active leadership.

His major problem was to encourage economic growth while containing inflationary tendencies. He met it through the establishment of wage-price guidelines pegged to productivity growth. The unions (the Teamsters aside) were generally willing to go along because of their political stake in the Kennedy presidency and because inflation was not a serious problem. Business, less supportive, could be faced down in a serious crunch.

In early 1962, the steelworkers' union agreed to a 2.5%-percent wage settlement with the large steel companies; the administration had helped induce the settlement under what it took to be a firm understanding that the steel industry would not increase prices. Two weeks later, U.S. Steel announced a general increase of $6.00 a ton. Wounded both politically and economically, Kennedy fought back with a public denunciation of the move as "a wholly unjustifiable and irresponsible defiance of the public interest." When other steel companies fell in line, the Justice Department threatened price-fixing investigations and possible antitrust prosecutions. The administration intimated that federal procurement officers might be ordered to buy cheaper foreign steel. Some of the smaller steel companies then refused to join in the markup, leaving the industry facing competitive pressures as well as official wrath. One by one, the remaining companies rescinded the hike, thereby keeping the lid on price inflation and removing any rationale for larger union wage demands.

A stunning success, Kennedy's action was nevertheless so traumatic for all concerned that it could not be repeated. The steel incident unleashed all the latent hostility that almost by definition existed between a liberal Democratic administration and a conservative business community. In a fit of private anger, Kennedy had declared, "My father always told me that all businessmen were sons-of-bitches, but I never believed it till now." Inevitably, the remark leaked to the press and precipitated a surge of resentment in business circles. On Wall Street, an already overbought stock market plunged sharply, underscoring a lack of confidence that could have impeded the president's push for economic growth. In the circumstances, there was nothing to do other than attempt a reconciliation. He met privately with business leaders in an effort to reassure them, worked for passage of his investment tax credit, and swallowed a more subtle round of price increases without protest in the spring of 1963.[2]

In all, Kennedy's economic record was strong. He managed to achieve a high degree of wage and price stability while establishing the foundations for a remarkable increase in economic growth. His success demonstrated the virtues of both presidential activism and presidential flexibility. Most fundamentally, however, he was able to function within a gray economic environment amenable to leadership. His successor would discover the difficulties of restraining prices and wages in an overheated economy and would experience the practical limits upon the theory of "fine-

---

[2]By then, poor profits probably gave the major steel firms some justification for higher prices. The underlying cause of the poor profits, however, appears to have been Big Steel's reliance upon rapidly obsolescing production facilities, a problem that continues into the present day, with intermittently disastrous consequences for the industry. In 1962, some of the smaller companies (Inland, Kaiser, and Armco) could afford to buck U.S. Steel's price trend because they were better managed, had more efficient facilities, and focused their production upon specific areas of the market.

tuning." It is possible to argue that Kennedy would not have faced these problems because he would not have overloaded the economy by plunging into Vietnam. Even if one accepts this unverifiable proposition, it seems certain that sooner or later the growth policies of the New Economics would have scouted some excesses that could have been contained only by a president of almost superhuman tactical skill, aided by a team of economic advisers with unusual powers of prediction. One may respect Kennedy and his economists without attributing such superlative talents to them.

The Roosevelt-Truman tradition had left the Kennedys with one other challenge, that of meeting increasingly militant black demands while holding the Democratic coalition together. From the Depression on, the condition of American blacks had presented Democrats with both great opportunities and great difficulties, with the promise of millions of new votes and the peril of party disintegration. To liberals, it represented a moral problem that could not be dodged. Roosevelt and Truman had met the situation by tendering as much recognition to black sensibilities and as many tangible concessions as seemed compatible with the continued survival of the party. During the 1950s, Adlai Stevenson had backed away a bit from the advance ground they had staked out. A moderate by temperament if a liberal by intellect, Stevenson had provided scant contrast to the racial conservatism of Eisenhower. The charismatic leader of the liberal intelligentsia, he did much by his own example to coopt that group for the status quo in American race relations.

By the time John F. Kennedy began his drive for the presidency, a substantial consensus had developed on the issue among those liberals who had outgrown the impatience and soaring idealism of youth. Reflecting Stevenson's moderation, it emphasized gradualism and tokenism. The new consensus was willing to accept a few black students in integrated schools or a few new black voters in scattered areas of the South as entering wedges, but it either ignored the plight of the vast majority of blacks altogether or sorrowfully dismissed it as a sore that could be healed only by slow progress over several decades.

It is hardly surprising that John Kennedy—as an admirer of Stevenson, a calculating politician, and a man of the fifties—

substantially adopted the new liberal consensus. He courted the black vote in the routine fashion of any Northern politician but was never as caught up in civil rights problems as Hubert Humphrey. As a presidential candidate, he avidly sought pockets of Southern support that for one reason or another were not available to his rival, Lyndon Johnson. In the tradition of Roosevelt, Truman, and other successful Democratic leaders, he attempted to gain support from both Northern blacks and white Southerners and was relatively successful in doing so.

Unlike Roosevelt and Truman, however, he found himself confronted by pressures that could not be avoided. Blacks themselves had rejected the moderate-to-liberal white consensus on tokenism and gradualism; instead, under the leadership of Martin Luther King, they were embarked upon a nonviolent revolution. Aided and abetted by the idealism of many white liberals and radicals, the new black movement created situations that required the administration to make an unequivocal choice between integration or segregation. Faced with the necessity for choice, the Kennedys followed both political realities and their instinctive sense of morality.

By education and background, both brothers were integrationists with an acquired patrician concern for the status of the American Negro. Disturbed that no black soldier was in the honor guard at his inaugural, the president ordered the military services to add black faces to the crack drill units assigned to visible duty in the Washington area. At a more substantive level, he tendered important policy-making appointments to prominent blacks such as Robert Weaver and Thurgood Marshall; he appears to have fully intended to be the first president to appoint a black cabinet member and a black Supreme Court justice.

Nonetheless, civil rights was not his highest priority. Cognizant of the mood of Congress, he offered no significant civil rights legislation during his first two years in office. Hoping to avoid offending key legislators on Capitol Hill, he delayed an executive order barring discrimination in federally subsidized housing until after the 1962 elections, and the document proved weak and disappointing in practice. His judicial appointments for Southern federal courts were, on the whole, trimmed to the veto of influential Southern senators; consequently, a few were blatant segregationists.

The attorney general's outlook, on the other hand, reflected his passionate moralism. Prone to see social questions as struggles of justice against injustice, holding an office that put him on the front line of the struggles between integrationists and segregationists, Robert Kennedy increasingly found himself the administration's point man for civil rights. He resigned from the prestigious Metropolitan Club, indignant at its policy of excluding blacks. He saw to it that the Justice Department recruited black lawyers, and he pressured the FBI to hire black agents. But what would really call forth a commitment from him, and eventually from his brother, were violent flashes from the South.

It is difficult, some two decades after the events, to recall the bitter militance with which Southern whites resisted the slightest movement toward integration. Convinced that their world rested upon subordination of the black race, they perceived even the slightest exception as an attack upon the natural order of things and a step toward a frightening, disorienting chaos. Many of them, feeling threatened to the core of their being, were prepared to sanction any intimidation, any violence, in the fight against change. No Southern political leader could stand up publicly against such a mood. A good many avoided the issue as much as possible. Some who could not do so, such as Mississippi senator James Eastland, managed their political survival with the time-honored cynicism of public racism and private moderation. Others, such as George Wallace or Ross Barnett, were, quite simply, irresponsible and vicious. It was this last type that would force the Kennedys to take sides in a way they originally had hoped to avoid.

The confrontations with the racist South began almost as soon as the Kennedys had taken office. Freedom riders busing through Alabama faced savage beatings and near-lynchings. The state of Mississippi nearly rose in revolt against the admission of a single Negro undergraduate to its university. The governor of Alabama pledged to "stand in the schoolhouse door" to prevent the matriculation of even one black student. The city administration of Birmingham fought integrationist demonstrations with high-pressure fire hoses, club-swinging policemen, attack dogs, and mass arrests. In each case, the pattern was similar. The Kennedy brothers attempted conciliation, urged moderation on both sides, and ultimately intervened on behalf of black integrationists with marshalls, troops, legal aid, and, finally, the proposing of major civil rights legislation.

At some point, first in the mind of Robert Kennedy, then probably in that of his brother, the problems of civil rights moved from the realm of the political to that of the moral. In June 1963, in the wake of King's Birmingham campaign, the president called for civil rights legislation in a televised speech that was both blunt and more idealistic on the issue than any ever delivered by an American chief executive.

> We are confronted primarily with a moral issue. It is as old as the scriptures and is as clear as the American Constitution.
> . . . If an American, because his skin is dark, cannot eat lunch in a restaurant open to the public, if he cannot send his children to the best public school available, if he cannot vote for the public officials who represent him, if, in short, he cannot enjoy the full and free life which all of us want, then who among us would be content to have the color of his skin changed and stand in his place? Who among us would then be content with the counsels of patience and delay? . . .
> We face, therefore, a moral crisis as a country and as a people. It cannot be met by repressive police action. It cannot be left to increased demonstrations in the streets. It cannot be quieted by token moves or talk. It is a time to act in the Congress, in your State and local legislative body and, above all, in all of our daily lives.

At Kennedy's death, the extensive legislation he proposed was moving very slowly through the congressional process. Whether it would have survived intact remains unsure. It does seem certain that Kennedy had decided, less for political reasons than for what he considered moral imperatives, to put his prestige and his office behind a cause that he once had tried to dodge. In doing so, he went farther than any president before, took considerable risks in the bargain, and built most meaningfully upon the liberal tradition he had inherited.

Cold War to Détente

John Kennedy's critique of Eisenhower's diplomacy had epitomized the divided mind of Democratic liberalism in its effort to
couple an idealistic encouragement of peaceful economic development and social revolution with greater military strength.
The liberals suffered from intellectual tensions similar to those of
the conversatives—they shrank from the unpleasant and dangerous implications of the Cold War, yet because they visualized the
United States as the world's primary defender of the values of
liberal democracy, they could not escape the urge to wage it
more vigorously. During the first year of the Kennedy presidency,
U.S.–Soviet relations remained at a low point. Berlin was on the
verge of armed combat. Until the fall of 1962, the Soviet Union
engaged in deliberately terroristic open-air testing of huge nuclear
weapons. Nikita Khrushchev himself seized every opportunity to
behave in a boorish, aggressive fashion. In such an atmosphere,
Kennedy's sense of urgency about the Cold War was natural
enough. What was surprising was his comparative restraint.

The new president faced the same array of problems with
which Eisenhower had grappled. The Third World drive for an
end to colonialism was spreading into sub-Saharan Africa. The
Soviet leadership remained opportunistic, committed to "wars of
liberation," and willing to pursue openings all over the globe.
Crises existed to varying degrees in Berlin, Southeast Asia, and
Cuba. Kennedy himself was an unknown quantity around the
world, his two most widely perceived characteristics being youth
and apparent inexperience.

Given Kennedy's range of travel and the extent and quality of
the thinking he had done about foreign policy, the appearance
was deceptive. He had in fact succeeded better than most of his
Democratic colleagues in reconciling idealism and realism. The
idealism was the more visible and exhilarating, expressing and
capturing the natural impulse of youth to remake an imperfect
world. The Peace Corps, the Alliance for Progress, greater attention to the aspirations of the Third World, a more informal, shirt-
sleeve diplomacy—however superficial, however flawed in execution, they gave American foreign policy a tinge of democratic

altruism it had lacked under Eisenhower. Kennedy's vision of an interdependent Western world united by free trading arrangements was a recreation of the liberal vision of global unity and prosperity. He made the Cold War seem a progressive crusade.

Underneath the crusading rhetoric, Kennedy was very much a realist, and a cautious one at that. Willing to think in terms of spheres of influence as one basis for a relaxation of tensions with the USSR, he was taken aback in his first meeting with Khrushchev to discover that the Soviet leader seemed a shrill ideological crusader unwilling to bargain calmly. The experience made him all the more determined to defend American interests when he perceived them to be vital; in Berlin, he would do so not only with displays of power but also with the idealistic sense of purpose that he projected so effectively. Nonetheless, he was willing to back away in areas such as Laos where American claims were dubious and American power seemed overextended. It was this capacity for rational calculation that Khrushchev found hard to understand and that he may have mistaken for weakness.

In no area of the world did Kennedy show more tenacity than in Berlin. Like Truman and Eisenhower before him, he realized that the Western commitment to the city, however ill conceived, was the linchpin of the North Atlantic alliance. He invoked memories of past American steadfastness by recalling to duty as his personal representative in the city General Lucius D. Clay, head of the postwar U.S. occupation and hero of the airlift of 1948–49. He sent the vice-president to make an emotional speech of support. He called up military reserves for duty in Germany, increased the defense budget, and tried to make it unmistakably clear that he was prepared to go to any lengths to defend the Western position in the city. In a notable interview, he calculatedly told the journalist James A. Wechsler, "If Khrushchev wants to rub my nose in the dirt, it's all over." In 1963, with the immediate crisis over but the city still in need of reassurance, he came in person to tell an electrified crowd, *"Ich bin ein Berliner!"*

Still, Kennedy was never committed to more than protection of ground the West already held nor does he appear ever to have been carried away by the powerful emotions that attached themselves to Berlin. This rational detachment ultimately gave him the capacity to defuse the situation through a de facto compromise:

the acceptance of the Berlin Wall. An illegal, immoral atrocity, the wall was also quite possibly the minimum condition for the avoidance of war. Its erection did not bring the Berlin crisis to a sudden end. Perhaps indeed the Russians had originally considered it only the first step in a larger plan to evict the West, but by solving the immediate problem of large-scale East German migration to the West, it inevitably lowered the pressure that had been building up since the later years of the Eisenhower administration. Kennedy held the Western position in Berlin while his Soviet adversaries managed to maintain theirs only by substituting one profound embarrassment for another.

From the beginning, Kennedy addressed the problem of Cuba more aggressively; the island had become a Communist outpost in a traditionally American sphere of dominance. It was the same sort of irritation for the United States that Berlin had been for the Russians, but the problem of how to proceed against it was even more difficult. An American military occupation of the island could be no more than a hypothetical possibility given the climate of mid-twentieth-century diplomacy and the restrictions that the liberal Democratic ethic put upon Kennedy's foreign policy.

It was natural enough for him to turn to the plan for an invasion by exiles. Left behind by the Eisenhower administration and already far advanced, blessed with the endorsement of the military and intelligence experts, the scheme resisted critical scrutiny. As is frequently the case with tempting opportunities that promise large gains, the result was a disaster. Coming near the beginning of Kennedy's administration, the Bay of Pigs fiasco seriously impaired his effort to establish himself as a leader of world stature and may have emboldened Khrushchev to press harder on Berlin. The subsequent decision of the president and his brother to lend themselves to a private fund-raising effort that eventually ransomed the prisoners was honorable but humiliating.

The Bay of Pigs incident may be written off as the result of bad advice and of the inexperience that any new president brings to his job, but one senses another element also—John Kennedy was incapable of dealing with Fidel Castro in the careful, moderate way that he approached most problems. His subsequent policy toward Cuba, intermittently overseen by Bobby Kennedy, appears as the effort of a frustrated idealist to strike out at a hated enemy. Sanctioning commando raids and various covert activities by Cuban exiles based on U.S. soil, he created only an annoyance for Castro. With no clearly defined invasion or mass uprising in prospect, sabotage activities and minor paramilitary sorties presented the Cuban dictator little real danger while providing him the sort of external threat he needed to rationalize and consolidate a totalitarian society.

In time, the secret war against Cuba came to involve repeated CIA designs on Castro's life. Subjected to rational analysis, these also seem foolish. Castro's assassination would have made a martyr, doubtless further entrenched Communist domination of Cuba, and stimulated anti-Yankee sentiment throughout Latin America. The morality of the project was quite obviously dubious, although perhaps more ambiguous than its critics admit. Castro, after all, was known to be supplying guerrillas and would-be assassins throughout Latin America, and his most prominent target was the democratically elected, reformist president of Venezuela, Romulo Betancourt. But most intriguing is the as-yet-unanswered question of how much the Kennedy brothers knew about the plots to kill their enemy. It seems astounding that they would not have known in at least a general way; yet their staunchest defender, Arthur Schlesinger, Jr., makes a strong case that they were unaware of what was happening. Whatever the case, their Cuban policy was among the most ill-conceived aspects of their administration.

After that time, it can be argued that the focus of misconception moved to Southeast Asia. A remote, minor problem at the beginning of the Kennedy presidency, Indochina was just beginning to emerge as a major challenge at its end. The Kennedy brothers avoided falling into the abyss; still, their actions eased the path for their successors. Few would maintain that the quality of thought and attention they devoted to Indochina was very high.

As in Cuba, the Kennedys faced challenges to the assumptions that distinguished their foreign policy from Eisenhower's—the belief that the Third World revolution was a progressive, democratic force in line with the interests and traditions of the United States and that it could be redirected along the lines of the American Revolution. These assumptions gave the Kennedy foreign policy a crusading quality that bumped squarely up against another element of the Kennedy approach—an understanding of the uses and limits of power. The Kennedy administration expanded the available means of coping with Communist-led guerrilla insurgencies, but the result was an inconsistent anti-Communist effort, increasingly based on wishful thinking. Kennedy, like his predecessors, was generally successful in his direct confrontations with Soviet power because he understood the milieu of Western politics. He failed, however, although in a very different way from Eisenhower, to grasp the politics and culture of the Third World.

The immediate Southeast Asian problem at the beginning of 1961 was the confused situation in Laos. Here, the Eisenhower administration had clearly miscalculated. It had overthrown a neutralist government and had attempted to install a pro-American regime with little support in a distant land where only a tiny minority of the population was touched by the passions of the Cold War. The day before Kennedy's inauguration, Eisenhower counseled intervention with American troops if necessary, but there is little indication that the new president gave the possibility more than passing consideration. Logistically, Laos was untenable. Strategically, it was insignificant compared to Berlin. Morally, it put the United States in the repugnant position of having abetted the deposition of a legitimate non-Communist government.

In all, Eisenhower's commitment was an offense to Kennedy's realistic and ideological sensibilities. Unable to repudiate it overtly, the president engaged in rhetorical displays of resolve and authorized mild increases in U.S. military power in the region. Nevertheless, he sought only a restoration of the old neutralist status quo. After a year and a half of diplomatic activity, the administration achieved an accord, signed at Geneva in July 1962, restoring the neutralist premier, Prince Souvanna Phouma—but making him the head of a coalition government with only nominal authority over Communist-held areas. The Laotian settlement did not disturb Communist gains, may have created an impression of American weakness in Hanoi, and surely stiffened Kennedy's determination to meet the Communist challenge more firmly in South Vietnam.

Unlike Laos, South Vietnam was an Eisenhower commitment that seemed tenable in every respect. Logistically, it presented only routine transportation and supply difficulties. Its strategic location on the rim of Southeast Asia was important. It possessed an apparently well-entrenched, indigenous anti-Communist government. In addition, it provided a logical testing ground for the new military flexibility that Kennedy, heavily influenced by General Maxwell D. Taylor, wanted to develop. The only feasible counter to Soviet-sponsored "wars of liberation," so the reasoning went, was the building of elite counterinsurgency forces for Third World governments fighting Communist guerrillas. Consciously assuming a test of its theory of Third World revolution, the administration raised both militarily and politically the already substantial U.S. stake in South Vietnam. By late 1963, it had placed over fifteen thousand American advisers in the country, the majority of them involved in combat operations with South Vietnamese units. Reaching for bipartisan support, the president named as American ambassador one of the leading symbols of Republican internationalist anti-Communism, Henry Cabot Lodge.

The theory was attractive, but the actuality was disillusioning. Far from being strengthened by American support, the South Vietnamese government of Ngo Dinh Diem grew weaker. It was unable to stem enemy gains in the countryside or quell an increasingly militant non-Communist opposition in the major cities. Diem's Buddhist opponents engaged in the ultimate media theater by setting themselves afire in front of news photographers and television cameramen, horrifying the American public and the administration. In November 1963, just weeks before John Kennedy's assassination, the president and Lodge decided not to oppose a planned military coup that would oust Diem and presumably install a more acceptable set of rulers in Saigon. Perhaps they had convinced themselves that Diem would be sent off into exile rather than killed; still, their behavior raises moral questions even more troubling than those connected with their policy toward Castro. By dealing confidentially with the conspirators and giving them a green light, they in effect sanctioned the assassination of an ally, albeit a weak and troublesome one. And, as Lyndon Johnson would discover, they had failed to establish an effective, popular Vietnamese government.

At the time, events in Vietnam seemed peripheral to the larger picture of U.S.-Soviet relations as they had been reshaped by the Cuban missile crisis. This is not the place to recount the familiar details of that episode, but its centrality to the Kennedy image and its formative impact upon the Cold War require close attention to the questions it raises.

The first and most fundamental problem involves Soviet motivation. Khrushchev's memoirs, a first-hand but fallible source, state some obvious considerations—protection for the still-harassed Castro government, the extension of Soviet influence into other areas of Latin America, and the need to counter what had become a clear American superiority in reliable long-range nuclear missiles. The Cuban gamble may have been the first step in a last-ditch attempt to force the United States out of Berlin, either by providing the Soviet Union much greater leverage in a showdown or by setting up the basis for a diplomatic trade—Soviet withdrawal of missiles from Cuba in exchange for Western withdrawal of troops from Berlin. Finally, although Khrushchev is silent on the point, the decision may have rested at bottom on an extremely unfavorable estimate of Kennedy's character. Basing his opinion on their encounter at Vienna and perhaps also on the Bay of Pigs, the acquiescence in the Berlin Wall, and the retreat in Laos, Khrushchev may have concluded that the young American president was prone to capitulate under pressure.

If one accepts Kennedy's premise that U.S. credibility would have been fatally impaired by an unchallenged installation of Soviet missiles in Cuba, it is difficult to fault his response. It seems especially odd that he has been criticized for impulsiveness when he sought the advice of an "executive committee" composed of most of the major foreign policy authorities of the United States or that he has been accused of playing out irrational machismo impulses when he accepted the most pacific alternatives seriously offered to him. Faced with an act of appalling recklessness, he responded with balance and flexibility. He rejected the advice not only of military leaders but of no less a Democratic eminence than Dean Acheson, and he chose to blockade Cuba rather than unleash bombers and an attack force. Using emissaries such as Acheson and Charles Bohlen, he brought the leaders of Western Europe behind him. When Khrushchev sent both conciliatory and belligerent communications at the height of the crisis, he responded only to the conciliatory letter, thereby setting in motion the process of resolving the situation. Finally, he compromised, promising explicitly to cease efforts to overthrow Castro and indirectly pledging to make a token withdrawal of relatively valueless U.S. nuclear missiles from Italy and Turkey.

When one separates the emotions of the moment from the issues, it is difficult to gauge whether the United States "won" the Cuban missile crisis. Khrushchev had secured a guarantee for his client and in return had done little more than bulldoze some uncompleted missile pads. Nevertheless, it was more immediately apparent that the Russians had made their most daring attempt ever to change the structure of the Cold War and had been forced to retreat in humiliation, not because Kennedy wanted to humble Khrushchev but because the very audacity of the Soviet ploy guaranteed humiliation for whomever capitulated. For *both* sides, the experience was profoundly traumatic. The prospect of its repetition was almost as unthinkable to American leadership as to that of the USSR. The result was a mutual impulse to change the surface tenor of the Cold War if not the underlying dynamics of Soviet-American rivalry.

The word *détente* seldom, if ever, appeared in the rhetoric of American-Russian dialogue or in the analyses of foreign affairs experts during the year after the resolution of the missile crisis; yet Kennedy now moved swiftly in that direction. He established an instant personal communications system with the Kremlin, authorized a large sale of U.S. wheat to cover the Russian grain harvest shortfall, and negotiated a rudimentary arms control agreement—a treaty to end atmospheric nuclear testing. Caught up in the effort for peace with at least the same intensity that marked his endorsement of civil rights legislation, he eloquently advocated reconciliation with the USSR, step-by-step movement toward "a relaxation of tensions without relaxing our guard," and even a concerted effort to understand the Soviet perspective.

It is difficult to imagine how far the drive might have proceeded had Kennedy lived through a second term as president and how successful it might ultimately have been. One must observe, however, that as was the case with the later détente and as had been the case with Roosevelt's diplomacy, Kennedy's initiatives did not proceed far beyond the realm of atmospherics. The hot line was a token gesture and the wheat sale a help to a regime that experienced periodic difficulty feeding its people. Although a welcome and praiseworthy step toward detoxifying the air, the test ban treaty was not a significant deterrent to nuclear weapons development. At his death, Kennedy had not even begun the process of ending the Cold War, but despite some initial missteps, he had displayed considerable qualities of diplomatic leadership and had established himself as both a popular hero and the leading statesman of the Western world.

Survivor in a New World

No person was more psychically wounded by the assassination of John Kennedy than his younger brother. Moody by nature and possessing deep emotional ties to his older sibling, Bobby Kennedy spent the next four and a half years drifting into periodic fits of depression. Through his adult years he had been his brother's helper and enforcer; it seemed natural that in some way he should attempt to carry on his brother's tradition. But the murder of the president was also a liberating experience. It put the younger man on his own, compelling him to establish an independent political identity, built to be sure on the heritage of JFK but expressing also the drives of a unique and, in some ways, quite different personality.

The two were of course similar in some very obvious ways. Both possessed good looks and a magnetism especially vivid in its sexual dimension. "Women squeal and bound when he passes by, as they did for his brother in 1960," Fletcher Knebel wrote of Bobby in the spring of 1963. Both indulged in displays of wry, frequently self-deprecating humor. Both were gripped by an inbred desire to climb to the top of American politics.

Their differences were equally important. The most obvious was Bobby's intense political passion, the quality that had always made him so visible a counterpoint to JFK. In his engagement with the issues, in his political relationships, he openly displayed strong, unambiguous feelings. He cared deeply about the problems of the poor and racial minorities and always had believed that American foreign policy should have a moral mission. During the executive committee sessions at the time of the Cuban missile crisis, he had denounced the idea of a surprise attack on Cuba as morally repugnant. In his trips abroad, both during and after the Kennedy presidency, he conspicuously sought out the ordinary people, the young, and the oppressed, making it clear that he considered them the proper objects of American diplomacy. Had he been born in another time and another culture, someone remarked, he probably would have become a revolutionary priest.

The same depth of feeling carried over to his relationships with other public figures. To members of his family and to those of his staff who won his confidence, he was totally loyal and solicitous. To those with whom he came in conflict, his attitudes varied from scarcely disguised contempt—as appears to have been the case with Chester Bowles or Eugene McCarthy—to raw hatred—as with Jimmy Hoffa or Lyndon Johnson. These emotions, widely known and unconcealed, earned him such a widespread reputation for "ruthlessness" that it qualified even so sinister a character as Hoffa for martyrdom among people intelligent enough to know better. The charge touched a deep vein of insecurity that otherwise displayed itself only in a somewhat inarticulate shyness that Kennedy often manifested in one-to-one encounters with strangers. His friends and biographers have recorded too many weak jokes that he made about this side of his reputation for us to believe that he was unaffected by it. It appears to have inhibited his public life and many have been as responsible as anything for his reluctance to challenge Lyndon Johnson in late 1967.

Nevertheless, some degree of bitter vindictiveness came easily to him. It informed his estrangement from the new Johnson administration and his consequent drive for political power. His hostility toward Johnson was well established, perhaps originating in an attack LBJ had made upon Joseph P. Kennedy, Sr., during the 1960 fight for the presidential nomination. Johnson, sensitive, vain, and easily offended, reciprocated fully. The result, almost from the time the nation emerged from the shock of a presidential assassination, was a cold war in Washington between a considerable number of Kennedy loyalists unwilling to accept the transition and Johnson people attempting to take hold of the government. Bobby Kennedy encouraged the process, in effect refusing to admit that the new occupant of the White House was entitled to have his own people in power. Then, in a bizarre effort to impose himself on the new administration, he began an underground campaign for the vice-presidency. When Johnson countered by excluding all members of the cabinet from consideration, Kennedy looked in other directions for a power base.

Although he possessed only a tenuous claim to residence in New York, he made himself overnight the major figure in New York Democratic politics. It was not from any skill at political maneuvering but simply from the sheer fact of his electability that he overwhelmed the mediocrities among the party leaders and took the nomination to oppose the incumbent Republican senator, Kenneth Keating. Audacious and weighted with overtones of arrogance, the move met resistance from both the professional politicians and the liberal intellectuals. With reason, the professionals saw Kennedy as a threat, a new power with whom they could not do business, and one openly disdainful of them. Able to operate over their heads, he ignored the pols, snubbed them, ridiculed them, and alienated them, but he never seriously challenged their control at the routine, working level of state politics.

The reaction of the liberal intellectuals was more complex. Far from presenting a threat to them, Kennedy espoused their causes with much more effectiveness than any other New York politician. Nor was their frequent hostility based on Kennedy's "carpetbagger" status on the New York scene; their own hero and preferred senatorial candidate was Adlai Stevenson. Rather, it rested in their perception of Bobby Kennedy as a person—as the man who had worked for Joe McCarthy, who had managed the drive that torpedoed the presidential hopes of the old liberal heroes Stevenson and Humphrey, who had pursued Jimmy Hoffa so relentlessly with so little regard for civil liberties, who had, many believed, pushed Stevenson aside in his quest for the Senate. James Wechsler, a Kennedy supporter, barely exaggerated the attitude of many of his liberal friends when he wrote that they considered Kennedy "a simple man, possessed by a diabolical power complex, a ruthless man bent on destruction of all who stand in his way, a mirthless man who detects no irony in the human comedy, an inflexible man who neither listens nor learns."

Such an attitude was of course a caricature—and a rather cruel one—but it was widely held enough to throw the votes of many liberal intellectuals to Keating and to earn the incumbent the editorial endorsement of the *New York Times*. For a time in the fall of 1964, Kennedy trailed Keating in the polls. Exhaustive campaigning—some of it in company with President Johnson—along with the enduring appeal of the Kennedy name and image turned the situation around. On election day, Kennedy defeated Keating by 700,000 votes, but Lyndon Johnson carried New York over Barry Goldwater by 2,700,000. It was a bitter irony for both men that the president had carried his most vehement personal enemy to office on his coattails.

As had his older brother, Robert Kennedy used the Senate as a launching pad for a presidential campaign. Like John Kennedy and quite unlike his younger brother, Edward, he was a loner with little interest in winning the esteem of the congressional establishment. He was not an effective senator in the traditional sense of the term. The destiny for which he was prepared by circumstance and temperament was to be leader of the opposition, and in the America of the mid-sixties this more than ever required not legislative dexterity, but the ability to mobilize a mass following.

Like John Kennedy, Robert aligned himself with the forces of liberal insurgency as a matter of both tactics and preference. It seemed so natural a thing that few observers questioned it; yet a scant five years had changed American politics so much that liberal dissent now stood for something very different. For John Kennedy, it had entailed attacking what had come to be widely perceived as a tired, conservative Republican administration; it had meant standing for activism in foreign policy and stepped-up social reformism at home. For Robert Kennedy, it required criticism of a vigorous, activist Democratic administration that had played out, however badly, many of the policy lines that his brother had set in motion. It was natural enough that he was a bit halting and uncertain, and it is perhaps surprising that in the end he handled the role so effectively.

The Kennedy-Johnson polarization provided a personal basis for the Kennedy challenge, and the rise of the New Left presented something of an ideological basis. After his move to New York, Robert Kennedy surrounded himself with young liberal intellectuals such as Pete Hamill, Jack Newfield, and Adam Wallinsky; while not adopting the full-blown New Left critique of American liberalism, they had been strongly affected by it and had incorporated it selectively into their thinking. Some of the older Kennedy advisers, most notably Arthur Schlesinger, Jr., and Theodore Sorensen, appear to have gone through a similar process. Aspects of New Left thought—its concentration on the oppressed, its indictment of American racism and materialist affluence, its advocacy of participatory democracy—appealed to them all and must have seemed especially attractive to Bobby Kennedy's crusading personality. Increasingly, snatches of the youthful radicalism of the sixties crept into his rhetoric providing what there was of his mass appeal that was distinct from the legend of his brother and the force of his own personality.

Most immediate among the issues upon which Kennedy would confront Johnson was the Vietnam War. He abhorred the general LBJ style in diplomacy and had been dismayed by such episodes as the Dominican intervention, but it was Vietnam that furnished a continuous, ever deepening source of discontent. Robert Kennedy's adoption of the issue had its obvious ironies and revealed the moralistic passion that lay at the core of his personality. It is hard to pin down with any degree of precision Kennedy's participation in his brother's decisions for increased involvement in Vietnam, but he had undeniably backed those policies and had fervently believed in them as the necessary means of stopping the evil of Communism. He could argue with much reason that Johnson had carried those policies past anything John Kennedy had contemplated and had done so at a once-unimaginable cost to the nation. Nevertheless, his conversion involved far more than a change of mind about degrees of force or about the most expedient means to an end. It entailed also a redefinition of the moral and a new emotional commitment that went far beyond any political calculation.

He never, it is true, broke with old friends who had helped orchestrate the war, such as Maxwell Taylor and Robert McNamara; nonetheless, he came to express horror at what it was doing to both Vietnam and America. As early as the spring of 1965, he was arguing against escalation, decrying the prospect of large-scale bombing, and urging negotiation with the Vietcong. By the end of that year, he was defending draft card burners and endorsing the giving of blood to the Vietcong. Still, he was unwilling to advocate unilateral withdrawal; nor did he at first make his qualms about the war a constant theme of his political identity.

By early 1967, he was speaking out more freely and more emotionally, exhibiting a conviction that transcended personal self-interest or any considerations of *Realpolitik*. He declared indignantly that the United States had betrayed its traditions by using military tactics that resulted in the napalming of civilians and the killing of children and women. He made the absurd and politically counterproductive assertion that "what we are doing to the Vietnamese is not very different than what Hitler did to the Jews." His determination to get the country out of the war and his revulsion at the war itself were on the verge of becoming obsessions, but he never produced an acceptable strategy for extrication.

The other issue upon which he challenged Johnson—the plight of the underprivileged in America—presented equally great opportunities for emotional involvement and equally great practical difficulties. Johnson, a genuinely dedicated social reformer, had initiated vaster social welfare programs than any president in American history and in the process had ignited unrealistic expectations of rapid progress for the deprived. But he had involved the United States in a massive military conflict that diverted urgently needed funds from his own social programs, and the underprivileged classes provided a disproportionate percentage of the troops who bore the brunt of combat in Vietnam.

To the New Left and left-liberal thinking of the time, the entire spectacle laid bare the bankruptcy of establishment liberalism, representative primarily of the well-to-do, manipulative of the underclasses but superficial in its concern for them, and prone to disastrous military adventures abroad. Kennedy and his advisers accepted much of this diagnosis. Moreover, they embraced the essentials of the general remedy that went along with it: the first step in bringing the full benefits of American life to the underprivileged was to stop the Vietnam War; the second step was to create a social program that would go beyond the Great Society.

Robert Kennedy's impulse to act as the tribune of the underclasses came to him naturally. His sincerity and dedication were undeniable, but like Martin Luther King—the political figure he most resembled in his appeal, his following, and his sense of mission—he found it difficult to develop credible prescriptions. He argued in general terms for an even greater Great Society— full-scale national health insurance, more government-subsidized housing, more food for the hungry—and he took up the new catchphrase of "participatory democracy." Yet at the same time he found himself criticizing an administration that had done far more about the problems of poverty and discrimination than any other in American history. Almost in the mode of King, he was accepting a prophetic role in American politics rather than a pragmatic one.

By the end of 1967, the senator faced a difficult choice. He had made himself the leader of a growing Democratic opposition to Lyndon Johnson and ran about even with the president in preference surveys. He was under increasing pressure to declare for the presidency from some advisers. Others, however, urged caution; it would be easier and surer to wait until 1972. Kennedy worried that he would be regarded as pursuing a vendetta against Johnson. He decided against an announcement, forced the antiwar liberals to turn to Eugene McCarthy, and thereby forfeited the opportunity to make himself the leader of all the groups and impulses that were on the verge of routing the old politics within the Democratic party.

Kennedy's initial decision hurt and angered many of the liberals who had counted on him. His change of mind, coming on the heels of McCarthy's stunning showing in the New Hampshire primary, deepened those wounds and created new ones. McCarthy had taken a serious risk, stepping forward only after Kennedy had decided against doing so. He had emerged morally triumphant and had gained an instant devoted following among antiwar students and liberal intellectuals. He and his new disciples greeted the Kennedy announcement with anger and contempt. The opposition of so substantial a portion of the liberals was probably more a handicap than that of the regular Democrats, who after Johnson's withdrawal lent themselves to Hubert Humphrey with notable lukewarmness, ready to jump to Kennedy if he could demonstrate that the country wanted him.

The situation dictated Bobby Kennedy's strategy, which was, as Adam Wallinsky put it, to win a presidential nomination in the streets. Like JFK, he had to run outside the establishment while seeking establishment support; like JFK, he had to stand as the second choice of the liberals and endure their skepticism without cutting what ties he had to them; like JFK, he had to prove that he was the candidate with the greatest personal appeal. Carrying both the memory of his brother and his own near-mythic presence, he demonstrated an almost fanatical following of his own among the underprivileged—the blacks, the Chicanos, the poor whites of Appalachia—and among the lower-middle-class blue-collar ethnics who revered his family's success story. When one added to this the fact that most of the liberal intellectuals and political pros could accept him as a presidential candidate, it was manifest that he alone could revive the old Roosevelt coalition.

His campaign showed, in addition, that of all the presidential candidates, he stirred the most passion. There were exceptions. WASP small-town Indiana treated him coolly, and Oregon, a predominantly middle-class state with a suburban ethos, dealt him his family's first electoral defeat—but in the main his travels around the country took on the appearance of a nearly continuous mob scene. A rally in a Washington, D.C., parking lot a few days after the announcement of his candidacy was described matter-of-factly in the *Washington Post*:

> Thousands of Washingtonians sang, cheered, grabbed at, and nearly pummeled Sen. Robert F. Kennedy . . . last night.
>
> Only a nest of microphones heard anything he said, but the screaming, waving crowd—estimated by police at between 5,000 and 10,000—couldn't have cared less.
>
> They tugged at his coat, they grabbed Ethel Kennedy's hands, they gave him a daffodil, pictures from their wallets, shreds of paper to autograph. Bands of policemen had a difficult time holding them back. . . .
>
> There were people on tops of telephone booths, on roofs, on parapets and in the closed-off street as police tried without success to clear a path for Kennedy to stumble down the steps and make his way back to his car.
>
> He and Mrs. Kennedy squeezed between a brick wall and a swaying panel truck that nearly toppled from the wave of yelling college students, children, and nervous women who smashed against the other side of the vehicle.

> A young blond fainted in front of Mrs. Kennedy and was
> scooped up by policemen and placed in the convertible that
> eventually plowed the Senator and his wife through the throngs
> encircling it. . . .
> On one corner down the street, a couple of Black National-
> ists urged the predominantly Negro crowd not to vote for
> "another whitey," but drew little attention.

The scene was typical in its demonstration of the power of
the Kennedy myth and personality. At times, Kennedy attempted
to talk above the hysteria, as when he urged programs to create
jobs for the poor rather than to dispense welfare to them, or when
he espoused the need for participatory democracy. At other
times, he was carried away by the emotion he created, calling
himself the candidate of "the people" fighting the "political
bosses," blaming Lyndon Johnson for every social malaise, declaring falsely that South Vietnam, in contrast to the United
States, did not draft eighteen-year-olds.

The substance of his campaign had little appeal to the average
middle-class American; as an exercise in the politics of personality,
it touched many middle-class voters with little interest in the issues
that drove Kennedy. Rather naturally then, the campaign became
an effort to intensify the emotions it called forth, even when doing
so at times meant a resort to near-demagoguery. To those who observed him closely, Kennedy's social concern was unquestionable,
but his strategy of using the crowd in a quasi-revolutionary effort
to take the presidential nomination out of the hands of the professionals had frightening implications.

However debatable the plan of battle, it nearly worked. The
night Kennedy edged McCarthy in the California primary, he
regained the momentum he had lost in Oregon and appeared on
the verge of creating an unstoppable public demand to which the
Democratic president makers would accede. Had he secured the
nomination, he surely would have defeated Richard Nixon in
November. It is harder to say whether he would have been an
effective president. His campaign produced no credible plans for
removing America from the Vietnam morass or for redoing the
Great Society in a way that would eliminate poverty and all its
symptoms from the nation's life.

In the last analysis, his supporters could only hope and believe that he possessed the character and strength of leadership to restore a sense of national purpose, but it was a hope that had more merit in his case than in that of any other politician of his day. To many in the United States and elsewhere, he had become a symbol of the American promise. The *Times* of London put it most simply the day he died: "If American Presidents were elected by the suffrage of all countries Robert Kennedy would have gone to the White House next January."

His assassination thus evoked tragedy in all its dimensions. It was the murder of a still-young man at the height of his powers, of the third brother in his family to die in national service, of a potentially great national leader. Finally, it was peculiarly senseless; the young Arab who shot him down might more rationally have attacked dozens of other politicians with closer ties to the American Jewish community and the state of Israel. John Kennedy's death at the hands of a left-winger, after he had refused to invade Cuba and had initiated a process of détente with the USSR, had been equally irrational. Both brothers, one concludes, were victims not of the policies they espoused but of the emotional responses that their personalities and physical magnetism generated among the alienated and the ineffectual.

This as much as anything sums up the Kennedy achievement. As compelling political personalities, the brothers had no peers. They aligned themselves with the dominant political trends of their era; they used the communications media with remarkable skill as a vehicle for projecting their charisma; they combined within themselves and within their constituencies the forces of the old and the new politics. But they were more than unusually talented political tacticians. Their importance stems in the end from the personal impact they made upon their times rather than from what they achieved or even what they stood for. In general, the most intense criticism of both men appears to have come from believers in ideological formulas as the key to political leadership. Those who most lament the fate that cut short their lives are likely to be persuaded, as were the Kennedys themselves, that in the end what matters most is the strength and talent of those who lead us.

6

The Politics of Excess:
Lyndon B. Johnson

Lyndon Johnson surely ranks near the forefront of those political leaders who will be remembered primarily for their negative personal qualities. Crude, arrogant, domineering, he gloried in a style of conduct calculated to emphasize the blemishes in his personality and to obscure his liberal sentimentalism. Although he preferred to think of himself as a conciliator, he is likely to be remembered as a warmonger who propelled his nation into its worst military disaster.

By temperament, Johnson was a man of excess and over-compensation. Assuming the presidency at a strategic moment in American history, determined to outdo all his predecessors, he carried the tradition of his old hero FDR to a breaking point. Wanting love for his benevolence, he overloaded the social welfare system and raised utopian hopes for the total eradication of poverty. Craving respect for his strength and will, he committed the nation to a war it could not win. Convinced that somehow he could resolve the classical dilemma of guns or butter, he put his nation's economy on the road to ruin.

This striving for hyperaccomplishment appears to have been the product of a deep insecurity, derived in the first instance from a difficult childhood, then amplified by the changing conditions of American political life after World War II. Long after the passage of time and the achievement of worldly success should have overcome boyhood traumas, Johnson remained an insecure man, aware that he was held in low repute by an increasingly cosmopolitan political culture. His neuroses reflected in large measure a sense of alienation from the mainstream world of American national electoral politics in the mid-twentieth century.

Possessing the energy and ambition of two men, Johnson drove most ordinary human beings before him. His brilliance at diagnosing political situations and skill in the manipulation of others made him a natural leader in legislative matters that placed a premium on hard work and intricate negotiation. By upbringing and political necessity, he was the quintessential provincial, who achieved recognition in an assembly of provincials, the U.S. Senate. In the larger world, his provincialism was a handicap he could not overcome. Fate seemed to favor him by elevating him to the presidency, an office he could not otherwise have obtained, but the result was to take him beyond his capacities and to leave him repudiated, bewildered, and tormented.

The Way Up

Lyndon Johnson's childhood seems to have been unusually tension-ridden; his parents, who possessed drastically different backgrounds and temperaments, were engaged in a perpetual state of hostility. His father, Sam Ealy Johnson, was a mercurial personality, a real estate trader and commodity speculator who moved the family finances from boom to bust. He drank hard, spun tall tales naturally, and appears to have exemplified the ideal of what W. J. Cash called the rip-roaring, hell-of-a-fellow so common to the hill country South. A Democratic politician of a liberal populist bent, he served several terms in the state legislature. There he made contacts that his son would later find useful, set an example for him as a campaigner, and gave him an ideology he would never abandon.

Rebekah Baines Johnson was from an altogether different mold. Well educated, patrician by temperament and aspiration, and impatient with the crudities of small-town Texas, she provided her children a difficult counterpoint to their earthy father. Granddaughter of the founder of Baylor University and the product of a long line of educated Baptist ministers, she appears to have been fundamentalist in her personal morality, refined in her appreciation of the Victorian arts and literature, and determined to pass her values along to her offspring. Her husband's life-style profoundly offended her. Their marriage strikes one as an unlikely mismatch explicable only on the principle that opposites attract. She also seems to have been a not-uncommon type—the small-town, middle-class housewife who conceives of her mission in life as the transmission of culture and the reformation of the coarse, uneducated male.

The boy himself seems to have been handled badly by both parents. Sam Johnson, a man of considerable virtues as well as ample weaknesses, gave his son examples of courage when he defended the rights of German-Americans during World War I and spoke out against the Ku Klux Klan in the twenties. He also gave young Lyndon a political education. Nevertheless, he could be oppressively domineering and demanding. Intimidating and forceful, he expected much of his children without having given affection easily. He imparted a sense of the requirements of masculinity that would stay with Lyndon Johnson always.

The approval of Lyndon's mother came even harder. Sam Johnson's style was of a piece with the cultural milieu of rural Texas. Rebekah's aspirations for her son—high achievement at school, training in the arts, exemplification of the genteel values—pitted her against young Lyndon's peers as much as against her husband. She had a volatile relationship with the boy in his adolescent years, moving from warm approval when he pleased her to extended periods of stony silence when he engaged in such periodic rebellions as his adamant refusal to take violin lessons. The experience left obvious scars; it was also one from which the young man learned in near-Pavlovian fashion the value of variable and unpredictable behavior in the manipulation of others.

As a schoolboy, Johnson appears to have been the type of child who today would be described as hyperactive—he was restless, seething with energy, frequently incapable of concentration, a mediocre student, and something of a problem for his teachers. When he first rejected his mother's advice that he go directly from high school to college, he did so, he recalled, because he could not stand the thought of being cooped up in a classroom for another four years. The decision reflected both his extra-glandular energy and his preference for action over contemplation.

Rather than attend college after high school, Johnson undertook what was probably a valuable course in the real world. He slipped off with some other boys to California where he picked fruit, washed dishes, worked in service stations, and spent the better part of a year on the fringes of hobodom. This tough and occasionally hungry existence gave him a needed taste of freedom from the difficult situation in which he had grown up, and it put him in sympathetic contact with ordinary people who spent their lives in manual, frequently transient work. He spent another year more comfortably, as a clerk to a well-known Los Angeles criminal lawyer, a cousin of his mother. Returning home in 1926, he worked for several months on a road crew, apparently to the dismay of both his parents, periodically drank to excess, and on at least a couple of occasions came out second best in brawls. Finally, in February 1927, he told his mother he was ready to go to the teachers college at San Marcos.

The oft-told story of Johnson's years at San Marcos is so incredible that the mind rejects belief; yet the testimony is so widespread as to leave no doubt about the facts. Entering the college as a scholarship student despite his poor secondary school record, compelled to work part-time, possessing next to nothing in the way of extra money, he made himself the dominant force on the campus as the president's student assistant, informal appointments secretary, and legislative relations adviser. It is some measure of the limits of his appeal that he himself was never elected student body president; nevertheless, he probably was the school's most powerful student. Before graduating, he became editor of the campus paper, a leading member of the debate team, and an honors student.

Along the way, he took a year off to work as principal and teacher of the Mexican-American elementary school in the small south Texas town of Cotulla. He arrived there, according to local lore, with a wardrobe of one suit and an old pair of dress slacks shiny from too many pressings. Most of his pupils were far more impoverished, and in later years he recalled that the miserable conditions in which their families lived had made a deep impression upon his social conscience. Johnson was a tough disciplinarian —firm, domineering, and, indeed, insensitive. He spanked male students freely, forbade the speaking of Spanish on the school grounds, and treated his Latino charges as if they were little Anglos right down to subjecting them to lectures on the glories of Texas history and the perfidy of Santa Anna. He made them begin each day with a declaration of personal loyalty to him, presumably followed by the pledge of allegiance to the flag. Nonetheless, he momentarily injected some badly needed vitality into the little school, introducing athletics, spelling bees, public speaking contests, and field trips.

Yet Johnson remained singularly dependent upon his mother. She helped him prepare for the entrance examinations at San Marcos, assisted him with some of his schoolwork, and at times polished his editorials for the college paper. "Your letters always give me more strength, renewed courage and that bulldog tenacity so essential to the success of any man. There is no force that exerts the power over me that your letters do," he wrote to her. Forty years later, he would describe his mother with such phrases as "perfect woman," "great lady," "brilliant," "beautiful," "sexy."

Over the long run, however, Johnson appears to have learned more from his father, who gave him whatever political savvy he did not acquire himself. Sam Johnson helped his elder son on many occasions, including the acquisition of his first job in Washington. Even as Johnson relied heavily upon his mother and eagerly sought her approval, his life took on patterns established by his father. As a young man, he did his share of drinking, carousing, and brawling. He became a wheeler-dealer politician, operating out of smoke-filled rooms, cutting compromises in secret, dealing with a good many individuals that his mother would not have considered respectable. He affected a rough Southwestern style of masculinity laced with copious doses of anti-intellectualism. It may tell us much about the sources of Lyndon Johnson's insecurity to understand that his life epitomized so much that he had been taught to despise.

Johnson liked to remember that he had chosen politics as a career that would please both his mother and his father. However, upon graduating from college, he became a high school teacher in Houston. At the same time, he kept his hand in politics.

In 1931, with the help of his father and another politician, he secured appointment as secretary, or chief of staff, to Congressman Richard Kleberg. When he began the long train ride to Washington, D.C., near the end of 1931, slim, hungry, inordinately ambitious, he passed a milestone in his life.

During his early years in Washington, Johnson was a near-caricature of the aspiring young man from the provinces—hard-working, manipulative, and self-promoting. Thrown into the little world of Capitol Hill with other ambitious young men of provincial background, he rapidly established himself as a dominant figure. He put in eighteen-hour days learning his job, doing much of Kleberg's work for him, and riding herd, sometimes roughly, on the rest of the staff. He asked questions incessantly, finding out how things were done on the Hill and where the power lay. For a time he worked also as a House doorkeeper to meet and observe other congressmen. Whenever possible, he watched the proceedings of the Senate; he especially admired Huey Long.

Kleberg assigned him the many constituent requests that came into his office, and he took to signing his name to return correspondence. His dealings with the federal bureaucracy enlarged his knowledge of how Washington worked. Usually successful at obtaining satisfaction for the folks at home, he gradually became known to many of them—especially those most deeply concerned with politics—as a promising young man who got things done. He joined the congressional secretaries' club (the Little Congress), quickly perceived that the organization was run by a tired, middle-aged coterie, and within a year got himself elected its speaker.

He could count on the interest and sympathy of two of the more experienced and important members of the House, Wright Patman and Sam Rayburn. Both had been personal and ideological friends of Sam Ealy Johnson when they served together in the Texas legislature. It was particularly fortuitous that Rayburn, already a nationally known figure high in the House leadership structure, was a bachelor. He would come close to adopting Lyndon Johnson. In the beginning, he was prepared, perhaps even eager, to give the bright, up-and-coming younger fellow a few words of advice every once in a while, a few minutes of company now and then, and, eventually, a key recommendation when the right opportunity came along.

It came in 1935 when President Roosevelt created the National Youth Administration, a New Deal work relief agency aimed at the young unemployed. Johnson lined up the support of Rayburn and other Texas congressmen for the job of Texas NYA director. He understood that the time was right for him to return home and establish a political base from which he could come back to take his place among all the other emissaries from the provinces who made the nation's laws. He also realized that in the Depression world of the mid-thirties, few positions would provide more opportunities for an ambitious young politician. At the age of twenty-eight, he returned to Texas, the youngest state NYA director in the country.

The job was a demanding one, and Johnson handled it superbly. Unlike the directors of the major relief agencies, he had a budget only for salaries and administration. His job was to find work for young people and pay them. He covered the state, meeting with individuals whose occupations ranged from librarianship to construction contracting, making contact with hundreds of state and local officials. He made himself highly visible, and he further developed his powers of persuasion. After six months, he had put eighteen thousand unemployed young people to work. In a typical episode, he perceived that the state highway department, suffering from sharp budget cuts, had enough unused equipment and material for the building of an extensive system of roadside parks. He secured the cooperation of its director, supplied the labor, and benefited all concerned. His successes won notice in Washington. Visiting Texas in 1936, Eleanor Roosevelt made a point of delivering her public congratulations. Aubrey Williams, the NYA's national head, praised Johnson as his best state director. Most importantly, thousands of young Texans knew him as a man who had given them employment in hard times.

Johnson thus was in a strategic position when James P. Buchanan, his home district congressman, died suddenly in early 1937. He quickly announced his candidacy and ran as the most vocal supporter of the New Deal in a field of seven serious candidates. It was a shrewd decision despite the growing tide of conservatism in Texas and despite the national reaction against Roosevelt's Court-packing plan. There would be no runoff. The winner would need only a plurality and Johnson, having distinguished himself from the rest of the contenders, was certain to draw the great bulk of the pro-Roosevelt sentiment. Moreover, whatever the innate individualistic conservatism of most of its inhabitants, the district itself was economically distressed enough that it needed the New Deal—or at least federal money—for such programs as irrigation and rural electrification. It also contained the center of Texas liberalism, the university at Austin.

In such circumstances, it is not surprising that Johnson won with 30 percent of the vote, more than double the total of his closest opponent. Given Roosevelt's own embattled position, the race had drawn national attention. A happy president, vacationing on the Gulf Coast, seized the opportunity to meet his young supporter; delighted with each other, they began a political friendship that endured until FDR's death.

Thanks both to his connections with the White House and his zeal in servicing his district, Johnson was soon a fixture in the Texas congressional delegation. He saw to it that his office handled the needs and requests of individual constituents with unusual dispatch. His relationships with Rayburn and Roosevelt helped bring a large amount of New Deal largesse—water projects, rural electrification, various agricultural assistance programs—into his district. He also sought and obtained powerful allies, including the Brown & Root Construction Company and the millionaire Austin publisher Charles Marsh. Helped by FDR's intercession, he got a seat on the coveted House Naval Affairs Committee; in 1940, he chaired the Democratic Congressional Campaign Committee. He became Roosevelt's most vocal Southern supporter on both domestic and foreign issues. When the war came, he went on active duty in the navy and survived the forced landing of a patrol bomber hit by Japanese fighter planes. In July 1942, he and other congressmen who had gone on military duty without resigning their seats were ordered back to Washington.

In the meantime, Johnson had fought and lost his first senatorial contest. The decision to wage it and the way in which it was resolved both indicated his driving ambition and did much to shape his future career. After 1941, he would be an increasingly complex and ambiguous political figure, searching for a new and surer way up the ladder.

When Senator Morris Sheppard died in early 1941, Johnson leaped at the chance to move ahead. On April 22, 1941, he met with FDR and declared his candidacy literally from the steps of the White House. Roosevelt all but endorsed him, and the word went out through the federal establishment to support him.

The race became a four-way contest between Johnson, Governor W. Lee "Pappy" O'Daniel, a former hillbilly radio personality known for his reactionary views, respected moderate Attorney General Gerald Mann, and Congressman Martin Dies, a vitriolic Red hater and labor baiter who chaired the House Committee on Un-American Activities. Alone among the candidates, Johnson emerged as the all-out New Dealer, military interventionist, and champion of FDR. Surprisingly, he almost won. Leading O'Daniel by five thousand votes two days after the election, he watched late rural returns eat away at his plurality. After several days, O'Daniel emerged the victor with a margin of thirteen hundred votes out of a total of six hundred thousand. Johnson had been counted out. Having been educated in the seamier realities of Texas politics, he would be prepared the next time. He also had learned another lesson: Rooseveltism was no longer a winning issue in Texas, nor was the populism on which Johnson had been nurtured.

The Texas in which Johnson had grown to manhood had been predominantly an agricultural debtor state that felt all the traditional grievances of American populism. A producer of cotton, cattle, and other rural commodities, it faced the economic hazards of volatile, highly competitive markets. Its farmers and ranchers carried heavy burdens of debt. Like hard-pressed agricultural debtors everywhere, they harbored a built-in resentment against the Northeastern financial centers upon which they ultimately were dependent. A strong current of Bourbonism notwithstanding, the old Texas had a tradition of elemental protest politics compatible with New Dealism.

The Texas of 1941 was in the midst of a dramatic change highlighted by the maturing of an oil industry that had been non-existent at the turn of the century and by the emergence of an aircraft industry that would expand rapidly during World War II. The transition from Cotton and Cattle Texas to Oil and Aircraft Texas brought powerful changes in the state's power structure and political climate. Non-agricultural big business interests wielded greater political power, and gained the acquiescence of many ordinary people who identified them with prosperity and economic growth. The new business class exemplified the crudest traits of a nouveau riche bourgeoisie, accentuated by a rampant frontier individualism—conspicuous consumption, intense fealty to the established social order, suspicion and hatred of federal bureaucratic regulation, a loathing of New Deal liberalism and all it stood for.

After the O'Daniel defeat, Johnson undertook what appears to have been a calculated campaign to make himself acceptable to the new Big Mules of Texas politics. He shrilly attacked strikes during the war, voting for virtually every piece of antilabor legislation introduced in the House of Representatives from 1943 to 1948. Once the war was over, he endeared himself to the aircraft industry by becoming a vociferous advocate of an air force twice the size that the Truman administration considered necessary. Although he dodged a vote on the Tidelands oil issue, he told those who were interested that he favored state control of the Tidelands deposits. To be sure, he did not wholly shed his old liberalism, especially on economic controls, which had broad appeal to ordinary people in their roles as consumers, and on agricultural subsidies, which remained quite acceptable throughout Texas. Nevertheless, he had made himself a moderate by local standards and had become more viable as a statewide candidate. By 1948, O'Daniel was retiring, and Johnson was ready for a second try at the Senate.

In the meantime, Johnson's personal life had proceeded along lines which doubtless contributed to his newfound moderation. His emergence from the fringes of poverty had begun with his marriage to Claudia "Lady Bird" Taylor in 1934. Unusually talented and always devoted to her husband, Lady Bird had been left a modest trust fund by her mother. It provided the start-up funding for the first Johnson congressional race. In January 1943, she drew on it again to buy a tiny radio station, KTBC, in Austin, Texas.

Under her active management, the station prospered, aided mightily by a series of favorable Federal Communications Commission rulings that permitted nighttime broadcasting and increased its transmitting power fourfold. Soon it had a national network affiliation and was cranking out cash far beyond what was needed to maintain its operations. The Johnsons began to acquire land, raise cattle on a large scale, and accumulate stock in a local bank. By 1948, Johnson was no longer a hungry young outsider; he told his friends that his family's assets were worth a million dollars. By then also he may have been eying the next step in the construction of his empire—the acquisition of an FCC license to operate the only VHF television channel in the city of Austin. In the style of many other Texans who had participated in the war and postwar boom, he was a highly successful entrepreneur approaching middle age in anticipation of increased wealth. It is hardly surprising that his one-time blazing liberalism became muted; it is remarkable that deep within himself he retained so much of it.

Johnson's decision to go for the Senate in 1948 was among the most critical of his life. He gave up his House seat and seems to have been prepared to become a full-time businessman if he lost. His opponent in a runoff primary was former governor Coke Stevenson, a right-winger friendly to the Dixiecrats. Ironically, Stevenson waffled on the Taft-Hartley Act in order to obtain the endorsement of the state AFL, thus laying himself open to an effective onslaught from the right by Johnson, who advocated state control of Tidelands oil, criticized organized labor, and attacked Truman's civil rights program. In truth, the two men differed mainly in the depth of their allegiances to the national Democratic party.

A million voters split nearly down the middle, and as in 1941, "late returns" began to trickle in from rural precincts, seesawing the count first one way, then the other. Three days after the election, Jim Wells County, one of the most notorious fiefdoms in Southern politics, reported an additional two hundred votes for Johnson, giving him an edge of eighty-seven votes over Stevenson. The fraud was so obvious that a New York or Chicago precinct captain would have blushed with shame, but Johnson made it stick. He secured the backing of the state Democratic Executive Committee by a vote of 29–28; the Truman administration and a number of prominent Washington liberals, headed up by his longtime friend, Abe Fortas, supported him, reasoning that he was a more reliable party man and a safer moderate in his inclinations than Stevenson. Beating back a legal challenge, he kept his name on the Democratic ticket and won the general election without significant opposition.

Johnson was only one among a remarkable group of Democrats elected to the Senate in 1948—Clinton Anderson, Paul Douglas, Hubert Humphrey, Estes Kefauver, Robert Kerr, and Russell Long were the others. In one way or another, they all outshone him—Anderson was a more respected Washington insider, Douglas a better economist, and Long a political operator who appeared to have inherited the intuitive brilliance of his father, the Kingfish. Yet none possessed Johnson's special combination of qualities—his intense ambition, inexhaustible energy, streak of ruthlessness, talent for manipulation, and long experience in the world of congressional Washington. Together these qualities would rapidly propel a fairly young junior senator to the leadership of the Capitol Hill establishment.

Into the Establishment

The Senate that Johnson entered in 1949 took a conscious pride in its position as the "upper house" of the Congress, but its political atmosphere was similar to that of the House. During most of Johnson's career on both sides of Capitol Hill, the Republican party could still reasonably aspire to national majority status, and an old-style conservatism was still the conventional wisdom. A conservative coalition, consisting of most Republicans and a substantial number of rural-oriented Democrats from the South and the West, was dominant on race, labor, and some social welfare issues, but it tended to evaporate when aid to agricultural interests came up for a vote.

The United States was an urban nation, but the ambience of the Congress remained predominantly rural and small-town. Most of its members maintained roots in nonmetropolitan areas. Their values, and frequently their prepolitical careers, were those of the small entrepreneur; and they were prone to belong to organizations that expressed the ethic of the provincial middle class—the Elks, Rotary, the American Legion, the Masons. Such was especially true of the Senate; the House, after all, provided representation for scores of irredeemably metropolitan districts. It would be misleading to describe this mood as an "ideology"; it was a climate of opinion, in many ways more subtle and more pervasive than any articulated ideology.

Another component of the congressional ambience was a broadly shared sense of toleration for the tending of local interests. In 1955, commenting on the proposed deregulation of natural gas, the respected old Vermont senator, George Aiken, remarked that if he lived in some gas-producing state, he probably would support it, but as an advocate of a consuming state, he would oppose it. This perception of an issue as the product of a natural interplay among legitimate interests was typical. Aiken reflected the conviction of most congressmen that opposites— however different their views—had to live and work together in a small club, that the need for a civil atmosphere demanded mutual respect on a personal basis, however forcefully one represented a cause in the legislative process. Few congressmen personally reviled each other or carried their disputes off the floor; of those who did, fewer could claim positions among the influentials of either house.

Embodied in the ethic of tolerance was the realization that all members of Congress had, in Harry McPherson's phrase, "sacred cows," interests or persuasions so central to their constituencies that they dared not fight them. For the Southerner, it was white supremacy; for many Midwesterners, it was the agricultural program; for a Texan like Lyndon Johnson, it was the oil interests. The exercise of tolerance necessary to the conduct of legislative business encouraged a widespread mood of moderation most apparent among the veterans who ran things.

The establishment that largely controlled the day-to-day operations of Congress consisted of men who were in a sense the ultimate provincials, those legislators who, however well they represented the sentiments of their states or districts, had become Washingtonians. They combined the values they had brought with them with a devotion to the Congress as an institution. Having abandoned whatever other ambitions they once had harbored, they expected that their careers would be played out on Capitol Hill. Through long years of service, which usually had led to major committee chairmanships, they had mastered the procedures of Congress and taken on an identification with its ways that verged on a religious commitment.

The men of the congressional establishment possessed certain common characteristics. Most were Democrats, although an occasional veteran Republican such as Joe Martin of Massachusetts in the House or Arthur Vandenberg of Michigan in the Senate—both of whom combined their partisanship with flexibility and geniality—qualified as members. The establishment was heavily Southern and Western in regional identity; the more remote from Washington one's constituency, the more one tended to stay in town and concentrate on legislative business. The Northeasterners, by contrast, were notorious for their four-day weekends. The men of the establishment invariably enjoyed safe seats, permitting the luxury of concentration upon the processes of Congress. Those who played the game most shrewdly could use their growing prestige in Washington to reinforce a position at home.

Suspicious of new ideas, concerned with the techniques of getting things done, emphasizing relationships between personalities, the establishment ostracized the zealots of the Left and the Right. Above all, it admired ability in all the facets of the legislative process—draftsmanship, bargaining, conciliation, mastery of parliamentary procedure. It was natural enough that Lyndon Johnson would attract its attention, but it also was Johnson's good fortune to secure as his sponsors the two great barons of the mid-twentieth century Congresses—Sam Rayburn and Richard Russell.

Although a generation older than Johnson, Rayburn had nevertheless come from relatively similar circumstances and was even more devoted to the populistic values of the Texas farm country. A bachelor whose one attempt at marriage had lasted only three months, he devoted his life primarily to the House of Representatives and secondarily to his brothers and sisters and to the ranch he developed near his hometown, Bonham. Visibly lonely for the son he never had fathered, he from time to time took promising young men under his wing—but always with the understanding that the rules and traditions of the House placed strict limits on the degree of preferment he could give them. Elected House majority leader in 1935 and speaker in 1940, he became a widely respected national figure, increasingly venerated as an incarnation of representative government, a public man of rigid integrity, and an intelligent compromiser who made the legislative process work. He epitomized the values of Capitol Hill and was an ideal patron for an ambitious young congressman.

Richard Brevard Russell, the dominant figure in the U.S. Senate, differed from Rayburn primarily in his patrician origins and outlook and in the intensity of his Southernness. Born in 1897 on the fringes of Georgia's Black Belt, he had been given the name of his father, a prominent attorney, cotton planter, and businessman who twice failed of election as governor before becoming the state's chief justice in 1922. The son was elected governor in 1930, the youngest chief executive in the history of the state. Taking office at the bottom of the Depression and following the example of Governor Harry Byrd of Virginia, he ruthlessly eliminated and consolidated state agencies, cut salaries (including his own), and simplified the tax system. In 1932, he was easily elected to the U.S. Senate to fill out an unexpired term; in 1936, he beat back a challenge from his one-time political ally, Governor Eugene Talmadge. Thereafter, he was invulnerable so long as he deferred to the imperatives of Georgia politics.

The first of these, of course, was white supremacy, discreetly packaged for national consumption as states' rights and strict construction of the Constitution. By 1935, Russell—brilliant, articulate, and highly skilled in parliamentary procedure—already had made himself the leader of a successful filibuster against a federal antilynching bill. By the postwar era, he was the acknowledged master of those Senate votes representing the Southeastern quadrant of the United States and able to swing them almost as a solid bloc in any matter involving race. In the manner of Southern spokesmen from the beginnings of the Republic, he depicted himself as a representative of a maligned agrarian way of life, purer and more noble than the crowded, impersonal hostility that plagued the uneasy tempo of urban America. This justified the other imperative: support for various forms of subsidy to Georgia agriculture. Russell routinely backed the whole spectrum of government enrichment of middle-class farm life—price supports, loan programs, the extension service, rural electrification.

In his foreign policy voting, Russell was a bit less disposed than Sam Rayburn to follow the lead of FDR or Truman, but in general he was a reliable backer of their diplomatic initiatives. In the Southern tradition, he supported the flag once it was committed, and an occasional quibble aside, he had no trouble siding with the escalating military expenditures of the Cold War. (Along with other powerful Southerners, including his Georgia colleagues, Carl Vinson and Walter George, he saw to it that his state contained numerous military facilities.) As a conservative economizer, he tended to be wary of foreign aid programs, frequently offering amendments to cut them and rarely voting for the full package. A nationalist, he was suspicious of any international agreements that might limit U.S. freedom of action or lead to outside meddling in domestic problems—especially the status of blacks. Still, like his fellow members of the Senate establishment, he fit easily into the foreign policy consensus of the forties.

His home base impregnable, Russell was the single most powerful figure in the Senate. By 1949, his sixteen years of seniority had given him tangible positions of strength. He was the key figure on the Armed Services Committee (its chairman beginning in 1951) and exercised authority over tens of billions of dollars in defense spending. Second in tenure among the Democrats on the Appropriations Committee and its de facto chairman, he possessed considerable influence over every section of the federal budget.

It is doubtful that any senator was more widely respected among Washington insiders. He won the awe of his fellows for his character and dignity, his hard work, and his legislative brilliance. Unable to achieve serious consideration for the presidency because of his role as a spokesman for the South, unmarried and single-mindedly devoted to his work, he made the Senate his life. In 1949, the affable Scott Lucas of Illinois had just assumed the formal Democratic leadership, but it took little discernment to realize that the pivotal force among the Democrats was Richard Russell. He would succeed Rayburn as the focus of Johnson's insatiable quest for advancement.

From the start, Johnson aspired to leadership of the Senate. Good luck, hard work, and a consummate skill at personal relationships gave him the prize within four years. First, however, he reinforced his weak Texas power base by continuing his move to the right. He opposed Truman's effort to repeal the Taft-Hartley Act, voted for the Kerr bill to deregulate the price of natural gas, and fought to conservatize the Federal Power Commission, the federal regulator of the energy industry. He made himself one of the leading opponents of Truman's reappointment of Leland Olds, the FPC's most prominent advocate of a tight government leash on the oil and gas interests. With Johnson highly visible near the front of the pack, Olds's opponents insinuated that he was a Red. Shabbily indulging in what eventually would be called McCarthyism, they smeared a devoted public servant instead of grappling with the legitimately debatable policy positions for which he stood. The Olds nomination was defeated, 53–13; Johnson had given the Texas power structure the bona fides it sought.

The drive for leadership of the Senate required infinitely greater subtlety and patience. Drawing on his experience with Sam Rayburn, Johnson instinctively grasped that swift advancement required one powerful patron—Richard Russell. Securing an appointment to the Armed Services Committee, a stroke that put him into almost daily contact with the Georgian, he began a long courtship.

There appeared at first to be little in common between the austere, conservative patrician and the young, flamboyant Texan; and Johnson underscored the differences when he politely but firmly refused to type himself as a neo-Confederate by joining Russell's Southern Caucus. Still, he closed the gap in other ways. His voting record differed little from that of the older man. He uncharacteristically subordinated himself to his adopted mentor. He invited Russell to his home at every excuse, was helpful to him whenever possible, and actually copied Russell's muted business suits and exquisitely polite manner. Russell was impressed by his young acolyte's talent and pleased by the discovery of a kindred spirit who shared his love of the Senate, the parliamentary process, and the give-and-take of politics.

The Democratic party's losses in the 1950 elections became Johnson's good luck. Among their senators ousted at the polls were Lucas, the party leader, and Francis Myers of Pennsylvania, the party whip. To maintain a semblance of party unity, their replacements had to be ideologically ambiguous. Both, in order to function at all, had to be acceptable to the establishment, and especially to Richard Russell. To succeed Lucas, the Democrats chose Ernest McFarland of Arizona, a genial, moderate South-westerner. To replace Myers, they picked Lyndon Johnson.

Neither job had been much sought after. McFarland would soon regret accepting the majority leadership. Johnson had won little more than an honorary position with no authority and little prestige; no other senator seems to have been seriously interested in it. His major activity for the next two years was the chairman-ship of a subcommittee that oversaw Korean War mobilization, a position that won him some favorable notice. As whip, however, he could from time to time be of service to his colleagues, and he would be a natural candidate for the majority leadership, when-ever it might open up. In 1952, McFarland became one of the casualties of the Eisenhower landslide; he was defeated by Barry Goldwater. Johnson, one of the few senators eager for the Demo-cratic leadership, was acceptable to most of his party colleagues other than a handful of Northern liberals. He handily turned back a token challenge from the old Montana wheelhorse James Murray.

At first, he ostentatiously deferred to the inner circle, asking Russell to move to a desk on the Senate floor just behind his. Throughout his tenure, he constantly drew upon Russell's counsel, but he had no intention of serving simply as a dutiful subordinate of the Old Boys. He ran the Senate, employing his capacity for hard work, his instinctive psychology, his talent for persuasion, and, occasionally, his penchant for bullying.

Like most politicians, Johnson had ideological preferences; above all, however, he sought power and recognition. He in-tended to use his position in the Senate—as minority leader (1953-54) and majority leader (1955-60)—to pursue those aims. More-over, although he was to become one of the quintessential Senate Men, he clearly saw the institution as a springboard for the presidency. He also knew that in the 1930s Joe Robinson of Arkansas had made the Democratic leadership into a post of considerable strength and influence. He intended not only to emulate Robinson's example, but also to make himself a national figure in a way that Robinson never had been.

His job had little inherent authority, but it occupied a strategic position from which a resourceful person could create power. He had more information about what was going on in the Senate than any other person in his party, and he could schedule consideration of bills in a way that might affect them positively or negatively, accommodating or inconveniencing their sponsors. Because he was involved in all his party's affairs in the Senate, he could expect a voice in almost everything. Johnson also controlled a limited number of hideaway offices in the Capitol building; they were visible, highly coveted status symbols that within certain limits could be distributed to senior colleagues whose goodwill was vital. Finally, he held substantial authority over the composition of delegations sent on foreign trips.

Other prizes, not inherent in the job, could be established. The leader easily could interest himself in the Senate Democratic Campaign Committee, claim a voice in its decisions, and gain a powerful hold on successful Democrats who felt he had helped them. He also persuaded Richard Russell and the other Senate grandees to allow for a modification of the seniority system to give every young senator a seat on one of the more sought-after committees and thereby put a number of newly elected colleagues in his debt. He managed occasionally to alter the system in other ways that either gratified his friends or punished his enemies.

In addition, he displayed small kindnesses of many varieties for colleagues and other politicians and for employees. There were gifts at Christmas time, offers of financial assistance during crises, birthday remembrances, and attendance at funerals. A considerable amount of calculation lay behind it all, but Johnson equally enjoyed playing the role of Big Daddy. Seldom, if ever, did he hand out favors on a quid pro quo basis; rather, he accumulated goodwill, basked in it, and subsequently used it as a basis to plead for support from the right person in the right circumstances.

The ability to do favors represented only half the story. The other half was Johnson's unusual talent for persuasion and bargaining, one worthy of the most adept horse trader or snake oil salesman. Rowland Evans and Robert Novak have described it in unforgettable terms.

The Treatment could last ten minutes or four hours. It came, enveloping its target, at the LBJ Ranch swimming pool, in one of LBJ's offices, in the Senate cloakroom, on the floor of the Senate itself—wherever Johnson might find a fellow Senator within his reach. Its tone could be supplication, accusation, cajolery, exuberance, scorn, tears, complaint, the hint of threat. It was all of these together. It ran the gamut of human emotions. Its velocity was breathtaking, and it was all in one direction. Interjections from the target were rare. Johnson anticipated them before they could be spoken. He moved in close, his face a scant millimeter from his target, his eyes widening and narrowing, his eyebrows rising and falling. From his pockets poured clippings, memos, statistics. Mimicry, humor, and the genius of analogy made The Treatment an almost hypnotic experience and rendered the target stunned and helpless.

The Johnson treatment was a highly personalized technique, most effective with individuals or small groups. It depended on knowing whom to approach on which issues; it required a knowledge of which buttons to push. It was fine for a small body such as the Senate but utterly useless in the larger world of national electoral politics to which LBJ aspired.

Johnson enjoyed a particularly favorable situation for party leadership. From 1953 to 1958, the Democratic party delegation in the Senate was never larger than forty-nine. An embattled group was more receptive to leadership than a large, characteristically undisciplined majority. At no time, moreover, did he face anything resembling the plight of Lucas and McFarland, who had been ground between the competing demands of a liberal Democratic president and a conservative Senate oligarchy. He was free to be his own man, steer an ideological course that would enhance his standing in Texas politics, and establish his dominance over the Senate as a personal triumph. If he received nearly constant criticism from Democrats outside the Senate, he could ignore it as irrelevant to the task at hand, never fully realizing how wounding it was to his White House ambitions.

Viewed from almost any perspective, Johnson's accomplishment was impressive. Never the absolute master of the Senate, he managed to control it more often than not. Rejecting the role of an obstructionist, he put together a positive record of moderately liberal legislation: a compromise increase in the minimum wage, a substantial public housing authorization, the addition of disability payments to the Social Security System, and the civil rights bills of 1957 and 1960. He quietly engineered the censure of Joe McCarthy in 1954. In 1958, he blocked legislation designed to curb the power of an increasingly liberal Supreme Court. Even a major heart attack in 1955 could do little more than put him out of action for several weeks. Aside from Eisenhower himself, no man in Washington was more formidable.

Although Johnson, in tandem with Sam Rayburn, established himself as leader of the congressional Democrats, he did not become the leader of the larger Democratic party that nominated and elected presidents. One of the most successful of American politicians, he was nevertheless singularly ill equipped by virtue of his temperament, personal style, region, and ideological front to capture a Democratic presidential nomination.

Politically, Johnson attempted a precarious balancing act throughout the fifties. He was an effective spokesman for the interests and outlook of his home state, so much so that he faced no significant opposition in the 1954 Democratic senatorial primary. But he also had to avoid being typed as a diehard conservative Southerner. He sought a compromise by depicting himself as a moderate and a Westerner.

The strategy seemed to fit the popular mood of the Eisenhower era. It was consistent with Johnson's home state politics (Eisenhower carried Texas in both 1952 and 1956), and yet it allowed for concessions to the liberals. Johnson usually followed a course of friendly cooperativeness toward the Eisenhower administration, from time to time depicting himself as a better supporter of the administration's more "modern" proposals than the numerous Republican right-wingers. He also supported liberal initiatives to the extent he deemed it feasible—even public housing, even civil rights.

Texas would tolerate various mild liberal deviations so long as he remained safe on such issues as organized labor and energy production. Moreover, as a man who was supremely result-oriented, he wanted to produce legislation, and he was ever willing to make compromises to do so. The liberal intellectuals failed to perceive his moderate reformism as home state heresy and found his compromising penchant positively repellent. Absolutists by temperament, they advocated political tactics that would reject compromise, sharpen the issues, rally the Democratic coalition, and put an unhesitating liberal reformer in the White House. What Johnson rejected as impractical, they found irresistible.

Throughout his years as Senate Democratic leader, Johnson clashed incessantly with the more ideological Northern liberals such as Joseph Clark of Pennsylvania, Paul Douglas of Illinois, or Herbert Lehman of New York. Such men were relatively insignificant in the politics of the Senate, but they and their supporters defined the outlook and aspirations of the Democratic presidential party—Northern and urban, oriented toward minorities and organized labor, pointing toward a new age of reform that would take America beyond the New and Fair Deals. Johnson's failure, indeed his inability, to identify himself with this group foredoomed his curious try for the presidency in 1960.

Johnson's 1955 heart attack had aborted his first dip into presidential politics. He had hoped to set off a small boomlet that would establish him as a national figure of White House stature, enlarge his range of contacts around the country, and perhaps gain him the vice-presidential nomination. Had he been nominated for the vice-presidency, the campaign experience would have been invaluable and might well have changed his career. As it was, the coronary took him out of the running, reduced him to a peripheral figure at the 1956 Democratic convention, and left him little more than the task of swinging the Texas delegation to a young senator whom he hoped to make into a reliable Capitol Hill loyalist—John F. Kennedy.

Johnson thus was in a poor position to move for a presidential nomination in 1960. Tied close to the Senate by his impulse to be a strong, effective party leader, he refused to enter the primaries and sought to transform weakness into strength by using the upper house as the basis for an unannounced campaign. He seems to have believed that success as a legislative leader, joined with the respect and support of powerful colleagues, would deliver him national esteem and the nomination after his rivals had knocked each other out in the primaries. It was a remarkable, indeed almost inexplicable, miscalculation.

Johnson seemed innocent of the fact that high standing in the Senate was, if anything, a liability in presidential politics. At best, legislative skills did not attract the popular imagination; at worst, they conjured up images of unprincipled back room dealing. Nor did the rural Southern and Western style, so natural and so pervasive in the Senate, appeal to the large masses of metropolitan voters who formed the core of the Democratic presidential party. Johnson's Texas-country-boy-made-good style, his displays of wealth, his old-fashioned oratory—all seemed corny, even vulgar, to many of the people a Democratic presidential candidate had to attract.

Finally, Johnson showed little understanding of the structure of the Democratic party; he appeared to confuse power within the Senate with control of the politics of the individual states. In state after state, the dominant powers were the governors, the city bosses, state and local party chairmen, labor or farm leaders, racial, ethnic, or religious spokesmen, liberal activists. At most, senators might be co-equals, possessing their own organizations; at the least, they were creatures of the machines that had put them in office. Even those with independent followings tended to have little leverage in other contests, and, operating from Washington, they could exert scant influence in a matter as local as convention delegate selection. One Democratic senator after another pledged his support to Johnson, but few were able to deliver living, committed delegates. Kennedy in the meantime paid little attention to the Senate but worked skillfully at the game of modern American politics—forming grass-roots organizations to attract unaffiliated activists, negotiating with traditional pols, utilizing the media with consummate skill, and projecting an image with incalculable appeal to the rank-and-file of the Democratic presidential party.

One must wonder if Johnson really failed to sense what was happening. He was a shrewd man, especially adept at the analysis of political structures. His peculiar try for the presidential nomination may have reflected in part an understanding of his own limitations as a national candidate. Yet until he demonstrated to the world that he could win votes outside the old Confederacy, how many Northern political bosses would support him? His noncampaign may also have reflected his deep personal insecurity. Afraid of rejection, he could make the Senate almost a hiding place and use his position as Senate Democratic leader as a built-in excuse if Kennedy prevailed.

Easily overwhelmed by the Kennedy juggernaut, Johnson was offered the vice-presidential nomination. His advisers were nearly unanimous in their opposition; yet he accepted, and despite the powerlessness of the office, despite the shakiness of the Democratic chances in November, he had made a sensible decision. The vice-presidency was the only chance he had left to establish a national constituency, and it offered a way out of the potentially difficult situation he would face as Senate Democratic leader. If the Republicans won the election, Nixon would precipitate bitter divisions. He was young, partisan, aggressive, and intensely hated even among Democrats who had liked Ike. Johnson would have been forced to lead an intense, vituperative opposition, a role that was unlikely to play well in increasingly Republican Texas. If Kennedy became president, the Senate leader would find himself trapped between the conservatism of the establishment and the liberalism of the White House. He would be frequently blamed for defeats, rarely given credit for victories, and placed in political jeopardy at home. In contrast, the vice-presidential nomination held out the promise of an honorable position that at worst would be a distinguished culmination for a remarkable career and at best could serve as a stepping-stone to the higher office that Johnson so coveted.

Johnson's hard campaigning through the South was vital to the Kennedy drive. It surely made the difference in Texas, perhaps in Louisiana, and in some other states as well. The vice-presidential candidate figuratively—and almost literally—shed blood for the ticket when he and his wife found themselves jostled and reviled by a mob of angry right-wing Republicans in Dallas. The incident created a backlash of sympathy that apparently convinced many Texans to vote Democratic on the theory that a ballot for Nixon could be taken as an endorsement of violent rowdyism. It demonstrated to the nation as nothing had before just what sort of political setting Johnson had been forced to function within; thereby, it created at least a small glimmer of sympathy and understanding among the liberals.

The new vice-president reaped meager rewards for his efforts; even more keenly than most of his predecessors, he found the position frustrating. He was, it was true, among the more visible vice-presidents of American history, making some eleven foreign trips in less than three years to points on the globe as diverse as West Berlin, Turkey, India, and Vietnam. He was given a considerable amount of authority over the burgeoning space program; he presided over equal employment opportunity enforcement for government contractors and developed good relations with prominent civil rights leaders. Yet he no longer could exercise power in the ways that had been so important to him. He had hoped to be able to continue as de facto Senate majority leader, but he quickly discovered that was unacceptable to the Senate Democrats. He soon realized that on matters of patronage or legislation, he no longer had the clout of a Sam Rayburn or a Robert Kerr.

His inability to command and dominate appears to have caused him to engage in a process of psychological withdrawal. Repeatedly, he passed over opportunities that he should have sought to speak in Northern cities and thereby enlarge his political base. He rarely offered his services to the Kennedy congressional liaison team (which itself acted foolishly in not seeking them more avidly). Reportedly, he was uncomfortable at the various state affairs Kennedy arranged for the great figures of the American world of arts and letters. From time to time, he displayed acute symptoms of inferiority about what he perceived as his cultural deficiencies and lack of social graces. The president good-humoredly but rather disparagingly privately called him the riverboat gambler. In the public eye, he seemed the uneasy country provincial within an administration that prided itself on its style and sophistication.

Increasingly, his powerlessness made him feel trapped and isolated. In general, his relationship with Kennedy was good, and the president treated him with much more thoughtfulness than Johnson himself would later treat Hubert Humphrey. Still, the occasional White House refusal of a Johnson request, the need to measure some Johnson claim against those of competing interests, the inevitable conflicts between rival staffs—all resulted in dozens of insults, real or imagined. From the beginning, moreover, Johnson and Bobby Kennedy displayed a visceral hatred for each other. By 1963, rumor mongers were circulating baseless stories that the vice-president was going to be dumped, and Johnson appears to have lent some credence to them. It was in this atmosphere that John Kennedy was shot and killed.

Well briefed on the issues, well prepared by his experience for the presidency, Johnson nevertheless came to the office under incredibly difficult circumstances. The obvious tangible tasks before him—handling the continuing foreign policy crises in Southeast Asia and elsewhere, picking up the pieces of the Kennedy domestic program in Congress—attracted the most attention. Perhaps, however, the greatest obstacles were within Johnson himself. He had achieved his highest ambition through the death of another man, murdered in Dallas, Texas; he must have known that here and there one heard ugly whisperings that he himself or his backers had been behind the assassination. To a person of his personality structure, it must have been a terribly guilt-inducing situation, compounded by his activist delight in having reached the position of supreme power and his determination to put his own mark on the office.

Typically, he dealt with such impulses by trying to overcompensate. In foreign policy, he sought to display strength and demonstrate to the world that the United States was capable of defending its interests and honor. In domestic policy, he intended to show benevolence and win the love of the people by making himself the greatest reformer of all time. Both designs contained more inherent difficulties than Johnson dared admit. In addition, they would be vitiated by the demons that Johnson carried within himself: the style and image that transformed his most benign impulses into something gross and vaguely repulsive; the insecurity that now led him to believe that flexibility and the moderate way were signs of weakness; the feverish drive that told him he was a failure unless he surpassed all his predecessors.

The Great Society and the Overextension of American Liberalism

The first year or so of Johnson's presidency was the summit of his career. Never before had he been so widely appealing—diffident, dedicated to the program of the murdered former leader, brilliant in his dealings with Congress, standing for election in his own right as a voice of sanity in a contest with a right-wing primitive. Never again would he be as popular. The experience of piling victory upon victory both built his confidence and unleashed aspects of his personality that he at first restrained—his domineering qualities, vulgarity, immoderateness, and jingoism. But through 1964, his energy, his lack of a sense of limits, and even his provincial mannerisms appeared dynamic and refreshing, bringing as they did a feeling of progress to a political world that had been mired in the deep ruts of a conservative stalemate for a quarter of a century.

Suddenly, Lyndon Johnson became the tribune of the liberals. The differences between them had involved styles of conduct, modes of thinking and divergent approaches to the relationship between principle and political expediency. It now became clear that the substance of Johnson's aspirations was more often than not identical to theirs. The cause of economic expansionism, so in vogue among the Kennedy economists, was, after all, part of the atmosphere of twentieth-century Texas. Help for the underprivileged, black and white alike, was an article of faith with roots in the populist heritage of the Johnson family and in Johnson's own experience as a young man. Liberated forever from the constraints of Texas conservatism, he was free to affirm his basic impulses in simple words and a rural accent, compensating for his lack of polish with a plain sincerity and Americanness.

Johnson and the liberals now also found themselves in agreement on the art of the politically possible. The new president realized that, for a season, compromise was no longer necessary. He transformed a feeling of national mourning into a feeling of national unity directed toward enactment of the Kennedy legislative program as a memorial to a national martyr. Unequaled at the art of persuasion, he could now pour forth his torrent of pleas and arguments from the strongest position he ever had occupied, invoking the memory of JFK and asking for help in a time of difficulty.

Possessing favors to trade as never before, he dealt directly and unsubtly with the Republican leader in the Senate, Everett McKinley Dirksen, swapping pork barrel projects and presidential appointments for votes on the tax cut bill or civil rights legislation or some other vital matter. A creature of the Congress, a politician incapable of leading a purely personal life divorced from his profession, he established relationships with leading congressmen and their families that broke down the wall of reserve characteristic of their contacts with Kennedy. Six months after Johnson's accession to the presidency, the tax cut and civil rights bills had been signed into law, having passed in what probably was stronger form than would have been the case had Kennedy survived. The president was now ready to adopt as his own and promote without delay the planned war on poverty.

Johnson's enthusiasm for the concept was genuine. Having lived on the fringes of poverty himself, he felt a deep empathy for the poor. His benevolent impulses, moreover, were reinforced by his need to be loved, by the nagging insecurity that led him to seek affection through the distribution of gifts and benefits to those around him and now to the needy throughout America. Yearning to be identified with social reform programs so large and ambitious as to dwarf the New Deal, the president coined as his own slogan the goal of a Great Society which would bring all Americans into the middle class.

Johnson pressed as hard for this new cause as he had for the Kennedy programs, and he pushed through Congress the Economic Opportunity Act of 1964, an omnibus bill that started up a broad range of educational, training, loan, and assistance programs for the underprivileged classes. Promising an end to poverty, he created an atmosphere of ebullience for a series of measures based on untested assumptions. In mid-1964, few realized the extent to which he was courting disillusionment. He had brought the nation back from a low point in its history, given it a greater sense of domestic progress and momentum than had any president since FDR, and all but guaranteed an election victory.

By mid-1964, Johnson had won the solid support of the American people. It was terribly important to him to be more than simply the executor of John F. Kennedy's presidency. Thus he was not simply justifiably annoyed when Robert Kennedy angled for the vice-presidency; he felt positively threatened. In his worst moments, he had visions of the Democratic convention stampeding away from him to nominate JFK's brother. He proclaimed with transparent circumlocution that he had decided to exclude any member of his cabinet from consideration for the second place on the ticket. Thereafter, he unabashedly dangled the prize in front of several prominent Democrats and kept them all waiting for his decision until he could announce personally to the delegates that he had chosen Hubert Humphrey. Although he could not avoid a memorial session for JFK, the convention was otherwise a vast tribute in which he gloried.

By nominating Barry Goldwater, a candidate who came across as a know-nothing reactionary bent on repealing the New Deal and starting World War III, the Republican party had made Johnson the consensus choice for the presidency and had guaranteed him overwhelming congressional majorities. A warm and affable man, Goldwater nevertheless espoused an aggressive frontier individualism more appropriate to a John Wayne movie than to the realities of the modern world. To vast numbers of Americans, he appeared dangerous, almost sinister. Johnson, by contrast, seemed appealing and humanitarian. He won the support of much of the corporate business establishment and many liberal or moderate Republicans. As the returns came in on election night, he reveled in a popular landslide even greater than those obtained by his old hero FDR. Johnson later told Doris Kearns: "For the first time in all my life I truly felt loved by the American people."

During the two years that followed, Johnson presided over an avalanche of social legislation—another civil rights bill, Medicare, aid to education, housing and urban development programs, increased Social Security benefits, enlargement of the multiple antipoverty efforts, even the subsidization of American "culture" through the establishment of National Endowments for the Arts and the Humanities. Formulated by task forces heavily weighted with academic social scientists, the Great Society programs represented the apogee of American liberal thought in the mid-sixties. Economic growth, so the assumption ran, would create the dividends necessary to pay for a wide range of social welfare efforts, eliminate poverty, and substantially equalize opportunity; the transformation of American society was within sight and would be managed without the friction of redistributionist politics.

For Johnson himself, the prospect had an almost miragelike allure. He was convinced that this was the way to the hearts of the

American people and, eventually, to the esteem of the historians. Typically, he demanded everything at once. In 1965 alone, he bombarded Congress with sixty-three separate messages requesting a multitude of important programs.

He understood that however much he might like to interpret his election triumph as a fond personal endorsement, it actually had been as much a vote against Goldwater. No doubt he shared the broader liberal impression that the time had come to put through urgently required proposals that had been gathering dust for the past ten to twenty-five years. Able to draw upon an overpowering Democratic congressional majority receptive to his lead, cultivating and neutralizing key members of the Capitol Hill leadership, mobilizing the leadership elite of America—union presidents, civil rights spokesmen, corporate directors, eminences of the professoriat—he got most of what he requested.

The result, of course, was not that for which he had hoped. By the end of 1966, the United States was experiencing considerable disorder and self-doubt. In the fall elections, the Democrats lost forty-seven seats in the House of Representatives. It was already clear that things were going wrong, but it was much harder to say why. No single answer seemed sufficient, but several answers in the aggregate explained the growing prevalence of discontent.

The domestic effects of the Vietnam War lay behind much of the public mood. Most tangibly, the war, financed by heavy federal deficits, spun off an inflation that contributed to social tensions and public unease in the way that inflation normally does, and it inevitably drained money away from many Great Society programs. The bitter debate about the war unavoidably carried over into domestic politics, casting doubt upon Johnson's accomplishments and focusing the wrath of the dissenters upon the Great Society as well as upon Southeast Asia.

Other problems, however, were inherent in the Great Society itself and in Johnson's methods of promoting it. It was by no means the well-formulated agenda that many people had taken it to be. The haste with which it had been rushed through Congress had discouraged careful examination of practical administrative problems and thoughtful debate about ideological implications. By dumping dozens of antipoverty and social welfare programs upon the political system, Johnson and his liberal followers grievously overburdened it.

Even the less controversial efforts, such as Medicare and Medicaid, were bedeviled by large-scale fraud, and numerous antipoverty programs became disaster areas of waste and corruption. In Washington, D.C., the local employment service, under Labor Department orders to recruit the hard-core unemployed for job-training programs, lured heroin addicts off the streets with $50 advance payments, signed them up, and let them float back into the drug culture; the result was to provide the bureaucrats with statistical proof of their success in grappling with a problem while actually having done nothing toward its solution. In other cases, the war against poverty enabled local politicians and their cronies to line their pockets and build political organizations.

The administration did little about such abuses, save when they became public. Johnson was persuaded that they would discredit and eventually destroy the Great Society; better to hush them up and to hope they could be resolved internally. "I knew that the moment we said out loud that this or that program was a failure, then the wolves who never wanted us to be successful in the first place would be down upon us at once, tearing away at every joint," he remarked privately. But was the public really so simpleminded? The president's attitude was intensely personal; much as de Gaulle confused himself with the nation of France, Johnson considered himself the embodiment of the Great Society. His fear of rejection provided a powerful motive for his refusal to face the practical difficulties of antipoverty welfarism more directly.

The result was a crisis of the spirit for American liberalism and for the country as a whole. While some of the Great Society's academic formulators considered it a series of "income transfer" programs, they had not presented it as such to Congress, and they evaded debate about the goal of income redistribution. Moreover, there was little preparation for the economic dislocations of massive social welfare spending, including diminished work incentives and an increasingly serious inflation. Among welfare recipients there suddenly emerged a sense of entitlement at variance with all past American tradition. Where the New Dealers had stressed the importance of work in exchange for federal benefits, advocates of "welfare rights" in the 1960s denounced work requirements. Soon such a position was the new orthodoxy of American liberalism. Tied in with the demands of a black population growing more and more militant, it became one of the major issues that precipitated the alienation of "middle America" from the administration and from the liberal ethos.

In the end, the results were disappointing. Johnson had established as a goal the elimination of poverty, and his supporters proudly displayed statistics that seemed to show that eight million people had been lifted out of poverty during his presidency. Yet the slums of urban America, many of them ravaged by riot, appeared as vast and inhospitable as ever; welfare costs climbed in a steep spiral; and the culture of poverty seemed untouched by his efforts. No doubt, he had succeeded in lending aid, comfort, and opportunity in tens of thousands of individual success stories, but he also had demonstrated that in the larger view, poverty involved more than the pocketbook.

Johnson's desire to be remembered as the second Great Emancipator suffered an even harsher disappointment. No president ever had done so much to aid the black community. Legislation labelled "civil rights" was hardly half the story; a large portion of the antipoverty drive was aimed primarily at blacks. But during the Johnson presidency, the black revolution reached its violent peak, leaving the president hurt and baffled and American liberalism confused and demoralized. After having given the civil rights establishment almost everything it had asked for, Johnson found himself facing a new wave of black militance with which he could not communicate. Dealing with Roy Wilkins or Martin Luther King and understanding the fundamental legitimacy of their demands had been easy enough. Here Johnson had been ahead of a majority of American whites, but not so far that he was unable eventually to carry them along. The fury of the militants was nearly impossible to manage.

During Johnson's first summer in office, angry blacks had engaged in isolated rioting in a few Northern cities. In 1965, the Watts section of Los Angeles had erupted. In 1966, Stokely Carmichael and other hitherto unknown blacks launched themselves into national notoriety screaming the slogan "Black Power." To be sure, the black power movement reflected in some ways a new sense of racial pride, but it asserted even more a rejection of the white America that the civil rights integrationists had wanted to join. Where the old movement had reflected the concerns and styles of the segregated Southern black and of the black middle class, the new movement expressed the rage of the Northern black urban underclass, especially its younger spokesmen. More than a protest against such relatively tangible matters as poverty and discrimination, it was also an expression of alienation from the larger society so deeply felt that neither the old civil rights leaders, the president, nor the liberal establishment could fully comprehend it.

Some liberals dutifully accepted every accusation of guilt, abandoned old-style integrationism, and docilely bared their backs to the lash as if they were slaves on a particularly harsh antebellum plantation. Others clung to the values of the older-style movement, but all took up the argument that "white racism" was the fundamental explanation for black-white divisions in American life and, by implication, an excuse for every manifestation of black militance, no matter how extreme. For Johnson, both as a political leader and as a private person, the adjustment was not so easy.

As a political leader, he felt his coalition crumbling under him. The charges of white racism bitterly divided the Democratic party, pitting white liberals and their black allies against the working-class white ethnics who so often found themselves in competition with blacks for jobs and housing. Johnson privately rejected the Kerner Commission's endorsement of the white racism thesis, and he understood that "law and order" was more than a code word for repression to most Americans. His public addresses, whether delivered to police conventions or black organizations, tended to emphasize themes of reconciliation and positive assistance to the black population. Yet in striving for a tone of moderation in what was becoming an era of extremism, he succeeded only in forfeiting his credibility with each side.

As a private person, he alternated between understanding the anger of many blacks and feeling wounded at their lack of appreciation for his accomplishments. In a philosophic mood, he was capable of remarking that he had after all done little more than raise the position of blacks from D+ to C−; he could understand their militance. And he always had realized that black leaders had to avoid an Uncle Tom label. But Martin Luther King's obdurate self-righteousness, his aloofness from the establishment, his brinks-manship in dangerous situations, his refusal to play the political game all alienated Johnson, who soon was referring to him as "Martin Lying King" and avoiding meetings with him. The un-varnished militants, the violent black racists, were properly enough beyond his tolerance, perhaps really beyond his comprehension. Assailed from the Right for his advocacy of civil rights and antipoverty legislation, he encountered little appreciation on the Left. The experience must have been profoundly embittering.

To American radicals, motivated by the vision of an egali-tarian democratic socialist polity, the fading dream of the Great Society was just one more not unexpected, not unwelcome, indi-cation of the bankruptcy of American liberalism. Their point of view, increasingly influential in the intellectual community, was aptly summarized by the economist Robert Lekachman:

> Perhaps Mr. Johnson went just about as far as a conservative politician in a conservative, racist country could have gone. The Great Society has distributed the nation's income even less equally than it was distributed before 1960. It has enlarged the prestige and influence of the business community. It has lost its token bouts with racism and poverty. The Great Society, never a giant step beyond the New Deal which was President John-son's youthful inspiration, has ground to a halt far short of a massive attack on urban blight, far short of the full integration of Negroes into American society, and far short of a genuine assault upon poverty and deprivation.

For many radicals, the United States was a more malign nation at the end of Johnson's administration than at its beginning. Underneath its surface prosperity and reformist aspirations, it was dominated by militarism and corporate capitalism. It op-pressed its poor and its minorities by refusing to engage in the meaningful economic restructuring which would lift them from poverty, and it oppressed its noncorporate middle classes by subtly stifling free thought in their educational institutions and inflicting a deadening sameness upon their lives.

For others—many of them once its enthusiastic supporters—
the Great Society was a disillusioning experience that led them to
question the liberalism in which they once had possessed un-
doubting faith. It seemed instead to show that government could
be too heavy-handed, too inefficient, too insensitive to manage
complex social problems. Some thinkers began to talk of the
futility of throwing dollars at a situation. Others began to question
the whole complex of assumptions that lay beneath American
liberalism—its faith in the plasticity of human nature and institutions, its assumption that people were fundamentally good and
that social engineering was fundamentally beneficient, its tendency to reject the values of private capitalism as crass and
greedy, its apparent indifference to social disorder in the name of
change.

The result of this reevaluation would be a retreat to a more
cautious reformism, characterized by a sense of limits and a
receptivity to values of traditional conservatism. It would manifest itself in the social policies of Johnson's successor.

Vietnam, the National Interest, and the Diplomacy of Power

Lyndon Johnson was hardly the first American president to come
to power with no claim to expertise in diplomacy. However, he
probably was the most ill prepared by virtue of experience and
temperament to conduct a measured foreign policy that would
clearly define the national interest and to employ force with
caution. Neither Johnson's education, experience, nor travel had
given him much of a sense of the larger world. His geography
appears to have been wretched and his sensitivity to cultural
differences virtually nonexistent. His numerous foreign assignments as vice-president were memorable primarily for their
gaucheries—his exultant war whoop within the Taj Mahal, his
haggling with native merchants, his insistence upon such elaborate
stopover accommodations as oversized beds, needlepoint shower
sprays, and cases of Cutty Sark scotch. Where John Kennedy had
used his extensive travel quite consciously as a means of education, Johnson traveled as if he were determined to minimize his

exposure. Narrowly educated and personally insecure, he was uneasy with the wider world.

For all his successes in imposing his will on others, for all the wealth and position he had acquired, Johnson was—by his own account—often a lonely and frightened man, periodically gripped by desperate feelings of anxiety. Beneath his arrogant facade, he was still the uncertain youth striving for success, seeking recognition and approval from parents and peers. Having grown up in a culture that celebrated aggressive masculinity, he took refuge in a self-image that exaggerated even the egocentric individualism of rural Texas. He compared himself to the rider at the head of a stampede, attempting to turn back a frightened, dangerous herd of cattle; he pictured himself as the man of strength facing down a foe at high noon. Inclined toward toughness almost as a reflex, he conceived of every foreign policy challenge as personal. He was not predisposed to weigh ends and means or to separate critical interests from peripheral ones. He turned naturally toward displays of strength and resolve, coupled with the use of force.

To these personality traits, Johnson added other characteristics commonly associated with the politician—a heavy reliance upon experience and a tendency toward caution. But these were not necessarily moderating influences. His relevant experience, like that of other men of his generation, came from Munich and from the failure of Western nerve in the 1930s. It resulted in the still widely held assumption that tolerance of any aggression anywhere represented a grave danger to all peoples everywhere. His politician's caution focused on the experience of McCarthyism. Johnson remembered vividly the way in which the Truman administration had been crippled for its alleged softness on Communism, and especially for the loss of China. McCarthyism had been the ultimate weapon against Truman's Fair Deal. Any losses in the Cold War, any signs of softness might wound the Great Society every bit as much as military conflict. Personality, experience, political calculation—all brought the president to the same conclusion.

Johnson's attraction to the hard line became apparent at first in his dealings with Latin America. For months, he refused to negotiate with Panama after its citizens rioted for control of the Canal Zone. When he finally agreed to discuss renegotiation of the Panama Canal treaty, he did so with little intention of reaching an agreement—and there would be none until the administration of the next Democratic president. Confronted with a revolution in the Dominican Republic, fearful that some of the revolutionaries were Communist or Castroite, he sent troops to enforce a cease-fire and establish a pro-American (if moderate) government.

Johnson's reaction to his critics was revealing; he dug in, characterized his opponents as Communist dupes or sympathizers, and lamented that he was being crucified for protecting the nation. Stubborn, prone to feel persecuted, lashing out at criticism, he demonstrated that he lacked the cool balance necessary to conduct a foreign policy and rally support for it at home.

When Johnson became president, he was quite familiar with Vietnam. Three months after taking office as vice-president, he had headed up a delegation to South Vietnam and had returned to Washington urging firm support of the Diem government. Nevertheless, he did inherit an ongoing policy that had been largely created by others. One of the strongest and most constant themes of his defense of military involvement in Vietnam was his insistence that he was following through on a course that had been laid down by John F. Kennedy. One need not dispute the sincerity of this belief in order to observe that at some point Vietnam became Johnson's responsibility, that in the process of continuing Kennedy's commitment, he took the United States into a conflict so different in degree that it became different in kind. He did so in part, no doubt, because he was carried along by the momentum of Kennedy's direction and by Kennedy's holdover foreign policy advisers. But in greater part, Johnson was receptive to the escalation of conflict in Vietnam because it fit his own temperament. He was too insecure to reexamine Kennedy's earlier moves or to give serious consideration to withdrawal in the face of an armed challenge. Ultimately, his own determination to fight Communism in Southeast Asia would outstrip that of the Kennedy people.

Typically, Johnson increased the American commitment in a series of responses to provocations. The Gulf of Tonkin incident produced not only a retaliatory air strike but also a congressional resolution giving the president open-ended authority to employ

American power in Southeast Asia. An attack against American military advisers in Pleiku precipitated the regular bombing of North Vietnam and the dispatch of the first large-scale U.S. combat units. When Johnson assumed the presidency in November 1963, seventeen thousand American troops were stationed in Vietnam. A year later, the number had increased to twenty-three thousand. During the first half of 1965, the total reached seventy-five thousand.

Guided, to be sure, by most of the holdover Kennedy foreign policy aides, Johnson had already gone far toward turning a relatively small, reversible commitment into a major military operation. Out of his depth in assessing issues of national interest or strategic considerations, he accepted an inflated estimate of the importance of Vietnam. He had neither the security nor the independent judgment to withdraw the small, largely noncombat U.S. presence in 1964 or early 1965 and let the American-supported government in Saigon fall of its own weight. At the same time, his instinctive political caution and his lack of self-assurance restrained him from proclaiming an all-out commitment to the independence of South Vietnam. Incapable of decisive action in either direction, he would find himself presiding over the worst of all possible worlds—for the morale and vitality of his country, and for himself.

The conflict that followed—not officially a war, of course—was the most contradictory and confusing in American history. At times, Johnson defended it with rhetoric appropriate to total war, asserting that to abandon a stalwart ally such as South Vietnam would be to place in jeopardy the entire post–World War II international order upon which rested the security of the United States. "There are great stakes in the balance," he declared in a notable address at Johns Hopkins University in 1965. "Let no one think for a moment that retreat from Vietnam would bring an end to conflict. . . . The central lesson of our time is that the appetite of aggression is never satisfied." Yet in the same address, he also offered friendship and extensive economic assistance to North Vietnam, right down to what journalists widely characterized as a TVA for the Mekong River Valley. Was North Vietnam an enemy or not? Were the stakes really as high as Johnson claimed? If so, why did he talk at times of concessions and friendship rather than total victory? Why at other times did he condemn "nervous Nellies" for not wanting to see the conflict through? And why did he exhort American troops to "nail that coonskin to the wall"?

The manner of waging the war was equally confusing. The world wars and Korea had been accompanied by reserve call-ups and conscription, by sharp slashes in domestic federal spending, and by economic controls to mitigate the inflationary pressures of greatly increased military spending. Johnson shrank from such commitments. He believed that mobilization of the reserves would have negative political reverberations at home, create a world diplomatic crisis, and denude the military of a ready force for employment elsewhere in the world. Instead, he planned to meet manpower needs through the use of the draft. Unwilling to cut appropriations for the Great Society programs, to install politically unpalatable and economically dubious controls, or to advocate increased taxes, he hoped that somehow the war could be fit into the economic expansion over which he presided. The military buildup itself became one of step-by-step escalation in bombing levels and military strength with each step purportedly the last or at least close to the last. At each point, administration spokesmen claimed, a small ray of light was visible at the end of the tunnel.

The style of combat was bewildering. The ground war was fought guerrilla-style with no well-defined front line and with great ambiguity about who and where the enemy was; for the American soldier, and ultimately the American populace as a whole, it became uncertain whether the war was being fought to save the Vietnamese people from Communism or whether the masses of the Vietnamese were the Communists against whom the war was being waged. The air war was managed with restrictions far more sweeping than those employed in Korea. Not only was China off limits, as it had been in the earlier conflict, but so was a vast range of targets in North Vietnam. The United States had not hesitated to bomb Japan, Germany, or North Korea into the stone age; the Johnson administration, however, was unwilling to countenance the overwhelming application of explosive power that would have rendered North Vietnam incapable of fighting. To do so, Johnson had convinced himself, would be to bring China, Russia, or both into the war. Perhaps so; but this may have been another manifestation of the caution and insecurity that marked Johnson's foray into a war that he did not quite understand and could bring himself neither to win nor lose.

This insecurity revealed itself in the way the war became an obsession, demanding his personal attention down to the smallest detail. Fearing excesses that might enlarge the conflict, he designated bombing targets, acquainted himself with the details of troop life, and learned about the newest weaponry. He was plagued by episodes of uncertainty and found sleep increasingly difficult; awakening in the middle of the night, he frequently sought refuge in the White House War Room.

The president also fought off feelings of guilt and doubt by interpreting disagreement, no matter how discreet, as disloyalty. Systematically he excluded the doubters from access to information, from the decision-making process, and, frequently, from the administration. George Ball, Bill Moyers, McGeorge Bundy, and Robert McNamara all experienced what amounted to presidentially imposed exile.

Johnson's path was especially difficult because Vietnam became the first televised war in American history. A nation already confused about the war could only have its doubts underscored when enterprising journalists filmed combat engagements, the relocation of bewildered peasants, the vice and corruption so open and pervasive in Saigon, the frequent protests against whatever South Vietnamese government happened to be in power, the barbarous treatment that the government meted out to political prisoners, the chaos of the Tet offensive, an occasional summary execution, the destruction of villages that presumably were being saved—all shown within hours of the event at dinnertime in every home in America. Demanding to go anywhere and film anything just as they did at home, and generally allowed to do so, American television journalists displayed to the country the nastiest aspects of a dirty war. They confirmed the fears and prejudices of the opposition, gave it an emotional self-assurance, and won converts for it. They shook the backers of the involvement day after day, gradually eroding their support for the war. Conversely, only an occasional print journalist gained access to North Vietnam, where he encountered tightly controlled exercises in totalitarian manipulation.

The reporters themselves, whether print or electronic, tended to be a new breed of war correspondent. They were highly educated, skeptical of the military, and resistant as a matter of principle to appeals to loyalty or patriotism that might have been used to curb their independence in an earlier era. Frequently more incisive and realistic in their observations than American authorities on the spot, they became rebels against official duplicity and self-deception. Usually liberals of one variety or another, they tended to dislike the American army bureaucracy and to view the South Vietnamese military government as fascistic. They came to see the war as both unwinnable and meaningless. Those with assignments that permitted overt editorializing expressed themselves openly; but the message often crept through in the tone and content of reporting that made an honest attempt to be objective.

In the circumstances, it is surprising that a majority of the nation supported the war for so long—at least when responding to public opinion polls. Gallup, Roper, and the others consistently found that through mid-1967 the public was much more constant and tolerant in its backing of Johnson's involvement in Vietnam than had been the case with Truman's intervention in Korea. But much of the public sentiment was little more than an inarticulate patriotic reflex based on support of the flag, opposition to Communism, and a frequently bitter hostility to the countercultural character of so many of the war's opponents. It was rooted in neither a clear-cut sense of national peril nor in ethnocultural affinities with an endangered people. Much of it was like Johnson's Rio Grande—broad but also shallow and prone to dry up in a difficult climate.

The opposition to the war, on the other hand, came primarily from the trend setters of American life—the intellectuals, the communicators, the middle-class college students. Articulate and adept at organization, they made their presence felt beyond their numbers from the beginning. Some of them proceeded from a reasoned critique of what was after all an ill-considered struggle. Increasingly, however, the vanguard of the antiwar movement became a species of domestic anti-Americanism, radical in politics and cultural styles. It outraged traditional America, to be sure, but it captured the imagination of a privileged, affluent middle class that was receptive to the new and the iconoclastic. By 1968, the country was bitterly divided over not only the war but a wide range of cultural issues for which the antiwar movement provided a focus.

America by then had become a political-cultural Vietnam, subverted by intellectual guerrillas who burned draft cards, expressed contempt for the stars and stripes, smoked pot, rejected conventional sexual mores, and mocked the values that the masses of their countrymen had taken for granted. Numerous developments in post–World War II American life—ranging from abundance to the rise of the intelligentsia to the baby boom to the pill—would have called forth new life-styles, but the war made their emergence all the more dramatic and immeasurably embittered what would have been under any circumstances a difficult confrontation between dominant and insurgent cultures.

The antiwar movement, primarily composed of representatives of the intelligentsia and their children, tended to be privileged and cosmopolitan. Many of its figures were contemptuous of affluence only because it had enveloped their lives to the point of making them feel smothered; their slogan "Make Love, Not War" indicated an expectation of a life characterized by low levels of pain and by an abundance of gratification. As the younger vanguard of an affluent, other-directed society, they confronted a president who had matured in an individualistic, economically impoverished culture, who was profoundly inner-directed in his values, acquisitive by instinct, and incapable of envisioning love and gratification as a given of human existence. Johnson and the dissenters soon developed a mutual hatred derived only in part from differing opinions about the war.

Ogre in the White House

At bottom, Johnson's plight was rooted in a negative conception of himself with which he had struggled unsuccessfully since childhood. As his tenure in office progressed, his attempts to manage this insecurity became increasingly counterproductive. His efforts to compensate resulted in behavior that undermined his public image. In 1964, he had established himself as the Great Healer of American society; by 1968, he had made himself an ogre lurking dangerously in the White House, feared, reviled, and ridiculed almost as if he were Quasimodo.

Throughout his life, Johnson had dreamt periodic nightmares of paralysis or impotence. Always, he was unable to move—tied or caged or the victim of a stroke. In the White House, as the Vietnam crisis deepened, he often dreamt that he had become totally immobilized and speechless, ignored by his advisers, who were bickering over how to divide his authority among themselves. Such dreams were symbolic of a deep fright encompassing his own profound self-doubt and a distrust of others that bordered on the paranoid.

No twentieth-century American president had experienced such profound apprehensions of inferiority vis-à-vis the social and political establishment of which he was the ostensible leader. Always feeling very much the despised provincial, he was especially sensitive to what he came to consider his cultural and educational inadequacies. The intellectuals' hostility toward Johnson was, it is true, much too heavily based upon contempt for his "cornpone style." But Johnson not only reciprocated their dislike; he actually came close to accepting the rationale for it.

The ghost of John F. Kennedy haunted his administration. The guilt-inducing fact of a Texas assassination, the omnipresent memories of Kennedy's polish and charisma, the ever-present threat of Bobby Kennedy—all ate away at Johnson, tapping his intellectual energies, reinforcing his feelings of inadequacy, contributing ultimately to feelings of irrational bitterness toward the martyred president's younger brother. His efforts to cope with these repeated feelings of inadequacy and threats from the outside took forms that ranged from constant activity to blatant egomania to crude domination. The sixteen to twenty hours a day studying reports, talking on the telephone, holding personal discussions, presiding over meetings, selecting military targets—all this became a way to avoid the feeling of fundamental miscalculation, of meriting self-pity, of escaping a sense of defeat or failure. Johnson fully epitomized James David Barber's model of the active-negative personality, frantically attempting to compensate for his unhappiness with himself.

At other times, he gloried in his Lincoln Continentals and his large Texas barbecue parties, in the imperial presidency and all its perquisites. Asked by a young journalist to identify his helicopter from among a group waiting on the White House lawn, he was perfectly capable of replying, "Son, they're all my helicopters!" He ordered the seats on Air Force One repositioned so that they faced the presidential compartment. He thought nothing of having a valet kneel and wash his feet as he conducted business with others. He insisted that photographers take only the "good side" of his face and refused to be photographed next to anyone taller than he. Where John Kennedy had accepted the trappings of wealth and power with a casual elegance, Johnson seemed to insist on their being noticed.

It was legendary that Johnson achieved a heightened sense of himself by abusing and humiliating those who worked for him. His demands for performance assumed that everyone possessed his energy and singleness of purpose—and that those who did not were inferior beings. "I don't get ulcers, I give 'em!" he boasted. He pushed some of his staff members to the point of collapse; he embarrassed others cruelly with his public displeasure. "The price Johnson exacted for the gifts he bestowed upon his aides—personal intimacy, access to the presidential office, power for themselves," Doris Kearns writes, "was often nothing less than their dignity."

Perhaps his most conspicuous target was his vice-president, Hubert Humphrey. Once the happy warrior of American liberalism, Humphrey found himself cut off from his original constituency by his efforts to defend Johnson, yet incessantly harassed by a leader who resented the opposition of the liberals, refused to give the vice-president adequate staff, and insisted upon prior approval of every move. By the time of his nomination for the presidency in 1968, Humphrey was a demoralized individual. His domination by Johnson had been uncomfortably close to an emasculation. Accepting the role of Johnson's faithful spokesman and defender, he forfeited his autonomy and, in Eric Goldman's words, "sounded more and more like a hawkish, maudlin, passé Throttlebottom."

Just as Johnson established his control over those who entered his service, he attempted to gain absolute mastery over everything that came within his reach, including a White House press corps that was fiercely jealous of its independence. In fact,

Johnson's dealings with the press constituted perhaps the most serious group of tactical errors in his administration. Failing to understand their sense of professional identity, he attempted to cut deals with reporters as if he were a senator log-rolling with his colleagues. The approach was unsubtle: Play along with me. Treat me favorably. I'll feed you inside information. I'll make an important person out of you. Few journalists went along, and those who displayed signs of doing so quickly suffered a loss of standing among their peers.

When deal-making failed to work out, the president turned to fits of pique and harassment. If, say, a reporter got advance information on the contents of an important speech, the speech might be thrown out for a declaration on a different subject altogether. If a member of the press had done something, deliberately or not, that offended the president, he might be denied one of the little gifts that Johnson distributed from time to time to those around him.

Worst of all, Johnson indulged in open displays of vulgarity as if to tell a highly influential group of image shapers that they were beneath his notice. The incidents were legion. Generally, reporters, operating under White House rules, treated them as off-the-record; inevitably, however, a few stories became public. At one time or another, the nation discovered that its president was a reckless driver who sped his car down Texas highways at ninety miles per hour with one hand on the steering wheel and the other curled around a cup of Pearl beer; a dog owner who enjoyed listening to his beagles yelp as he pulled them up on their hind legs by the ears; a swimmer who skinny-dipped in the White House pool with his aides; and a recuperated surgical patient who thought nothing of pulling up his shirt and displaying his scar to an entire country.

Yet these intimations of undignified behavior were pale compared to other practices that Johnson routinely engaged in. These ranged from the free use of profanity (his favorite word seems to have been *chickenshit*) to a near obsession with the sexual characteristics of animals (once, showing off a prize bull on his ranch, he asked UPI White House correspondent Frank Cormier, "How would you like to be hung like that?") to an utterly unself-conscious tendency to adjourn meetings to a nearby toilet as he attended to his bodily functions. It was almost as if he managed his feelings of inadequacy about his crudeness and lack of sophistication by flaunting these qualities and taking a perverse pride in them. The emperor, he seemed to reason, was always clothed, and journalists usually found themselves forced to toe the line. More than he realized, however, he must have greatly offended the sensibilities of those who were his primary interpreters to the outside world.

Johnson's more direct confrontations with the American people only underscored the poor image he had built for himself with the press. Television, John Kennedy's great ally, was his great nemesis. In the heady days of 1964, it is true, he had appeared folksy and benign in contrast to Barry Goldwater, and his forceful leadership of Congress had won general approval from a nation ready for new departures and willing to grant a honeymoon period to the successor of a slain president. Nevertheless, his flaws were evident from the start, and as in many marriages, they became increasingly noticed as the honeymoon ended. His lack of polish on television stirred inevitable comparisons to his predecessor. Kennedy had used the frequent televised press conference to project an attractive and authoritative personality; Johnson was unable to do so. Ill at ease in the few scheduled press conferences he held, he exuded evasiveness and insecurity. His discomfort at appearing before a vast audience as a national leader amounted to a statement about his own self-doubt.

His set speeches might at times take on some eloquence, as in his advocacy of the Civil Rights Act of 1965 before Congress, but generally they ranged from the humdrum to the disquieting. When he adopted the pose of a reasoned moderate, Johnson was a dull speaker; when he lapsed into the flamboyant oratorical style of his youth, he was out of key with the temper of metropolitan America. A country whose opinion shapers and educated classes rejected the standards of rural Texas tended more and more to notice the negative: their president lacked the qualities that in combination had made Kennedy so compelling—coolness, glamour, self-assurance, command.

Although he oversaw the conduct of the Vietnam War with nearly obsessive caution, Johnson tended to make emotional public statements that revealed a deep, almost irrational commitment, whether he was telling troops at Camranh Bay of a fictitious grandfather who had died fighting for freedom at the Alamo, flailing away at the nervous Nellies who opposed his course, or utilizing the White House rose garden to award medals to combat heroes. Privately, or at least semiprivately, he indulged in ugly innuendoes about his critics—Walter Lippmann took his cues from the Soviet ambassador; J. William Fulbright, frustrated at not being named secretary of state, had launched himself on an ego trip. With such conduct, Johnson made himself increasingly perceived as a president who was mean and perhaps psychologically erratic. "What may well be a majority of American people are persuaded that the President is a dishonest and dishonorable man," declared Richard Rovere in early 1967.

Victim of the New Politics

Johnson's particular combination of policy failures and personality deficiencies left him especially vulnerable to a style of political opposition derived from the intellectual outlook, organizational skills, and emotional sensibilities of the liberal intelligentsia. Somewhat misleadingly called the "New Politics" by its advocates, it actually was the latest manifestation of a tradition of middle-class reformism that periodically had surfaced in American history and that had provided much of the distinctive tone of early-twentieth-century progressivism. Its proponents were highly educated, affluent, moralistic, and alienated from the worlds of business and commerce. The New Politics dated from Adlai Stevenson's accomplishment in bringing the intellectual and professional classes into grass-roots politics during the fifties, and it reflected the radicalizing effect of the New Left upon those classes.

Advocates of the New Politics conceived of politics as a moral and intellectual exercise and were contemptuous of the jockeying for relatively marginal advantages that characterized the interplay of organized interest groups. They saw themselves as uniquely suited to be protectors of the poor and unorganized, arbiters of the national good, tribunes of peace and order in an irrational world. Their leaders of 1968 and 1972, Robert Kennedy, Eugene McCarthy, and George McGovern, all adopted the same stance of outrage at war, racism, and poverty. All operated on the fringes of the traditional business-as-usual establishment of unions, political machines, and old-line racial and religious organizations. Rejecting conventional pragmatic deal-making, they behaved as crusaders for a just cause. It was no coincidence that Kennedy was the most pietistic male of his family, McCarthy an authority on Catholic theology, and McGovern a former aspirant to the Protestant ministry. Nor was it surprising that they were all in some way devotees of humanistic learning. Kennedy avidly read and quoted classical poetry; McCarthy wrote poetry and would later teach literature; McGovern held a Ph.D. in American history.

The catalyst of the New Politics was the Vietnam War. Vietnam intensified the natural liberal middle-class revulsion from wars that lacked indisputable moral justifications and encouraged doubts about the legitimacy of force under any circumstances. Vietnam also deepened the New Politics outrage at racism and poverty. Black soldiers were a disproportionately large percentage of the American combat forces engaged in a war against other nonwhite peoples who were trying, it was believed, to achieve their legitimate national aspirations. The conflict unquestionably cut into the amount of federal money available for welfare programs at home, leading many liberals to envision it as a war against the American poor. Finally, the New Politics drew heavily upon the indignation of the intellectuals against Johnson himself—against his crudeness, his perceived callousness, his apparent disregard for political principle (ideological consistency) throughout his career, his assumed lack of character.

On all counts, Johnson was vulnerable, but his downfall was surely hastened by the strategic importance of the class he had offended. The cartoons, editorials, columns, and articles denouncing him in such publications as the *New York Times*, the *New York Review of Books*, the *Washington Post*, the *Atlantic Monthly*, and their numerous counterparts represented what had become a consensus viewpoint among an intellectual elite with a mass following of liberal-minded, highly educated middle-class people. This elite jostled up, it was true, against other, more conservative elites in business and allied professions, but these possessed neither the articulateness, the public standing, nor the sense of moral certitude necessary to compete in forums of public discussion on broad policy issues. Functioning politically within a narrow band of their own interests, the business-oriented elites tended toward loosely held right-wing ideological prejudices but were far from having achieved a shared, coherent vision of politics and society. For the most part, they confined their organizational talents to their own enterprises and entered the world of politics only with reluctance.

To the intellectuals and their followers, on the other hand, political concern and political action were in one way or another integral components of one's everyday life. Unlike the business-oriented elites, they thought of politics as an exercise in the higher morality rather than in the enhancement of personal interests. Communicators above all, they had become dominant factors in a society in which mass communication was increasingly the foundation of political achievement. They defined the issues and set the framework of perceptions within which the public weighed them. Their educated followers, especially among the young, could be used as highy motivated battalions of campaign workers tireless in their devotion to a just cause. Not superrich, but possessed of a substantial measure of upper-middle-class affluence, the intellectual elite and its adherents could finance a national campaign with an ease that earlier liberal insurgent movements in American politics could never have imagined. The intelligentsia did not of course constitute a ruling class, but by the mid-sixties it had emerged as a class whose consent was necessary for the smooth functioning of the political system, necessary indeed for an administration to govern.

Johnson faced an angry challenge from another traditionally Democratic quarter. George Corley Wallace was succeeding as had no other politician before him in carrying the appeal of Southern racist populism to a Northern working-class constituency that felt threatened by the erosion of traditional cultural values and by the black revolution of the sixties. Playing to the blue-collar, lower middle class of the New Deal–oriented industrial states, Wallace moved his rhetoric across taut nerves with the skill of an angry maestro. He drew his first support with his vehement stance on such racial issues as the movement of blacks into the inner suburbs, busing for school integration, and the rapid growth of welfarism. He built on it by flailing away at the liberal intelligentsia and all those aspects of American life that it had either encouraged or amiably accepted over the past decade—not just the civil rights movement, but also the antiwar crusade, long hair, pot-smoking, draft-card–burning, and the whole panoply of social and political dissent. A seditionist within the Democratic party, he urged the commoners within it to overthrow its ruling elite.

At first blush the archnemesis of the New Politics, Wallace employed many of its methods. From the time he had ostentatiously forced federal troops to order him aside as he attempted to block the registration of a black student, he had manipulated the news media, especially television, with a shrewdness rivaling that of Martin Luther King. When he drew hippielike hecklers in the North, he utilized them as demonstrations of the cultural decadence that he was fighting. When he lashed into "limousine liberals" and "beatniks," he spoke to an accumulation of frustrations that transcended any particular issue. Meanspirited, ill informed, and demagogic, he nevertheless aroused identification as a little man speaking for other little people in opposition to the machinations of a self-contained elite alienated from the mainstream of American life. His organization quickly developed substantial direct mailing lists, stuffed envelopes with smoothly conceived campaign material, and raised the funds for a major campaign effort. The technique was similar to that employed by McCarthy and, four years later, by McGovern.

The New Politics and Wallace between them demonstrated the fragility of the Roosevelt coalition as it had evolved over a generation. The death of Robert Kennedy, the only candidate who might have held both the intelligentsia and the blue-collar classes, ensured its disruption. By the time of Kennedy's assassination, Johnson had confessed defeat. Done in by the insuperable burden of Vietnam and by all the other offenses of character and personality he had inflicted upon the various alienated groups of American life, he had taken himself out of the running for the presidential nomination. Ready at last to acquiesce in the deescalation of the Vietnam War, he hoped to preserve the Great Society and repay political loyalty by throwing the presidency to

Hubert Humphrey. Instead, a nation in revolt against its president's flaws would turn to a man of equal ambiguity, abundant in talent but at least as deficient in character. Having expected to lead America into a new era of power and domestic prosperity, Lyndon Johnson had succeeded in taking it into an epoch of frustration, bitterness, and diminished expectations; somehow, he had managed only to prepare the nation for Richard M. Nixon.

7

The Flawed Challenger:
Richard M. Nixon

Richard Nixon reminds one of Clyde Griffiths, the antihero protagonist of Theodore Dreiser's *An American Tragedy*. Like Griffiths, he was born into poor but pietistic circumstances and indoctrinated with the American success ethic. Like Griffiths, he pursued wealth and recognition and was guilty of criminal behavior in the process. Griffiths was driven to murder and paid with his life; Nixon betrayed the trust that the American people had traditionally placed in their presidents and forfeited his political life, leaving the presidency in serious disrepair. Griffiths's short, unhappy life was of course a metaphor for the way in which the American Dream and the values connected with it could be perverted by the pressures of social reality. Nixon's career may tell us much the same thing; to the extent that it does, it tells us not simply about Nixon but about ourselves, and that perhaps as much as anything accounts for our national fascination with him.

Nixon's failure of character has obscured the fact that his presidency presented the contemporary American political tradition with its most coherent challenge yet. In the main, this challenge, as opposed to the man who advanced it, enjoyed widespread popular support. During his years in the White House, Nixon sensed that the old internationalist liberalism had approached the point of exhaustion. He quite consciously adopted a

282

set of "neoconservative" alternatives that contrasted sharply with traditional GOP right-wingism and sought to build a new majority in American politics. He was well along the road to success when forces within himself brought him down and aborted the effort.

Making It

It is difficult to read of Richard Nixon's childhood without experiencing feelings of considerable sympathy, even pity. Almost every feature of his youth conspired to deny him a sense of security and self-worth. He was born in 1913 in suburban Los Angeles, the second of five children, and grew to maturity in a family existing precariously at the margin of middle-class socioeconomic status. As a teenager, he managed the produce section of the family grocery store and filling station and made daily predawn drives into the city for fresh vegetables.

His father, Frank, must surely rank among the most difficult parents in the history of the presidency. A trolley conductor, farmer, carpenter, and finally the operator of a mom-and-pop general store, Frank Nixon spent his life struggling to make ends meet, never establishing an atmosphere of success or financial security for his children. Temperamental, quick to take offense, a stern disciplinarian, irritable, ulcer-ridden, he must have seemed at times a terrifying figure to a young child. As Richard Nixon has described it, his father was a classical totalitarian who expected instant obedience and did not flinch at the prospect of inflicting pain. "I learned early that the only way to deal with him was to abide by the rules he laid down. Otherwise, I would probably have felt the touch of a ruler or the strap as my brothers did."

The mother, Hannah Milhous Nixon, provided, it is true, an oasis of gentleness and stability in a hard, small world. Universally described as saintly and loved in the community, she was a source of reassurance and protection. Yet for some two years—crucial, formative years for a boy—she was away from home, having taken young Richard's tubercular older brother Harold to a nursing home in Arizona, where she did menial labor to pay the bills. A younger brother, Arthur, also fell prey to a degenerative disease, tubercular meningitis. Both necessarily received greater attention, and both died while Richard was in his teens. It is not surprising that the boy is widely remembered as quiet, introverted, studious, and hard-working.

In many respects, Richard Nixon grew up as a Horatio Alger type, a diligent poor boy aspiring to greater things. At home, he absorbed all the values of pietistic Protestantism and the petit bourgeoisie. At school, he was a grade grubber, a successful student politician, and a determined, if woefully inadequate, member of the football squad. Behind his model-child exterior, he seems to have harbored an intense, combative aggressiveness. This was possibly a reaction to all the frustrations that surrounded him, possibly an emulation of his father. Football, with its special blend of discipline and violence, always would hold a special attraction for him. It encouraged a tendency to envision combat as a metaphor for life. It gave to its heroes an acclaim and devotion that Nixon always would covet.

After graduating from little Whittier College, Nixon went off to Duke University Law School. Living on a scholarship in povertylike conditions, he was again an unsuccessful football player but a star student. His academic success he attributed, frankly and perhaps a bit too self-disparagingly, to his incessant study, characterizing himself as a young man with an "iron butt." He graduated second in his class.

He had practiced all the Horatio Alger values, but the world did not give him a Horatio Alger payoff. Along with a couple of friends, he traveled to New York to interview with some prestigious law firms. He did not receive a job offer. He sent a letter of application to the FBI, but nothing came of it. Instead, he wound up back in Whittier, practicing law with an older family friend. One has to wonder how hard he had tried. Perhaps like many an introvert, he found a return to a familiar, easily manageable environment preferable to the threats of a high-powered, uncertain world well beyond his experience.

As a young attorney handling routine cases, he worked tirelessly, occasionally sleeping overnight at the office. He earned a modest living and secured some community standing. Soon he was a trustee of Whittier College and an aspiring businessman. With some friends, he organized the Citra-Frost Company to produce frozen orange juice. Displaying his usual intense commitment, he was both president and sometime juice squeezer. The firm was thinly capitalized and it was unable to develop suitable packaging. After a year and half, it failed, leaving Nixon with a considerable financial and—no doubt—emotional loss. He could at least find a large measure of consolation in his marriage to Pat Ryan in 1940.

As it did with so many of the young men of his generation, World War II profoundly affected Nixon's future. He and his wife went to Washington and landed jobs with the Office of Price Administration. He later remembered the experience as distasteful and disillusioning. A conservative Republican who had grown up in a milieu of small-town individualism, he found himself working in a haven for New Deal Democrats, infamous for its miles of bureaucratic red tape. In August 1942, he obtained a commission in the U.S. Navy.

Eventually, Nixon wound up in the South Pacific as a supply officer, working on the edges of combat zones. He was an efficient, first-rate young commander who displayed considerable initiative in cutting rear supply areas and landing strips out of the bush; he took care of his men, and won rapid promotions. Along the way, he met and became a friend of the actor Jimmy Stewart. He also learned to play poker so skillfully that he came out of the service several thousand dollars richer. By 1945, he was back in Washington, working on the navy's legal staff, renegotiating procurement contracts. Several weeks after the surrender of Japan, he was discharged with the rank of lieutenant commander.

By now, Nixon had acquired a range of personal, administrative, and legal experience beyond anything he could have achieved in a lifetime of practice in Whittier. He felt ready to look for opportunities in Washington or New York. Then, unexpectedly, he received an offer that touched an ambition he had long harbored and brought him back home without hesitation.

A committee of Republican businessmen searching for a strong candidate to oppose Democratic congressman Jerry Voorhis paid Nixon's travel expenses for what amounted to an audition. The young veteran delivered a brief, forceful speech, contrasting the virtues of individual self-reliance with the evils of New Deal bureaucratic paternalism, then concluded with the somewhat incongruous assertion: "If the choice of this committee comes to me, I will be prepared to put on an aggressive and

vigorous campaign on a platform of progressive liberalism designed to return our district to the Republican party." He won a
top-heavy endorsement.

Voorhis was a respected four-term veteran of the House,
widely admired in Washington and the author of a book on
Congress that had won national attention. Still, he faced difficulties. The district belonged to neither party, and the year was a
very bad one for any Democrat outside a safe district. Starting
out as an underdog, Nixon aggressively rode the tide while his
opponent was pulled under by it.

He personally put half his savings, $5,000, into the campaign.
His supporters secured him the part-time help of a shrewd if
rather unscrupulous campaign operative, Murray Chotiner, who
had run Earl Warren's successful first bid for the governor's
mansion and was devoting most of his time to William Knowland's
race for the Senate. Chotiner's advice meshed well with the
candidate's temperament: nothing was more important than hard
work; always take the battle to the enemy; respond to an attack
by going on the offensive; never play to the strengths of the
opposition.

From January on, Nixon slugged away, his opponent in
Washington most of the time. He faced Voorhis in a series of
debates that fall and soon had him on the ropes, pounding at him
on the two big national issues of the election—price controls and
the spreading revulsion against Communism. Increasingly, he was
prone to emphasize Communism, an easily manipulable vehicle
for personal attack. Nixon never accused Voorhis of being a
Communist as such, but he dredged up alleged radical statements
from Voorhis's past and claimed he had accepted support from
Communist-dominated labor organizations. Printed advertisements alluded to Voorhis's younger days as a registered Socialist.
An anonymous telephone campaign, its extent uncertain and its
relationship to the Nixon organization unknown, flatly labeled
Voorhis a Communist. The same sort of tactics were used by
many other Republican candidates across the country in 1946
and were frequently effective.

The challenger had more going for him than an instinct for
the jugular. Like a good many returning servicemen who went
into politics, he advertised his veteran status and was not shy

about reminding his constituency that his opponent had spent the war in Washington. He occupied the middle of the road by pushing Voorhis over to the left and by evading a firm ideological stance of his own. He seemed an attractive young personality with his humble beginnings, his war record, his smooth yet sincere speaking style, and his attractive young wife and infant daughter.

On election day, he defeated Voorhis handily. The incumbent, an idealistic liberal deeply interested in the consumer cooperative movement, was of course neither a Communist nor a Communist sympathizer. Given the unfavorable political situation of 1946, he might well have lost on other issues. Nonetheless, many observers thought that the charges of Communism had been decisive, and Richard Nixon went to Washington believing that he had found a winning technique. He also had demonstrated that in the real world, the young man who constantly works and fights to get ahead cannot be overly fastidious. It was a lesson he accepted.

Nixon's two terms as a young congressman displayed his skill at the game of self-advancement. He made himself a leader among the Young Turk Republicans. He obtained coveted appointments to the House Education and Labor Committee (where one of his Democratic colleagues was John F. Kennedy) and the Un-American Activities Committee. He did his homework well, spoke effectively when he ventured into debate, and serviced his constituency faithfully. Ideologically, he remained hard to classify. On domestic issues, he usually voted as a Republican conservative. He was especially vehement in his criticisms of organized labor, which he tended to represent as an offshoot of the Communist conspiracy or a fraud against the American worker; he was a strong advocate of the Taft-Hartley Act.

In foreign policy, however, Nixon stood apart from the Taft "isolationist" bloc and reflected the experience of many young veterans of World War II. He supported most of the major Cold War initiatives of the Truman administration and was willing to incur some risks in the process. When informed in 1947 that his position in favor of the Marshall Plan was unpopular at home, he returned to his district, made some fifty speeches, and got his viewpoint across to the voters. Adopting the Cold War without reservations, he criticized the Truman administration only when he found its policies too soft.

He was always remarkably successful in identifying himself with the Communist issue. As a member of the Un-American Activities Committee, he avoided demagoguery and displayed some concern for the rights of witnesses. Nevertheless, he was anything but a civil libertarian. In 1948, with Sen. Karl Mundt of South Dakota, he sponsored legislation that would have required Communists to register with the government, denied them passports or the right to apply for federal employment, and made them subject to deportation if they were not U.S. citizens. The bill was pigeonholed after Thomas E. Dewey, the leading candidate for the Republican presidential nomination, denounced it as "nothing but the method of Hitler and Stalin." In 1950, it would be exhumed and incorporated into the McCarran Act.

The Alger Hiss controversy made Nixon a national figure. Among the Republican members of the Un-American Activities Committee, he most quickly overcame his doubts about Hiss's accuser, Whittaker Chambers, and emerged as the leader in the drive to obtain Hiss's eventual indictment for perjury. Whatever the truth about the Hiss case and whatever Nixon's own exaggeration of Hiss's importance as a Communist agent, there is no evidence to suggest that the young congressman engaged in any violation of Hiss's rights, made charges frivolously, or undertook in a frame-up. He simply felt that Hiss was guilty and stayed with the case; eventually, a jury agreed with him. In the process, he gained fame and positioned himself for a shot at a Senate seat. In 1950, he faced Congresswoman Helen Gahagan Douglas in one of the most notorious elections of the era.

A noted singer and actress before her move into the political world, and wife of the movie star Melvyn Douglas, Helen Douglas had spent three terms representing a liberal Los Angeles constituency. She was not especially popular among her House colleagues—Nixon recalls that Jack Kennedy delivered to him a $1,000 contribution from Joseph P. Kennedy and added his own best wishes—but the media attention that she orchestrated so naturally had made her one of the better-known figures in Congress. Glamorous, idealistically liberal, embodying the chic reformism of the Hollywood set, she was a perfect foil for Nixon.

Although her political career had taken shape on the left wing of the Democratic party, Helen Douglas was in no way a Communist sympathizer. Like many liberals of the period, she was a reluctant cold warrior who had swung behind Truman's foreign policy only after being attracted by the idealism of the Marshall Plan. She had opposed the presidential candidacy of Henry Wallace, voted for the military aid to Western Europe, and supported the Korean War. Her husband was a leader of the California Americans for Democratic Action, the focus of anti-Communist liberalism in the state. (Another important figure in the state ADA was Ronald Reagan.)

Nixon and his managers chose to ignore these facts in a campaign that painted a mainstream liberal a virulent shade of hot pink. They distributed a highly selective list of congressional votes and quotations purporting to show that Mrs. Douglas's record was comparable to that of the notorious fellow-traveling New York congressman, Vito Marcantonio (who actually had supported Henry Wallace, voted against military aid to Western Europe, and opposed the Korean War). Shouting "pink" at every opportunity, Nixon and his supporters succeeded in making their opponent the issue.

On the defensive, the Democrats asserted that Nixon's negative voting record brought more comfort to the Communists than Douglas's. The tactic had no chance of success against the man who had gotten Alger Hiss. On election day, Nixon won by a wide margin. Apparently experiencing no twinges of regret about the crude innuendo that had helped bring him victory, he was capable of writing twenty-eight years later that the Douglas campaign, unequaled "for stridency, ineptness, [and] self-righteousness," had smeared *him* and that he had saved the state from being represented in the Senate by "one of the most left-wing members of Congress."

Twice Nixon had defeated well-known figures who at most might have been criticized for a liberal idealism a bit fuzzy around the edges. He had done so by implying that they were either subversives or dupes of subversives. As a senator, vice-presidential candidate, and at the beginning as vice-president, he frequently resorted to such methods. He was at most a half-step removed from the worst aspects of McCarthyism. A 1952 characterization of Adlai Stevenson epitomized the style: "Adlai the appeaser . . . who got a Ph.D. from Dean Acheson's College of Cowardly Communist Containment." Among Democrats, he became the most hated Republican, detested by many fellow congressmen, indelibly caricatured for the rank and file by the cartoonist "Herblock" as the dark-jowled compatriot of Joe McCarthy.

Nixon could plead with some justice that his use of the Communist issue was of a piece with the Republican rhetoric of the time, as employed by no less a figure than Robert A. Taft. After the conviction of Alger Hiss, Herbert Hoover had sent Nixon a telegram of congratulations that asserted: "AT LAST THE STREAM OF TREASON THAT HAS EXISTED IN OUR GOVERNMENT HAS BEEN EXPOSED IN A FASHION ALL MAY BELIEVE." Even Thomas Dewey would from time to time lob charges of pinkness at the Democratic opposition. For Hoover or Taft or Dewey—and no doubt for Nixon—such declarations delivered a powerful emotional satisfaction that went beyond considerations of rationality. For a politician seeking a response from a partisan Republican audience, the Communist issue was the rhetorical equivalent of 101-proof bonded whiskey. It was not altogether surprising that a young up-and-coming GOP figure would seize on it.

But Nixon's anti-Communism was also imbedded deeply in his background and value structure. His Republicanism had not come from the study of economics; rather it was rooted in the assumptions and aspirations of the Protestant, entrepreneurial lower middle class with its belief in religion, patriotism, hard work, and traditional morality, its faith that the virtuous would get ahead in the world. The liberalism of the New and Fair Deals—most coherently expressed by secular intellectuals openly contemptuous of old absolutes, most visibly supported by the labor unions, most epitomized by the phrase *welfare state*—was an affront to the fundamental beliefs of Nixon and the many Republicans like him who constituted the most durable core of support for the party. From their perspective, Communism could seem just more of the same. Throughout his career, Nixon's appeal would be strongest not in the more sophisticated metropolitan areas of America but in the small towns and cities where the values of his youth remained strong.

Nothing in Nixon's career demonstrated the point more graphically than the "secret fund" crisis that nearly drove him from the Republican ticket in 1952. The charge itself was pressed hardest by sophisticated liberal intellectuals who tended to snicker at traditional ideals and who despised Nixon as a sanctimonious fraud. Nixon's famous television response, however cornpone it may have been, amounted to an instinctive reassertion of those ideals and a rallying of a vast constituency that still adhered to them. He talked of his modest background, his military service, his fight against Communism, his mortgages, his two-year-old car, and his family—the wife with the respectable Republican cloth coat, the two daughters, and the little dog they loved so much.

Whether or not he had depicted himself as he really was, he had put across the self-image he sincerely idealized. A groundswell of support kept him on the ticket. The defeat of Adlai Stevenson, denounced by Republican campaigners as an egghead sophisticate, provided a final confirmation of the way in which the GOP drive as a whole had been a "crusade" to reassert hallowed values. Nixon was not simply *in* this crusade; he was *of* it: "I felt instinctively negative toward Stevenson. I considered him to be far more veneer than substance, and I felt that beneath his glibness and mocking wit he was shallow, flippant, and indecisive."

Nixon had been chosen for the vice-presidential nomination largely because he appeared to embody the domestic world view of the Taft Republicans without sharing their isolationism. Based on the classic considerations of political balance, his selection occurred without Eisenhower's active participation. For the remainder of his career, his relationship with the Northeastern establishment would be distant. For the balance of the fifties, his relationship with Eisenhower would be ambiguous.

Superficially, the two men appeared to form a mutual admiration society. Nixon seized every opportunity to declare the general's greatness and profess a doglike loyalty to him. Eisenhower in turn referred to Nixon as one of the fine young men in the party. Actually, however, there was a degree of tension between them. It had begun with the fund crisis when Eisenhower nearly dropped Nixon from the ticket. It persisted in the president's seeming lack of interest in utilizing his young vice-president for substantive assignments. It manifested itself in Eisenhower's public indifference to an effort to dump Nixon from the Republican ticket in 1956. It finally culminated in an odd misunderstanding over the presidential role in the 1960 campaign and in Eisenhower's even stranger remark to a press conference that if given a week, he might be able to think of some contribution by Nixon as vice-president. Their personal relationship was formal and businesslike. Nixon lamented that his chief treated him like a junior officer. His advance through the politics of the 1950s toward a presidential nomination was the product of his own effort rather than of presidential preferment.

Nevertheless, Nixon's vice-presidency was not hollow. He observed and participated in the deliberations of an administration attempting to govern a nation positively, a distinct change from his congressional experience as a rising young figure in a negative, obstructionist minority party. He was involved in most important decisions, even if his counsel was rarely heeded. To the surprise of many observers, he made a relatively successful foray into labor relations when he helped mediate the steel strike of 1959.

His extensive foreign travel, although usually ceremonial, was profoundly educational. He met and had an opportunity to gauge established international leaders and younger men on the way up. He saw first-hand the conditions of life in the underdeveloped world. In two instances, his trips brought him substantial popular acclaim and sympathy at home. In 1958, he displayed considerable courage when left-wing rioters attacked his entourage in Venezuela and Peru. In 1959, sent to Moscow to help open an American trade exhibition, he seized upon an opportunity to engage in an impromptu debate with Khrushchev as U.S. newsreel cameras ground away. In all these ways, he not only gained valuable experience and knowledge; he also established a public image as a statesman.

The president's reservations, however, remained painfully apparent. Regarding the younger man as inexperienced and a bit superficial, Eisenhower suggested to Nixon in 1956, probably without devious intent, that it would be best to leave the vice-presidency, take a major cabinet post, such as Defense, and gain some *real* administrative seasoning. Nixon was also too close to the Taft/McCarthy Republicans to suit both the president and most of the big business–big publishing establishment that surrounded Eisenhower. To put it another way, Richard Nixon was not a Charles Percy, the kind of up-and-coming young progressive Republican Eisenhower liked to boost. The president must also have found Nixon's combative style unattractive. A chief executive whose leadership was based upon skill at conciliation, a warm smile, and the cultivation of a father image could hardly help being put off by a person whose concept of politics seemed to be built around lethal swipes at an opponent.

Yet Nixon's aggressiveness made him the Republican party's chief campaigner. Especially in the midterm contests of 1954 and 1958, he was the point man (hatchet man, the Democrats might grumble) who led the national attack on the opposition. He was astute enough to understand the counterclaims he would someday be able to make upon the support and loyalty of thousands of state and local party leaders and workers. Furthermore, he was drawn to the effort. Throughout the decade, he made increasing efforts to look like a young statesman, only to have them largely undone by his tendency to throw rhetorical raw meat to the partisan animals who packed his speaking engagements. In 1954, he worked the Communist issue so hard that he could justly be described as a slightly sanitized McCarthy; by 1958, he was in only a slightly lower key. Journalists tended to interpret Republican losses in both years as a repudiation of the vice-president; actually, Nixon had laid the basis among the party faithful for a presidential nomination.

Taking the nomination in 1960 was in fact almost effortless. Nelson Rockefeller, the recently elected governor of New York, assayed a challenge, but he quickly discovered that all his considerable strengths as a campaigner, all his appeal to the independent voter, and all his vast wealth counted for little with the state and local functionaries who ultimately controlled the Republican convention. As a running mate, Nixon shrewdly chose Henry Cabot Lodge, Jr., ambassador to the United Nations, former senator from Massachusetts, widely popular for his tough retorts to the Russians in UN debates, and a leading figure among the

Northeastern establishment Republican types who were still put off by Nixon.

It is difficult to ascribe Nixon's loss to any one or two factors. He was of course the candidate of the minority party, and he struggled against a soft economy. Nonetheless, two other important circumstances stand out even more—the debates and Nixon's relations with the working press.

Nixon's decision to meet Kennedy in a series of televised debates, foolish in retrospect, was understandable at the time. From his school days, he had been a polished debater. He had bested Voorhis in 1946 and had used television effectively in 1952. But in 1960, he was a quasi-incumbent with wider national recognition and a generally acknowledged lead in the presidential race. He forfeited an advantage when he agreed to meet Kennedy on equal terms and gave his opponent a special exposure. Nixon had forgotten, if he ever had understood, that television transmitted images and personalities; it was this function that had saved him in 1952, not his recitation of his fund's audit. In 1960, however, he was not alone in front of the camera, and pathos was not an acceptable tool for a presidential candidate. Kennedy was handsomer, and his style more in keeping with the expectations of American trend setters. Nixon's hot, impassioned demeanor and his uptight conventionality contrasted poorly with Kennedy's cool detachment and witty humor. He never had stood to gain much from the debates; he lost a great deal.

The loss was compounded by his relationship with the working press. Unable to accept the possibility that the negative side of his reputation was his own doing, he had long believed that most reporters misrepresented him to the public and engaged in a continuous smear campaign against him. He avoided them as much as possible, and his staff treated them with hostility. Correct in perceiving that most reporters leaned toward liberalism and the Democratic party, he surely was wrong in believing that a conspiracy was at work against him. Yet his behavior and that of his aides went far toward creating one.

Kennedy, in contrast, understood the media and was a master manipulator. He joked, ate, and drank with journalists, occasionally asked their advice, and saw to it that his staff treated them as respected old friends. For a newsman to move from the Nixon campaign to the Kennedy campaign, Theodore H. White has written, "was as if one were transformed in role from leper and outcast to friend and battle companion." By election day, Nixon had managed to alienate many of them who had begun the campaign with a determination to be scrupulously fair toward him. Kennedy had won their friendship and devotion; when he appeared at his first press conference as president-elect, they rose to applaud him. Televised across the nation, the scene must have profoundly embittered the defeated Republican.

Nixon's difficulty with the journalistic world exemplified certain personality problems that would forever haunt his political career. Absolutely central to his sense of identity was a self-image as a crusading underdog fighting against a host of privileged, unscrupulous enemies. He was incapable of admitting to himself that on occasion he had done wrong or had abandoned principle for opportunism. In his own mind, he never smeared his opponents; he just told the truth about them. It was he who suffered constant smears—from Helen Gahagan Douglas, from the Kennedys, from Pat Brown in 1962, and above all, from the press, which never had forgiven him for exposing Alger Hiss.

Having relieved a sense of guilt by transferring his own misdeeds to others, he could exhibit an indefatigable self-righteousness that was not simply a typical politician's hypocrisy. Feeling beset from all sides and mistreated by others, he could also lapse easily into a maudlin self-pity, reminding listeners of his humble origins, his hard work for the right causes, and the insufficient appreciation he received from the American people. He possessed an unhealthy suspicion of others and a lack of respect for the integrity of his opponents.

Nothing became Nixon more during the 1960 campaign than his decision to concede defeat. He had lost by only 113,000 votes out of 68.3 million cast for himself and Kennedy. He was down by a hairsbreadth in Illinois amid charges of extensive fraud by the Chicago machine. He lost Texas, with its long tradition of creative tabulation, by 46,000 out of a grand total of 2.3 million, and came within one percentage point of a majority in five other states. Some Republican leaders counseled him to demand a recount, and although he quickly convinced himself that the election had been stolen, he decided to accept the reported result. As a practical matter, he must have realized, there was little chance of a reversal. Nonetheless, he had made a statesmanlike gesture. It is reasonable enough to accept his word that he did not want to divide the country.

The election also showed that Nixon enjoyed a substantial, loyal following concentrated in the Republican heartland. It admired both the Nixon record as a fighting partisan and the way in which he had identified himself with the traditional values still strong in that part of the country. No doubt, the vote also reflected a fair degree of grudging respect by political independents for the man's demonstrated ability. He remained a major figure in American politics, still hungry for the presidency.

Nixon attempted to establish a power base by running for governor of California in 1962. The decision almost destroyed his career. His opponent, the amiable incumbent, Pat Brown, was a difficult target for any challenger. Nixon's widely perceived lack of interest in state governance compounded the problem. And most observers believed, correctly, that he considered the governorship of California nothing more than a means to achieve a larger goal.

Bereft of a winning issue and dangerously low in credibility, the Republican challenger trailed in the polls from the beginning. Attacks on the Brown administration for fiscal irresponsibility, a growing crime rate, and high taxes all made little impact. Nixon fell back on his old standard—he began to attack Brown for alleged softness on Communism. It was a preposterous tactic against a pot-bellied, cigar-chewing old pro. The Democrats, for their part, unfairly insinuated that Nixon was somehow improperly involved in his brother's financial dealings. In his final television address, the night before the election, Nixon, exercising his well-developed penchants for self-pity and guilt transference, asserted that he had been the victim of the worst smear campaign in the history of California politics. The next day, he lost to Brown by three hundred thousand votes even as the popular Republican senator, Thomas Kuechel, carried the state by a seven hundred thousand margin.

Nixon also gave in to his worst impulses in another way. The morning after his defeat, he tore into the journalists who had covered him. What he called his "last press conference" was an astonishing performance, displaying bitterness, petulance, and a bit of unexpected vulgarity. ("If they're against a candidate, give him the shaft, but also recognize that if they give him the shaft, put one lonely reporter on the campaign who will report what the candidate says now and then." Afterward, he was heard to say to his press secretary, "I gave it to them right in the behind.") Of course, the most famous line was "You won't have Nixon to kick around anymore." Almost everyone who witnessed the spectacle assumed that Nixon had written finis to his political life.

Within months, he and his family had moved to New York. Assisted by Thomas Dewey, who had become a close friend and adviser, he accepted a position as senior partner in a leading Wall Street law firm. The job yielded a high six-figure income and placed him in more frequent and intimate contact with the corporate and financial leaders of America than ever before. He bought a large, luxurious apartment in the same building that housed the personal residence of his genial political enemy, Rockefeller, traveled extensively on business, and enjoyed long vacations with his family. In all, it was the sort of existence envied by people with a normal amount of self-indulgence. For Richard Nixon, it quickly became unsatisfactory.

However bitter he may have been in the months immediately after the California debacle, Nixon quickly regained his obsessive interest in politics and in the presidency. His business trips and vacations often included visits with Republican leaders in the United States and dignitaries overseas. He spoke frequently at party gatherings; by maintaining a high degree of visibility, he quietly established himself as the primary force for moderation in the Republican party between the extremes represented by Rockefeller and Barry Goldwater. He spent the fall of 1964 working hard for the Goldwater ticket; preaching unity at every turn, he cast himself in the role of healer of the GOP's self-inflicted wounds. Nixon fully expected the electoral disaster that occurred, and he knew that he would emerge as the figure around whom the party would most likely rally. Two days after the election, he underscored his new position for the unsubtle by holding a press conference at which he denounced Rockefeller as a spoilsport and a divider.

The next four years played out with an almost inexorable logic. Nixon campaigned tirelessly for Republicans across the country in 1966. He stepped up his foreign travel. He prepared intelligent, thoughtful essays for journals of opinion. He even managed to establish friendly contacts with a few influential journalists such as Theodore H. White. In the meantime, the Johnson administration collapsed of its own weight, and the Democratic party suffered near-disintegration with the Wallace secession, the McCarthy revolt, the emotional insurgency and assassination of Bobby Kennedy, and the convention riots in Chicago. Easily nominated by the Republican convention, Nixon had somehow placed himself near the center of American politics with the liberal Humphrey on the left and the pseudo-populist, race-baiting Wallace on the right. He capitalized on the position by turning his television campaign over to shrewd media experts who packaged him as a reasonable, competent, relatively attractive statesman answering questions from groups of ordinary people seated around him.

On election day, Nixon squeezed out a narrow victory, running ahead of Humphrey by half a million votes. He polled 43.3 percent to 42.6 percent for the Democrat and 13.5 percent for Wallace. The election capped the most remarkable comeback in the history of American presidential politics. Moreover, it seemed to portend sharp shifts of direction both in foreign policy and in the trend toward liberal welfarism at home.

The Richard Nixon who won the presidency in 1968 was different from the candidate who had lost in 1960. He was more reflective, more inclined toward moderation, more pragmatic. He already had talked and written of the need to establish a relationship with mainland China, and he was pledged to pull the country out of Vietnam. His foreign policy would be "conservative"—not in the sense of being dogmatically anti-Communist but rather in the more authentic sense of being attuned to power relationships on a global scale with ideology a secondary consideration. At home, he would seek to control and limit the Great Society welfare state but not to destroy it. In a period of economic crisis, he would not hesitate to take strong federal action. To use a term that had not yet come into vogue, he had become something of a "neoconservative," alarmed at the excesses of the New Deal liberal tradition and determined to reconcile it with the classical values of conservatism. This objective was frustrated in the end less by any national doubts about its merits than by Nixon's considerable deficiencies of the spirit.

For all his immersion in the world of politics during most of his adult life, Nixon remained a distinctly unpolitical personality. He found little pleasure in the ritual camaraderie of handshaking and eager socializing so essential to the practice of American politics. A veteran political warrior who bore the psychological marks of years of nearly continuous, no-quarter combat, he was remarkably lacking in human warmth, uncomfortable meeting strangers, and inordinately fearful of their hostility or rejection. He was a self-conscious outsider who never ceased to resent a social and intellectual establishment that never had accepted him. Acutely conscious of the hatred of the liberals, he convinced himself that they were engaged in a constant conspiracy against him.

His behavior was that of a man who was markedly insecure and every bit as erratic as his predecessor. As president, he isolated himself from many of his cabinet members and congressional leaders and in fact, from all but a few trusted friends and advisers who for one reason or another did not threaten him. He surrounded himself with men who were second-rate (Spiro Agnew), or lacking strong substantive convictions (H. R. Haldeman and John Erlichman), or without an independent power base (Henry Kissinger, Daniel Moynihan). He was quick to engage in petty displays of displeasure with aides who seemed to get too much favorable press notice. Almost as if he felt too little to occupy the Oval Office, he frequently retreated to a smaller workplace in the Executive Office Building. At other times, as when he ordered the White House police dressed in European palace-guard–style uniforms, he seemed to take refuge in the imperial presidency. Plainly, he was uncomfortable with the position he had so arduously achieved.

Yet however insecure he felt, whatever the impulse to withdraw, he behaved as if he conceived of politics as a struggle for survival in a jungle. Having used spurious tactics against his opponents time and again, he was willing to employ almost any method that might bring victory. For all his service under Eisenhower, he somehow had failed to learn that presidents were not supposed to resemble alley fighters. His political Darwinism constituted a moral Achilles heel.

All the same, he was as much a moralist as any president in American history. Deeply attached to the values his parents had taught him, he perceived also that they constituted about the only politically useful common bond he had with many ordinary, working-class Americans who had tended to vote Democratic since FDR. Typically, he planned to rebuild the Republican party with a ruthless, no-holds-barred defense of the old morality.

In many respects, the neoconservatism he would adopt was simply the old liberalism of the 1940s and 1950s, as espoused by Truman or Kennedy at the working level and conceptualized by such thinkers as Reinhold Niebuhr at the intellectual level. Seen from the enthusiasm of the New Left or the expansiveness of the Great Society reformers, the old liberalism had come to look stodgy and dated. From the perspective of Vietnam, it appeared dangerously prone to Cold War military ventures. To a younger, more ambitious generation of liberals, unfettered by a sense of limits and anxious to distance itself from its elders, the old persuasion seemed unliberal.

The old liberalism had in fact moved in the direction of accepting some identifiably conservative values—the fragility of human nature, the futility of social engineering, the centrality of power in relationships between nations. To this, it had added a ferrent conviction, developed by social thinkers who had witnessed and had sometimes personally experienced the parallel rise of German Nazism and Soviet Communism in the 1930s: totalitarian states were fundamentally alike beneath their different ideological masks; whether of the Left or the Right, they constituted abhorrent menaces to democracy.

Arthur Schlesinger, Jr., had codified these principles for the liberals in the 1940s as the "Vital Center." His work had become the point of departure for self-conscious efforts to square the liberal tradition with conservative principles in the 1950s, such as the New Conservatism and the New Republicanism. The neoconservatives who began to emerge in the late 1960s tended to have their intellectual roots in the old Vital Center liberalism more than in the New Conservatism. For the most part, they were one-time liberals who had occupied a position well to the left in American politics—many had been supporters and formulators of the Great Society. By the time Nixon was elected president, however, they had come to question both the assumptions and the techniques of liberalism as it had developed under Lyndon Johnson in the sixties. The Great Society, they believed, had become too ambitious, too wasteful, too redistributionist, too antimeritocratic.

They had, it is true, incorporated in their thinking some of the standard premises of American conservatism. Skeptical about extensive government intervention in the economy, they accepted the ethic of classical individualistic capitalism and argued in favor of greater leeway for free-market decision-making. Still, they fell well short of embracing laissez-faire or Social Darwinism. (The intellectual leader of the movement, Irving Kristol, found himself able to muster only *Two Cheers for Capitalism* in a volume published after Nixon left the presidency.) Reacting to the disorderly environment of the sixties and early seventies, they valued social stability. They emotionally supported the old-style liberal principle of equal opportunity and merit advancement as contrasted with the loose egalitarianism and advocacy of affirmative action of the newer liberals. Several of their leading figures— Daniel Bell, Irving Kristol, and Daniel Patrick Moynihan—had made their way up in society from unpromising beginnings and were disposed by experience to value effort, self-help, and opportunity even as they favored certain social reforms that might encourage those qualities.

They approached foreign policy in much the same spirit. Militant anti-Communists, they accepted the Cold War as a struggle of transcendent historical significance between liberal democracy and totalitarianism absolutism. Willing to concede in general terms the need for economic assistance and development in Third World nations, they nevertheless viewed the moral posturings and more extravagant material claims of the Third World as hypocritical. Almost always, they rejected the assertions that the difficulties of underdeveloped nations stemmed from Western imperialism, preferring instead to cite corruption, social disorganization, the absence of a liberal-democratic tradition, and ill-conceived efforts at socialism. Power, they believed, was in the last analysis the most important aspect of international diplomacy.

A final attitude underlay neoconservatism, one with which Nixon possessed a reflexive agreement. The neoconservatives were hostile toward the "New Class" of liberal and radical intellectuals who, it seemed, had come to dominate American culture in the sixties and whose beliefs clashed with theirs at every point.

It is difficult to estimate how aware Nixon was of the neo-conservative movement. He read and was influenced by Irving Kristol. He appointed Daniel Patrick Moynihan as a chief domestic adviser. In casting about for intellectuals willing to join a Republican administration, he and his aides undoubtedly recruited hundreds of third- and fourth-echelon operatives who identified with many aspects of the neoconservative outlook. Having become a national figure during Eisenhower's gropings at a Modern Republicanism, having witnessed the futility of Taftite traditionalism, and having lost an election in 1960 to a dynamic young candidate who promised new frontiers, Nixon was well aware of the inadequacies of the Old Republicanism and ready to experiment with new approaches that might bring him a reelection victory and establish the Republican party as the majority force in American politics. The neoconservative approach, situated somewhere within the broad center of the political spectrum, was so ideally suited for the purpose that it quickly became the dominant policy tone of his administration.

The World After Vietnam: Neoconservative Diplomacy and Its Limits

Richard Nixon had taken office as president with one clearly stated priority: to get the United States out of Vietnam. But he faced the equally difficult, if less emotional, problem of constructing a diplomacy that would take into account the emergence of a new world order in the 1960s. He had to deal with the rising visibility and influence of the Third World, the emergence of Japan and Western Europe as economic superpowers, the seeming diffusion of global power, and, as Vietnam appeared to have demonstrated, the limitations of American military strength. In this, as in no other area of his presidency, Nixon achieved considerable intellectual and emotional maturity. He possessed a strong grasp of world affairs, analyzed them with considerable dispassion, and was, above all, willing to recruit a strong figure to act as his aide.

His selection of Henry Kissinger as his chief foreign policy adviser was both surprising and inspired. While Kissinger came from and lived in worlds wholly removed from Nixon's, there also were personal similarities. Both men carried the scars of traumatic childhoods; both by nature were introverts; both saw themselves removed from an establishment that disdained Nixon and fell short of tendering Kissinger full acceptance. But most importantly, both had acquired as a result of their experiences a conservative view of human nature and, by extension, diplomacy.

Nixon's view of the world, an outlook that expressed the cynicism of a weary street fighter, had grown from the rhythms of victory and defeat in years of constant struggle. Kissinger's view, darker and more profound, stemmed from his childhood in Nazi Germany. He had witnessed brutal persecution first-hand and, with his family, had been fortunate to escape it. Like every Jew of European background, he found the slaughter of the vast majority of his people to be an inescapable presence in his mind. It imparted the certain knowledge that the human race harbored within itself a nearly inexhaustible capacity for inhumanity. Having once lived among Nazis, he naturally rejected the optimistic sentimentality that characterized so much of American liberalism. In a manner few Americans could comprehend, he had looked evil in the face and had measured its intractability.

Nixon and Kissinger both accepted the premise that power was the predominant factor in world politics and the balance of power the only reliable basis for relations among nations. These ideas were so alien to the American mind that it became necessary to conceal them. Depicting themselves as shapers of "détente" or "a generation of peace," they compromised their convictions to maintain their political support. Finally, they faced the handicap of having to lead a nation that was above all weary of power and its burdens, frustrated beyond measure by Vietnam, and increasingly attracted to the vision of withdrawal from an unpleasant world. Functioning in these difficult circumstances, they pursued the national interest much more effectively than would their immediate successors.

When Nixon took office, the American public demanded extrication from Vietnam. But where the opinion-shaping intelligentsia and its young followers expressed themselves in a style of moral indignation and quasi-pacifist outrage, Middle America tended more simply to be exhausted and disillusioned. To the opinion shapers, the war was immoral and should be terminated at once, even at the cost of delivering South Vietnam to the Communists. To Middle Americans, however, the war was a more ambiguous evil that needed to be brought to an end, but without national embarrassment. In adopting the objectives of Middle America, Nixon and Kissinger dealt themselves an extraordinarily difficult task.

Vietnam had destroyed Lyndon Johnson; it is remarkable that it did not destroy Richard Nixon. Public opinion, as measured by the polls, had swung toward withdrawal only in the last year of the Johnson administration; it weighed on Nixon from the beginning. Johnson had enjoyed the acquiescence—if not the active support—of many moderate-to-liberal Democrats motivated by caution and party loyalty. Nixon could count on little tolerance from the Democrats, nor could he expect any sustenance from the foreign policy establishment that had invented the war and now was well along in the process of abandoning it.

Finally, there was the obstacle of the North Vietnamese themselves. They and their allies in the South had endured a quarter-century struggle to unify Vietnam under Communist rule; they were determined to carry on whatever the cost. Negotiation, if undertaken at all, was to be another tactic in the march toward total victory. Masterful, if crassly cynical, in manipulating U.S. public opinion, they played upon popular feeling for captured Americans by displaying them at periodic press conferences in Hanoi. Already enjoying a large measure of sympathy among the antiwar intellectuals, the North Vietnamese convinced many of them that an acceptable solution was blocked only by Nixon's intransigence. Public negotiations with the enemy and periodic secret talks dragged on fruitlessly. Meanwhile, the pressure for withdrawal continued to build and all but required the administration to move publicly toward extrication.

Nixon's objectives were at bottom the same as those of the Johnson administration. Both sought to preserve an independent South Vietnam and United States influence in Indochina. Nixon would carry on the war while winding down U.S. participation and strengthening the South Vietnamese forces. To pursue victory while staging a withdrawal was a task so paradoxical that the most accomplished statesman would have found it difficult to explain. Nixon handled the job of gathering public support with particular ineffectiveness—indeed, with counterproductivity. Tactically, the job was well handled; it is possible to believe that had it not been for the destruction of his authority by Watergate, Nixon might have succeeded in maintaining South Vietnamese independence. Politically, it was managed in a way that displayed the president's inadequacies as a public leader.

To those most vehemently opposed to the war, Nixon was a hated, devious politician and a hard-line anti-Communist. He needed to conduct himself in a way that reached out to the antiwar intellectuals and neutralized at least some of them. Instead, he behaved in a way that inflamed the movement. He sent out contradictory signals, some of which could easily be taken as indications that the war was to be enlarged. He practiced confrontation instead of conciliation with the antiwar forces, and he displayed an emotionalism that no doubt reflected his own inner turmoil over having to orchestrate a policy of retreat so in conflict with his own combative instincts. The result was to lower the level of rationality in American politics, divide the country further, and bring antiwar sentiment to a point of near-hysteria.

If the intellectuals loathed Nixon, he accepted a fight with them eagerly. He never quite had learned one of the most elemental lessons of politics—that it usually made more sense to attempt to win over one's enemies than to alienate them. "The American leader class," he noted to himself, disgusted him with its effeminate complaining and abdication of responsibility. The university intellectuals were haters, frustrated, alienated failures. Antiwar demonstrators were "bums" whose Washington rallies he pointedly ignored. After New York hard-hat workers had beaten up war protestors, the president ostentatiously met with their union leaders and praised their patriotism.

The speech in which he announced the invasion of Cambodia in April 1970 demonstrated his almost willful failure to get his message across. The Cambodian incursion was a rear-guard action, designed primarily to destroy Communist supply stockpiles and buy time to turn the war over to the South Vietnamese. There was no way to announce even a limited military offensive into Cambodia without generating protest, but Nixon did it in a way almost guaranteed to ignite hysteria.

The Cambodia speech demonstrated the way in which live television could reveal insecurities and exaggerate every sign of instability. Since Nixon knew he would receive vehement denunciation, he primed himself by watching *Patton*, by persuading himself (most likely only half-persuading himself) that he was a strong leader making difficult decisions in lonely isolation. He decided to go on nationwide television to explain the move personally to the American people rather than to let it be announced and backgrounded in a matter-of-fact, low-key way by military officials.

The address was a disaster. After a relatively restrained presentation of the limited nature of the military operation and its utility in facilitating American withdrawal from the war, he used rhetoric one might employ to announce a major escalation. America could not be "humiliated"; it could not behave as "a pitiful, helpless giant." He himself was prepared to make any sacrifice in support of his decision; his own reelection would count for nothing. He would rather do the right thing, rather preserve the nation's status as a first-rate power than accept the first defeat in its proud history.

As Kissinger has observed, Nixon had made Cambodia into "an earthshaking, conscience-testing event." The antiwar movement responded in kind, and after jittery, ill-trained National Guardsmen killed four demonstrators at Kent State University, the nation was submerged in a politics of hysteria that the president had done much to set off. Cambodia injured the cause it had been designed to promote—that of a deliberate, carefully phased withdrawal.[1]

But the wound was not mortal. Despite the indignation of the antiwar movement, Nixon was able to cling to his objective. Whatever qualms one might have about his timetable, he did in fact go about the unappetizing task of leading the nation out of Vietnam and thereby out of the poisonous atmosphere that had come to dominate American politics during the last years of the Johnson administration. Sadly, he could not find the personal

---

[1] Nixon may have felt it necessary to go on the air and speak as he did because of his belief that successful diplomacy in the contemporary world could be facilitated both by displays of resolve and appearances of unpredictability, even irrationality. In an era of the retreat of American power, such behavior presumably would confuse the enemy and deter unbridled aggressiveness. One must feel, however, that Nixon should have been able to manage it without touching off hysteria at home, that indeed a cooler approach might have been taken with more gravity in unfriendly chanceries.

style and resources of leadership commensurate with the goal. A policy initiated to heal the divisions in American life was presented in a confrontational style that perpetuated them. In part, this development was an outgrowth of a strategy of cultural politics that the Nixon administration consciously pursued for partisan advantage. But even the larger strategy reflected Nixon's own emotional combativeness, the source of his ultimate failure as a leader who had declared that he wanted to bring the nation together.

It is clear in perspective that Nixon was steering a course toward extrication from the start. At the time he took office, 545,000 American troops were based in Vietnam. Throughout his first term, the withdrawals continued steadily. By September 1972, just in time for the beginning of the presidential campaign, only 39,000 American troops remained. Nixon also proclaimed the so-called Guam Doctrine—a declaration that America's Asian allies would have to bear the greatest share of their own defense. And, he did much to cool the greatest source of domestic unrest by carrying through a long-overdue reform of the military draft, then by ending conscription altogether.

Amazingly, all the hostility between Nixon and his critics boiled down to little more on the rational level than an argument about the pace of withdrawal from Vietnam. Opponents might have argued compellingly in favor of a faster movement, questioned the feasibility of Vietnamization, or asserted that the continued expenditure of lives and treasure were not worth the gamble, but it is fair to observe that especially after Cambodia, the antiwar protestors were impelled by more than rational argument.

A bit of their motivation was partisan. In and out of Congress, the antiwar groups were predominantly Democratic or Democratic-leaning. A good many Democratic politicians who had remained relatively silent under Johnson now felt free to express themselves openly and vehemently in a fashion that took the onus of the war off their party and placed it upon the Republicans and Nixon. Partisan calculation, however, was perhaps the smallest part of the answer.

For the vast majority of the antiwar movement, Vietnam had become a burning moral issue not susceptible to a gradualist solution. American policy was a supreme immorality, directed toward prolonging an unjust war for the benefit of a repressive puppet government. Geopolitical thinking made little impression upon people who had come to live by such slogans as "Stop the Killing" and "Give Peace a Chance."

Nixon himself, however, made no substantial efforts at dialogue; his preferred stance toward the antiwar demonstrators was either disdainful silence or harsh denunciation. As in so many other ways, he made himself part of the problem. His own meanness of spirit had a way of spreading to his opponents, many of whom really *had* come to relish kicking him around. Incapable of reining himself in and attempting conciliation on the grounds of national interest, the president, as happened so frequently, readily succumbed to his worst impulses. Unable to achieve total victory in Vietnam, he sought the destruction of his enemies at home.

It was ironic that in the process of finally achieving peace in Vietnam, Nixon was treated as if he were continuing the war full tilt. The blame for the venomous character of debate over the war could be spread generously. Yet much of the failure in the end was Nixon's. His character and reputation had preceded him, leaving many Americans with strong reservations about his intentions and trustworthiness. The tense, emotional style of his leadership served only to reinforce those doubts; and his irrepressible impulse to vilify and destroy his enemies created a bitter atmosphere. A major achievement of the Nixon presidency, the extrication from Vietnam also was a major example of Nixon's failure as a leader.

The rest of Nixon's diplomacy was in many respects attuned to the theme established by his Vietnam policy—that of an orderly retreat from an overextended position, an exercise made palatable by rhetoric extolling the goal of "a generation of peace." With the nation's sense of purpose and conviction of righteousness all but wiped out by Vietnam, American power, already barely useable, grew weaker in real terms as Congress cut military appropriations. There was an occasional surreptitious effort to wield power through Central Intelligence Agency operatives, as in Chile or Laos, but in the main Nixon and Kissinger attempted to conduct diplomacy while foregoing the military capabilities upon which diplomacy usually rested.

Both men understood the limitations of their course. It is noteworthy that after they left office, each wrote a book (*The Real War*; *The White House Years*) that implicitly rejected numerous attitudes he had displayed while still in power. Consummate realists, they had opted for retreat because they saw no other choice. Given the situation, they managed American diplomacy about as well as could be expected.

More was involved in what Henry Brandon has called "the retreat of American power" than the collapse of national will in the wake of Vietnam. It rested also upon the judgment that the post–World War II bipolar power struggle between the United States and the Soviet Union had given way to a situation in which there were five global forces—the United States, the USSR, China, Japan, and Western Europe. But in truth the world still contained only two superpowers capable of exerting a reach almost anywhere on the globe. One of them was growing in its capabilities; the other was declining. When they thought and acted in terms of raw power, Nixon and Kissinger clearly had as their point of departure a triangular relationship between China, the Soviet Union, and the United States. It was this conception that guided their most creative efforts.

At the time Nixon became president, the Cold War appeared on the wane. Intermittent disturbances—most serious among them the Soviet invasion of Czechoslovakia—had shaken but had not terminated the quest for mutual accommodation that had followed the Cuban missile crisis. Nixon understood full well that the old-style virulent anti-Communism no longer paid political dividends. Accepting the reality of the national mood, he attempted to defend American interests while cultivating friendship with the USSR.

Both in terms of public relations and even private conceptualization, the effort involved two diametrically opposed images of the Soviet Union: the rapacious aggressor and the benign, if somewhat backward, aspirant to full membership in the modernized, civilized community. Inconsistent conceptualization necessarily encouraged an inconsistent policy. Indeed, Nixon's approach to the Russians with its emphasis upon personal relations and manifestations of goodwill was not unlike Roosevelt's. As was the case with Roosevelt, it could boast of substantial accomplishments, but it encouraged illusions far grander than what it achieved.

On the surface, few nations appeared more receptive to a new diplomatic beginning than did the Soviet Union. Under Leonid Brezhnev, the USSR had taken on a bland, mediocre, nonthreatening appearance quite in contrast with its image under the evil Stalin or the blustering Khrushchev. The Brezhnev regime found itself more afflicted by open dissent than had any of its predecessors and gave the impression of having greater difficulty in dealing with a number of social and economic problems ranging from alcoholism to poor grain production. In fact, however, the Brezhnev government was the most adventurist in the history of the Soviet Union. As Nixon presided over a retreat of American power, Brezhnev oversaw a vigorous expansion of Soviet strength. While the American military budget was being effectively eroded by inflation and by the day-to-day demands of Vietnam, the Soviet Union was in the middle stages of what probably was the largest sustained buildup of armed might in human history. Khrushchev had marched into Hungary only after that nation had broken out into an open anti-Communist revolution. Brezhnev invaded Czechoslovakia for tendencies toward liberal democracy and enunciated the doctrine that the Soviet Union would use force to maintain its species of totalitarian socialism wherever it had been established. Under Brezhnev, Soviet military power, most often in the form of advisers, penetrated into the Middle East and Africa on a scale that Stalin most likely would have found unimaginable.

The USSR thus presented two faces to the West. It was convenient to deal with the less threatening, and almost necessary to do so considering the lines of policy already established by Kennedy and Johnson and the way in which Vietnam had discredited the Cold War. Practically forced to proclaim a policy of "détente," Nixon and Kissinger were given neither the resources nor the time to engage in the sort of negotiations that might have produced real meaning for such a relationship. Thus, the character of détente was never definitively established. Neither the

United States nor the Soviet Union really was prepared to abandon every opportunity for gain in international politics. Where then was the quest for influence permissible and where not? Was it all a matter of geography or of degree?

Nixon and Kissinger were more specific in their enunciation of the doctrine of "linkage," the assertion that good relations in one area of concern depended upon good relations in others. But in reality, this seems to have been little more than a statement of preference, however forcefully it was asserted from time to time. The Russians never accepted the proposition in the abstract and routinely ignored it whenever opportunities for gain presented themselves, whether in the India-Pakistan conflict of 1971 or the Yom Kippur War.

Finally, there was the question of whether the American political system could muster the flexibility that détente and the doctrine of linkage assumed. Behind the theory and practice of détente was the assumption that the United States could reward good behavior and punish bad conduct. Actually, the administration could do neither.

Détente, in fact, became more important to Nixon than to Brezhnev. The proclamation of an end to the Cold War paid off politically. The theme of détente, highlighted by a summit meeting with Brezhnev in Moscow, played a major part in Nixon's 1972 reelection. Even at the very end, in 1974, the president would use a visit to Moscow in an effort to stave off impeachment. The politics of détente quickly overrode diplomatic considerations and became the chief drive behind its practice. Rather than a careful, sophisticated effort to deal for a better relationship with an old enemy, it became an exercise in atmospherics.

Still, détente had a hard side, and nothing represented that better than Nixon's China policy. Writing in *Foreign Affairs* the year before he was elected president, Nixon had declared, "Any American policy toward Asia must come urgently to grips with the reality of China." The policy he advocated was sound, moderate, and remarkably un-Nixonian. The United States did not have to rush to give mainland China unreciprocated concessions, and it had to continue efforts to contain Chinese tendencies toward expansionism. But it also needed to make conciliatory gestures designed to bring China back into the international community and had to undertake a diplomacy that would *persuade* China to abandon foreign expansionism and turn to the solution of its domestic problems.

At once practical and idealistic, the argument was a remarkable departure from Nixon's early dogmatic anti-Communism. Behind it, moreover, there lay an unspoken but major assumption —China represented an important military counterpoise to Soviet power in East Asia. The China card was a way of cementing the balance of power in a region that could not be stabilized by a militarily powerless, if economically prosperous, Japan. Nixon and Kissinger translated their design into reality with daring and opportunism.

The China policy was also good politics, and as was the case with U.S.–Soviet relations, political hype obscured both the hard intentions behind the opening to China and the limitations of the policy. Nixon visited China in February 1972, almost as the opening event of his presidential campaign. Television lent powerful immediacy to the event by transmitting one dramatic scene after another back to the United States.

The president proclaimed his efforts to be important steps in the building of a structure of peace. Understandably enough, neither he nor Kissinger dwelt on the limited character of what had been done. The reopening of diplomatic intercourse with China was all to the good, but as Kissinger himself would later write, the United States had not acquired a "China card" to play at will. What the China connection had done was to create a three-cornered relationship that with agile diplomacy the United States might use to its advantage. Nixon exaggerated his accomplishment, although his exaggeration was nothing compared to the euphoria that followed his trip among journalists and intellectuals.

The lasting results of détente and three-cornered diplomacy are hard to measure. Détente did bring China back into the world community and may have provided some support to its relative moderates in their deadly struggle with the hard-line Maoists. It produced the Strategic Arms Limitation Treaty, which at least moderated the arms race a bit. It encouraged efforts toward a general relaxation of tensions in Europe, exemplified by the *Ost-*

politik of West German chancellor Willy Brandt and, after Nixon had left office, by the Helsinki Pact.

Yet behind the mood of a new era (curiously, it was during the Nixon years that it became common for observers to speak of the Cold War in the past tense), the reality remained more constant than most people, inside and outside the administration, wished to admit. The USSR did little to assist in ending the Vietnam War; in fact, the North Vietnamese were able to prolong it to a successful conclusion only because they received massive Russian aid. The Russians did not display restraint in their efforts to expand their own imperial position, especially in Africa and the Middle East where they continued to employ the classic methods of subversion and armed force. Indeed, the rhetorical proclamation of the age of détente underwrote a general idealism about the character of world politics hardly congruent with the base realities that would continue to govern international conduct.

If the style of the Nixon-Kissinger diplomacy appears more impressive than its substance, that may be the consequence of having to wage a holding action from a position of ebbing power. Both men appear to have understood the limits of what they could accomplish, but neither proclaimed these limits to the American people. They propagated an illusion of accomplishment far grander than the reality. Whether in the long run this public relations feat served the national interest remains questionable.

When Nixon took office, he also had to deal with a far more volatile situation than the carefully orchestrated encounters that characterized most Soviet-American friction. From the end of World War II on, Russia and America had skillfully measured each other's intentions during such confrontations as the Berlin blockade, the Hungarian insurrection, and the Cuban missile crisis. Each usually yielded to an opponent's territorial imperative, invariably taking care to avoid backing the other side into a position that might make war inevitable. The conflict between Israel and the Arab states since 1948 was marked neither by comparative rationality nor by a mutual acceptance of the right to a continued existence. Taking place in an area of great strategic and economic importance, it threatened constantly to draw the superpowers into a conflict substantially beyond their control.

For successive American administrations since Truman's, the Arab-Israeli conflict presented a dilemma enveloped in a muddle. The strategic and economic interest of the West in a friendly Arab world was obvious. Yet the American cultural and moral ties to Israel were profound and were cemented by a U.S. Jewish community politically, economically, and intellectually influential far out of proportion to its size. Consequently, one administration after another had fudged the issue, attempting to please both sides, striving in a typically American way for a compromise settlement, never having to face squarely the ultimate problem of whether to underwrite Israel's survival or watch it be destroyed.

Nixon's first term in office was largely a continuation of what had become an old story. Trying somehow to find the elusive solution that would please all sides, or at least to keep the lid on the problem, his State Department labored mightily and unsuccessfully to achieve a disengagement between Israeli and Egyptian forces that had faced each other across the Suez Canal since the Six Day War of 1967. By then, the Soviet Union had become the military patron of Israel's most determined enemies, the United States was Israel's major military supplier, and the Middle East had turned into the most dangerous theater of the Cold War.

The Jordanian crisis of September 1970 illustrated the forces that affected Middle Eastern politics and diplomacy. It started with a series of airplane hijackings by Palestinian guerrillas, at least some of whom had been trained in the Soviet Union, progressed through a two-week buildup of U.S. military power in the eastern Mediterranean, led to the expulsion of the Palestine Liberation Organization from Jordan, and culminated with the Jordanian repulse of an armored invasion from Syria. Nixon had displayed resolution and moderation in dealing with a dangerous situation that had come close to touching off a general Middle Eastern war, but the Jordanian crisis would become little more than a footnote to history after the challenge of the Yom Kippur War.

The Syrian-Egyptian attack upon Israel in October 1973 threatened to change the face of world politics in a way gravely damaging to American interests. For the first time since its war of independence, Israel faced a genuine threat to its survival. Nixon confronted the prospect that the USSR would have played a vital role in the accomplishment of the most cherished goal of Arab nationalism, that an ally would have been destroyed, and that American influence in an area nearly as important as Western Europe would have been all but eliminated. He had to meet the challenge having been already seriously wounded by the unfolding Watergate affair and by the separate scandal involving his vice-president. On October 6, the Yom Kippur War began; on October 10, Spiro Agnew pled *nolo contendere* to income tax evasion and resigned from office; on October 20, the president staged the "Saturday Night Massacre" firing of the special prosecutor, the attorney general, and the deputy attorney general in a desperate effort to put an end to Watergate. He and his administration were under such public suspicion that nearly anything he did would be subjected to criticism and disbelief.

Nixon was not, Kissinger has written, by nature a courageous man; but at critical moments he was capable of steeling himself to acts of considerable bravery. The Yom Kippur attack was one of those moments. Acting in a situation that weaker men would have met with inaction, he decided quickly to sustain the Israeli military effort with an American airlift, overrode foot-dragging within the administration, and consequently laid the groundwork for yet another Israeli victory. In the closing days of the conflict, the Soviet Union delivered a scarcely veiled threat of military intervention; acting on the advice of Kissinger, now secretary of state, and other officials, Nixon instituted a U.S. military alert that apparently dissuaded any Russian action. Whatever the shabbiness of other aspects of his presidency, he had acted with nerve and decision; yet he had fallen into such disrepute that the need for the military alert was widely questioned as a political ploy. In fact, he had won next to no recognition as the savior of Israel.

At the same time, he had to cope with the realization that the nation had paid a high price, well beyond the value of the military hardware he had ordered shipped to the Jewish state. The Organization of Petroleum Exporting Countries (OPEC) used the war to increase prices fourfold, and its Arab members instituted a boycott against the United States and other pro-Israel Western nations. The Arab boycott was only semieffective, but it ended the margin of petroleum abundance that the nation long had taken for granted. The higher OPEC prices amounted to a heavy and unexpected tax on the American economy. The resulting spectacle of long lines of cars waiting for suddenly expensive gasoline exemplified the nation's shock and frustration. The economic recession touched off by these developments illustrated in a more serious way how the United States could be harmed by Arab hostility.

Having satisfied the national interest in the preservation of Israel, Nixon now faced the task of placating the Arabs. The stakes were high—the restoration of the American economy and the reestablishment of U.S. influence as a positive force in the Middle East. During the last ten months of his presidency, as he lurched from one political setback to another at home, he managed to accomplish this extraordinary objective. He had, he has written, decided that peace was possible in the Middle East only with the establishment of a military balance of power, which he had achieved with his aid to Israel. Now he offered the services of the United States as honest broker and would-be peacemaker. It was a role that no other country, assuredly not the USSR, could fulfill. With Kissinger shuttling across the Middle East in late 1973 and early 1974, skillfully seizing upon every opportunity to negotiate the first limited disengagements between Israel and its enemies, Nixon brought an eventual end to the oil boycott. He made substantial progress toward both restoring the American position and reducing Soviet influence in the region. He began the long process that eventually would lead to a measure of normality between Egypt and Israel. Symbolically, he, not Brezhnev, eventually would be embraced by President Sadat and hailed by Egyptian crowds. This was only the most visible measure of his last and perhaps greatest achievement as a diplomat.

The Politics and Economics of Neoconservatism

During the 1960s, Richard Nixon had educated himself for the presidency primarily by acquiring a new expertise and sophistication in foreign policy. But he had inherited from Lyndon Johnson pressing socioeconomic problems, intensified no doubt by Vietnam but not likely to go away with the end of the war. Inflation was running at a then-frightening rate of about 5 percent. The sprawling jumble of Great Society programs, some of them functioning well, others a wasteful shambles, all had enormous potential for growth in their demands upon the federal treasury. The black revolution, embittered by the murder of Martin Luther King and exhilarated by the vocal rage of numerous militants, had become an angry force threatening to tear America into two societies. War-related dissent had been the catalyst for unusually acerbic political divisions and had created a large cadre of radicalized political activists disposed to continue their struggle against other aspects of the system once the war was over.

Nixon long had sensed that old-style orthodox Republicanism was not sufficient to deal with these challenges. He intended to continue leaning toward the Right, but he believed that the rigid Republican economics of the 1950s had severely damaged the party and sabotaged his 1960 bid for the presidency. As he took office in 1969, he was groping for an approach that would be both conservative and acceptable to the American people, one that would fit within the liberal tradition of Roosevelt and Truman yet maintain a critical attitude toward the Great Society. It would also have to mesh comfortably with his deeply felt personal belief in hard work and self-discipline.

The emergence of neoconservatism gave Richard Nixon a perspective that provided whatever coherence one can attribute to his policies and political strategies. Under the tutelage of Daniel Moynihan, a man of great charm and powers of persuasion, Nixon came to think of himself as a Tory reformer, an American Disraeli. Under the guidance of less likable men, he would become the spokesman of traditional Middle America leading a nasty crusade against the intellectuals.

In a general way, Nixon's domestic policies proceeded from certain assumptions largely held in common by thinkers who later would claim the neoconservative label. Moynihan had expressed some of these points of departure in an address, fittingly entitled "The Politics of Stability," to the National Board of the Americans for Democratic Action as early as 1967:

> 1. Liberals must see more clearly that their essential interest is in the stability of the social order; and, given the present threats to that stability, they must seek out and make much more effective alliances with political conservatives who share their interest and recognize that unyielding rigidity is just

as great a threat to continuity of the social order as an anarchic desire for change.

2. Liberals must divest themselves of the notion that the nation—and especially the cities of the nation—can be run from agencies in Washington.

3. Liberals must somehow overcome the curious conde-scension that takes the form of defending and explaining away anything, however outrageous, which Negroes, individually or collectively, might do.

Speaking to the liberal establishment of the nation, Moynihan had delivered blunt challenges to the bulk of what had become the orthodoxy of reform in the sixties. Yet he had not abandoned the objective of reformist social change. Nixon found himself receptive to Moynihan's quest for alternative techniques that would combine conservatism and social activism; the most noted result of their collaboration was, of course, the Family Assistance Plan (FAP), destined to become the most significant failed initia-tive in the history of American social welfare politics since Truman's universal medical insurance proposal. Although ortho-dox GOP conservatives were aghast at its central concept of a guaranteed annual income for every American family, it appealed to many on the Right. It sought to bypass the bureaucracy as much as possible; by making direct payments to the poor accord-ing to nationwide standards, it would minimize casework sur-veillance and with it the demeaning psychological consequences of receiving welfare. "We hoped," Nixon has written, "to cut down on red tape, and before long to eliminate social services, social workers, and the stigma of welfare." The FAP intended to preserve family structures by removing the common prohibition against assistance to dependent children whose fathers were alive, well, and living at home. It would have encouraged work by requiring able-bodied recipients to accept jobs or vocational training and by providing benefits to those accepting low-paying employment.

Praised by a wide range of liberal and conservative observers who found its conceptual framework appealing, the FAP never-theless was quickly ground to bits in the political process. Its projected cost alienated most Republican conservatives and divided Nixon's own administration; yet its rock-bottom benefits irritated many liberals. Moynihan put his finger on a large measure of the truth when he told Nixon that the Republicans, by and large, were not resisting efforts to kill the bill and that the Democrats wanted to deny the president an "epic victory" while blaming him for the defeat.

Understandably, however, Moynihan omitted one important factor—the president's own equivocal attitude about his creation. In retrospect, Nixon would defend the FAP mainly as a gamble worth taking in the hope of rehabilitating a discredited welfare system; his analogy suggests he felt considerable doubt. The president announced the plan, spoke out for it a few times, perhaps did a bit of serious lobbying for it, but failed to make it an urgent priority or an emotional cause. FAP might well have died in Congress anyway; by declining to give it the same sort of effort as, say, G. Harrold Carswell's appointment to the Supreme Court, Nixon ensured its demise.

Equally consistent with the mood of neoconservatism was the general concept of a "New Federalism" and its most specific incarnation, revenue-sharing. Republican moderates from the Eisenhower era on, Nelson Rockefeller among them, had sought a middle ground between the old conservative outlook and the centralizing tendencies of Democratic liberalism. Nixon and his brain trusters, William Safire and George Schultz among them, asserted the need for a New Federalism in which the national government would make broad policy and establish basic standards while leaving administration and determination of details to the states.

Revenue-sharing, the most visible embodiment of this approach, was attractive in its simplicity. The national government would remit to the states a portion of its revenue inflow with as few strings attached as possible. Along with the FAP, revenue-sharing was designed to deflate the growing power of the federal establishment. Nixon claimed that it would "start power and resources flowing back from Washington to the states and communities and, more important, to the people all over America." Nonetheless, it also had been advocated by such liberals as Walter Heller, and it left a good many conservatives disturbed by its easygoing separation of the power to spend from the power to tax. In 1972, Congress passed a modified version providing an important new source of funds for state and local governments but scarcely reversing the flow of power and resources to Washington.

Race relations was another area in which neoconservatism sought an approach midway between the older conservatism and Great Society liberalism. Typically, the old conservatives had accepted segregation and all its consequences as a more or less justifiable, if occasionally unfortunate, exercise of personal choice, or matter of states' rights, or demonstration of black inferiority. Great Society liberals had developed an increasing obsession with racial injustice. They had been mightily impressed by the anger of black militance and had attempted to mobilize federal authority to put an end not simply to segregation but to every vestige of black inequality—social, political, economic.

Moynihan had exemplified the neoconservative reaction in his speech to the ADA. By 1970, he was advising Nixon that government had gone about as far as it could and that the issues of race had been "taken over by hysterics, paranoids, and boodlers on all sides." In a memorable sentence, soon leaked to the press and widely misunderstood, he declared, "The time may have come when the issue of race could benefit from a period of 'benign neglect,'" which he went on to define as one in which "Negro progress continues and racial rhetoric fades." Other influences were at work also, foremost among them the president's hope of making political gains in the South.

The Nixon approach to civil rights was far cooler than that of the Johnson administration, but it was well beyond anything Eisenhower could have envisioned and shocking to many old-style Republicans. The administration advocated a go-slow, voluntary approach to school integration, denounced the technique of busing children away from neighborhood schools, and at one point even sent Justice Department attorneys to file briefs in support of a Mississippi appeal for delay. Nevertheless, it did encourage the process of desegregation in the South, although it did so by employing financial incentives rather than pursuing adversary litigation. When Nixon became president, school districts across the country faced a Supreme Court order for immediate desegregation; when he left the presidency, the die-hard South had been almost entirely desegregated, at least in the sense of the dismantlement of racially separate school systems. And however much he might denounce racial quotas in hiring, the president countenanced affirmative action programs that came very close to mandating quotas, especially in education and construction employment.

Nixon assuredly perceived himself as a moderate on the race issue, and even when one takes all his backtracking from the Johnson years into account, one can argue that his self-image was correct. Yet he became widely perceived as a reactionary, hostile to the cause of civil rights at every point. This turn of events was a result in part of the nearly unlimited expectations generated by the black revolution and encouraged by the Great Society. But it was also a product of the curious politics of the Nixon era, a politics in which the president cultivated appearances frequently at variance with the reality of what he did, and openly, if unsuccessfully, asked to be judged on actions rather than words.

Nixon left most of the Great Society programs intact. He endorsed a national health insurance program and accepted the cause of environmental reform. He signed and put into effect the Basic Opportunity Grant program, which appropriated a billion dollars for outright grants to low-income college students. It was true, of course, that Nixon acquiesced to liberal initiatives for the most part; still, he did acquiesce, and his administrators usually followed through in good faith. The White House, however, neither publicized this tendency nor attempted to appeal to Great Society constituencies.

Moynihan has suggested persuasively that "Nixon and his opponents joined in a strange and almost sinister symbiosis." Liberal Democrats, who long had hated Nixon, were naturally inclined to see him as an enemy of the underprivileged and politically anxious to deny him any credit for advancing the goals of American liberalism. Their viewpoint may have been overly narrow-minded, but it was understandable, indeed quite normal. What was remarkable, as Moynihan has susggested, was that Nixon and those around him did not protest; instead, they seemed almost as anxious as the Democrats to conceal the liberal side of the administration. Nixon signed the Basic Grants bill into law with no official ceremony whatever; LBJ, Moynihan opines, would have staged a barbecue. The Republicans, Nixon included, found it hard to "internalize" the ethic of liberal government; they remained uncomfortable with it and had difficulty incorporating it into their rhetoric.

Finally, Nixon's natural political constituency—the heartland Republican middle class—and his potential following from the Democrats—the Southerners and the blue-collar workers—were profoundly alienated from those elements most identified with the Great Society. These were the "New Class" of intellectuals, professionals, and bureaucrats who formulated, administered, and legitimized American social welfare liberalism; and the client groups who received its benefits, especially blacks and other minorities. Nixon had great potential appeal to those Democrats who felt bypassed by their own party, but not if he were perceived as a trimmer making compromises with the forces they hated. His penchant for combat and confrontation sealed the situation; it would have been ludicrous to claim credit for advancing the goals of liberals whom he assailed bitterly in public.

If with a little effort one can envision the main lines of Nixon's social policies within a loose pattern of neoconservatism, it is more difficult to find any sort of coherent pattern for his economic policies. These reflected the same impulse to escape the restrictions of traditional Republican conservatism while avoiding the excesses of Democratic liberalism. They demonstrated also that Nixon was both an activist and an opportunistic experimenter, more in the tradition of FDR than of Hoover. Still, as had been the case with FDR's improvisations, his zigs and zags fell far short of a coherent pattern, did little to cure the economic ills he had inherited, and may have made them worse.

Nixon faced an uncomfortable economic situation when he took office. The prosperity he had inherited from Johnson was war-induced and dangerously feverish. The new president's first impulse was to follow the tradition of twentieth-century Republicanism and launch a strong effort against the menace of inflation with relatively little concern for employment. The result won only wide depiction as the worst of both possible worlds. An administration policy of fiscal conservatism, supplemented by Federal Reserve credit tightening, induced a mild recession that did little more than add a second edge to the nation's economic problems. During Nixon's first two years in office, unemployment nearly doubled; and prices crept upward, if at a slower pace.

Like Eisenhower before him, Nixon was discovering that inflation was easily ignited in the post–New Deal political economy and not easily extinguished. He was doubtless correct in his intuition that a draconian wringing-out would be politically suicidal. He had learned in the Eisenhower years that Republican recessions lost elections. Yet by holding himself to halfway measures, he succeeded only in raising the national misery level and rendering his party vulnerable in the midterm elections. With mild stringency having failed and strict austerity an impossibility, Nixon staged a leap even more improbable in the economic realm than his rapprochement with China in the diplomatic realm. Powerfully influenced by his secretary of the treasury, John B. Connally, the president swung all the way over to stimulative economics and price-wage controls.

In his own way, Connally exemplified the stirrings of neoconservatism within the Nixon administration. Considered a conservative within the Democratic party, he had nevertheless matured in Depression-era Texas and moved into politics under the tutelage of Lyndon Johnson. However much he might give the appearance of a flamboyant, nouveau riche millionaire spokesman for oil barons, he retained within himself traces of the social activism and populist economics that had motivated Johnson. His vigor and decisiveness awed Nixon and tipped the balance in favor of a new departure.

Nixon accepted for the first time in his career the principle of stimulative deficit spending. Pronouncing himself a Keynesian, he submitted to Congress a "full employment budget," one at which the amount of federal spending was pegged to the estimated revenues that full employment would have produced. Having committed himself to one of the oldest ideas of the Keynesian left, he instituted a program of wage and price controls, an almost unimaginable heresy. His international monetary actions were if anything even more an affront to traditional Republican economics. Roosevelt had taken the dollar off the gold standard as far as domestic convertibility was concerned; Nixon cut it loose from gold internationally. Roosevelt had formally devalued the dollar in an attempt to stimulate foreign trade; Nixon became the next president to do so.

The results were disappointing by any standard. Nixon's "new economic policy" temporarily brought inflation to a crawl and cut into unemployment, but it provided little more than a scant respite. Unemployment remained higher than formerly had been considered acceptable; controls merely postponed wage and price increases, both of which took off as soon as Nixon initiated decontrol in early 1973. The administration had in fact done relatively little to attack the underlying causes of stagflation —low productivity, the "guns-and-butter" mentality that Lyndon Johnson had encouraged, and an out-of-control federal budget whose deficits invited increasingly severe Federal Reserve credit policies. The dollar devaluations amounted to a probably unavoidable recognition of international reality, but they also were inflationary.

In his memoirs, Nixon concludes that the new economic policy was largely a failure. It is unmistakable that when he left office, the economy, reeling from the oil shock that followed the Yom Kippur War, was in worse shape than when he had been inaugurated; and it seems relatively certain that even without the war and the Arab economic retaliation that followed it, he would have been lucky to return the nation to the uncomfortable economic situation in which Johnson left it. His best defense in the end was that the Democrats had no better ideas. His economic failures were to a great extent those of a nation unwilling to face up to more fundamental problems. Of course, his economic measures, like those of most politicians, were less a matter of ideological conviction than of a rational calculation of the best means of staying in power. On this account, they would be successful, laying as they did the economic basis for the president's reelection in 1972.

Although he had been elected with less than an absolute majority of the popular vote, Nixon took office with a distinct mandate from those groups in America who were in revolt against one aspect or another of the Great Society and the countercultural left-liberalism that had flourished alongside it. The George Wallace following added to Nixon's constituted a potentially unbeatable coalition of the disaffected—if Wallace were neutralized and if the administration's economic performance were satisfactory enough to allow blue-collar Middle America to vote its cultural prejudices. Republican political strategist Kevin Phillips optimistically proclaimed the emergence of a new Republican majority. No American political leader was better equipped by temperament and outlook than was Nixon to engage in a politics of cultural confrontation designed to build a new majority of the resentful.

Nixon and his political strategists were especially influenced by *The Real Majority*, a book written by Democrats Richard Scammon and Ben Wattenberg in an attempt to influence the course of their own party. Scammon and Wattenberg reminded their readers that the majority of Americans were unyoung, unpoor, and unblack. The Economic Issue that had loomed so large in partisan politics since the Depression was giving way, they contended, to the Social Issue, a web of doubts and concerns about all the cultural and political upheavals connected with the newer liberalism of the sixties. Much in the vein of Daniel Moynihan, they argued for a reconciliation between the new brand of liberalism and the older party constituencies—the blue-collar lower middle classes, the union workers, the ethnics, the old-style political organizations—openly regarded with scorn by the new liberals. They had little effect on the Democratic party; but to a large extent they defined the targets of Nixon's political strategy.

No part of that strategy had more visceral appeal for the president than its vocal opposition to the influence of what the neoconservatives called the New Class. The intellectuals, the media people, the bureaucrats, many nonentrepreneurial professionals, large portions of the college-educated public—all, according to the neoconservative diagnosis, had come to constitute a New Class in American life. Alienated from the traditional business ethic, the New Class leaned toward the politics of the Left, envisioning itself as the protector and leadership elite of the poor and the oppressed, the promoter of a more just society, the executor of a planned, welfarist economy. The New Class was the dominant force in governmental bureaucracies at all levels, in the educational establishment, in the print and electronic communications media. It had acquired a vested interest in welfarist government and in hostility to corporate enterprise. Daniel

Moynihan greatly impressed Nixon with a memorandum attacking "the service dispensing groups in the society—teachers, welfare workers, urban planners, nutrition experts, etc.," many of
whom he characterized as in the "resentment business":

> They earn very good livings making the black poor feel put
> upon, when they are, which is often the case, and also when
> they are not. . . . On average, I would suppose, for example,
> that the white women who teach Head Start children earn
> about three times as much per hour as the black men who
> fathered the children. And for all this the results are really
> rather marginal so far as the children are concerned. In the
> meantime the black poor *seem* to be favored over the white
> near poor, the loud mouths get louder and temperatures rise.

Such an analysis touched almost every impulse in Nixon's
personal and political experience, impugning as it did groups
with whom he always had felt a reciprocal hostility and depicting
the white lower middle class, a group with whom he identified, as
ignored by an uncaring bureaucratic class. He also made caustic
comments to his diary about what he called the "American leader
class": "It's really sickening to have to receive them at the White
House as I often do and to hear them whine and whimper and
that's one of the reasons why I enjoy very much more receiving
labor leaders and people from middle America who still have
character and guts and a bit of patriotism." The political coalition
he wanted to build—traditional Republicans plus Southerners,
hard hats, and middle Americans—had as its common denominator a shared resentment against the New Class and the excesses of
Great Society liberalism. Roosevelt had built a coalition with a
politics of hope and benefits-dispensation; Eisenhower had established an unconquerable personal following with a politics of
strength and warmth. Nixon characteristically would seek vindication and reelection through a politics of attack and resentment.

The leader of the offensive against the New Class was, of
course, Vice-President Spiro T. Agnew. Agnew shared Nixon's
values and personal experience to a remarkable degree. Like
Nixon, he came from humble origins, having made his own way
in the world. An inner-directed man who stopped just short of
Social Darwinism, he exhibited open distaste for the welfare state

and all but the neediest of those persons who made their liveli-
hoods from it. He was ostentatiously traditional in his appearance
and family life—a solid countersymbol to almost every cultural
change that had made an impact on American life in the sixties. A
stern law-and-order man, he had won his first modicum of national attention by delivering an angry lecture to Maryland black
leaders in the wake of the Baltimore riots that followed the
shooting of Martin Luther King, Jr. Agnew suddenly became the
most visible Greek-American in the United States, and a prominent symbol to many of the scorned ethnics who still conceived of
America in terms of the ethic of upward mobility and the morality
of their parents. He would become the administration's most
formidable rhetorical weapon.

With Nixon's encouragement and with the assistance of the
Menckenesque speechwriter, Pat Buchanan, Agnew undertook a
rhetorical offensive against the New Class that was entertaining
and attention-grabbing in its use of alliterative phraseology ("nat-
tering nabobs of negativism," "hysterical hypochondriacs of history") but also unsettling in its bitter, divisive character. He acidly
portrayed the liberal intellectuals as the source of every ill in
American life. They were effete, impudent snobs, presumably
oblivious to the needs of the ordinary working American. They
were advocates of permissiveness, responsible, one might gather,
for every manifestation of indiscipline and purposelessness in
American life from disorder in the schools to the drug culture to
crime in the streets. They were "radical liberals" lacking faith in
their country and ultimately subversive of the American way of
life.

It was tough talk—almost McCarthyite in its tone—yet it was
not altogether baseless. The well-to-do leaders of liberal opinion
did live in a refined, privileged world removed from the grubbier
realities of everyday life. They did tend to extend an easygoing
tolerance to educational disorder, narcotics, and criminality. What
was disturbing was the inflation of Agnew's rhetoric and the
vehemence with which he sought to make one class a scapegoat
for developments that transcended any mushiness of which it
might be guilty. He voiced not only his own personal prejudices and
those of his chief but also appealed to millions of Americans, some

of them traditional Republicans, some of them George Wallace followers, some of them Archie Bunker–type blue-collar workers.

No segment of the New Class came under stronger assault than Nixon's old bête noire, the press. Agnew attacked the world of journalism with special gusto, arguing that the leaders of the print and electronic communications media were in the vanguard of a liberal effort to topple the administration. As with his larger comments, Agnew grossly exaggerated a germ of truth. Most leading journalists were indeed liberal in their personal politics, but whether that problem was best handled with a blunt instrument was quite another question.

Agnew's rhetoric was but the most noticeable aspect of a concentrated effort to attack the administration's perceived enemies. In several federal prosecutions around the country, the Justice Department attempted to subpoena notes reporters had taken in the process of developing a story. The administration secured the dismissal of at least one liberal-minded commentator from the national public television network. It set up challenges to the renewal of television licenses owned by its archenemy, the *Washington Post*. It ordered an FBI investigation of a hated TV correspondent. In these and numerous less specific ways, the tone of the relationship between Nixon and most of the working press became one of unmitigated hostility at a level even more insidious than that which had prevailed during the Johnson administration.

Like Johnson, Nixon was guilty of a tactical error, the seriousness of which would prove to be almost incalculable. In 1960, he had damaged his presidential campaign gravely by treating the press as an enemy unworthy of consideration or friendship. In 1962, he had made himself ridiculous at his "final press conference." His political experience should have taught him the futility of antagonizing the people who interpreted him to the world; instead, it led him only to redouble his efforts to beat them down, and they freely returned the attack. So long as the president could preserve his political power, all the noise made little difference. But neither he nor any other chief executive could render the press subservient; what he had done was to make it resentful, ready to pounce on his every misstep, and eager to bring him down at the first serious malfeasance.

Through 1972, however, the president seemed well beyond the touch of the people he had made his enemies. It was not that Nixon achieved any strong measure of personal popularity or that he had brought the nation unalloyed prosperity or that he had healed its divisions. By focusing their political strategy upon the Social Issue and the New Class, Nixon, Agnew, and their operatives had nevertheless advanced their cause by aligning themselves with a number of widely held resentments. But there were dangers in the approach. It carried with it a temptation toward an overkill that could make one look silly, or perhaps sinister. It also was a technique that demanded a highly visible, stationary target. Although the administration failed to avoid those pitfalls in the 1970 congressional elections, in 1972, it took advantage of its experience and of a much more favorable situation.

In 1970, in the wake of Cambodia and Kent State, a climate of bitter social disorder had emerged, characterized by scattered bombings around the country. It was natural enough for the Republicans to seize upon the Social Issue as a weapon for dealing with liberal Democratic opponents, but in practice it was hard to make the issue stick against a shrewd candidate. Agnew, barnstorming the country, ever more extreme in his rhetoric as he played to one party rally after another, became almost a parody of himself. Nixon, justifiably angry at the way an unruly mob of California peace demonstrators had stoned the presidential car, made an angry, arm-waving speech denouncing "the terrorists, the far left . . . violent thugs" who had assaulted him and leaving the implication that they were representative of the Democratic opposition. Incredibly, he ordered the performance televised the evening before the election as the finale of the national Republican campaign, giving the public yet another demonstration of his lack of balance at crucial moments.

The Democrats, by contrast, were able to assume the role of moderates, make ritual gestures of patriotism, affirm the principles of law and order, and cater a bit more visibly to their traditional working-class ethnic constituencies. Most prominent administration targets retained their seats. The 1970 election was a standoff that demonstrated the limitations of the Social Issue.

Nixon's 1972 victory demonstrated what the Social Issue

could do when handled with restraint against an easy target. Self-described practitioner of the "New Politics," George McGovern was a living representation of the New Class. He was a certifiable egghead with a Ph.D. in history and experience as a college teacher. Long in the forefront of the antiwar movement, he verged on a commitment to pacifism and neoisolationism; one of his campaign slogans was "Come Home, America." He had no roots in the traditional Democratic party, which his campaign perceptibly bypassed. Ideologically, he was on the far left wing of the Democratic party in his concern for extended social welfare, women, and blacks. As chairman of a committee that established the procedures for representation at the 1972 Democratic convention, he had presided over the development of a quota system that outraged old-style white ethnic Democrats. Personally, he appeared irresolute when he withdrew a pledge of support to his chosen running mate, Senator Thomas Eagleton, after it was discovered that Eagleton once had undergone psychiatric shock therapy.

However much McGovern's nomination demonstrated the power of the liberal intelligentsia in the Democratic nominating decisions, his campaign displayed the isolation of that class in the broader arena of American politics. Scorned by the traditional Democrats, he had little chance of victory unless Nixon united the opposition himself. The president refused to do so and made certain that Agnew and other fire breathers were kept on a tight leash. His own campaign was a muted, barely visible affair that effectively utilized the tactical advantages and moral prestige of incumbency, leaving McGovern in the position of the wild-lunging attacker. Perhaps for the first time in his life, Nixon won a strong personal endorsement over his opponent. With nearly 61 percent of the ballots and forty-nine states, he could claim a solid vote of confidence, no matter how much of the total was based primarily on negative reaction to McGovern. He could even represent himself as a man above party, given the concurrent Democratic victories in Congress.

Nixon looked to his second term with ambitious objectives. He eliminated the system of economic controls that had kept prices down at the expense of disrupting important areas of the economy. He undertook a concerted effort to establish genuine presidential control throughout the executive branch by appointing trusted White House lieutenants to key managerial positions in one cabinet department after another. The Vietnam War finally over, he hoped to continue the delicate diplomatic processes he had set in motion involving détente and three-power diplomacy. Seemingly, he had established himself as a capable president who might achieve standing as a near-great chief executive. No one could imagine in January 1973, as he took the oath of office for the second time, that Richard Nixon would be destroyed by a third-rate burglary.

Breach of Faith

In June 1972, the District of Columbia police took into custody five burglars who had broken into the offices of the Democratic National Committee at the fashionable Watergate complex in Washington, apparently to plant a listening device. A trail of clues led incredibly from the perpetrators—three Cuban émigrés and two native-born Americans, all with CIA connections—to E. Howard Hunt, an administration consultant who a dozen years earlier had helped plan the Bay of Pigs invasion, and to G. Gordon Liddy, a Republican campaign official. All seven men were indicted; the head of the Nixon campaign committee, the president's close friend, former Attorney General John Mitchell, denied prior knowledge but resigned all the same.

As the Watergate Seven awaited trial that fall, the Democrats attempted unsuccessfully to make an issue of the episode. The American electorate, apparently unwilling to face the prospect of a McGovern presidency, behaved almost as a willing conspirator in the increasingly dubious pretense that the break-in had been the work of a few overzealous underlings. In fact, Nixon himself had secretly allowed his top domestic aide, H. R. Haldeman, to dissuade the FBI from a serious investigation that would have demonstrated otherwise.

Throughout 1973 and into 1974, the cover-up slowly came apart, partly because of pressure from a determined opposition, partly because Nixon and those around him displayed monumental ineptitude and inexplicable irresolution in dealing with a matter of political life and death. The events are well known: the conviction of the original Watergate burglars; the decision of their leader to implicate hitherto untouched administration figures; an investigation conducted by a special Senate committee headed by Sam Ervin of North Carolina; indictments of more administration figures; the resignations of FBI Director L. Patrick Gray and Attorney General Richard Kleindeinst; the appointment of Archibald Cox as special prosecutor; the discovery that the president had taped most of his confidential conversations; the inexorable push to make the tapes public; the Saturday Night Massacre firing of Cox and others in October, 1973; the conviction of various administration officials on charges such as perjury and obstruction of justice; continued pressure from a new special prosecutor, Leon Jaworski; the issuance of some "sanitized" transcripts; court orders mandating full release of the tapes. Along the way, there also occurred the forced resignation of Vice-President Agnew under charges of taking illegal payoffs, an Internal Revenue Service assessment against the president for back taxes, and the revelation that some of the Watergate burglars had been part of a White House "plumbers" unit that had engaged in other illegal activities. During the last week of July 1974, the House Judiciary Committee recommended impeachment. A few days later, Nixon was forced by his own angry lawyers to release the "smoking gun" transcript of June 23, 1972, proving conclusively that the president long had known about cover-up efforts. On August 8, 1974, he became the first chief executive in American history to resign from office.

As with any series of events played out on the level of epic drama, Watergate was utterly fascinating in itself—for its human interest, its complexity, and its alteration of the course of American history. Beyond the public view of powerful men parading from the Senate committee rooms to the courtrooms and thence to public disgrace, however, there remain compelling questions. How could Watergate have happened in the first place? And how could a trivial surreptitious entry about which a president almost certainly had no advance knowledge be allowed to become a national obsession for nearly a year and a half? And how could this obsession bring down a leader who had been elected by overwhelming majorities? The answers appear to reside within Richard Nixon—in his own insecure, meanspirited personality and the responses it aroused.

Why did it happen in the first place? The break-in occurred on the evening of June 17, a week and a half after George McGovern had won the California primary, locked up the Democratic nomination, and thereby assured Nixon of an easy victory in November. Manifestly, it was not required by the exigencies of a close campaign. Nor was it particularly mitigated by the fact that other administrations had engaged in political bugging and other dirty tricks. At bottom it was yet another reflection of Nixon's reflex combativeness and anything-goes approach to politics. Nixon, Agnew, and Mitchell had passed down to the third and fourth echelons an attitude that the opposition was illegitimate and that the political contest with them might reasonably have a dimension of secret warfare not unlike that waged by the CIA against its Soviet counterparts.

Nixon's team not only reciprocated the hatred of the Democrats but also acquired the vindictiveness and ruthless amorality that always had characterized their chief's approach to politics. Nixon recalls of Charles Colson, one of the central figures of the cover-up, "I had always valued his hard-ball instincts." It followed naturally enough that Colson sensed his leader's priorities. So also did many of the other operatives close to the president: H. R. Haldeman, John Erlichman, John Dean, and John Mitchell all demonstrated no qualms about the destruction of evidence, perjury, and hush money payments. *Their* subordinates imbibed the mood also.

Thus, the Watergate break-in seemed a plausible enough course of action. It was simply another battle, however poor the tactical conception, in a continuing war. A stern denunciation and a sincere effort to hunt out the culprits probably never seriously entered the mind of the president and those around him. Instead they instinctively moved to control the damage by initiating a cover-up; rather than remove themselves from the problem, they made themselves part of it.

Curiously, Nixon knew better. In one of his last meetings with John Dean, he recalled the fatal mistake of his old adversary, Alger Hiss: "That son of a bitch Hiss would be free today [*sic*] if he hadn't lied. If he had said, 'Yes I knew Chambers and as a young man I was involved with some Communist activities but I broke it off a number of years ago.' And Chambers would have dropped it. If you are going to lie, you go to jail for the lie rather than the crime. So believe me, don't ever lie." Strangely, he proved incapable of taking his own good advice.

Why and how did Watergate become a national obsession? Nixon has argued, not altogether fallaciously, that bugging and other political "dirty tricks" had been practiced by both political parties and virtually every president since FDR. From his perspective, Watergate was still another cause, magnified beyond its actual importance, to be used by all those forces in American life that long had delighted in kicking Dick Nixon around. As the cover-up was in the early stages of its slow but inexorable collapse in March 1973, Nixon held a press conference. "The questioning kept returning to Watergate with a relentlessness, almost a passion, that I had seen before only in the most emotional days of the Vietnam war," he recalls. "For the first time I began to realize the dimensions of the problem we were facing with the media and with Congress regarding Watergate: *Vietnam had found its successor.*"

There was something to be said for this analysis; yet it was at most a slanted, woefully incomplete explanation. It was true enough that Nixon had long been detested by both the Democratic party and the adversary culture in American life and that he had a hate relationship with the majority of the journalists who covered him. What it does not explore is the question of why this was the case; other Republican leaders, Nelson Rockefeller the prime example, did not carry such burdens. Nixon's cut-and-slash attacks against liberal Democrats, the intelligentsia, and the press had inflicted scars beyond the norms of most political combat. It was hardly surprising that the *Washington Post* should take up the issue of Watergate with special gusto against an administration that had publicly impugned its integrity and organized challenges to the renewal of its television licenses. And it was natural enough that many Democrats retained ugly memories of the fate of Jerry Voorhis and Helen Gahagan Douglas. Nixon's past, a past he had never repudiated, had made him the most vehemently hated man in American politics and left him peculiarly vulnerable.

Throughout 1973, one development after another, from the defection of John Dean to the desperate Saturday Night Massacre, destroyed Nixon's credibility. Even in their sanitized, "expletive-deleted" state, the transcripts released in April 1974 made Nixon and his aides appear to be sleazy, foul-mouthed, amoral operators who thought only of public relations. They showed that the president had at least come close to sanctioning a cover-up. They demonstrated that no later than March 21, 1973, John Dean had informed Nixon of an ongoing situation that included perjury, obstruction of justice, and payment of blackmail by White House functionaries, and that the president had treated it all as a problem to be handled pragmatically rather than a series of crimes to be exposed. The transcripts contained numerous passages in which the president had anticipated the maximum use of federal power against the administration's enemies.

By this time, something else had emerged as an indicator of the moral atmosphere of the White House—the efforts of some of the people enmeshed in Watergate to save themselves by implicating others. John Dean, counsel to the president, an ambitious young man not overly burdened with scruples, had participated in the early stages of the cover-up with few qualms, but he began to worry when it became clear that the opposition would not let the issue die a natural death. He jumped ship when he perceived that the president was setting him up to take the rap. Dean's suspicions probably were well founded, and his testimony before the Ervin Committee, truthful if a bit self-serving, was crucial in destroying the president whom he had served.

Dean's sense of betrayal seems to have been felt by numerous individuals, ranging from Howard Hunt, who engaged in what amounted to blackmail demands for money and clemency, to Haldeman and Erlichman, who felt the ground collapse under their feet when their chief fired them under pressure and ultimately refused to grant them a presidential pardon before leaving office himself. It was a measure of Nixon's confidence in his own aides that, by his own admission, he worried for months that John Dean might have surreptitiously taped some of their Watergate-related conversations.

Had Nixon acted more decisively at two critical points, he could have survived Watergate. His reputation would have been damaged, but he still could have functioned as chief executive. The first critical point came a few days after the break-in, when he could have come down against a cover-up and disowned any aide guilty of complicity in a shabby little crime. He might have done the same thing with more difficulty after the election. The second critical point came with the public discovery of the president's taping system. Only a group of audio tapes over which the president possessed full authority could confirm the charges brought against him. Their destruction would have made his removal from office almost impossible. Nixon's refusal to act doomed him. His inability to make the moves necessary to save himself strikes one as not simply the product of mistaken calculation but of deep-seated insecurity and self-destructiveness.

Why didn't he act? Nixon himself has faced this question with some openness, and much of what he says deserves to be taken at face value.

He probably was concerned, as he has claimed, with the fate of his close friends and associates, Mitchell, Haldeman, and Erlichman, whom he surely knew beyond a doubt to be involved in obstruction of justice. To let them down and face their rejection would have been an unpleasant prospect for a stronger man. To an individual of Nixon's insecurity, it was a nearly unendurable possibility. Characteristically, he attempted to transmute his reluctance to face the facts into a virtue, a nonpartisan virtue. "Whatever we say about old Harry Truman," he told John Erlichman at a point when Erlichman was desperately in need of reassurance, "while it hurt him, a lot of people admired the old bastard for standing by people who were guilty as hell, and, damn it, I am that kind of person. I am not one who is going to say, look, while this guy is under attack, I drop him."

Aside from exaggerating Truman's tolerance of criminal behavior, Nixon had also evaded the question of his responsibility as the nation's chief executive. As Henry Petersen, the federal prosecutor in charge of the Watergate investigation at that time, told Nixon, his reluctance to fire Haldeman and Erlichman might speak well for him as a man but poorly for him as a president. Two weeks later, events forced him to accept their resignations all the same, leaving them angry and disillusioned. Later, Nixon would recall the old British maxim that a successful prime minister had to be a good butcher. With self-pity and some hope of exculpation, he would declare that he had not been a good butcher. True enough; and, like most acts of bad butchery, his irresolute behavior had made a situation worse. Ultimately, what was at issue was the national interest, the duties of the presidency, and the preservation of the office itself; it was these Nixon butchered devastatingly.

Nixon also has addressed the problem of why he failed to destroy the tapes. Until very late in the game, the tapes were an unknown quantity, recorded, stored, and never reviewed. After their existence became known, after the Ervin Committee had subpoenaed them and the issue had become a matter for the courts, it became positively dangerous for White House staff members to listen to them. Knowledge of the tapes entangled one in a steadily growing web; it might entail embarrassing appearances before congressional committees or courts of law and expensive legal representation. Not knowing precisely what was on the tapes, Nixon probably did not realize how damaging they were. He has written that he believed they would exonerate him rather than convict him!

Still, it is hard to imagine that he ever really believed that they could be more helpful than harmful. It is equally difficult to assume that he thought that over the long haul he could withstand what was certain to be an intense public campaign for their release. One is driven to wonder whether Nixon preserved the tapes precisely because he knew he had done wrong and possessed some need to be punished.

Like many individuals who receive and internalize a set of rigid behavioral standards in their youth, Nixon had departed from values that had been deeply instilled in him in order to get ahead in the hard adult world; yet, far from abandoning those values, he proclaimed them at every opportunity and sought to make himself their personification. The contrast between his behavior and his rhetoric might appear a simple case of conscious hypocrisy, but in all probability it was a guilt-inducing situation that plagued him constantly.

Throughout Nixon's account of Watergate and many other episodes in his career, one finds a defensive, self-pitying tone that must indicate an attempt to cope with intimations of guilt. Envisioning his life as that of a man who moves from one extreme situation (crisis) to another, he places himself in settings that require more than ordinary morality. Constantly employing *tu quoque* argumentation, he asserts that his behavior is no different from that of others in the real world, that the indulgence of his opponents in various dirty tricks requires him to do the same sort of thing. Invariably depicting himself as a man set upon by implacable enemies, he attempts to shift the reader's attention from his motivation to that of those who are out to get him. The difficulty of managing this burden may well be the ultimate explanation of Nixon's politically suicidal behavior during the last year and a half of his administration. In his forced resignation from office, he at last experienced the judgment he probably had come to feel he deserved.

Tragically, that judgment extended not just to the man but to the political and diplomatic principles with which he had attempted to identify himself and, finally, to the office of the presidency as it had evolved by the end of the sixties. Nixon's major domestic and foreign policies were flawed, to be sure, and scarcely as successful as his defenders would have us believe. Nonetheless, they represented interesting, important efforts to adjust American life and American diplomacy to new realities. At his best, Nixon the domestic policy maker attempted to come to grips with problems that his liberal opponents had brought into being and had consistently dodged. Nixon the diplomatist engaged in an earnest and, for the most part, constructive effort to adjust U.S. foreign policy to an increasingly difficult world in which the nation no longer could assume either military or economic preeminence. A better man with fewer psychological burdens and more substantial qualities of leadership might have avoided many of the negative aspects of the Nixon presidency and won recognition as an above-average president. Nixon achieved only a personal disaster. Worse, he left the presidency itself an object of suspicion and scorn, awaiting a new Roosevelt or Eisenhower to restore its standing and provide a demoralized public with a sense of movement and purpose that could come only from the occupant of the White House.

8

The Roosevelt of the Right: Ronald Reagan

Time and again in his memoirs as he describes the twists and turns, the low points followed by the lucky breaks, of his early life, Ronald Reagan asserts his conviction that God had a plan for him. It is the sort of remark that drives his critics to a fury, illustrative, they are convinced, of a simplemindedness that made him ill-equipped to lead the United States in the penultimate decade of the twentieth century. It is equally emblematic, however, of Reagan's enduring appeal to millions of Americans who found him a reassuring tribune of the values of an earlier and possibly simpler America.

Reagan's adversaries envisioned him as a chief executive who had emerged from a time warp, attempting to inflict a callous individualism on a diverse, interdependent, urban society that desperately needed a caring state. They saw him as a foreign policy leader appealing to a base jingoism and indiscriminately squandering the wealth of the country on military hardware in a new age in which military strength was increasingly irrelevant and American hegemony neither possible nor appropriate. His followers praised him as the moral leader of a "revolution" that was attempting to restore the values that had brought America greatness, reverse its decline, and reassert its mission in the world.

Like most such partisan interpretations, both visions possess grains of truth but are unlikely to be accepted as serious evalua-

339

tions by those who strive for detachment. It will be many years
before scholars can measure the ultimate impact of the Reagan
presidency, but it is surely possible to undertake a preliminary
assessment of its immediate effects and of Reagan's own mark on
his times. What emerges is a picture of a revolution that never
happened because neither its leader nor his followers were certain of their objectives, of a presidency rivaled only by that of
Franklin Roosevelt during this century in its rhetorical accomplishment, and of a style of conservatism that was more populist
than elitist, more prone to risk taking than to prudence, more
flexible in its methods and more successful in elections than any
of its twentieth-century predecessors.

In Reagan, one finds a shrewd politician who amassed support by speaking his mind bluntly, won even a measure of grudging respect from his enemies for his stubborn constancy, and yet
systematically compromised his objectives. If his rhetoric seemed
that of a revolutionary, his actual program was that of an incre-
mentalist who fully understood the limitations of his political
situation. His inconsistencies of intellect and political behavior
simply softened his image and likely made him acceptable to a
larger number of the electorate than otherwise might have been
the case. Like other presidents before him, he gained appeal by
expressing the divided mind of the American people, but he did
so at the expense of leaving behind him not so much a fully
developed ideological legacy as a collection of resentments and
leanings that could be either exploited or ignored by his heirs as
their own political needs dictated.

Ambition, Self-Promotion, Politics

In what no doubt is destined to become one of his most famous
lines, Ronald Reagan has declared that if he had gotten a job
managing the sporting goods department at the Montgomery
Ward store, he probably never would have left Illinois. Coming
from a public figure who built much of his career around the
construction of a persona as Mr. Everyman from small-town
America, the observation seems plausible enough and may constitute a pleasant daydream for a generation of liberal Democrats. Yet Reagan clearly was a much different type than the
mythical amiable Joe who never got out of Dixon, Illinois, married the girl next door, raised a family, worked at an obscure job,

then died, briefly lamented and quickly forgotten. It is a measure of his political skill that he made us believe that he could have been a contented provincial nonentity.

Actually, he seems to have been more the extraordinary small-town boy, who, to be sure, absorbed the values of his environment but also possessed aspirations that were unlikely ever to have been satisfied within the limited confines of his youth. In this and numerous other respects—a childhood on the margins of poverty, an ineffectual father, a saintly mother, a history of difficult social adjustment, an upbringing built around the values of church and hard work—Reagan's experience resembled Richard Nixon's. But something in it—or perhaps something within him—gave him a personality far more suited to politics and public leadership.

Dixon, Illinois, a small city of 10,000, was the fifth town in which Ronald Reagan had lived when the nine-year-old and his family moved there in 1920. His father, Jack, a genial Irishman with a gift for salesmanship and a weakness for the bottle, had achieved what proved to be the high point of his life, a partnership in a local shoe store. In the boom years of the 1920s, the business provided little more than subsistence for the family; during the depression, it would go bust. His mother, Nell, a hardworking, devout member of the Disciples of Christ, sometimes did sewing to augment the family income. She imparted to her sons a sense of faith, ambition, work, and optimism along with a diet of hamburger and oatmeal and a wardrobe of hand-me-down clothing.

As Reagan remembers it, he came to Dixon a somewhat introverted, bookish child, small for his age, and a miserable athlete, always picked last whatever the game when the boys chose up sides. At the age of thirteen, he finally was diagnosed as terribly nearsighted; eyeglasses gave him the confidence of clear vision and apparently did not constitute much of a social handicap. In high school classes and student theatricals, he discovered gifts as a speaker and actor. He began to get his growth at last, worked as a lifeguard at a local park, became a startling lineman on the football team, and was elected student body president.

His high school experience set a pattern for his four years at tiny Eureka College, where he joined a fraternity, played football, ran on the track team, helped organize a swim team, worked on the yearbook, performed in one campus play after another, participated in student government, and became student body president. Majoring in economics, he made respectable grades, but, as he has freely admitted, the extracurricular activities were his real major. He graduated in 1932, a tall, handsome, young man with hopes for a job as a radio sports announcer and secret aspirations for a career as a movie actor.

Reagan's own account stresses the difficulties, disappointments, and near-failures he suffered in obtaining and keeping his first job. But by the standards of depression America, he was remarkably successful. His early career is best understood not as a succession of lucky breaks or as a romantic rags-to-riches story but as the progression of a risk-taking entrepreneur shrewdly selling his one asset, his personality. As a sports announcer at WHO, a powerful clear-channel station in Des Moines, he quickly established himself as a regional celebrity and pulled down an upper-middle-class income. In 1937, accompanying the Chicago Cubs to spring training in southern California, he got an appointment with a talent agent, did a screen test with Warner Brothers, and was signed to a contract as a B-movie player. Leaving his comfortable job in Iowa, he moved out to California that May, a twenty-six-year-old would-be matinee idol who had taken his biggest chance yet in the quest for fame and fortune.

He became, as he recalls, "the Errol Flynn of B pictures," making twenty-five hastily-ground-out low-budget features in his first three years. Then, he has asserted, he conceived the idea of a film on the life of Knute Rockne, the famous Notre Dame football coach, recruited Pat O'Brien for the role, and sold himself to the producers as Rockne's most famous star, the ill-fated George Gipp. Whether his account of the origin of the film is altogether accurate may be less important than his belief that his initiative and ambition propelled him to stardom. *Knute Rockne, All-American* was a foreordained box-office success; Reagan had the most memorable scene, that of Gipp on his deathbed asking Rockne to tell the boys someday when the going was tough to win one for the Gipper. Other big roles followed, including a leading part in *King's Row*, his finest dramatic performance ("Where's the rest of me?"), and seemingly assured him of a long and distinguished career.

In the meantime, Reagan had met and married Jane Wyman, a promising young actress. They seemed a picture-book couple, exuding a wholesome Hollywood glamour, apparently devoted to each other and to their daughter, Maureen. The dominant figure in terms of achievement and fan appeal, Reagan cultivated the personality of Mr. Everyman. In August 1942, a feature article in *Photoplay Magazine* quoted him as declaring that he was no Errol Flynn or Charles Boyer, just an average guy. His favorite actress was his wife, his favorite meal steak with strawberry shortcake for dessert, his favorite recreations swimming and hiking.

On the surface, World War II did little to disrupt his life. He had joined the Reserve Officers Corps in the 1930s, largely out of a love of horseback riding. Three months after Pearl Harbor, he received orders to report for duty. Ineligible for a combat assignment because of his myopia, he spent most of the war living at home, shooting training, morale, and bomber-mission briefing films. It was useful, perhaps valuable, work of the sort performed by a number of movie stars.

The army allowed him to make one feature film, *This Is the Army*, the proceeds of which went to the Army Emergency Relief Fund. (His army duties, however, apparently did prevent him from being given the role of Rick Blaine in *Casablanca*; whether he could have developed it into the career-making vehicle it became for Humphrey Bogart will never be known.) When he was discharged in September 1945, he had a lucrative seven-year, million-dollar contract waiting for him. Yet his Hollywood ascent stalled. In February 1946, not yet assigned a role, he spent a lot of time by himself, racing up and down Lake Arrowhead in a rented speedboat. As he recalled it, he told the owner: "I just want to know that the boat is there at the dock any time I want to take a drive on the water. I can't walk on it anymore."

The parts began to come, of course; some were pretty good, others rather dreadful, but none were career-builders. Unhappy with his ties to a production company that refused him the roles he wanted, Reagan asked for and received a release from his Warner Brothers contract in 1950. A poor decision, it left him scrambling for whatever he could get, which was not much in a Hollywood depressed by increasing competition from television. By then, his marriage to Jane Wyman had ended. As Reagan floundered after the war, her career took off with a stunning Academy Award performance in *Johnny Belinda*. Having surpassed her husband professionally, she seems increasingly to have found him humdrum and insensitive. At the end of 1947, she announced they were separating; in mid-1949, she won a divorce. The breakup of his marriage left Reagan, by his own admission, in something approaching a state of emotional numbness; the unsatisfactory trajectory of his career surely amplified a feeling of distress and aimlessness that would have afflicted most persons in such circumstances.

Reagan's initial foray into Hollywood politics had begun in July 1945, when his friend, George Murphy, president of the Screen Actors Guild, appointed him to the Guild's Board of Directors. Almost immediately, he found himself involved in a complex labor dispute between an old-line stagehands union and a new Communist-influenced one. The Guild directors, unwilling to take sides in a jurisdictional dispute, authorized members to cross the new union's picket lines. Reagan personally presented the board recommendations to the entire membership, which adopted them by a margin of more than five to one.

Months of bloody labor violence followed, with both sides employing goons. Reagan crossed picket lines while making his own films and quickly emerged as the Guild's most visible spokesman. An anonymous caller threatened to disfigure his face. For the next seven months, he wore a gun and had an around-the-clock guard. FBI men called on him to ask for aid in their inquiry into Communist influence in Hollywood; they told him he had become one of the party's most-hated enemies. Soon he was convinced—not necessarily wrongly—that he was fighting a Communist bid to take over the film industry unions.

In February 1947, the insurgent action collapsed. On March 10, the Board of Directors of the Screen Actors Guild named Reagan to fill out Robert Montgomery's unexpired term as president. Two days later, Harry S. Truman appeared before Congress to enunciate the Truman Doctrine and request aid for Greece and Turkey, thereby crystallizing a developing national obsession with Communism at home and abroad. By then, Reagan had provided information to the FBI about the membership and activities of the Hollywood Independent Citizens Committee of the Arts, Sciences, and Professions, the local chapter of a national liberal group well along in the process of being converted into a Communist front. He discovered also that he had become a pariah in the local American Veterans Committee, apparently also for his anti-Communism. He resigned from both organizations.

Reagan would be elected president of the Guild five times by the membership. After stepping down in November 1952, he would serve on the board for nine more years, then spend another half-year as president before leaving the Guild for good. Much of his first presidency was dominated by the Communist issue, which he handled in a fashion similar to that of many other union leaders, including Walter Reuther, Philip Murray, and James B. Carey. He drove whatever open Communist influence existed out of the union, pushed sympathetic leftists to the margins, and, in practice if not in theory, supported a blacklist of known Reds and their sympathizers.

Did such behavior make Reagan a McCarthyite? No more than most other anti-Communist liberals, who believed it both a moral imperative and a tactical necessity to expose Stalinists and purge them from liberal organizations. The process was a nasty one, made all the more difficult by the tendency of party members and fellow travelers to dissemble about their allegiances. In Hollywood it brought ostracism and near-ruin to a number of artists; in the CIO, it meant dual unionism for the electrical workers; among the liberal intellectuals, it led to schisms that would be keenly felt and fought over by children and grandchildren a generation later. Still the anti-Communist liberal distinguished himself from the McCarthyite by the touchstones of proof and responsibility—one exposed only genuine Communists or fellow travelers. To call a Communist a Communist was not to red-bait; to drive that person from an organization was to purify it; if the consequences were harsh, they were not nearly as harsh as would be the case if the Stalinists were in control with the power to eliminate their opponents.

From a contemporary perspective, Reagan was a responsible anti-Communist liberal. As president of the Screen Actors Guild, he was the one person in Hollywood most capable of clearing an unjustly accused performer; he appears to have taken the responsibility seriously and to have performed it fairly. Moreover, he established a process by which former Communists could "rehabilitate" themselves through cooperating with government investigators (which usually meant naming former party associates) and renouncing their former affiliations. At its shabbiest, the process could damage disillusioned former Communists who had quietly left the party; in practice, individuals usually named persons already known to the investigators.

By 1948, Reagan was a leading Hollywood political figure. He had made himself one of the mainstays of the southern California Americans for Democratic Action, headed by Melvyn Douglas. He spoke earnestly for Truman in the 1948 campaign, and was seated on the platform when the president visited Los Angeles. Two years later, he campaigned (and apparently voted) for Helen Gahagan Douglas in her losing campaign against Richard Nixon, whom he claims to have distrusted until they actually met in 1960. His first departure from the mold came in 1952, when he worked as a Democrat for Eisenhower. He would not change his party registration until 1962.

Reagan's political ideology before the mid-1950s appears to have been little more than a vague outlook built around his experiences as a small-town boy who had witnessed the depression, an ambitious young man who had achieved fame and fortune by dint of initiative and risk taking, a Democrat by inheritance who had admired Franklin D. Roosevelt, a film celebrity who had taken on the chic liberalism of most of his friends, and an instinctive anti-Communist who led the attack on the Reds in the internecine battles of postwar Hollywood. Never very firm in his liberalism, he already had moved decisively into Hollywood anti-Communist politics before his marriage to Jane Wyman came apart, but his pronounced move to the right did not come until after he had resolved many of his personal difficulties by marrying Nancy Davis in 1952 and had settled into a comfortable career pattern as host of television's *GE Theater* and traveling spokesman for the General Electric corporation.

It seems likely that Reagan's political change was less a response to a midlife crisis, as the political psychologist Betty Glad has suggested, than a return to older values, encouraged by the different environment in which he moved by the 1950s. His new wife and his physician father-in-law were very conservative. He had become to all intents and purposes a highly paid employee of General Electric and rather naturally absorbed its corporate viewpoint. As he toured GE factories and spoke to local groups, invariably business-oriented, he was constantly exposed to two different but altogether compatible varieties of American conservatism: that of the well-compensated, property-owning working class and that of the smaller businessman. Both shared a generalized resentment of big government and the high taxes it exacted from its citizens.

Even before he became a businessman himself as a partner in a production company after mid-1960, Reagan felt firsthand anger at a system that imposed high marginal tax rates on persons who (like himself) had ambition, took risks, and were financially successful. "I was in the ninety-four percent tax bracket, which meant the government took most of what I earned," he has written of his years as an actor, remarking that he had seen too many brief careers end with little money left after the extractions of the tax collector.

Old incidents in his life took on a new salience. He began to tell audiences how the local relief bureaucracy had discouraged recipients from taking short-term WPA jobs when his father had managed the New Deal work program in Dixon, how his army unit had requested permission to destroy old records and had received it subject to the provision that a copy should be made and retained of every piece of paper to be burned, how he had spent four months of 1948 making a film in England and had been shocked by the way in which Labourite socialism had destroyed the incentive to work. By the late 1950s, he had become an ideological free-market conservative who extended his attacks from the aggrandizing tendencies of bureaucracies to such specifics of the New Deal–Fair Deal tradition as the progressive income tax and the Social Security program. By 1962, asserting that a growing federal bureaucracy had become a drag on the economy and a danger to freedom, he had become convinced that many liberal Democrats wanted to "impose a subtle kind of socialism" on America.

Reagan's recollections of his personal experiences were probably accurate; almost anyone who has been in public service knows that bureaucracies tend to expand, rarely turn back excess funding, and frequently outlive the purposes for which they were originated. His perception that big government was itself an organized, powerful interest had much to commend it. What was jarring about his arguments was their categorical character. Perhaps because his mind favored stark simplicity over complexity, perhaps because he sensed that political constituencies do not react well to ambiguity, he rarely put many qualifiers into his rhetoric.

No national political figure played a greater role in Reagan's transformation than Barry Goldwater, whom he came to admire greatly. By 1964, he was a fervent supporter of Goldwater's presidential candidacy. Theodore H. White remembered watching him on television appealing for funds, then visiting a shabby Goldwater headquarters on Wilshire Boulevard a few days later:

> A long plank table rested on several sawhorse supports; women sat at it opening envelopes. Out of them came one-dollar bills, five-dollar bills, even an occasional Social Security check endorsed to Goldwater or Reagan. The Reagan personality had tapped a hidden mother lode of money—poor people's money, the contributions of those who must be called the underclass of conservative populism.

By his own estimate, Reagan raised at least $8 million for Goldwater in 1964. Deluged with pleas to run for governor of California, he spent the last half of 1965 developing support; at the beginning of 1966, he announced his candidacy to become chief executive of the most important state in the country.

Perhaps his greatest problem was to avoid identification with Goldwater-style extremism; here, both his own personal style and the pace of history were helpful to him. The Goldwater of 1964, hard-edged and shrill, had laid himself open to typing as a "radical rightist." Reagan's geniality and self-representation as Mr. Everyman made it hard to pin that tag on him. Instead, he successfully merchandised himself as a tribune of the ordinary Middle American, resentful of high taxes, big government, a visibly growing class of welfare dependents, crime in the streets, and increased civic disorder from big-city ghettos to university campuses. He backed away from radical rightism and appealed to many registered Democrats by stressing the more conservative side of the Roosevelt-Truman policies—the New Deal emphasis on work relief, for example, and the rhetorical priority both had given to budget balancing. It helped also that he was supported by the Democratic mayor of Los Angeles, Sam Yorty, a vehement critic of black militance.

The momentum of history was equally with him. In 1964, Goldwater had run up against a wall of optimism and had seemed to a majority a threat to continued peace and prosperity. Less than two years later, America had become deeply involved in a rapidly escalating war in Vietnam, inflation was beginning to pinch the affluence of the middle class, riots were occurring in one black ghetto after another, the campuses of major universities were consumed with protest. In California, these developments had a special impact. The state's cost of living and tax rates were both high; its major university at Berkeley was in turmoil; it had experienced the biggest and most violent racial upheaval of the postwar era in Watts; its population was growing at a breakneck rate sure to intensify social strains. The political atmosphere contained resentment aplenty; Reagan capitalized on it by campaigning to "the man in the suburbs working sixty hours a week to support his family and being taxed heavily for the benefit of someone else."

Relying notably on television skills honed to a fine edge by a quarter-century of experience in front of the camera, Reagan reshaped the California Republican party in 1966. Carrying fifty-three of the state's fifty-eight counties, he defeated a moderate primary opponent, Mayor George Christopher of San Francisco. In the general election, he administered a drubbing to Edmund G. "Pat" Brown, Sr., the two-term liberal Democratic incumbent who previously had disposed of such heavyweights as William Knowland and Richard Nixon. His subsequent two terms as governor demonstrated that he could manage the state in a manner satisfactory to a majority of its voters. They also established in many respects a paradigm for his future presidency.

Perhaps simply because he faced a legislature controlled by the Democratic party, his rhetoric tended to be more ideological than his policies; in fact, at times they rather clearly contradicted each other. Neither then nor later would he let reality stand in the way of a good campaign speech, but by the same token, once he had the power to govern, he would not let the good speech stand in the way of practical necessity. For example, after being elected on a campaign platform that excoriated high taxes, he came into office faced with a state budget crisis that he felt compelled to solve in part with yet higher taxes. There would be other increases before his term expired. Not surprisingly, he would prefer in later years to emphasize periodic tax rebates he was able to give to the state's citizens. Some observers found the spectacle ironic, but the tactic of making necessary compromises while continuing to profess broader objectives as a long-term goal was neither illegitimate nor politically counterproductive.

He was, all the same, capable of dramatic and decisive action. Perhaps the strongest was his determination to reimpose "law and order" on the troubled campus at Berkeley at almost any cost. First, he and his supporters on the university Board of

Regents dismissed President Clark Kerr, whom they considered a mushy liberal. Then when radical activists—some of them enrolled students, some of them not—determined to force a showdown on the unlikely issue of converting a university-owned vacant lot into a "people's park," Reagan accepted the gambit, right down to mobilizing the National Guard. In the confrontations that followed, the campus was saturated with tear gas dropped from helicopters, more than five dozen demonstrators were injured in clashes with police, one policeman was stabbed, one student was killed and another blinded when shotgun-wielding deputy sheriffs fired at them. Whether because of gubernatorial toughness or the natural exhaustion of a cycle of activism, campus disorder had subsided by the end of Reagan's first term.

Despite specific compromises, he succeeded in turning the overall direction of California politics to the right. He cut the rate of increase in state spending in a number of areas, including higher education. As a result, the state colleges and universities had to levy a tuition charge. He secured a welfare reform package that tightened restrictions for public assistance and instituted some experimental programs with work requirements while providing higher benefits for those persons who continued to qualify.

Yet these developments deserved neither the admiration they received from the ideological Right nor the horror they elicited from the ideological Left. In these and numerous other instances, Ronald Reagan, dogmatic conservative in principle, functioned as a slightly-right-of-center accommodationist in practice, making deals and giving the liberals about as much as he got from them. Higher education, for example, continued to be supported in California more generously than in most states, but with the tuition charge, conservatives got recognition of the principle that users of state services should pay at least a portion of the cost. The new welfare system was a billion dollars cheaper during its first year of operation, but in order to get the assent of Democratic legislators, Reagan had agreed to automatic cost-of-living increases that soon made it once again one of the costliest in the nation.

If Reagan was adept at declaring victory, however ambiguous the reality of things, the skill was by no means inconsequential. By the end of his years in office, the political tone of California and the terms of public discourse had undergone significant change. His successor, Edmund G. "Jerry" Brown, Jr., may have been "liberal" in many senses of the word and unconventional in ways that only a New Age Californian could truly appreciate, but he assuredly was not a free-spending liberal in the image of his father. Brown's own successors, right-leaning Republicans, underscored the sense of governmental limits that Reagan had imparted to California politics.

He was a conspicuously detached administrator. On certain issues—among them welfare reform—Reagan was capable of mastering considerable detail and wading personally into the give-and-take of negotiation. For the most part, however, he envisioned executive leadership as rhetorical leadership on the big issues and was content to let expert subordinates handle the nitty-gritty. He preferred to have major questions boiled down to "mini-memos" of about a page that quickly summarized alternatives, made a recommendation, and left a line for approval or disapproval. The method, in effect, turned issues over to subordinates who might or might not have the same ideological commitment on the specific decisions as did the boss. Yet there was much to be said for the proposition that in an age of increasingly large and complex government no single administrator could possibly master the details of dozens of issues and programs. Reagan doubtless realized also that great executives have seldom, if ever, been remembered for their micromanagement.

On balance, Reagan's governorship was successful. He left the state with solid finances, did no injury to its services, and maintained substantial popularity among both his immediate constituents and his larger national following. He also had passed an eight-year intensive course in the politics of governing. It had not been easy. As he would admit later on, he had been too dogmatic at first, had not fully understood the art of public relations as it must be practiced by politicians, and in all had made enough fumbles to put to shame his old football image as the Gipper. But he had been flexible enough to learn from his mistakes and emerge a shrewder and wiser man. What else could lie ahead for a successful outgoing governor of California? Only the presidency itself.

The Transit of Power and Ideology
from Nixon to Reagan

Ronald Reagan took the oath of office as thirty-ninth president of the United States just a little less than six and a half years after the resignation of Richard Nixon. In that short interval, the American political pendulum had swung to the left, then back to the right in presidential politics largely because neither party had been able to provide a convincing leader or a compelling ideology for a nation that seemed increasingly in drift and decline.

Perhaps in the end the most remarkable aspect of the Nixon presidency was the way in which it continued without Nixon. With Gerald Ford benignly overseeing their efforts, the chief policy makers of the late Nixon years continued to steer the nation's course. At home, the trials of an economy battered by an oil-induced recession cum inflation were the most pressing problem. With Council of Economic Advisers Chairman Alan Greenspan most responsible for policy, the administration did what Republicans often do best; it concentrated on fighting inflation and reduced a soaring rate of price increases from 11 percent in 1974 to 5.8 percent in 1976, but did so at the cost of raising unemployment from 5.6 to 7.7 percent over the same period.

In 1975, the Vietnam era came to an end as Saigon fell to a North Vietnamese offensive facilitated by congressional refusal to continue aid to the South Vietnamese. That same year, Secretary of State Henry Kissinger and Soviet leaders reached an important agreement at Helsinki. Many conservatives denounced it because it recognized Eastern Europe as a sphere of special Soviet interests. However, it also required the USSR to respect basic liberties in the region and thereby provided some small additional measure of legitimacy for the democratic opposition. Fifteen years later, Helsinki would be given considerably more credit than it deserved for the demise of Communism on the Continent. At the time, however, it clearly was an act of expediency in line with the retreat of American power rather than an effort to set in motion a liberation movement.

All the same, the country might well have opted to keep Ford in office had he maintained a semblance of presidential leadership. Far more likeable than Nixon, he possessed little of his predecessor's talent and none of his vision. Appointed rather than elected to the vice presidency, he had no claim to electoral legitimacy. After he slipped on a flight of airplane steps, comedians and cartoonists unfairly lampooned him as a stumblebum. Yet the caricature was not a bad analogy for a political personality who at a crucial moment in the 1976 presidential debates kept stubbornly insisting: "There is no Soviet domination of Eastern Europe." The line might have been understood and applauded at a meeting of the Sons of Kosciusko in Grand Rapids; a baffled nation decided it was time for a change.

Jimmy Carter seemed the ideal leader for a nation still reeling from Watergate. A former governor of Georgia, a Southerner with a commitment to civil rights, an appealing personality who strove for an identification with the ordinary individual, and above all an outsider not identified with the Washington establishment, he was in many respects a model Democratic candidate. Although he emphasized his record as a strong fiscal manager in Georgia, Carter was an ardent supporter of the tradition of Democratic liberalism from Roosevelt through Johnson. It was misleading to call him, as have some observers, a conservative. He was interested in eliminating waste, subjecting federal expenditures to cost-benefit analysis, and cutting pork-barrel projects, not in undertaking an ideological offensive against social programs. Above all a "good man" in the best sense of that term, he was honest, deeply religious, and motivated by a highly developed social conscience. Few presidents have possessed greater integrity; few have failed so badly. Histories of the Carter presidency must invariably be dominated by the question "What went wrong?"

From the beginning, Carter's appeal was broader than it was deep. His Southernness and his pietistic Baptist faith disconcerted many Democrats outside Dixie. Neither Northern ethnics (both Catholic and Jewish) nor the intelligentsia quite knew what to make of a leader who affirmed a fundamentalist faith in the literal truth of the Bible, publicly confessed the sin of adultery in his heart, taught Sunday school, neither drank nor smoked, and spoke with a deep-South accent that set him apart from the old-line Democratic mainstream. It was indicative of his tenuous hold on the American imagination that in the end he barely defeated Ford in the presidential election.

Deficient in inspirational capabilities, possessing no well-defined constituency, inexperienced on the national scene, Carter was utterly without the resources to impose his will on the

Washington establishment and was able to govern effectively only with its cooperation. Instead of coming to terms with Washington, however, he and his circle displayed an almost perverse hostility and ineptness that alienated many of the leaders of his own party. Earnest, all business, he disliked politicians, did not know how to deal with congressmen, never mastered the bureaucracy, and ultimately wearied the American people.

Carter did not even have the following of the committed activists he needed to staff the policy-making positions of the executive branch. Aside from a small number of Georgia loyalists, he had no political cadre with a strong belief in him or his point of view to which he could turn for recruits to staff the government he headed. Consequently, most of his non-White House appointments came from the main source of intellectual ferment and activist experience within the Democratic party: the left-liberal intelligentsia. After calling for a moderate reassessment of Great Society liberalism, he appointed to one office after another members of the New Class (to use the neoconservative terminology) who either had formulated the Great Society or had staked out positions to the left of it. It was eloquent testimony to the exhaustion of post–Great Society liberalism that their policies demonstrably worsened matters.

Carter had attacked Ford for allowing the "misery index," a pseudo-statistic that combined the rates of inflation and unemployment, to rise unconscionably to a peak of 17.6 in 1975. (In 1976, it declined to 13.5.) Carter followed the classic Democratic approach of concentrating on lowering unemployment, injected considerable stimulus into the economy with little regard for inflationary impact, and then found himself caught in the oil crunch that followed the overthrow of the shah of Iran. By 1980, the misery index, reflecting a roaring inflation and a mounting recession, had climbed above 20. To calm the financial markets, Carter had been all but forced to appoint as chairman of the Federal Reserve Board Paul Volcker, a monetarist determined to defend the dollar. Carter's energy program equally evolved into a debacle. It stressed controls, provided no incentives for domestic exploration, and poured funds into alternative-fuels programs that promised much but accomplished practically nothing. As Iranian production dried up and the price of oil soared to nearly forty dollars a barrel, the administration relived the Nixon nightmare of lines at service stations and nagging shortages.

Foreign policy became almost as great a nightmare. Carter scored an impressive personal triumph when he negotiated a peace agreement between Israel and Egypt, but even this remarkable achievement became all but lost in the intractability of the larger Middle Eastern conflict. One stunning success could not obscure setbacks on other crises—setbacks largely rooted in a failed conceptualization of the meaning and objectives of diplomacy. The Carter team trumpeted an end to Nixon-Kissinger *Realpolitik* and announced it would make human rights the major concern of American foreign policy. The new stance sought to replace power as the basis of diplomacy with morality and did so with little understanding of the complex relationship between power and morality that characterized the thinking of Kissinger at his best. By renouncing interventionism in the affairs of other nations and the use of military force as tactics of diplomacy, Carter had little left but diplomacy by concession—when concession was possible.

The reversals that followed soon overshadowed the luster of the Egyptian-Israeli agreement. Unwilling to meddle in the politics of Nicaragua, the administration failed to give strong support to moderate elements in the coalition that secured the long-overdue exile of dictator Anastasio Somoza. Consequently, political power went to the men with the guns, anti-U.S. Sandinistas openly pledged to emulate Castro's Cuba and spread their revolution to other Central American countries. The administration's hope of winning the Sandinistas over to a democratic path by extending aid proved so futile that it cut off the assistance. The Soviet invasion of Afghanistan was even more stunning; it dashed hopes of a general resolution of the Cold War, ruined plans for disarmament progress, forced Carter to reverse a policy of slashing defense spending, and elicited from the president an agonized statement that he had totally misjudged the USSR.

Carter's greatest setback, however, came in Iran. There, as in Nicaragua, he resolutely abstained from efforts to channel growing discontent with an incumbent regime into a moderate, pro-American direction. In consequence, Shah Reza Pahlavi was replaced by the Ayatollah Khomeini, who to the apparent stupefaction of the State Department displayed a genuine belief in the bitter anti-Americanism he had professed before coming to power. On November 4, 1979, Khomeini followers seized the U.S. embassy in Tehran and initiated a fifteen-month hostage crisis that left the nation with feelings of impotence and was more responsible than any other issue for Carter's downfall.

Subsequently, many observers, mostly disillusioned liberal Democrats, would argue that the major problem of the Carter administration was Jimmy Carter. It was true that the president displayed transparent deficiencies in the skills and experiences traditionally prerequisite to the office. A plodding speaker of narrow background, an individual with no practical foreign policy experience, a legislative leader unable to relate effectively to his own party chiefs in Congress, a workaholic whose obsession with detail often caused him to miss the big picture, he was well-endowed with numerous qualities that spelled failure in the modern presidency.

It was equally true, however, that the policies that led him to disaster were not of his making. They expressed the imperatives of Democratic liberalism as it had developed after Lyndon Johnson. Few liberals, however, then or after the subsequent defeats of Walter Mondale and Michael Dukakis, would be willing to accept the conclusion that somewhere along the line liberalism had made a series of wrong turns. By 1980, they were under an increasingly vehement assault by a rejuvenated conservatism, far more coherent and confident than the fuzzy neoconservatism that had provided the Nixon administration with a modicum of ideological coherence.

The Reagan coalition as it emerged in 1980 contained many of the elements of the old Nixon following: a still disaffected Middle America, a white South increasingly moving toward the Republican party out of resentment of the Democratic embrace of affirmative action, a significant number of hard-hat blue-collar workers, and traditional heartland Republicans. The neoconservative movement remained on board, but a New Right, composed of Protestant evangelicals and an emergent class of policy intellectuals, increasingly overshadowed it.

The evangelicals, although naturally drawn to traditional morality and frequently from Republican backgrounds, were little more than a fringe phenomenon before the Supreme Court decision in *Roe v. Wade* (1973) legalizing abortion. For many, the fight against abortion was as grave a moral cause as had been the struggle against segregation for civil rights workers in the sixties. Those with the most intense feelings actually adopted tactics of civil disobedience.

Television facilitated the evangelical mobilization. One minister, Pat Robertson, put together his own cable network. Another, Jerry Falwell, founded the Moral Majority. Scorned as modern-day Elmer Gantrys by the secular intelligentsia, they were in fact a long way from the old-time revivalistic rogues so effectively lampooned by Sinclair Lewis and H. L. Mencken. Reaching a vast audience, projecting benign personalities, they were equally at home on either side of a talk-show interview desk and in a pulpit on Sunday morning. They spoke effectively not only to abortion but to a wide range of other issues, foremost among them the disintegration of the family and the traditional values associated with it. Attracting a following of millions of alienated ordinary people in search of moral stability and a sense of purpose, they guided a flock that had become increasingly apolitical back toward politics.

The New Right policy intellectuals were by and large a different breed, less drawn to their advocacy by a quest for stability and tradition than by a zest for change and a classical nineteenth-century liberal view of political economy. Willing to take on New Deal–Great Society liberalism at its core, not simply nibble at the margins, they believed they could prevail because they had discovered that policies once identified with such symbolic types as "robber barons" and "gluttons of privilege" could be packaged so as to take on a "populist" tinge with broad appeal to a hard-pressed middle class. In addition, they sought to tap an even deeper impulse, presenting their policies as a means of reversing a sense of American decline that had set in during the seventies.

The centerpiece of the new viewpoint was "supply-side economics." Popularized by the economist Arthur Laffer and the *Wall Street Journal* editorialist Paul Craig Roberts, the doctrine attacked the liberal Keynesian formula of promoting economic expansion by moving money to "the demand side" (the consumer) through numerous income-transfer programs financed by high taxes. Rather "supply" (in the form of creative investment) was the driving force behind growth. Thus, the revival of the economy required strong steps to free up additional investment capital. The preferred method was across-the-board tax cutting.

To those who argued that nonprogressive tax reductions would be inequitable, benefitting primarily the rich, the supply-siders had two replies: a lowering of tax rates at the high end would produce more revenues from the rich, who would quit looking for tax shelters; and it would still make available more discretionary capital from the investing classes. What about the federal budget deficits that big tax cuts inevitably would produce? Increasing budget deficits were irrelevant if they abetted an economic growth that was even greater. What about a possible collapse of the dollar on international markets if the budget deficit grew too rapidly? A conservative monetary policy could maintain the value of the dollar; a return to the gold standard would be even better.

That supply-side economics caught on quickly among Republican conservatives was scarcely surprising. The new doctrine was in many respects a reformulation of traditional Republican dogma that had been written off by a generation of liberal intellectuals as "normalcy," or "trickle-down economics." The fundamental idea had been forcefully stated and effectively implemented in the 1920s by Secretary of the Treasury Andrew Mellon. To the liberals, that alone was enough to discredit it; to the conservatives, it was a reminder that the 1920s had been a period of unprecedented prosperity.

It was not, however, that they wanted to turn the clock back with no adjustments. The supply-siders, quite unlike their predecessors of fifty years earlier, were relentless free traders and advocates of competitive economics. They tended to find the origins of the Great Depression not in the 1929 stock market crash but in the 1930 Hawley-Smoot tariff and the resulting contraction of world trade. Economic growth within the United States, most believed, required worldwide growth fueled by a continued easing of trade restraints. Supply-side economics had in truth a special relevance to a world in which the United States no longer functioned as a largely self-contained economic unit. By 1980, the focus of support for open international trade had shifted from an increasingly protectionist Democratic party to the Republicans.

The major policy objective of supply-side economics, lower taxes, came naturally to most Republicans; for all their traditional talk about budget balancing, they long had lunged at any opportunity to cut taxes, assuming that lower revenues would sooner or later whittle down the size and functions of government. In the end, the reduction of government was as essential to the supply side as the provision of capital, for it was government—liberal welfarist government to be precise—that exacted a relentless toll on the supply of capital in the form of higher taxes and expenditures. It was government that bore primary responsibility for the constant inflation that increased the cost of capital in the private markets, exerted upward pressure on public spending, and inexorably pushed taxpayers into ever-higher marginal tax brackets.

In his influential book, *Wealth and Poverty*, George Gilder summarized the process: "The programs multiplied, the money supply grew, inflation raised taxes, and the spurious yield of federal programs—which often gave no valuable service—and of government bonds—which often financed waste—remained as high or higher than the real profits of private capital." In brief, the public sector was crowding out the private sector, which alone could produce real wealth.

No aspect of big government was more destructive, both economically and morally, the New Right argued, than its social-democratic, welfarist features. Few were willing, at least in public debate, to advocate a Social Darwinist society, but all were convinced that the quest for security and protection in the modern industrial state needed to be curbed and that its products needed to be trimmed back. The old-age and survivors insurance program of Social Security, for example, had grown from an inexpensive retirement supplement to a vast, costly program on the verge of insolvency, sustained by heavy payroll taxes, returning to many of its beneficiaries less than would have been the case had they pursued a private investment program.

Worst of all, however, were most of the welfare programs aimed at poverty, especially Aid to Families with Dependent Children. In general, welfare, rather than working to eliminate poverty, entrenched it, creating a culture of dependency sustained by various subtle or not-so-subtle devices that discouraged the initiative and self-reliance that alone could take one out of poverty. Four years into Ronald Reagan's presidency, Charles Murray's *Losing Ground* would provide the definitive statement of the critique and conclude that the immediate elimination of the welfare system would ultimately be better for the poor and for American society than halfway measures to reform it. The message was as politically ineffective and irrelevant as it was despairing.

Finally, the New Right extended its principles vigorously to foreign policy. Assuming that capitalism and the free market were the most durable sources of liberty and democracy, it embraced a revival of anti-Communism, repudiating both the détente of the Nixon administration and the flaccidity of the Carter years. Determined to renew the Cold War, it saw the struggle against the USSR as another dimension, quite possibly the most important one, of the struggle for freedom and prosperity at home.

The American New Right was one component of an international movement gathering strength throughout the developed world by the end of the seventies. The most prominent European leader—and one who in many ways set an example for Ronald Reagan—was Margaret Thatcher. Elected leader of the British Conservative party in 1975, becoming prime minister in 1979, Thatcher preached the doctrines of free enterprise, entrepreneurship, and individual initiative in a strident fashion discomforting to paternalistic, old-line Tories. A scathing critic of socialism, she waged war on large, expensive social welfare programs, sold public housing units to their occupants, and privatized one publicly owned industry after another. A product of evangelical Protestantism, she attempted to revive the Protestant ethic in capitalism by equating hard work and economic success with virtue. The most anti-Communist prime minister since Winston Churchill, she also turned back to the Cold War.

Thatcher was the most well-defined example, but events elsewhere in Europe confirmed the general drift of politics and ideology during the late 1970s and 1980s. In France, the Socialists came to power under François Mitterand in 1981, soon found themselves forced to confront the failures of their traditional panaceas of greater public ownership and increased welfarism, and renounced large portions of their old agenda. In the meantime, the French Communist party, scorned by an intelligentsia that had been sympathetic for a generation, sank to its lowest ebb of the postwar era. In Germany, the Social Democrats lost power after repudiating their moderate leader, Helmut Schmidt, and moving to the left; they became increasingly irrelevant for the balance of the eighties. Few observers understood it in 1980, but Ronald Reagan was the American representative of an idea whose time had come.

Reagan himself was that new idea's greatest asset in the United States. The amiable Mr. Everyman personality that he had assiduously cultivated for so much of his life connected him to an earlier, simpler, and (so many believed) more successful America; it possessed a powerful nostalgic appeal to many voters. Relatively ineffective in genuinely extemporaneous situations, he could deliver a prepared text with the facility of a man who regularly had faced microphones and cameras for forty-odd years. Not an intellectual in any strict sense of the word, already known for his lack of interest in detail, he was nonetheless both intelligent and among the most ideological of presidential candidates in American history. Hence he possessed a harder edge and exuded more confidence than his opponents in either party. And, as Aaron Wildavsky has put it, if he was not "fact smart," he was "strategy smart."

By 1976, he already was well along in his quest for the presidency. Clearly the most charismatic Republican, he narrowly missed ousting the sitting president, Gerald Ford. At the advanced age of sixty-nine, he was back on the campaign trail in 1980. It said much about his appeal that he rather easily defeated a Republican rival, George Bush, who was much younger, successful in business, experienced in a number of high-level Washington positions, and favored by the hitherto ascendant moderate wing of the party. It said much for his strategic sense that, having begun the campaign as a factional candidate favored by the party's right wing, he adeptly brought Bush onto the ticket as his running mate and united his party in a fashion that Barry Goldwater had not even approached sixteen years earlier.

Still it was not foreordained that Reagan would beat Carter (who himself had to turn back a challenge from Senator Edward Kennedy). Yet he emerged as the dominant figure very quickly, bringing together both regular Republicans and the diverse forces of the New Right. His promises of an America resurgent— "number one again"—appealed to many voters demoralized by the Carter years. His use of the "misery index" as a measure of Carter's failure was devastating. On election day, he won easily, polling 51.6 percent of the vote to 41.7 percent for Carter and 6.7 percent for the independent, John Anderson. His devoted followers waited joyously for the implementation of the coming revolution.

What Happened to the Revolution?

The Reaganites liked to distinguish themselves from the mushy accommodationists who had staffed earlier postwar Republican presidencies. All the same, they clearly existed on a continuum with the Nixon administration in terms of both policy goals and political strategy. Reagan, every bit as much as Nixon, expressed the values of culturally conservative working and middle classes who resented a new morality that was gaining ascendancy in American life and felt overtaxed for the benefit of nonproductive groups. Like Nixon, Reagan deplored abortion on demand, sought out judicial conservatives for his court appointments, denounced racial quotas, praised the traditional family ethic, and preached individual self-help.

Like most Republican presidents of the twentieth century, if considerably more than Nixon, he had an adversary relationship with organized labor, even if he once had been a union president. When federal air safety controllers called an illegal strike at the beginning of his administration, he ordered every single striker dismissed, then staffed the air control system with supervisors and retirees until an entire new work force could be hired and trained. The move enjoyed substantial support from a public fed up with large and growing government-employee unions that from the sixties on had called strikes of teachers, sanitation workers, police, and fire fighters. It also sent a powerful symbolic message to private business, which thereafter bargained more toughly with unionized employees than at any time since the thirties. Calvin Coolidge, whose portrait Reagan ostentatiously displayed in the oval office, would have thoroughly approved.

Reagan's inaugural address established a determination to establish a new order in Washington:

> Government is not the solution to our problem; government is the problem. . . . It is my intention to curb the size and influence of the Federal establishment and to demand recognition of the distinction between the powers granted to the Federal Government and those reserved to the states or to the people. . . . [W]e are too great a nation to limit ourselves to small dreams. We're not, as some would have us believe, doomed to an inevitable decline. . . . It is time to reawaken this industrial giant, to get government back within its means and to lighten our punitive tax burden.

Yet so sweeping an agenda was never possible. Every existing federal program possessed a constituency determined to defend it. Liberal Democrats retained a firm grip on the House of Representatives, although the Republicans had won narrow control of the Senate. Just as Reagan was among the most ideological of American presidents, so had the Democrats become ideologically committed to the idea of the state as dispenser of benefits; the beneficiaries, ranging from the urban poor to farmers and businessmen were also the political underwriters. Not even practical Republican politicians were willing to target significant existing programs for demolition.

The sentiments on which Reagan had capitalized included a middle-class reaction against high taxes, mounting welfare expenditures, an apparent deterioration of the quality of life in much of America, and a sense that the nation's global standing was in decline. In practical politics, this cluster of attitudes boiled down to a willingness to cut someone else's benefits, but the built-in safeguards of a governmental system characterized by federalism and checks and balances provided a degree of protection for practically every existing program. Presenting his first budget to Congress, Reagan affirmed his commitment to the New Deal "safety net."

His strategy would be to nibble around the edges of numerous programs by imposing various restrictions that would limit their growth; although characterized as "cuts" in the surreal world of Washington budgeting, this tactic actually entailed the acceptance of larger dollar amounts year after year for most "social programs." The administration got $39 billion in such "cuts," but it was neither selective nor daring in setting priorities. Inevitably, those programs that possessed the strongest—not necessarily the most deserving—constituencies survived with the least damage.

Social Security, for example, had increasingly become an expensive entitlement for the elderly middle class and faced serious financing difficulties. The administration talked initially about a thorough reexamination but backed off quickly when lobbyists for older Americans and most Democrats launched a preemptive strike of vituperative criticism. Reagan quickly adopted the time-honored strategy of turning the problem of the system's pending bankruptcy over to a bipartisan committee of "wise men" who proposed no fundamental changes. They recommended substantially higher payroll taxes that would keep the Social Security trust fund solvent, increase the federal fiscal drag on the private economy, and, not incidentally, help fund the soaring national debt. Congress happily adopted these "reforms." Adapting well to the prevailing rules of the game, Reagan announced in 1984 that Social Security recipients would get a cost-of-living increase although the rate of inflation had fallen so much that the law did not require one. Farm subsidies, another well-entrenched program, fared about equally well.

The social "safety net" programs aimed at the poor suffered a few cuts, but in general they survived without major damage, the passionate rhetoric of their supporters to the contrary. At most, Reagan succeeded in stabilizing "safety net" spending. Here and there, various special interest programs took more substantial hits, but rather ironically, the only death sentence of consequence was imposed on revenue sharing, the cornerstone of Nixon's "new federalism." For all his talk of a balanced budget, Reagan never presented one to Congress, in large measure because he pressed hard for, and received, enormous increases in defense spending.

On one strategy, substantial deregulation of the economy, Reagan won relatively broad cooperation from the Democrats. The Carter administration had already scrapped regulation of airlines and trucking companies. In principle there was much to commend the policy, so long as it did not involve safety. In transportation especially, but in other areas also, federal regulation had evolved into government-sanctioned cartelism that restricted competition while delivering ever-higher revenues to managers and ever-higher wages to employees at the expense of the general public.

Unfortunately, both Democrats and Republicans moved toward general financial deregulation and in particular agreed on a policy of allowing savings and loan associations to invest in almost anything. Neither party gave much attention to the probability that the new direction might impose severe strains on the federal deposit insurance system; instead they more than doubled its potential liabilities by increasing its coverage. Over the next several years, much of the S & L industry found itself taken over by wheeler-dealers, real estate entrepreneurs, incompetents, and outright crooks. Federal regulators were neither numerous enough nor energetic enough to deal with them expeditiously. On the occasions they did attempt to act quickly, they frequently encountered trouble from influential congressmen.

By 1989, the savings and loan insurance fund was depleted and much of the industry on the brink of collapse. The administration of George Bush would have to deal with the mess, the tab for which threatened to run into the hundreds of billions. The lesson was pretty clear: any thorough deregulation program had to have the risk to fail as one of its components and could not involve government guarantees. Whether either Democrats or Republicans had absorbed it, however, seemed doubtful.

The Reagan budget proposals brought forth an apocalyptic deluge of rhetoric from the Democratic opposition about a return to Social Darwinism and a war against the poor. The ideologists of both parties notwithstanding, the processes of government resembled those of the Eisenhower administration considerably more than those of a revolution. After four frustrating years, Reagan's budget director, David Stockman, resigned in disillusionment and wrote an embittered memoir, *The Triumph of Politics*. The book was aptly named; whether the process of accommodation it recounted was a good thing, a bad thing, or simply necessary is not so clear.

Reagan and his advisers from the beginning preferred to concentrate on an objective less painful than budget cutting. The president proposed a 30 percent cut in income taxes. The argument was seductive: a large tax cut would stimulate the economy and thereby produce increases in federal revenues that would make up for short-term declines; moreover, it would free up large amounts of money for use as investment capital needed to pay for the retooling of a declining economy. To the untutored eye, the rationale appeared quite similar to the arguments that John F. Kennedy had employed in arguing for his tax-cut plan nearly two decades earlier.

Yet only a few of the surviving veterans of the Kennedy era, most notably Gardner Ackley, supported the Reagan tax cut. Walter Heller, the father of the New Economics, was perhaps the most vociferous and articulate opponent. Partisanship no doubt explained a portion of the reaction, but hardly all of it. The political struggle over Reagan's tax proposal said much about the change in climate between the early sixties and the early eighties. The post–Great Society Democratic party had become wedded to a host of programs with constantly expanding revenue requirements that tended to exceed the average rate of economic growth. Falling into the same pattern that characterized European social democratic parties, the Democrats now emphasized entitlements over a steadily increasing Gross National Product.

The Reagan tax program was very much in line with tradiional twentieth-century Republican conservatism. Whether under the ideological leadership of Andrew Mellon or Robert A. Taft, Republicans always had been willing to cut taxes and anxious to do it on an across-the-board basis that would inevitably deliver the largest dollar gains to the prosperous middle classes and the wealthy. While they had been intellectually committed to budget balancing, it never had been at the top of their priority list. As a tangible and near-universal benefit, tax cuts were well-nigh irresistible, and they were most attractive to two constituencies: the traditional GOP middle class and the hard-pressed, angry blue-collar and lower-middle-class voters whom first Nixon and now Reagan were trying to convert to Republicanism. Tax cuts, moreover, were the central component of a siege strategy that attempted to reduce the growth of Democratic-generated entitlements through revenue starvation.

An integral (and critical) part of the Reagan tax proposal was the elimination of "bracket creep" through a procedure that would index tax brackets to the rate of inflation. Indexing had become popular in the seventies as a means of maintaining federal benefits against the constant erosion imposed on them by inflation, but it never before had been applied to taxation. Bracket creep had been crucial in producing the ever-mounting stream of federal revenues needed to pay for the rising costs of social programs and every other government operation. It made the federal deficit smaller than it might otherwise have been, but only at the cost of a steadily increasing drain from the private economy. It also had become a widely perceived and increasingly bitter grievance of middle-class taxpayers, who saw much of the nominal dollar growth of their incomes siphoned out of their paychecks. Only the administration's most dogmatic opponents dared argue against it.

A big tax cut coupled with bracket indexing was too popular to resist. Democrats protested and numerous Republicans had qualms—Senate leader Howard Baker called the proposal "a riverboat gamble"—but the public loved it. It meshed well with the traditional Republican faith in a liberated capitalism and attracted support from a minority of Democrats (most notably

Senator Bill Bradley of New Jersey), who saw it as an economic recovery program. The proposal, named for its chief sponsors, Representative Jack Kemp of New York and Senator William Roth of Delaware, passed Congress in 1981 with only small modifications. It enacted a 25 percent reduction in federal income taxes, to be phased in over three years, subjected brackets to indexing, and accelerated the investment tax credit provisions.

The most immediate and persistent result of the new policy (predictably and drearily tagged "Reaganomics" by journalists) was an enormous increase in the federal deficit. Carter's last budget (Fiscal Year 1981) resulted in a deficit of $78.9 billion; Reagan's first (Fiscal Year 1982) had a deficit of $127.9 billion and pushed the cumulative national debt over $1 trillion. The last budget for which Reagan was responsible (Fiscal Year 1989) was $152 billion in the red with a cumulative debt surging toward $3 trillion. At the beginning of the Reagan presidency, the cumulative debt represented about one-third of the annual Gross National Product and interest on it consumed around 14 percent of the federal budget. By the end, the debt was 56 percent of GNP and interest payments amounted to more than 20 percent of the budget. Although more than 80 percent of the national debt was still held by American citizens, an increasing amount was being funded by the Japanese and other foreigners, who had acquired large dollar holdings as a result of an unfavorable balance of trade that ballooned from $28 billion in 1981 to just under $160 billion in 1986 before receding to $127 billion in 1988. By 1989, moreover, the United States had transformed itself from a creditor of awesome financial power to the biggest debtor nation in history in terms of net dollars owed to foreign sources.

A critic who focused on such figures could argue with considerable force that Reaganomics had in the end done enormous damage to the American economy by burying the country under a mountain of debt, reducing the financial flexibility and independence of the federal government, and giving foreigners considerably more economic influence over the nation's destiny than at any time since World War I. Yet Reagan's defenders could argue with equal impact that his administration had given birth to a strong economic recovery and a degree of prosperity unknown since the late sixties.

Reagan had inherited from Carter a sagging, inflation-ridden economy. When he took office, unemployment was over

7 percent, inflation at 13 percent. In 1980, the prime interest rate (the rate charged by major banks to their most creditworthy corporate borrowers) had averaged 15.27 percent and home mortgages, the safest of all loans, 12.66 percent. Both were on the way up. Not since Franklin Roosevelt had a new president faced so serious an economic challenge. Unlike Roosevelt, moreover, Reagan could not enjoy the option of sealing off American economic activity from the rest of the world; the nation had become far too plugged in to the international economy.

In addition, Reagan faced a quasi-independent Federal Reserve Board with far more power than a half-century earlier and headed by perhaps the most imposing and independent figure in its history. No matter how hard the medicine, Paul Volcker was determined to wring inflation out of the economy. The economic "populists" in the administration grumbled bitterly but to no effect as Volcker pushed interest rates up through 1981 and eased only with agonizing slowness over the next few years. Unemployment followed predictably, peaking at above 10 percent and averaging more than 9.5 percent for 1982 and 1983. Yet Volcker's draconian policies may have been the only way of restoring economic prosperity; moreover, as severe as they were, the return to the gold standard favored by the supply-siders would likely have delivered even harsher results and would have allowed virtually no managerial flexibility.

It was a measure of the depth of public dissatisfaction with Carter and the Democrats that Reagan was able to survive the worst economic trough since the Great Depression with little damage. In the 1982 midterm elections, the Democrats picked up twenty-four seats in the House of Representatives but lost two in the Senate. The nation was willing, in the words of the Republican campaign slogan, to "stay the course" and hope that sacrifice in the present would mean better times in the future.

By 1984, the economy was on the rebound, if hardly in a runaway boom. Interest rates remained high—up a percent or more from 1983 levels, in fact—but unemployment had come down sharply, averaging 7.4 percent for the year, and inflation had been brought to an acceptable 4.3 percent. The final phase of the three-year tax cut was in place, leaving people with more disposable funds in their paychecks and a consequent feeling of prosperity. The economy was not the only issue in the presidential election, but its comeback undergirded every

Reagan theme of strength and renewal, thereby almost assuring his reelection.

During the president's second term, the recovery would continue apace, avoiding the excesses of an inflationary boom and giving the nation the longest period of slow but steady economic growth in its peacetime history. By the end of 1988, unemployment was below 5.5 percent, a rate that came close to effective "full employment" in an age of large numbers of two-earner households; inflation was running at 4.1 percent, a sum that would have caused great concern as late as Richard Nixon's first term but now seemed mild. Reagan had cut Carter's misery index in half.

In terms of immediate results, his accomplishment was impressive; still it was messy. The budget deficits were worrisome, largely because they grew more rapidly than the economy and thereby imposed an increased demand on the supply of private capital. Moreover, administration tax policy did little to stimulate the individual and corporate savings essential to the rebuilding of America. Indeed, the annual tug-of-war between president and Congress on tax policy resulted in one alteration after another to the Internal Revenue Code, the net effect of which was to place added burdens on savings and investment.

By 1988, thanks to a Democratic concentration on "revenue enhancement" and a Republican fixation on low marginal personal tax rates, numerous features designed to channel individual incomes into savings accounts and other investments (small exemptions for interest earned on savings accounts, tax-sheltered Individual Retirement Accounts, tax preferences for capital gains, the investment tax credit) had been eliminated or severely restricted. By the same token, most corporations found that federal tax policy made debt an ultimately more advantageous way of financing their operations than plowing earnings back into their business.

In such ways American policy ran counter to those of other, and, in the estimate of most observers, greater economic success stories of the decade, notably Japan and Germany, and all but guaranteed that the United States would be unable to finance its own budget deficit and business expansion needs from internal resources. The failure of the tax codes to encourage conventional savings and investment also stimulated the waves of takeover speculation and high-risk "junk bond" financing that hit Wall Street in the eighties. Neither was evil in itself, but their widespread visibility signaled a deeper economic malaise. Takeovers were the product of a sense that the market undervalued the assets of many corporations and thus a sign that long-term investment in underlying value had become difficult in America. Junk bonds and high business debt levels were rational responses to tax codes that accommodated such activities while failing to reward careful, low-debt management. Contrary to many of Reagan's critics, the eighties no more amounted to a "decade of greed" than did any other ten-year period in American history. The corporate financial foolishness of the period was a result of rules of the game for which Reagan's critics were at least as responsible as he.

Moreover, the high budget deficits kept interest rates at double-digit levels for much of the decade. (Money moves in the same fashion as any other commodity on the international markets; the greater the demand, the higher the price.) While this did little to stimulate domestic savings, it did attract foreign investors in both U.S. government securities and the private economy. High real interest rates also pegged the international value of the American dollar at a stratospheric level through the first half of the decade. The strong dollar contributed powerfully to the struggle against inflation at home; in 1986, the Consumer Price Index increased by only 1.9 percent. By making foreign alternatives to American goods cheap, the high-value dollar provided a strong competitive spur to American manufacturing. Unfortunately, there also was a serious downside; by making American goods expensive on foreign markets, it brought American exports to a standstill and gave rise to a ballooning trade deficit that became almost impossible to control.

A 1985 decision to let the dollar drop sharply led to a growing export revival but also helped bring inflation back up to the 4 percent level by the end of the Reagan presidency. Moreover, a cheap dollar encouraged a wave of foreign acquisitions of American companies, a development that was not necessarily economically bad but certainly disquieting politically; it raised a specter of foreign control over the nation's economy that could not be met simply by theoretical arguments about the desirable consequences of the free flow of capital. For many Americans it was all the more disturbing that much of the increased international presence was Japanese.

Administration critics argued that Reaganomics had paid a high long-run price for a false sense of well-being. By the late eighties, they asserted, real earnings for most Americans had not gained from their levels at the beginning of the 1970s; thus, only the fortunate few had experienced real gains in their standard of living. Yet the statistical foundation for such arguments generally rested on a baseline that began well before the Reagan years. Statistically, it appears that many Americans suffered declines in real income during the seventies and recouped them in the eighties, a period in which all groups enjoyed real increases. Much of the indignation was directed at an increasing inequality of distribution; without question, the "rich" (that is, the top 20 percent) enjoyed increases at twice the rate of the "poor" (that is, the bottom 20 percent). Whether quantitative inequality was evil more than ever divided Democratss and Republicans; the rising tide had nonetheless lifted all ships, if not at the equal rate that the analogy implies. Qualitative issues, resting as they did on widely varying normative assumptions, remained unamenable to empirical inquiry.[1]

The nature of Reagan's accomplishment remained unclear. His liberal critics believed that he simply had initiated a form of "reactionary Keynesianism"—stimulating the economy through tax cuts that gave the greatest benefits to the rich and through deficit spending that emphasized a military buildup at the expense of social programs. His conservative defenders praised him for liberating the economy and slowing, although not stopping, the growth of a wasteful, parasitical federal establishment.

In terms of current conditions, he clearly had left the country more economically confident than he had found it. Most Americans in 1988 felt they were better off than they had been in 1980,

---

[1]How, for example, did one take into account the development and distribution at increasingly lower prices of numerous items that simply had not existed at the beginning of the seventies, ranging from a dazzling array of electonic products to personal computers to new medical technologies and ethical drugs? Moreover, many of the more mundane staples of life, such as household appliances, had become cheaper in terms of inflation-adjusted income. So had luxuries such as air travel. Other areas involved trade-offs that were all but impossible to quantify—automobiles that were smaller but more fuel-efficient and considerably safer; environmental quality paid for in the form of higher prices on many items but of value to most Americans. One wondered if many Americans in 1989 would have opted to travel back in time twenty years or more and make their lives in an earlier era.

and most statistical measurements bore them out. Manufacturing productivity, which had sagged badly in the 1970s, increased sharply throughout the 1980s; by the end of the decade, the United States was once again fully competitive with the other large trading nations, and manufacturing was as large a share of GNP as at any time since World War II. Still most American products competed on the basis of price rather than perceived quality. The United States had generated more jobs than the rest of the industrial world combined but had been unable to manage the best-of-all-possible-worlds combination of a strong currency and high productivity gains accompanied by truly low inflation and low interest rates. By these criteria, Japan and (with some qualification) West Germany had been more successful. Thus the economic prospect remained unclear. That Reagan had "brought the country back" seemed a fair evaluation, as indicated by the statistics in Table 8.1. "At what cost?" remained a fair question with no certain answer, particularly when one considered the increasingly large debt owed to foreign investors.

Winning the Cold War

However controversial his social and economic policies, nothing separated Ronald Reagan's view of the world from that of the reigning intelligentsia more clearly than his approach to international relations. The dominant foreign policy theme of his administration was laid out most memorably in a 1983 speech to a group of evangelical churchmen. Much of the talk consisted of simple affirmations of fundamentalist positions on the major social issues and of rather conventional pieties about such matters as the power of prayer. For those who read it carefully and fully, however, the speech belied those who argued that Reagan avoided serious ideas. It was a statement about human nature in terms of what once had been called "neo-orthodox theology," which under the aegis of Reinhold Niebuhr had enjoyed a considerable vogue among liberals of the forties and fifties. (It was yet another indicator of the transformation of liberalism that Niebuhr had long since either fallen out of fashion or been reinterpreted into meaninglessness by those who still professed allegiance to his ideas.)

Asserting the persistence of evil in the world, Reagan denounced the notions that the concept of personal responsibility

Table 8.1. Reagan Administration Economic Statistics (U.S. Dollar Sums Unadjusted for Inflation)

	1981	1982	1983	1984	1985	1986	1987	1988
GNP ($ billions)	3,052.6	3,166.0	3,405.7	3,772.2	4,014.9	4,231.6	4,524.3	4,880.6
% Increase	11.7	3.7	7.6	10.8	6.4	5.4	6.9	7.9
adjusted for inflation	1.9	−2.5	3.6	6.8	3.4	2.7	3.7	4.4
CPI	90.9	96.5	99.6	103.9	107.6	109.6	113.6	118.3
% Increase	10.3	6.2	3.2	4.3	3.6	1.9	3.6	4.1
FY deficit ($ billions)	78.9	127.9	207.8	185.3	212.3	221.2	149.7	155.1
National debt ($ billions)	994.3	1,136.8	1371.2	1564.1	1,817.0	2,120.1	2,345.6	2,600.8
% Increase	9.4	14.3	20.6	14.1	16.2	16.7	10.6	10.9
% Unemployment	7.5	9.5	9.5	7.4	7.1	6.9	6.1	5.4
Trade deficit ($ billions)	28.0	36.4	67.1	112.5	122.1	145.1	159.5	127.2

Source: Economic Report of the President, 1990

was reactionary and irrelevant in modern society, that instead government could perfect human nature. Living in the real world, he declared, meant dealing with what philosophers called the phenomenology of evil and theologians called sin; thus, it was the duty of the Christian to join the struggle against sin, not to try to transcend it. The fight, to be sure, had a home front; in America, evil manifested itself in such forms as racism, anti-Semitism, and other hate movements. "The focus of evil," however, was overseas.

Marxist-Leninist movements repudiated traditional morality, preached class war, and employed any means, no matter how reprehensible, to achieve their ends. Given the fact of evil, "simple-minded appeasement or wishful thinking about our adversaries is folly." So was the tendency of increasing numbers of liberal churchmen to opt for neutrality in the Cold War. "I urge you to beware the temptation of pride—the temptation of blithly declaring yourselves above it all," he declared in Neibuhrian terms. It would be wrong to "label both sides equally at fault, to ignore the fact of history and the aggressive impulses of an evil empire, to simply call the arms race a giant misunderstanding and thereby remove yourself from the struggle between right and wrong and good and evil."

The phrase "evil empire" became to most liberals an instant barometer of Reagan's simplemindedness, a confirmation that his worldview was a product of the action-adventure films he had made with co-stars such as Errol Flynn in the 1940s. Many of his conservative supporters found the phrase rather embarrassing, however gamely they might defend it. Such reactions were in the broadest sense logical outgrowths of an increasingly pervasive "postmodern" mentality inclined to abandon all clear-cut distinctions, especially those that pertained to truth, morality, or meaning, in favor of a universe characterized by pervasive ambiguity. In the more specific sense of ideas about the nature and purpose of American foreign policy, however, the negative reaction to "evil empire" revealed a generational difference between those who, like Reagan, had been deeply affected by World War II and clung to what might be called the worldview of 1945 as opposed to those who had to one degree or another been shaped by the experience of Vietnam and had adopted the worldview of 1968.

The 1968 outlook was the culmination of the long, unproductive American involvement in Vietnam, brought into being by the

Tet offensive and the subsequent jelling of a national consensus in favor of disengagement. It also had its origins in a presidential campaign that would be remembered for the repudiation of a sitting president, the assassination of a chief contender, and riots in the streets of Chicago. It had sources in the economic and social problems that Vietnam seemed to intensify, from racial bitterness and urban violence to rampant inflation and declining national competitiveness. To a good many on the right, including Richard Nixon and Henry Kissinger, the 1968 experience mandated acceptance of a waning U.S. hegemony in the world, the retreat of American power, and détente with the Communist world. To most liberals, it increasingly suggested not just the need for retreat and détente but also loss of faith in an affirmative American purpose, a feeling that the nation had played a negative, oppressive role in recent world history, and a determined rejection of future "imperial" ventures in such places as Nicaragua or Iran. Thus, most liberals rejected sharp moral divisions between the United States and the Communist world and assumed that accommodation was a positive good.

Reagan by contrast, embodying the outlook of 1945, possessed no doubt that America had an affirmative moral mission in the world and was certain that American power was capable of prevailing over any challenge. Total victory, or something approaching it, was possible over Communism; as had been the case with the World War II Axis, it should be a rehabilitative victory rather than a vengeful one. His objective, at once consistent with militant affirmations of the Cold War and professions of generosity toward one's foe, was to reorient the world toward American ideals of liberty and democracy.

An observer in the early 1990s looking back at the Soviet Union of the early 1980s is most likely to recall the tired, sclerotic image of its leaders—Brezhnev, Andropov, Chernenko—and one state funeral after another. In 1981, however, the USSR still seemed an aggressive expansionist power bent on extending its influence into northern Africa (Ethiopia and the Sudan), the Middle East (Afghanistan, Iraq, Syria, South Yemen), and the Carribbean (Nicaragua and Grenada). Soviet power still held a firm grip on Eastern Europe, vigorously suppressing the most visible challenge to its authority, the Solidarity movement in Poland. The USSR had achieved an enormous, and superficially intimidating, margin over the United States in numbers of land-based intercontinental ballistic missiles (ICBMs), was clearly gaining in nuclear attack submarines, and could observe with satisfaction the increasing obsolescence of the B-52 bomber as a nuclear delivery vehicle. It seemed a very real possibility that the Soviet empire, capitalizing on the leftward drift of social democratic parties and the increasingly vocal sentiment for nuclear disarmament might be capable of achieving a hegemonic position over Western Europe in the coming years.

The United States, by contrast, appeared tired, irresolute, and humiliated by the Iran hostage crisis. Reagan himself had asserted in the presidential campaign that the country faced a "window of vulnerability," created by Carter's weak defense policy. As the new president saw it, his task was twofold: to strengthen the nation's military capabilities and to repair its self-confidence. The first job was the source of much of the increase in the national debt during his years in office. Jimmy Carter's last budget had included approximately $134 billion for national defense; Reagan's final budget, eight years later, had brought the total to $298 billion despite strong Democratic resistance. Even after adjusting for inflation, the increase was about 71 percent, devoted to a wide variety of acquisitions: exotic electronic warfare systems as well as bigger and presumably better versions of such old standbys as tanks, bombers, nuclear submarines, and aircraft carriers. Few could have imagined that their first real test would come not on the plains of north-central Europe but in the Arabian desert.

The second job, the restoration of confidence, would be largely a matter of rhetoric and presidential image. Here Reagan excelled, utilizing words and phrases that would have come naturally to presidents from Roosevelt through Kennedy but that seemed to have lost their sincerity and authenticity after having been uttered by Lyndon Johnson in support of Vietnam. In Reagan's rhetorical world, America stood for freedom, wanted only peace, pursued military strength for the good of humankind, and was approaching the greatest period of its history. A critical intelligentsia snickered at the lines, and produced long treatises proclaiming the inevitable decline of America as a world power. Reagan's broader audience found his words inspiring.

At times, as when he saluted "the boys of Pointe du Hoc" at Omaha Beach on the fortieth anniversary of D-Day, the president could be emotionally overwhelming. Perhaps no past chief executive had so frequently or so eloquently sought to link the inspirational moments of the past with the promise of the future. Liberals such as Sidney Blumenthal might lament "the long national daydream" that Reagan had inflicted on America. The president and his writers were nonetheless perceptive in believing that the preachments of a chief executive could boost the self-esteem of a nation and that a country that felt good about itself was likely to achieve more than one that did not.

The problem of confidence may have been primarily an American one, but it extended also to Europe and the NATO allies. In part because of a growing lack of faith in America, in part as a consequence of growing left-wing sentiment against nuclear weaponry, in part as a reaction to a Soviet policy that combined nuclear menace with a promise of political and economic détente, the Western European nations appeared perilously close to effective abandonment of the alliance. The immediate issue that Reagan faced was the need for the NATO military forces to deploy a new generation of intermediate-range nuclear force (INF) missiles.

Throughout most of Europe, antinuclear demonstrators dominated the streets and spoke with the loudest voices in public debate. For a time, the Labour party in England and the Social Democratic party in West Germany appeared controlled by advocates of unilateral nuclear disarmament. On the surface, it seemed doubtful that Ronald Reagan, generally considered a know-nothing cowboy actor by the European intelligentsia, could have an impact on public opinion in the NATO countries. Still, the president stood firmly for deployment, thereby assuring proalliance Europeans of American resolve; at the same time, he proclaimed verifiable nuclear disarmament as his ultimate goal, thus challenging assertions that he was a simpleminded warmonger.

Whether despite Reagan or because of him, the proalliance forces prevailed in one country after another. His stock remained low among the articulate classes of the Continent, but one doubts that Jimmy Carter would have been a more convincing symbol of American resolve. Moreover, the INF debate was an indicator of the strength of anti-Communism in Europe and yet another indication that Reagan was part of a transnational resurgence of the Right in reaction to the excesses of the Left throughout the Western world.

Missiles played a key role in the rest of Reagan's Cold War strategy. While his administration pressed for a new generation of ICBMs with the goal of matching the USSR, his own major energy and emotional commitment went into support for an antimissile defense system. The Strategic Defense Initiative (SDI) was designed to overturn what had become the accepted doctrine of Cold War strategic stability, Mutual Assured Destruction (MAD). MAD had established an enduring equilibrium because the two great nuclear powers concentrated on targeting each other's civilian population centers, possessed the military capacity to survive a first strike, and thus could inflict unimaginable devastation upon each other.

Professing moral horror over MAD, Reagan argued for development of an advanced laser-based defense system that could throw up an impenetrable curtain against missile attacks. It would not only provide the United States with a comprehensive defense, he argued, but could be the basis for disarmament and a new doctrine of mutual assured protection. He proposed, once the system was perfected, to share it with the Soviet Union and employ it as the tool that would make nuclear disarmament safe. Reagan's sincerity was genuine and contagious; and SDI, like all huge weapons systems, meant jobs and money for many congressional districts. All the same, the critics were legion, attacking SDI as a potentially destabilizing element in U.S.-Soviet relations and ridiculing it as a Hollywood fantasy ("star wars").

It was eminently reasonable to question whether any defense system could be absolutely foolproof against hundreds of ICBMs, but although Reagan oversold the system, much SDI research was certain to have more plausible defense applications. This probability, along with the political pork barrel benefits, won it congressional appropriations. In the end, its most critical element was its complexity and its expense. After the Soviet Union at enormous cost had achieved parity or something close to it with the United States, Reagan had thrown down the gauntlet for a new weapons race that the USSR, deficient in technological capabilities and financial resources, could not win.

Ironically, Reagan (or his policy of continued Cold War consciousness) was more successful in Europe than in the Western Hemisphere. Here the stakes seemed smaller, the issues cloudier, and the opportunities for partisanship consequently well-nigh irresistible. Like every president since Kennedy, Reagan posed no threat to Fidel Castro's Cuban regime, but he was determined to draw the line against any further expansion of pro-Soviet Communism into the Americas. Most Republicans tendered the cause visceral support. Most Democrats reflected a new party sensibility that had emerged from the experience of Vietnam, been ratified by the McGovern candidacy, and institutionalized in the Carter presidency.

Consisting of a generalized wariness about using military force and especially a reluctance to become involved in wars of liberation, the new Democratic attitude had strong roots in a broader public opinion. It had impacted upon Jimmy Carter himself when his secretary of state, Cyrus Vance, had resigned in protest against a military effort to rescue the Iranian hostages. In addition, the new sensibility included an emotional revulsion against dictatorships of the Right, with which previous Democratic leaders from Roosevelt through Johnson had routinely dealt. The other side of this revulsion was a far more frequent tendency to identify with revolutionaries who claimed to represent the masses against forces of imperialism, militarism, and right-wing dictatorship.

Among some political intellectuals most affected by the 1960s, even Castro remained a compelling figure. But the Nicaraguan Sandinistas had replaced him as the chic guerrilla attraction. Conversely, even those Central American regimes with democratically chosen leaders remained afflicted with powerful independent armies that attempted to suppress insurgencies with little regard for human rights. In El Salvador, for example, a social democratic president was unable to control a military that periodically killed reformist nuns and priests, thereby outraging not just the left-liberal intelligentsia but more traditional and moderate Americans.

Throughout his presidency, Reagan faced stiff Democratic opposition to a U.S. presence in Central America. Successful in obtaining congressional ratification of aid to El Salvador, he was unable to secure anything more than meager and sporadic assistance to *contra* guerrillas fighting the Nicaraguan government. Congressional opponents, implicitly rejecting a tenet of American foreign policy that dated back to Theodore Roosevelt, tended to assert that the United States had no vital interests in Central America and invoked the specter of a Vietnam-style war. A good many of them, moreover, argued with varying degrees of openness that the victory of revolutionary forces in the region was preferable to the continued repressions of the Right. Administration leaders, persuaded that they were promoting emerging forces of democracy and individual liberty against efforts to impose Soviet-style totalitarianism, stopped just short of accusing the Democratic opposition of softness toward Communism. Reagan's one major coup, the invasion of the tiny island of Grenada and the displacement of a pro-Castro regime there was possible only because he acted without congressional authorization and met no significant military resistance. The Iran-contra affair would be the climax to what had become a muddled partisan and ideological stalemate.

Reagan and his aides were nothing if not determined and inflexible in their commitment to win the Cold War. Dealing with the equally critical and even more intractable problems of the Middle East was quite another matter. The ideological fault lines of the Cold War were at most a subtheme in the region. The U.S. special relationship with Israel was a fixed part of the political landscape subject only to the most minor alterations and hence a consistent obstacle to good U.S.-Arab relations. The Arab world seethed with contradictory currents of moderate pro-Westernism, Islamic fundamentalism, ethnic hatreds, sectarian hostilities, conflicting national ambitions, and intense personal rivalries among various leaders. The post-1973 shock of oil dependency simply made an almost hopeless situation worse. Even Jimmy Carter's one heroic achievement, the Egyptian-Israeli peace agreement, could not break the logjam in the way of a general Middle Eastern peace; its Egyptian signatory, President Sadat, would pay for it with his life.

From the beginning, consequently, the Reagan administration, much like its predecessors, would find itself immersed in a series of ad hoc efforts: to contain and resolve the Arab-Israeli conflict; to protect Western access to oil by bolstering friendly regimes and maintaining a precarious regional balance of power; and to deal with hostage-taking fundamentalists who made anti-Western statements by snatching Americans and Europeans from the streets of Beirut. Almost by definition, full success was impossible; only the degree of failure was at question.

Neither the Arabs nor the Israelis were willing to make the sort of compromises necessary for further meaningful progress. The fall of the shah had transformed Iran from a friendly state into the vanguard of revolutionary (more properly, reactionary) anti-Western sentiment in the region; consequently, the administration would tilt toward Iraq as the lesser of two threats during the long Iraq-Iran war. Given the invisibility of the hostage takers, the hostage situation became a long-running sore that evaded diplomatic resolution. Periodically, it reemerged into newspaper headlines and television news shows that featured the anguish of victims' families and the impotence of the government.

Reagan's two major attempts to handle the ongoing Middle Eastern crises both demonstrated the apparent impossibility of management, much less progress, in the region. The first was an effort to restore stability in Lebanon, more strife-torn than ever. Beset by Israeli attacks, a Palestine Liberation Organization presence, bitter division between numerous Muslim and Christian factions that all were armed to the teeth, and pressure from Syria, Lebanon was a far more difficult and dangerous place than the little country that had reacted so benignly to a brief American occupation in 1958. In 1982, the administration sent a detachment of marines to Beirut; along with a French contingent, the marines were supposed to be a force that would facilitate the evacuation of Palestinian guerrillas, allow the Israelis to disengage, and then promote the establishment of a semblance of order in a city that had fallen into anarchy.

Yet, beyond securing the airport, the marines never had a clear mission; nor did they have the numbers to establish anything more than a limited presence. Tightly controlled through a complex chain of command more sensitive to diplomatic implications than military realities, they soon became daily targets for snipers in nearby apartment buildings. Nor did their commander implement sound security procedures. On October 24, 1983, a fanatic drove a speeding truckload of high explosives through a lightly guarded checkpoint and smashed into a barracks, killing 241 men. Shortly thereafter, Reagan ordered an evacuation of American military personnel. Lebanon continued its descent into chaos. The president's apparent lack of resolve appears to have left an indelible impression of U.S. unreliability in the minds of numerous Middle Eastern leaders, including the Iraqi leader Saddam Hussein. His decision to send warships to the Persian Gulf in 1986 to escort Western oil tankers would not erase it.

The administration would display once again the slipperiness of its grip on the Middle Eastern situation when it opened back-channel negotiations with Iran in 1986. The objectives were worthy—freedom for several American hostages held by pro-Iranian forces in Lebanon and a broad *modus vivendi* with the Iranian government. The policy execution was wretched. The Iranians requested and received a "demonstration of good faith" in the form of secret weapons sales, gave back little in return, and ultimately leaked news of the dealings to Middle Eastern press sources on the day Americans were voting in the midterm congressional elections. The revelations may have cost the Republicans a few close contests; over the next several months, they made administration diplomats look amateurish.

The situation took on the proportions of a major scandal when it became known that proceeds from the arms sales had been diverted to the aid of the Nicaraguan contras in defiance of a congressional resolution, the Boland amendment. For a time, it appeared that Reagan was at the center of a political firestorm comparable to Watergate. National Security Adviser Admiral John Poindexter and his aide, Lieutenant Colonel Oliver North, were forced to resign. Also let go under pressure was White House chief of staff Donald Regan; when former Senator Howard Baker succeeded Regan, it appeared that a new regency, controlled by a moderate establishment figure, had been established. A special counsel, appointed as the result of intense pressure, began to look around for people to prosecute. The Senate undertook a Watergate-style investigation of the entire affair; here and there, one heard the word *impeachment*.

Yet Reagan was far from through. He freely admitted knowledge of the negotiations with Iran and the arms sales, but denied being aware of the diversion of funds to the contras. No convincing evidence could be found to rebut him. The Senate investigation never really caught fire; rather than revealing the sort of stark lying and wrongdoing that had characterized Watergate, it partially opened the curtain on an ambiguous world of international intrigue hard to judge in terms of Sunday school morality. For all the outrage among Capitol Hill Democrats, most Americans were not incensed by under-the-table assistance to Central American anti-Communists or by disregard of a congressional resolution that specified no penalties for its violation. In the end, a few individuals pled guilty to some peripheral charges. North and Poindexter went to trial on a long list of accusations and were convicted of a few of them.[2] The moral import of the whole business became even fuzzier when in 1990 the Sandinistas, reacting largely to the pressure Reagan had initiated, agreed to free elections, and were promptly thrown out of office by an ungrateful Nicaraguan electorate.

Reagan in the meantime, far from being a figurehead for the duration of his presidency, had gone on to what would be its ultimate triumph. Despite the distractions of the Middle East, he was within sight of renewed détente with the Soviet Union and victory in the Cold War. During his first term, serious diplomatic intercourse with the Soviet Union had been all but impossible. Given the precarious health of the Soviet leadership, there was literally no one with whom the most accommodationist American chief executive could hope to negotiate a lasting deal. All that changed dramatically when Mikhail Gorbachev came to power in March 1985.

Younger, more vigorous, better educated, and more cosmopolitan than any Soviet leader before him, Gorbachev from the beginning raised the hopes of the Western world for a new era of détente with the USSR. Although his ultimate objectives were uncertain, it became apparent early on that he was determined to reform a stagnant economy through policies of *glasnost* (openness) and *perestroika* (restructuring). Rather too hopefully, some observers saw him as a closet liberal planning to toss overboard the entire apparatus of dictatorship and party control; he appears instead to have been from the start an abler version of Nikita Khrushchev striving to rescue a collapsing system. Still, he was a far more liberal-minded and consistent Marxist than his Chinese counterparts, who were trying to bring their country the benefits of capitalism while maintaining a rigid policy of political repression.

From the beginning, Gorbachev preached the benefits of relaxed tensions with the West. Reagan was receptive. The resulting diplomatic exchanges and personal meetings between the two men were by no means an unalloyed story of steadily growing fraternal comradeship; the Cold War carried too much bag-

---

[2]North's conviction was subsequently reversed by an appellate court order under a ruling that seemed likely to benefit Poindexter. The disposition of his case remained unclear as this edition went to print.

gage for that. Yet Reagan felt comfortable with his new adversary, and Gorbachev apparently concluded he could do business with the American president. Despite numerous bumps in the diplomacy that followed their first meeting, Reagan and Gorbachev revived détente. In the United States, the most heralded achievement was an INF agreement negotiated in 1987, providing for the destruction of intermediate-range missiles by both sides.

By the end of the Reagan presidency, Gorbachev had liquidated the Soviet presence in Afghanistan (where semicovert American aid had done much to maintain a strong resistance), encouraged liberalization in Eastern Europe, and introduced democratic political reforms in the USSR. Less than a year after Reagan left the White House, the Berlin Wall had come tumbling down, and from Poland to Bulgaria the old Soviet-supported regimes were either dead or dying. All but the most adamant of his opponents had to admit that Ronald Reagan *must* have had something to do with it.

Political Mastery, Political Stalemate: The Reagan Riddle

Through eight years, Ronald Reagan held onto a remarkably durable popularity. His approval ratings, as measured by the polls, had far more ups than downs. His skills as a communicator clearly were formidable, his personality appealing to all but his most unregenerate critics. To their everlasting chagrin, he emerged early on as a "Teflon president"—one to whom bad news did not stick, not even such fiascos as the Lebanon intervention or the Iran-contra episode. Much of the news media and a substantial majority of those engaged in public discourse in America openly held attitudes about him that ranged from somewhat cautious skepticism to outright disdain. Yet in 1984, he won a landslide reelection, defeating the most experienced candidate the opposition could put up against him. Four years later, he left the White House, still a recipient of admiration from a majority of the public.

Reagan's achievement was in many ways strikingly similar to that of Franklin D. Roosevelt. Roosevelt's presidential style also was heavily based on communication skills. Roosevelt had relied heavily on ideological appeals that made him sound much less moderate than he actually was. Like Reagan, he had been attacked by a large portion of the news media. Like Reagan, he frequently had been contemptuous of detail and often inconsistent in the mix of specific policies that went into his overall program. Like Reagan, he had been a stunningly successful electoral politician.

Yet for all the goodwill he had amassed, for all the policy successes at home and abroad, Reagan was not as important a president as Roosevelt. The one goal that consistently eluded him, and the one that Roosevelt achieved, was that of an enduring political realignment in the form of a broad coalition of interest groups loosely held together by an ideology. In that sense Reagan's presidency was more similar to Eisenhower's. One can fathom the failure of both only by understanding the limits of their commitment to change and by grasping the transformation of American politics from the New Deal to the Reagan Revolution.

Above all, as Eisenhower had impatiently written to his brother a generation earlier, no viable conservative movement could pose a frontal challenge to the New Deal state. Too many interests were enmeshed in its preservation; the loose ideological commitment to its essentials pervaded American thinking about government and had become (as Jefferson remarked of Lockean contract theory two hundred years earlier) "the common sense of the subject." A successful conservatism could have an impact on the character of national political discourse through rhetorical invocations of traditional values, a strategy Reagan employed with substantial success. Programmatically, however, conservatism could be little more than a containment operation, nibbling here and there at the perceived excesses of the Great Society.

To ideological purists of the Right, such tactics smacked of "me-tooism" and hence deserved only scorn; yet Barry Goldwater's 1964 campaign remained a vivid demonstration of what would happen to any Republican conservative who went beyond me-tooism. The widespread disenchantment with an old order of things that had made possible the Roosevelt realignment of the 1930s simply did not exist in the 1980s. Thus Reagan's conservatism was more rhetorical than substantive. One suspects that it reflected both his own shrewd sense of the politically possible and a fundamental uncertainty in his own mind about how far to the right he wanted to go. In this sense, he was wiser than many of his most devoted followers.

The steady erosion of the party system from 1945 on made any sort of "realignment" next to impossible. By the 1980s, political scientists wrote more of "dealignment." Among political professionals and activists, partisanship and ideological commitment remained intense, but for the majority of Americans, party affiliation had become a peripheral commitment scarcely worth making and ideology a somewhat offensive irrelevance. (In national polls, the percentage of the public calling itself independent was likely to be slightly larger than the groups describing themselves as Democratic or Republican.) By the 1980s, neither party could call on loyalties forged during periods of intense experience such as the Civil War or the Great Depression–World War II era. Nor, except in isolated and highly limited instances, could parties win allegiances through control of government jobs and the administration of informal charitable systems. Institutionalized civil service and welfare systems had supplanted those practices; mass affluence had made them largely irrelevant anyway. The rise of electronic communications had severely weakened one other critical function of political parties: the selection of candidates. In an era of disintegrating parties, realignment was a chimera.

What Reagan, like Nixon before him, could do was take advantage of the way in which the developments of the postwar generation had impacted the Democrats more negatively than the Republicans. New Deal pluralist liberalism continued to be the reigning ideology and predominant mode of political organization, but, especially after the 1960s, it loomed as a big, vulnerable target with numerous soft spots. Most vividly, it increasingly became open to attack as a conglomerate of diverse special interests—labor unions, blacks, feminists, homosexuals, environmentalists, disarmers, counterculturalists—that had little support in the larger body politic and no compelling vision of a general public interest. After 1968, Democratic presidential nominating campaigns and conventions appeared to lend visual support to the accusation.

The failure of Reagan's 1984 presidential opponent, Walter Mondale, told the story. The Democratic party possessed no abler presidential candidate. A person of widely recognized personal character and a remarkable fund of experience, Mondale nonetheless was hard-pressed to win the nomination against Senator Gary Hart of Colorado, who sensed the widespread public uneasiness with the direction of Democratic liberalism and talked in general terms about the need for "new ideas." Ultimately Hart was defeated because of the murkiness of his new ideas and doubts about his overall substance. But Hart also lost because Mondale drew heavily on his own old alliances with organized labor and blacks, promising both groups that he would do more for them than any other Democrat. In close major primary races, he made the same sort of pledge to the electorates of entire states, thus obliterating any sense that he was driven by a vision of the common good.

After winning the nomination, Mondale made two other decisions certain to hurt him with the larger electorate. To appease feminists, he selected as his vice presidential candidate, Geraldine Ferraro, a New York congresswoman whose qualifications to become president were at best speculative. In his acceptance speech, he pledged to balance the budget by raising taxes, thereby allowing the Republicans to pillory him as a tax-and-spend liberal determined to expand government programs for the benefit of his interest group coalition. Reagan responded by constantly asking the question "Are you better-off now than in 1980?" A blatant appeal to self-interest, it was nonetheless aimed at no explicitly targeted group, promised no special federal benefit, and was thereby less jarring to traditional American sensibilities.

Yet in broad strategic terms, even Reagan's landslide victory of 1984 was little more than a component in a continuing pattern of stalemate. Republicans (conservative to one degree or another) appeared increasingly to have a lock on the presidency; Democrats possessed untouchable majorities in the House of Representatives and usually controlled the Senate. (Republicans, it is true, had the Senate during Reagan's first six years, but by thin majorities; they had last controlled the upper chamber in 1953–1954.) One could produce a number of structural explanations for the continued Democratic ascendancy on Capitol Hill, among them the gerrymandering of congressional districts and the many advantages of incumbency: large staffs, name recognition, big campaign contributions, easy access to the news media. Still it remained hard to believe that larger issues were not determining.

At least from Nixon on, possibly from Eisenhower's time, a majority of the public appears to have been more in tune with Republicans on issues of foreign policy and national security. Moreover, majorities tended to register agreement with Republicans on such domestic matters as generalized control of spending, distrust of the growing Washington establishment, and such sociocultural debates as drug policy, racial preferences, or crime. Still, the appeal of federal benefits was strong. Since James Madison had written of the dangers of "faction" (special interest politics) in *The Federalist*, Americans had deplored the machinations of interest groups in the abstract while zealously using the political process to pursue their own interests. Congress long had been the cockpit of special interest politics, its members always expected to bring as much pork as possible back to dominant groups in their home districts. The game long had been a bipartisan one, but it was fair to characterize the Democrats as more receptive to it.

Ronald Reagan was never likely to alter that pattern. Nor were he and the Republicans altogether in the ascendancy on the sociocultural issues. The problem of abortion divided both the party and conservative thinkers; according to the polls, moreover, the wider public consistently favored a substantial degree of access to abortion for women. Other polls revealed with the same relative consistency that many who approved of Reagan as president disapproved of his positions on numerous issues. Larry Schwab, a close student of American opinion in the eighties, has argued that on the whole attitudes actually moved toward the left during the decade. That thesis may be questioned, but Reagan assuredly did not achieve a broadly-based ideological revolution.

His accomplishment was nonetheless remarkable. Whatever the long-term implications of his economic policies, he had turned around a sagging economy. Possibly his critics were correct in declaring that he had sown the seeds of long-term disaster; it is equally possible that John Maynard Keynes's caustic reminder that in the long term we are all dead remained apt. In foreign policy, Reagan had achieved the most stunning triumphs since Roosevelt beat the Axis and Truman achieved the Marshall Plan and NATO. He had brought back the presidency from its lowest ebb since Hoover. Most of all, he had restored the nation's confidence and had affirmed its faith in the future. If there had been plenty of bumps along the way, so had there been with FDR.

Epilogue: The Exhaustion of Liberalism, the Limits of Conservatism, and the Enduring Deadlock of Democracy

The presidential election of 1988 provided for those who needed it proof that Ronald Reagan had dramatically changed the tone of political debate and the agenda of American politics. He had done so not by gaining widespread assent for the ideology of the New Right but by legitimizing the Middle American reaction against the Great Society and thereby continuing a political strategy that Richard Nixon had begun. It demonstrated equally that the Democratic party, the near-exclusive vehicle of liberalism, remained formidable in its appeal to individual constituencies but hapless in producing either a leader or an appeal that convincingly projected a sense of strength and a broad common interest. Consequently, despite many changes in tone and substance, American politics remained in a pattern of deadlock that had emerged in the late 1930s and had been broken only temporarily by Lyndon Johnson in the mid-1960s.

Reagan's successor as leader of the Republican party, George Bush, was in many ways an unlikely heir. While he had loyally served the Gipper as vice president, he also had been his chief opponent for the Republican nomination in 1980, when he had called supply-side theory "voodoo economics." An instinctive moderate (some had even said "liberal") Republican, he had no roots in the New Right. Despite his formal residence in Texas, he was a product of the old Northeastern establishment that had dominated the Republican party in the days of Dewey and

Eisenhower. A New England patrician by background, an Ivy Leaguer, he envisioned politics as a matter of civic duty as much as of ideology; a good many Washington-watchers, in fact, questioned whether he possessed an ideological core.

Bush's opponent, Michael Dukakis of Massachusetts, was an even more unlikely choice. He had won the nomination over several other second-rank Democrats in a field noted for the absence of the party's strongest figures, all of whom seemed to possess characteristics that disqualified them with at least one key party constituency. Governor of a medium-sized state with no experience in foreign policy, he ran on the generalized issue of "competence," depicting himself as a pragmatic, "neoliberal" problem-solver who combined a social conscience with realistic budgetary management. A more poised and experienced television personality than Bush, he nevertheless registered as disquietingly passionless to many observers.

Later events would show that Dukakis's vaunted skill as a budget manager was vastly overstated, but that was among the least of his campaign problems. The Republicans would bring him down by combining a distinctly Reaganite slogan—"Read my lips: 'No New Taxes'"—with a hard-hitting version of the "social issue" that could trace its lineage to Richard Nixon and Spiro Agnew. The GOP campaign tore into Dukakis for vetoing a bill that would have required Massachusetts school teachers to lead their classes in the Pledge of Allegiance to the flag. It attacked him also for a prisoner furlough program that had given a weekend pass to a convicted first-degree murderer named Willie Horton; Horton had fled the state, raped a Maryland woman, and nearly killed her fiancé. The Republicans linked these incidents to Dukakis's comment that he was a "card-carrying member of the American Civil Liberties Union," and depicted the Democratic nominee as an example of the bankruptcy of liberalism in contemporary America.

Dukakis and his supporters dealt poorly with the attack, thereby putting themselves on the losing side of issues that stirred visceral emotions. Democrats heaped scorn on the pledge issue, arguing fairly enough that there would have been a presumption of unconstitutionality against the law Dukakis had vetoed but failing utterly to understand that many voters cared little for complex constitutional issues, revered the flag, and saw no harm in symbolic affirmations of patriotism. They dismissed the Horton case as an unfortunate glitch in a basically good rehabilitation procedure, noted that Dukakis had already excluded first-degree murderers from the furlough program, and accused the Republicans of racist demagoguery (Horton was black). From the late sixties on, many Republicans had asserted that liberal Democrats were deficient in patriotism and soft on crime; such responses simply lent credibility to the accusations.

Behind the Republican campaign lay the understanding that "liberalism" had become a political dirty word. Dukakis himself avoided it until near the end, thereby allowing his opponents to define it in a manner unacceptable to an electoral majority. Anguished liberal intellectuals wrote scholarly letters to newspapers and took out advertisements in an effort to remind voters of the origins of the word and of liberalism's promotion of individual liberty over three centuries. Such efforts missed the point: the voters had no quarrel with John Locke or John Stuart Mill or Franklin D. Roosevelt. They were unhappy with a contemporary variant of the tradition that seemed to promote license rather than liberty and was increasingly seen as the creed of a privileged elite that had little interest in the problems of ordinary people.

Bush had begun the campaign with little public esteem, and polls at first showed him running far behind an opponent who seemed an attractive newcomer. By the final weeks he was well ahead. On election day, he polled 54 percent of the popular vote and won thirty-eight states. Substantial though the victory was, it was based more on a widespread perception of Dukakis's deficiencies than the winner's merits. For the first year and a half of his administration, the new president enjoyed a widespread popularity; most students of American politics, however, analyzed it as a shallow appeal based on an amiable personality and a relatively prosperous economy.

In his speech accepting the Republican nomination, Bush had pledged himself to "a kinder, gentler America." As president, he did not deviate in major ways from the Reagan program, but New Right conservatives would consider his approach to domestic problems mushy. Bush's reservations about their agenda were relatively minor and won him few friends among liberal Democrats. Still, his concern about environmental values, education, and black sensitivities disturbed hard-core Reaganites; many of his key appointees, moreover, appeared more visible for their pragmatism than for their ideological commitment.

The worst fears of the New Right appeared vindicated when in 1990 the president agreed to break a budget impasse with congressional Democrats by accepting a marginally higher income tax rate and increased excise taxes. The decision to break his "no-new-taxes" pledge, coinciding with an emerging economic recession, seriously eroded his popularity in the public opinion polls. However justifiable as a pragmatic expedient, the budget compromise injured Bush's credibility by apparently exposing him as a politician who would not keep his word and who, unlike Reagan, possessed no solid core of values.

International developments in the first year and a half of the Bush presidency, while encouraging for American interests and heartening to all friends of human liberty, did little for the president's standing. During the last half of 1989 and into 1990, Communist rule collapsed in one Eastern European country after another, and democratic institutions seemed on the verge of terminating the Soviet dictatorship itself. The policies of Ronald Reagan, and by extension George Bush, had done much to set the stage for the vast drama that played itself out on the Continent. Still, America seemed by and large a spectator, reduced to applauding interesting new actors such as Vaclav Havel or old favorites such as Lech Walesa; the primary stage managers seemed to be Mikhail Gorbachev and Helmut Kohl.

The downfall of the Soviet empire and the end of the Cold War raised fundamental questions about the nature and purpose of American foreign policy, both in Europe and around the world. Francis Fukuyama, a Department of State policy analyst who had been schooled in both conservatism and political thought at the University of Chicago, proclaimed "the end of history" in a widely read article. He was writing, of course, of a perceived final triumph in the realm of political ideology, not of an end to conflicts between states. Moreover, China brutally repressed dissident democrats, and Gorbachev episodically appeased authoritarian forces, leaving considerable doubt about whether "history," even by Fukuyama's constricted definition, had come to an end. (The failed coup of August 1991 appears to have removed much of that doubt.)

Nonetheless, throughout 1990 a new and apparently irreversible order emerged in Europe, most indelibly symbolized by the unification of Germany and by a Soviet-German detente. In the new Europe, it seemed that the major actors would be the USSR, by virtue of its acquiescence in the dismantlement of its own empire, and Germany, which would be the banker and chief financier of change from the Elbe to the Urals. The prospective role of the United States to say the least, was ill-defined. The Cold War had provided a nation once dogmatically committed to isolationism with a guiding purpose for its international presence. Its end left America still a major player in the world but without a compelling mission. Paradoxically, victory opened up a prospect of aimlessness comparable to Bush's domestic drift.

If his future were to hinge on domestic developments, George Bush would be in serious difficulty—unloved by the liberals, attacked by the conservatives, presiding over a presidency without a purpose. In this sense, he was fortunate to be confronted with a foreign policy challenge that engaged his deepest feelings and allowed him to display formidable skills of crisis leadership.

Iraq's invasion of Kuwait on August 2, 1990, revealed the fallacy of the "end-of-history" argument. The Cold War, by creating a reasonably neat bipolar framework for international diplomacy, had actually been a suspension of the normal course of affairs in international politics. Its end meant a reversion to a more typical historical process, infinitely messier, relatively non-ideological, heavily affected by the ambitions of dominant personalities, developing from the interplay of interests and values of diverse peoples. Saddam Hussein's aggressive dictatorship and militaristic quest for conquest was in the end far more representative of "history" than the ideological dialogue between Marxian socialism and liberal capitalism.

The Iraqi attempt to absorb Kuwait and the implicit threat to Saudi Arabia presented an affront to American moral values and a serious challenge to U.S. strategic-economic interests. Thereby it gave a largely directionless presidency an opportunity to define itself. Far from being indecisive and valueless, the George Bush who confronted Saddam Hussein emerged as possibly the most masterful commander of foreign policy in the history of the presidency. One of the few twentieth-century American presidents to have experienced military combat, he shared as fully as Ronald Reagan the worldview of 1945. Outraged by the spectacle of "naked aggression," concerned by the threat to national interests, he revealed himself as a leader with deeply held values, steely determination, and a willingness to take big political risks.

He secured one United Nations resolution after another, orchestrated a largely effective economic embargo against Iraq, built a precarious coalition of Western and Arab states, put a half-million troops into Saudi Arabia, got a UN authorization to use force, and, most remarkably of all, obtained the functional equivalent of a declaration of war from a Democratic Congress. The American military triumph that followed, the quickest and most one-sided in the history of the republic, appeared to vindicate him in every respect. It also inevitably enhanced the reputation of Ronald Reagan, went far toward justifying his arms buildup, and gave the American military establishment an esteem it had not enjoyed since World War II.

Victory over Iraq did not, of course, begin to address every problem the United States faced in the world or even the Middle East. Nor did it answer the question of whether America could live comfortably in a world characterized by classical balance of power conflicts and intrusive depredations by egomanical pirates. Bush's own assertion that the United States was fighting for a "new world order," suggesting as it did the goal of establishing American (liberal) ideals as the planet's central organizing principle, was enough to give pause even to those who saw such an objective as desirable but doubted that it was possible. The goal came as naturally to George Bush as it had to Franklin Roosevelt a half-century earlier, but it likely would be as difficult to attain. In the end, a new world order could no more serve as a defining principle for American diplomacy in the post–Cold War era than could anti-Communism.

The spectacle of a conservative Republican president espousing international ideals and taking actions in the tradition of Roosevelt and Truman was a measure of the transformation of American politics nearly sixty years after FDR had taken the oath of office on the steps of the Capitol. Most liberals (in the political language of 1990), caught up in the worldview of 1968, had opposed going beyond economic sanctions against Iraq. America's sweeping victory in the desert left them more vulnerable than ever to charges that they were incapable of managing foreign policy and national security issues. In the near term, the liberals, and the Democratic party, would have to base their hopes for a return to power more heavily than ever on domestic issues in general and, most specifically, the possibility of gross economic mismanagement by conservative Republicans.

Yet on domestic issues, once beyond the pocketbook, the liberals, on the whole, occupied a defensive stance in American politics. The results of the Roosevelt revolution, as exemplified by Social Security, were beyond recall, the programs of the Great Society more mixed in their continuing appeal. Moreover, liberalism, as generally understood by the 1990s, had identified itself with a cluster of cultural attitudes and minority interests that had little support among the majority of the population. Liberals attempted to build a winning coalition by distributing benefits, not simply to the poor but to broad segments of the middle class. Americans were happy enough to take the benefits, reluctant to pay for them, and still disposed to view liberalism as a species of special interest politics.

Nonetheless, liberalism in the larger twentieth-century sense of reverence for individual rights, an acceptance of majority rule, a basic welfare state, and a commitment to American international involvement remained the basic American ideology. The two major political parties, one of them usually called "conservative," had laid claim to different aspects of it. With members of Congress expected to look after constituency interests, liberal Democrats could anticipate an electoral edge in legislative races. With the president expected to manage foreign policy and represent a broad national interest, conservative Republicans likely would continue to have an advantage in presidential contests—at least until some disaster, economic or otherwise, discredited their leadership.

As the United States moved into the last decade of the twentieth century, a historian striving to be a forecaster might most plausibly predict an enduring deadlock of democracy. Neither a largely exhausted liberalism nor a largely negative conservatism was likely to achieve a clear dominance among an electorate enervated by ideological politics and uncertain of its own priorities. The prospect of continuing divided government and uncertain direction was unattractive to political intellectuals and quite possibly downright dangerous for the future security of the nation. Still, the American experiment, in a way consistent with the fundamental liberalism that motivated it from the Declaration of Independence on, had never exemplified the virtues of orderliness and neatness so cherished by the intelligentsia.

Selected Bibliography

Introduction

While portions of this book rest upon primary research in printed and manuscript sources, what I have attempted is basically a synthesis of research and ideas generated by a host of scholars and journalists who have contributed to our understanding of American politics since FDR. Their work has made mine possible, and I hope that this bibliographic essay will both adequately acknowledge my debt to them and express my gratitude for their efforts.

In the most general sense the conceptualization for this book emerged from reading I have done in American political history over the past twenty years or so. However, a few books require special acknowledgment, even at the risk of slighting others. Richard Hofstadter, *The American Political Tradition* (New York: Knopf, 1948), inspired the format and approach for this much more limited attempt to use biography as a means of illustrating the progression of a "political tradition." The two classic general works on the modern American liberal tradition are Eric F. Goldman, *Rendezvous with Destiny* (New York: Knopf, 1952), and Richard Hofstadter, *The Age of Reform* (New York: Knopf, 1956). James David Barber, *The Presidential Character* (2nd ed.; Englewood Cliffs: Prentice-Hall, 1977), is an influential, common-sense attempt to deal with the psychology of presidential leadership. Christopher Lasch, *The New Radicalism in America* (New York: Knopf, 1965), was one of the first works by a historian to

397

examine "the intellectual as a social type" drawn to liberal and radical politics, a theme that has been taken up from quite a different perspective by numerous "neoconservative" writers cited for Chapter 7. James Sundquist, *Politics and Policy: The Eisenhower, Kennedy, and Johnson Years* (Washington: Brookings, 1968), remains the most thorough guide to the reassertion of American liberalism in the post-Truman years.

A number of general works on foreign policy are quite valuable: Norman Graebner, *Cold War Diplomacy* (2nd ed.; Florence, Ky.: Van Nostrand Reinhold, 1977), a brief but suggestive essay; Louis J. Halle, *The Cold War as History* (New York: Harper & Row, 1967); Adam Ulam, *The Rivals* (New York: Viking, 1971); Walter La Feber, *America, Russia, and the Cold War* (4th ed.; New York: John Wiley, 1981); and two books by John Lewis Gaddis, *Russia, the Soviet Union, and the United States* (New York: John Wiley, 1978), and *Strategies of Containment* (New York: Oxford University Press, 1982).

1. Franklin D. Roosevelt

Samuel I. Rosenman, ed., *The Public Papers and Addresses of Franklin D. Roosevelt* (13 vols.; New York: Random House, 1938–1950) and Elliott Roosevelt, *F. D. R.: His Personal Letters* (4 vols.; New York: Duell, Sloan and Pearce, 1947–1950) are the most valuable published primary sources.

The most thorough account of Roosevelt's early life and the beginnings of his presidency can be found in four notable volumes by Frank Freidel, published under the general title, *Franklin D. Roosevelt* (Boston: Little, Brown, 1952–1973). Freidel is now at work on a comprehensive one-volume biography. James Mac-Gregor Burns, *Roosevelt: The Lion and the Fox* (New York: Harcourt Brace, 1956), and *Roosevelt: The Soldier of Freedom* (New York: Harcourt Brace, 1970), sympathetically criticize Roosevelt's personality and policies. Joseph P. Lash, *Eleanor and Franklin* (New York: Norton, 1971), is a sensitive treatment of FDR's most important personal relationship. Kenneth S. Davis, *FDR: The Beckoning of Destiny, 1882–1928* (New York: Putnam, 1972), is a first-rate popular biography. Alfred Rollins, *Roosevelt and Howe* (New York: Knopf, 1962), examines Roosevelt's early political career from the perspective of his relationship with his closest political adviser. Among the important assessments of Roosevelt's character and personality by those with whom he worked are Rexford G. Tugwell, *The Democratic Roosevelt* (Garden City: Doubleday, 1957); Frances Perkins, *The Roosevelt I Knew* (New York: Viking, 1946); and Samuel I. Rosenman, *Working for Roosevelt* (New York: Harper & Row, 1952). Joseph Alsop, *FDR: A Centenary Rememberance* (New York: Viking, 1982), is perceptive.

On the New Deal itself, William E. Leuchtenburg, *Franklin D. Roosevelt and the New Deal* (New York: Harper & Row, 1963), remains the best one-volume account. Arthur M. Schlesinger's three volumes, published under the general title, *The Age of Roosevelt* (Boston: Houghton Mifflin, 1957–1960), remain the most monumental account of the Depression and FDR's first term. Paul K. Conkin's extended essay, *The New Deal* (2nd ed.; Arlington Heights, Ill.: AHM Publishing, 1975) is the most widely noted scholarly radical critique. Two volumes edited by John Braeman, et al., *The New Deal: The National Level* and *The New Deal: The State and Local Levels* (both Columbus: Ohio State University Press, 1975), contain original essays by many important New Deal historians. Alonzo L. Hamby, ed., *The New Deal: Analysis and Interpretation* (2nd ed.; New York: Longman, 1981), is a collection of secondary readings on its topic's major themes.

Among the many important specialized works, the following stand out: Otis L. Graham, *Encore for Reform: The Old Progressives and the New Deal* (New York: Oxford University Press, 1967); James T. Patterson, *The New Deal and the States: Federalism in Transition* (Princeton: Princeton University Press, 1969); Patterson, *Congressional Conservatism and the New Deal* (Lexington: University Press of Kentucky, 1967); John M. Allswang, *The New Deal and American Politics* (New York: John Wiley, 1978); Harvard Sitkoff, *A New Deal for Blacks* (New York: Oxford University Press, 1978); Theodore Saloutos, *The American Farmer and the New Deal* (Ames: Iowa State University Press, 1982); Irving Bernstein, *Turbulent Years* (New York: Houghton Mifflin, 1969); Ellis W. Hawley, *The New Deal and the Problem*

of Monopoly (Princeton: Princeton University Press, 1966); and
Albert U. Romasco, *The Politics of Recovery* (New York: Oxford
University Press, 1983). Richard Polenberg, *War and Society*
(Philadelphia: Lippincott, 1972), remains the best study of Ameri-
can society during World War II; Philip J. Funigiello, *The Chal-
lenge to Urban Liberalism: Federal-City Relations during World
War II* (Knoxville: University of Tennessee Press, 1978), focuses
more specifically on New Deal-style issues.

For Roosevelt's diplomacy, see especially Robert Dallek,
Franklin D. Roosevelt and American Foreign Policy, 1932–1945
(New York: Oxford University Press, 1979). Edgar B. Nixon, ed.,
*Franklin D. Roosevelt and Foreign Affairs, January, 1933–January,
1937* (3 vols.; Cambridge: Harvard University Press, 1969), is an
important collection of primary sources. Among the more important works covering Roosevelt's pre-Pearl Harbor diplomacy
are Robert A. Divine, *The Illusion of Neutrality* (Chicago: University of Chicago Press, 1962), and *The Reluctant Belligerent*
(2nd ed.; New York: John Wiley, 1979); Herbert Feis, *The Road
to Pearl Harbor* (Princeton: Princeton University Press, 1962);
Paul W. Schroeder, *The Axis Alliance and Japanese-American
Relations, 1941* (Ithaca: Cornell University Press, 1958); and two
semi-official volumes by William L. Langer and S. Everett Gleason,
The Challenge to Isolation, 1937–1940 and *The Undeclared War,
1940–1941* (both New York: Harper & Row, 1952–53). Charles C.
Tansill, *Back Door to War* (Chicago: Henry Regnery, 1952), is a
vitriolic revisionist interpretation, as are two works by Charles A.
Beard: *American Foreign Policy in the Making, 1932–1940* and
President Roosevelt and the Coming of the War, 1941 (both New
Haven: Yale University Press, 1946, 1948).

On the war itself, three classic works are Robert E. Sherwood,
Roosevelt and Hopkins (New York: Harper & Row, 1950);
William H. McNeill, *America, Britain, and Russia, 1941–1946*
(London: Royal Institute for International Affairs, 1953); and
Herbert Feis, *Churchill, Roosevelt, Stalin* (Princeton: Princeton
University Press, 1957). John L. Gaddis, *The United States and
the Origins of the Cold War, 1941–1947* (New York: Columbia
University Press, 1972) is an important "post-revisionist" work.
Gaddis Smith, *American Diplomacy during the Second World
War* (New York: John Wiley, 1965), criticizes Roosevelt from a

moderate-liberal and anti-Soviet perspective. Gabriel Kolko, *The Politics of War* (New York: Random House, 1968), provides a critique from the perspective of a Marxist radical.

2. Harry S. Truman

This chapter, more than any other in the book, is based heavily on my own primary research into the personality and presidential career of Harry S. Truman. I am especially indebted to the staff at the Truman Library for their friendly, patient assistance over a twenty-year period.

The standard, nearly definitive, compilation of Truman's addresses, statements, and press conferences during his presidency is *Public Papers of the President: Harry S. Truman, 1945–1953* (8 vols.; Washington, D.C.: U.S. Government Printing Office, 1961–66). They should be supplemented by Robert H. Ferrell, ed., *Off the Record: The Private Papers of Harry S. Truman* (New York: Harper & Row, 1980); Merle Miller, *Plain Speaking: An Oral Biography of Harry S. Truman* (New York: Putnam, 1973); and Truman's own *Memoirs* (2 vols.; Garden City: Doubleday, 1955–56).

For Truman's early life, see Jonathan Daniels, *Man of Independence* (Philadelphia: Lippincott, 1950); Robert H. Ferrell, ed., *The Autobiography of Harry S. Truman* (Boulder: Colorado Associated University Press, 1980); Ferrell, ed., *"Dear Bess"* (New York: Norton, 1983); Richard S. Kirkendall, "Truman's Path to Power," *Social Studies*, XLIII (April, 1968), 67–73.

The most important attempt at a full-scale scholarly biography to date is Harold F. Gosnell, *Truman's Crises* (Westport, Conn.: Greenwood, 1980). Margaret Truman, *Harry S. Truman* (New York: Morrow, 1972), is a valuable personal account. There are several general studies of Truman's White House years. Cabell Phillips, *The Truman Presidency* (New York: Macmillan, 1966), is competent, but overly selective. Bert Cochran, *Harry Truman and the Crisis Presidency* (New York: Funk & Wagnalls, 1973), is a thinly researched left-liberal interpretation. Robert J. Donovan's two volumes, *Conflict and Crisis* and *Tumultuous Years* (both New York: Norton, 1977, 1982), are comprehensive but relatively noninterpretive works by a distinguished journalist.

Alonzo L. Hamby, *Beyond the New Deal: Harry S. Truman and American Liberalism* (New York: Columbia University Press, 1973), concentrates on the relationship between Truman and the liberal movement of the day. Barton J. Bernstein, ed., *Politics and Policies of the Truman Administration* (Chicago: Quadrangle, 1970), contains several original "revisionist" essays. Richard S. Kirkendall, ed., *The Truman Period as a Research Field: A Reappraisal, 1972* (Columbia: University of Missouri Press, 1973), and Alonzo L. Hamby, ed., *Harry S. Truman and the Fair Deal* (Lexington, Mass.: D.C. Heath, 1974), provide introductions to the academic debates.

For the politics and economics of the Fair Deal, the following works are especially relevant: Richard E. Neustadt, "Congress and the Fair Deal: A Legislative Balance Sheet," in Carl J. Friedrich and John Kenneth Galbraith, eds., *Public Policy* (Cambridge: Harvard Graduate School of Administration, 1954); Francis H. Heller, ed., *Economics and the Truman Administration* (Lawrence: Regents Press of Kansas, 1981); Susan Hartmann, *Truman and the 80th Congress* (Columbia: University of Missouri Press, 1971); Irwin Ross, *The Loneliest Campaign: The Truman Victory of 1948* (New York: New American Library, 1968); Richard O. Davies, *Housing Reform during the Truman Administration* (Columbia: University of Missouri Press, 1966); Allen Matusow, *Farm Policies and Politics in the Truman Administration* (Cambridge: Harvard University Press, 1967); R. Alton Lee, *Truman and Taft-Hartley* (Lexington: University of Kentucky Press, 1966); Arthur McClure, *The Truman Administration and the Problems of Postwar Labor* (Rutherford, N.J.: Fairleigh-Dickinson University Press, 1969); and Monte M. Poen, *Harry S. Truman versus the Medical Lobby* (Columbia: University of Missouri Press, 1979). On civil rights, see Donald McCoy and Richard Ruetten, *Quest and Response* (Lawrence: University of Kansas Press, 1973); William Berman, *The Politics of Civil Rights in the Truman Administration* (Columbus: Ohio State University Press, 1970); and Richard Dalfiume, *The Desegregation of the U.S. Armed Forces* (Columbia: University of Missouri Press, 1969).

Truman's diplomacy has been the most-debated aspect of his presidency, calling forth both important memoirs and an outpouring of contentious scholarly literature. Among the memoirs, the most important in addition to Truman's are Dean Acheson, *Present at the Creation* (New York: Norton, 1969); George Kennan, *Memoirs, 1925–1950* (Boston: Little, Brown, 1967); Charles Bohlen, *Witness to History* (New York: Norton, 1973); and W. Averell Harriman and Elie Abel, *Special Envoy to Churchill and Stalin, 1941–1946* (New York: Random House, 1975). Important collections of primary sources are Walter Millis, ed., *The Forrestal Diaries* (New York: Viking, 1951); Thomas Campbell and George Herring, eds., *The Diaries of Edward R. Stettinius, Jr., 1943–1946* (New York: Franklin Watts, 1975); and Arthur H. Vandenberg, Jr., ed., *The Private Papers of Senator Vandenberg* (Boston: Houghton Mifflin, 1952). Truman's discussions with Lilienthal and Sulzberger are in David E. Lilienthal, *Journals: The Atomic Energy Years, 1945–1950* (New York: Harper & Row, 1964), and Cyrus L. Sulzberger, *A Long Row of Candles* (New York: Macmillan, 1969).

Lloyd Gardner, *Architects of Illusion* (New York: Quadrangle, 1970), and Gabriel and Joyce Kolko, *The Limits of Power* (New York: Harper & Row, 1972), focus on the Truman years and the Cold War from a revisionist perspective. On the origins of the Cold War, the following books are particularly relevant: John L. Gaddis, *The United States and the Origins of the Cold War*, cited for Chapter 1, and the early chapters of Gaddis's *Strategies of Containment*, cited for the Introduction; George Herring, *Aid to Russia* (New York: Columbia University Press, 1973); Lynn Ethridge Davis, *The Cold War Begins* (Princeton: Princeton University Press, 1974); Lisle A. Rose, *Dubious Victory* (Kent, Ohio: Kent State University Press, 1973); and Thomas G. Paterson, *Soviet-American Confrontation* (Baltimore: Johns Hopkins University Press, 1973). The career of Truman's most important Secretary of State is treated in Gaddis Smith, *Dean Acheson* (New York: Cooper Square, 1972), and David McLellan, *Dean Acheson* (New York: Dodd, Mead, 1976).

On Far Eastern policy, see especially Tang Tsou, *America's Failure in China* (Chicago: University of Chicago Press, 1963), John Spanier, *The Truman-MacArthur Controversy* (rev. ed.; New York: Norton, 1965), and Francis Heller, ed., *The Korean War: A 25-Year Perspective* (Lawrence: Regents Press of Kansas,

1977). Truman's pithy summary of his decision to fight in Korea is in Robert Alan Aurthur, "The Wit and Sass of Harry S. Truman," *Esquire*, LXXVI (August, 1971).

H. Bradford Westerfield, *Foreign Policy and Party Politics: From Pearl Harbor to Korea* (New Haven: Yale University Press, 1955), remains a valuable introduction to its topic. For McCarthyism and Truman's response, consult the works listed for Chapter 3.

3. Dwight D. Eisenhower, Robert A. Taft, Joseph R. McCarthy

The only full-scale biography of Eisenhower to date is Peter Lyon, *Eisenhower: Portrait of the Hero* (Boston: Little, Brown, 1974), a hefty volume that is most successful in providing a good account of Eisenhower's early life, but is less useful for the study of his World War II command or his presidency. Stephen E. Ambrose, *Eisenhower: . . . 1890–1952* (New York: Simon & Schuster, 1983), begins a major biography. Eisenhower's own informal memoir, *At Ease: Stories I Tell My Friends* (Garden City: Doubleday, 1970), provides his own version of key events in his pre-presidential career. Stephen E. Ambrose, *The Supreme Commander* (Garden City: Doubleday, 1970), covers Eisenhower's World War II role, as does Eisenhower's *Crusade in Europe* (Garden City: Doubleday, 1948). Robert Ferrell has edited *The Eisenhower Diaries* (New York: Norton, 1981), and *The Diary of James C. Hagerty* (Bloomington: Indiana University Press, 1983). Alfred Chandler, Jr., has prepared an edition of *The Papers of Dwight D. Eisenhower: The War Years* (5 vols.; Baltimore: Johns Hopkins University Press, 1970).

For Eisenhower's presidency, see *Public Papers of the Presidents: Dwight D. Eisenhower, 1953–1961* (Washington: U.S. Government Printing Office, 1957–1964), and Eisenhower's memoirs, collectively entitled *The White House Years* (2 vols.; Garden City: Doubleday, 1963–65). The most important personal histories of the administration are Arthur Larson, *Eisenhower: The President Nobody Knew* (New York: Scribner's, 1968); Emmet John Hughes, *The Ordeal of Power* (New York: Atheneum, 1963); and Sherman Adams, *Firsthand Report* (New York: Harper & Row, 1961). Important scholarly accounts are Herbert Parmet, *Eisenhower and the American Crusades* (New York:

Macmillan, 1972); Charles Alexander, *Holding the Line* (Bloom-ington: University of Indiana Press, 1975); and Elmo Richardson, *The Presidency of Dwight D. Eisenhower* (Lawrence: Regents Press of Kansas, 1979). Fred Greenstein has recently emerged as a leader in the academic reevaluation of Eisenhower; see especially his "Eisenhower as an Activist President: A Look at New Evi-dence," *Political Science Quarterly*, XCIV (Winter, 1979–80), 577–86, 596–97, and his book, *The Hidden-Hand Presidency: Eisenhower as Leader* (New York: Basic Books, 1982).

The literature dealing with politics and the domestic scene during the Eisenhower years is thin. James Sundquist, *Politics and Policy: The Eisenhower, Kennedy, and Johnson Years*, cited for the Introduction, does a fine job of surveying the major issues from the perspective of a liberal activist interested primarily in setting the scene for the New Frontier and the Great Society. Samuel Lubell, *The Revolt of the Moderates* (New York: Harper & Row, 1956), remains a valuable interpretation of the period by its shrewdest political journalist. Heinz Eulau, *Class and Party in the Eisenhower Years* (New York: Free Press, 1962), is significant. By far the best monographic contribution is Gary Reichard, *The Reaffirmation of Republicanism* (Knoxville: University of Ten-nessee Press, 1975), an excellent analysis of the administration and its objectives from the vantage point of Eisenhower's dealings with his first Congress. See also David A. Frier, *Conflict of Interest in the Eisenhower Administration* (Ames: Iowa State University Press, 1969); Aaron Wildavsky, *Dixon-Yates* (New Haven: Yale University Press, 1962); and William R. Willoughby, *The St. Lawrence Waterway* (Madison: University of Wisconsin Press, 1961). The woes of Secretary of Agriculture Benson are detailed in Benson, *Crossfire* (Garden City: Doubleday, 1962), and in Edward and Frederick Schapsmeier, *Ezra Taft Benson and the Politics of Agriculture* (Danville, Ill.: Interstate, 1975). The two civil rights bills of Eisenhower's second term are covered in J. W. Anderson, *Eisenhower, Brownell, and the Congress* (University: University of Alabama Press, 1964), and Daniel Berman, *A Bill Becomes a Law* (New York: Macmillan, 1962). For Chief Justice Warren's recollection, see *The Memoirs of Earl Warren* (Garden City: Doubleday, 1977). For economic policy, consult Harold Vatter, *The American Economy in the 1950s*

(New York: Norton, 1963); and Nathaniel R. Howard, ed., *The Basic Papers of George M. Humphrey* (Cleveland: Western Reserve Historical Society, 1965).

On the idea of a celebratory "national religion," see Will Herberg, *Catholic, Protestant, Jew* (Garden City: Doubleday, 1956); for the pseudo-religious atmosphere on the Washington scene, see William Miller, *Piety Along the Potomac* (Boston: Houghton Mifflin, 1964). For the New Conservatism in general, Rossiter, *Conservatism in America*, cited above, Chapter 3, is essential; for the New Republicanism in particular, Arthur Larson, *A Republican Looks at His Party* (New York: Harper & Row, 1955), is the definitive text. On the quest for a sense of national purpose, see Rockefeller Brothers Fund, *Prospect for America: The Rockefeller Panel Reports* (Garden City: Doubleday, 1961).

Several of the volumes cited for Chapter 2 are useful for Eisenhower's diplomacy. Robert A. Divine, *Eisenhower and the Cold War* (New York: Oxford University Press, 1981), is favorable. Blanche Wiesen Cook, *The Declassified Eisenhower: A Divided Legacy* (Garden City: Doubleday, 1981), is as the title suggests, more equivocal. There are many studies of John Foster Dulles: Ronald W. Pruessen, *John Foster Dulles: The Road to Power* (New York: Free Press, 1982), an excellent beginning to a projected two-volume biography; Louis Gerson, *John Foster Dulles* (2 vols.; New York: Cooper Square, 1967), a rather exhaustive contribution to the *American Secretaries of State* series; Townsend Hoopes, *The Devil And John Foster Dulles* (Boston: Little, Brown, 1973); Richard Goold-Adams, *The Time of Power* (London: Weidenfeld and Nicholson, 1962); and Michael Guhin, *John Foster Dulles* (New York: Columbia University Press, 1972). George B. Noble, *Christian A. Herter* (New York: Cooper Square, 1970), another work in the *American Secretaries of State* series, chronicles American diplomacy during the brief tenure of Dulles's successor.

Treatments of specific issues and episodes include Richard A. Aliano, *American Defense Policy from Eisenhower to Kennedy* (Athens: Ohio University Press, 1975); Douglas Kinnard, *President Eisenhower and Strategy Management* (Lexington: University Press of Kentucky, 1977); Bennett Kovrig, *The Myth of Liberation* (Baltimore: Johns Hopkins University Press, 1973); Melvin Gurtov,

The First Vietnam Crisis (New York: Columbia University Press, 1967); Robert Randle, *Geneva, 1954* (Princeton: Princeton University Press, 1969); Hugh Thomas, *Suez* (New York: Harper & Row, 1967); Theodore Draper, *Castro's Revolution* (New York: Praeger, 1962); Ramon Ruiz, *Cuba: The Making of a Revolution* (Amherst: University of Massachusetts Press, 1968); Jean E. Smith, *The Defense of Berlin* (Baltimore: Johns Hopkins University Press, 1963); Jack M. Schick, *The Berlin Crisis, 1958-1962* (Philadelphia: University of Pennsylvania Press, 1971); Robert Slusser, *The Berlin Crisis of 1961* (Baltimore: Johns Hopkins University Press, 1973); David Wise and Thomas Ross, *The U-2 Affair* (New York: Random House, 1962).

I have examined Robert A. Taft's papers in the Library of Congress and have drawn upon his addresses in the *Congressional Record*. However, the major source for any historian writing a short sketch of Taft inevitably will be James T. Patterson's *Mr. Republican* (Boston: Houghton Mifflin, 1972). Intensively researched, scrupulously fair, eminently readable, and consistently intelligent in its analysis, it is among the finest examples of contemporary political biography. I have relied upon it heavily and can claim to have added nothing to it. Russell Kirk and James McClellan, *The Political Principles of Robert A. Taft* (New York: Fleet Press, 1967), is a useful exploration of Taft's ideology.

In the domestic realm, Taft's efforts to compromise with liberal ideology have stimulated two scholarly articles: Richard O. Davies, "'Mr. Republican' Turns 'Socialist': Robert A. Taft and Public Housing," *Ohio History*, LXXIII (Summer, 1964), 135–143; and Charles C. Brown, "Robert A. Taft: Champion of Public Housing and National Aid to Schools," *Bulletin of the Cincinnati Historical Society*, XXVI (July, 1968), 225–253. On the Taft-Hartley Act, see R. Alton Lee, *Truman and Taft-Hartley*, cited for Chapter 2; Fred Hartley, Jr., *Our New National Labor Policy* (New York: Funk & Wagnalls, 1948); and Harry A. Millis and Emily Clark Brown, *From the Wagner Act to Taft-Hartley* (Chicago: University of Chicago Press, 1950).

For Taft's foreign policy, see Robert A. Taft, *A Foreign Policy for Americans* (Garden City: Doubleday, 1951). An influential critique of the approach that the Senator represented may be found in Norman Graebner, *The New Isolationism* (New

York: Ronald Press, 1956). Support from that might loosely be called the New Left can be found in two articles by Henry Berger: "A Conservative Critique of Containment: Senator Taft on the Early Cold War Program," in David Horowitz, ed., *Containment and Revolution* (Boston: Beacon, 1971), 125–139, and "Senator Robert A. Taft Dissents from Military Escalation," in Thomas G. Paterson, ed., *Cold War Critics* (Chicago: Quadrangle, 1971), 167–204. Also important is the sympathetic assessment of Taft by Ronald Radosh in his *Prophets on the Right* (New York: Simon & Schuster, 1975).

There is a large, hotly debated literature on McCarthy and McCarthyism. Thomas C. Reeves, *The Life and Times of Joe McCarthy* (New York: Stein & Day, 1982), and David Oshinsky, *A Conspiracy So Immense: The World of Joe McCarthy* (New York: Free Press, 1983), are the two most important biographies. Richard Rovere, *Senator Joe McCarthy* (New York: Harcourt Brace, 1959), remains valuable. Roy Cohn, *McCarthy* (New York: New American Library, 1968), is a sympathetic treatment by the Senator's most influential and controversial aide. Among the works that focus tightly on McCarthy's impact are Robert Griffith, *The Politics of Fear* (Lexington: University of Kentucky Press, 1970), and Richard Fried, *Men Against McCarthy* (New York: Columbia University Press, 1976). Books dealing with more specialized topics are Edwin Bayley, *Joe McCarthy and the Press* (Madison: University of Wisconsin Press, 1981); Donald F. Crosby, *God, Church, and Flag: Senator Joseph R. McCarthy and the Catholic Church, 1950–1957* (Chapel Hill: University of North Carolina Press, 1978); David Oshinsky, *Senator Joseph R. McCarthy and the American Labor Movement* (Columbia: University of Missouri Press, 1975); and Michael O'Brien, *McCarthy and McCarthyism in Wisconsin* (Columbia: University of Missouri Press, 1980).

Works dealing with the wider phenomenon of "McCarthyism" have taken several approaches. Earl Latham, *The Communist Controversy in Washington: From the New Deal to McCarthy* (Cambridge: Harvard University Press, 1969), stresses Republican partisanship. Daniel Bell, ed., *The New American Right* (New York: Criterion Books, 1955), published in a revised edition as *The Radical Right* (New York: Anchor Books, 1964), stresses "status politics" and mass irrationality. Michael Paul Rogin, *The Intellectuals and McCarthy: The Radical Specter* (Cambridge: MIT Press, 1967), attempts to refute Bell, et al., whom the author considers conservative "pluralists" distrustful of democracy. Richard Freeland, *The Truman Doctrine and the Origins of McCarthyism* (New York: Knopf, 1971); and Athan Theoharis, *Seeds of Repression: Harry S. Truman and the Origins of McCarthyism* (Chicago: Quadrangle, 1971), blame the anti-Communist rhetoric and politics of the Truman administration. Alan Harper, *The Politics of Loyalty: The White House and the Communist Issue, 1946-1952* (Westport, Conn.: Greenwood Press, 1969), takes a more balanced approach.

4. Martin Luther King, Jr.

There is a vast literature on the civil rights movement before the emergence of King. Some representative selections are Charles Flint Kellogg, *NAACP, 1909-1920* (Baltimore: Johns Hopkins University Press, 1967), the first volume of a projected multi-volume history; Roy Wilkins and Tom Matthews, *Standing Fast* (New York: Viking, 1982), the autobiography of the long-time NAACP director; Richard Kluger, *Simple Justice* (New York: Knopf, 1976), the story of the school desegregation cases; and Jervis Anderson, *A. Philip Randolph* (New York: Harcourt Brace, 1973), a biography of the leader whose tactics foreshadowed King's. Anthony Lewis, *Portrait of a Decade* (New York: Random House, 1964), provides coverage of the ten years after the *Brown* decision, including the emergence of King. Other new forces in the civil rights movement receive attention in August Meier and Elliott Rudwick, *CORE* (New York: Oxford University Press, 1973); Howard Zinn, *SNCC: The New Abolitionists* (Boston: Beacon, 1964); and Clayborne Carson, *In Struggle: SNCC and the Black Awakening of the 1960s* (Cambridge: Harvard University Press, 1982).

David L. Lewis, *King: A Critical Biography* (2nd ed.; Urbana: University of Illinois Press, 1978), first published in 1970, provided the first good biographical account and was quickly followed by John A. McWilliams' causticly entitled *The King God Didn't Save* (New York: Coward McCann, 1970). Stephen B. Oates, *Let the Trumpet Sound* (New York: Harper & Row, 1982),

Bibliography

has established itself as the standard biography. I am indebted to
Professor Oates for allowing me to read it in manuscript form.
The two most important analytical works on King and his move-
ment are by David Garrow: *Protest at Selma* (New Haven: Yale
University Press, 1978), and *The FBI and Martin Luther King, Jr.*
(New York: Norton, 1981). Coretta Scott King, *My Life with
Martin Luther King, Jr.* (New York: Holt, Rinehart & Winston,
1969), is useful for its many personal insights.

King's own works are, of course, essential. I have relied most
heavily upon his three "movement" books, *Stride toward Freedom* (New York: Harper & Row, 1958), *Why We Can't Wait*
(New York: Harper & Row, 1964), and *Where Do We Go from
Here: Chaos or Community?* (New York: Harper & Row, 1967);
two other volumes, *Strength to Love* (New York: Harper & Row,
1963), and *Trumpet of Conscience* (New York: Harper & Row,
1968), are collections of sermons. King's final published article, "A
Testament of Hope," appeared in *Playboy* (January, 1969), 175,
194, 231–35.

5. *John and Robert Kennedy*

Arthur M. Schlesinger, Jr., *A Thousand Days* (Boston: Houghton
Mifflin, 1965), and *Robert Kennedy and His Times* (Boston:
Houghton Mifflin, 1978), are fundamental sources by a distin-
guished historian, whatever their "memorial" qualities. Theodore
Sorenson, *Kennedy* (New York: Harper & Row, 1965), and *The
Kennedy Legacy* (New York: Macmillan, 1969), are tributes by an
even closer family associate. The best biography to date by an
independent scholar is the two-volume work by Herbert Parmet:
Jack: The Struggles of John F. Kennedy and *J.F.K.: The Presi-
dency of John F. Kennedy* (New York: Dial Press, 1980, 1983).
Among the critical treatments of the Kennedy brothers are Bruce
Miroff, *Pragmatic Illusions* (New York: David McKay, 1976);
Henry Fairlie, *The Kennedy Promise* (Garden City: Doubleday,
1973); and Garry Wills, *The Kennedy Imprisonment* (Boston:
Little, Brown, 1982). Jim S. Heath, *Decade of Disillusionment*
(Bloomington: Indiana University Press, 1976), is a balanced,
scholarly treatment of the Kennedy and Johnson years. For John
Kennedy's early years, see especially Joan and Clay Blair, *The*

Search for J.F.K. (New York: Berkeley, 1976). Kennedy's pre-presidential thinking on political leadership may be found in his books, *Why England Slept* (New York: Wilfred Funk, 1940), and *Profiles in Courage* (New York: Harper & Row, 1956). Theodore H. White, *The Making of the President, 1960* (New York: Atheneum, 1961), remains a classic account of its subject.

Important aspects of the domestic side of the Kennedy presidency receive treatment in James Sundquist, *Politics and Policy*, cited for the Introduction; Grant McConnell, *Steel and the Presidency—1962* (New York: Norton, 1963); Jim F. Heath, *John F. Kennedy and the Business Community* (Chicago: University of Chicago Press, 1969); Victor Navasky, *Kennedy Justice* (New York: Atheneum, 1971); Carl M. Brauer, *John F. Kennedy and the Second Reconstruction* (New York: Columbia University Press, 1977); Walter Heller, *New Dimensions of Political Economy* (Cambridge: Harvard University Press, 1966); and Benjamin Bradlee, *Conversations with Kennedy* (New York: Norton, 1975).

For JFK's foreign policy, see the favorable Roger Hillsman, *To Move a Nation* (Garden City: Doubleday, 1967), and the critical Richard Walton, *Cold War and Counterrevolution* (New York: Viking, 1972). For the Cuban missile crisis, consult Graham Allison, *Essence of Decision* (Boston: Little, Brown, 1971); Robert F. Kennedy, *Thirteen Days* (New York: Norton, 1969); and Robert A. Divine, ed., *The Cuban Missile Crisis* (Chicago: Quadrangle, 1971). The basic scholarly account of Vietnam is George C. Herring, *America's Longest War* (New York: John Wiley, 1979).

On Robert Kennedy, see in addition to many of the works cited above David Halberstam, *The Unfinished Odyssey of Robert Kennedy* (New York: Random House, 1968); Jules Witcover, *Eighty-five Days: The Last Campaign of Robert Kennedy* (New York: Putnam, 1969); and Jack Newfield, *Robert Kennedy* (New York: Dutton, 1969).

6. Lyndon B. Johnson

The best single book yet published on Johnson is probably Doris Kearns, *Lyndon Johnson and the American Dream* (New York: Harper & Row, 1976), surely one of the most interesting applications of oral history yet achieved by an academic writer. By contrast, Merle Miller, *Lyndon* (New York: Putnam, 1980), is thin and contrived. Alfred Steinberg, *Sam Johnson's Boy* (New York: Macmillan, 1968) is a caustic journalistic biography.

The best books on Johnson's early career are Ronnie Dugger, *The Politician* (New York: Norton, 1982), a thick volume that carries its subject into the beginning of his Senate career, and Robert Caro, *The Years of Lyndon Johnson: The Path to Power* (New York: Knopf, 1982), an even heftier work that ends with Johnson's defeat in his first try for a Senate seat. Both are the initial volumes of multi-volume biographies, and both are characterized by a hostility seldom found in biographical studies. William S. White, *The Professional* (Boston: Houghton Mifflin, 1964), is uncritical, as are Booth Mooney, *The Lyndon Johnson Story* (New York: Farrar, Straus, 1964), and Sam Houston Johnson, *My Brother Lyndon*, ed., Hank Enrique Lopez (New York: Cowles, 1970). Harry McPherson, *A Political Education* (Boston: Little, Brown, 1972), is a thoughtful memoir by a figure who intermittently served as an aide to LBJ in the fifties and sixties. Rowland Evans and Robert Novak, *Lyndon B. Johnson: The Exercise of Power* (New York: New American Library, 1966), is a shrewd journalistic account of Johnson's life through the first year of his presidency. Joe B. Frantz, "Opening a Curtain: The Metamorphosis of Lyndon B. Johnson," *Journal of Southern History*, LXV (February, 1979), 3–26, analyzes Johnson's ideological zigs and zags. T. Harry Williams, "Huey, Lyndon, and Southern Radicalism," *Journal of American History*, LX (September, 1973), 267–293, places LBJ in a broad context.

For Sam Rayburn, see in addition to the other sources listed in this essay C. Dwight Dorough, *Mr. Sam* (New York: Random House, 1962), and Alfred Steinberg, *Sam Rayburn* (New York: Hawthorne, 1975). There is no adequate biography of Richard Russell, but his Senate career is well covered in several works already cited. I have also drawn upon his numerous speeches in the *Congressional Record*. One may gain some insights into his early career by reading Magner White, "Father and Son Serve Their State," *American*, CXIV (December, 1932), 65, and Walter Davenport, "States Righted," *Collier's*, LXXXIX (June 4, 1932), 11, 45–47. A long obituary in the *New York Times*, January 22, 1971, provides a useful overview of Russell's life.

For Johnson's presidency, see *Public Papers of the Presidents: Lyndon B. Johnson*, 5 vols. (Washington: U.S. Government Printing Office, 1964–1970); Jim F. Heath, *Decade of Disillusionment*, cited above for Chapter 5; Eric F. Goldman, *The Tragedy of Lyndon Johnson* (New York: Knopf, 1969); and Robert A. Divine, ed., *Exploring the Johnson Years* (Austin: University of Texas Press, 1981). Theodore H. White, *The Making of the President, 1964* (New York: Atheneum, 1965), provides good, if not very critical coverage of Johnson's first year in office and his victory over Goldwater. Marvin Gettleman and David Mermelstein, eds., *The Great Society Reader: The Failure of American Liberalism* (New York: Random House, 1967), more than compensate for White's celebratory tone; a second edition (1970) is entitled *The Failure of American Liberalism: After the Great Society*. Michael Harrington, *The Other America* (New York: Macmillan, 1962), was the intellectual source of the war on poverty.

On foreign policy, see Philip L. Geyelin, *Lyndon B. Johnson and the World* (New York: Praeger, 1966); George C. Herring, *America's Longest War*, cited for Chapter 5; and Herbert Y. Schandler, *The Unmaking of a President: Lyndon Johnson and Vietnam* (Princeton: Princeton University Press, 1977).

Johnson's personality and image receive devastating treatment in Michael Davie, *LBJ* (New York: Duell, Sloan and Pearce, 1966), and Frank Cormier, *LBJ: The Way He Was* (Garden City: Doubleday, 1977), a rather chilling, if matter-of-fact, description of Johnson's imperious vulgarity. Jack Valenti, *A Very Human President* (New York: Norton, 1976), is a loyal, valiant, and unsuccessful attempt to counter the "ogre" image.

7. *Richard M. Nixon*

It will be years before the definitive biography of Nixon emerges, but no American political figure in recent times has inspired so diverse and interesting a group of biographical works. Earl Mazo and Stephen Hess, *Nixon* (New York: Harper & Row, 1968), and Stephen Hess, *Nixon: A Political Portrait* (New York: Harper & Row, 1968), are friendly; William Costello, *The Facts about Nixon* (New York: Viking, 1960), is vehemently hostile. Garry Wills, *Nixon Agonistes* (Boston: Houghton Mifflin, 1970), remains the best of the critical interpretations. Bruce Mazlish, *In Search of Nixon* (New York: Basic Books, 1972), and Fawn Brodie, *Richard Nixon* (New York: Norton, 1981), are psycho-biographies of dubious utility. Nixon tells his own story in *Six Crises* (Garden City: Doubleday, 1962), and *RN* (New York: Grosset & Dunlap, 1978).

For the story of the Nixon presidency, one must rely on memoirs and works by journalists. Rowland Evans and Robert Novak, *Nixon in the White House* (New York: Random House, 1971), provides first-class coverage of the first two years of the Nixon presidency. For the election campaigns, consult Joe McGinniss, *The Selling of the President* (New York: Trident Press, 1969), and two works by Theodore H. White: *The Making of the President, 1968* (New York: Atheneum, 1969), and *The Making of the President, 1972* (New York: Atheneum, 1973). John Osborn's five volumes, all published under the general title *The Nixon Watch* (New York: Liveright, 1970–74), provide some of the best journalistic coverage. James Keough, *President Nixon and the Press* (New York: Funk & Wagnalls, 1972), covers an important issue. Among the many memoirs by White House aides, two of the best are William Safire, *Before the Fall* (Garden City: Doubleday, 1975), and Raymond Price, *With Nixon* (New York: Viking, 1977). *Public Papers of the President: Richard M. Nixon* (6 vols.; Washington: U.S. Government Printing Office, 1971–75), constitute the basic documentary record.

The concept of neoconservatism and its impact on the Nixon presidency are examined in James Reichley, *Conservatives in an Age of Change* (Washington: Brookings, 1981), a fine scholarly study of the Nixon and Ford presidencies. Daniel P. Moynihan, *Coping* (New York: Random House, 1973), an episodic personal memoir of the author's White House service, *Maximum Feasible Misunderstanding* (New York: Free Press, 1969), an early critique of the Great Society, and *The Politics of a Guaranteed Income* (New York: Random House, 1972), all lay out the viewpoint of Nixon's most influential domestic advisor. Vincent J. Burke, *Nixon's Good Deed: Welfare Reform* (New York: Columbia University Press, 1974), is a scholarly account of the administration's most important domestic initiative. Kevin Phillips, *The Emerging Republican Majority* (New Rochelle: Arlington House, 1969), and Richard Scammon and Ben Wattenberg, *The Real Majority* (New York: Coward-McCann, 1970), both influenced administration political strategy. On the neoconservative impulse, see also Peter Steinfels, *The Neoconservatives* (New York: Simon & Schuster, 1969), a critical analysis, and the following representative works: Irving Kristol, *On the Democratic Idea in America* (New York: Harper & Row, 1972), and *Two Cheers for Capitalism* (New York: Basic Books, 1978); Daniel Bell, *The Cultural Contradictions of Capitalism* (New York: Basic Books, 1978); Norman Podhoretz, *Breaking Ranks* (New York: Harper & Row, 1979).

For foreign policy, see Henry Brandon, *The Retreat of American Power* (Garden City: Doubleday, 1973); Lloyd Gardner, *The Great Nixon Turn-Around* (New York: New Viewpoints, 1973); and Tad Szulc, *The Illusion of Peace* (New York: Viking, 1978). Nixon's intentions before assuming the presidency are partially laid out in "Asia after Viet Nam," *Foreign Affairs*, LXVI (October, 1967), 111–125; his post-presidential sentiments can be found in Nixon, *The Real War* (New York: Warner, 1980). Henry Kissinger's two volumes of memoirs, *White House Years* and *Years of Upheaval* (Boston: Little, Brown, 1979, 1982), are monumental, fascinating, and controversial.

There is no end to works on Watergate. Theodore H. White, *Breach of Faith* (New York: Atheneum, 1975), is the single best secondary account. Memoirs, each with a distinctive slant, abound; but many readers will find the primary sources more fascinating. Three documentary compilations by the staff of the *New York Times* are convenient and useful: *The Watergate Hearings* (New York: Viking, 1973), *The White House Transcripts* (New York: Viking, 1974), and *The End of a Presidency* (New York: Viking, 1974).

8. Ronald Reagan

The literature on Reagan is already large and threatens to grow exponentially in the first several years after his departure from the White House. One might begin with his own autobiography, *An American Life* (New York: Simon & Schuster, 1990), which builds on his *My Early Life or Where's the Rest of Me?* (London: Sigdwick & Jackson, 1965). See also Nancy Reagan *My Turn* (New York: Random House, 1989). Among the memoirs of members of the administration are Donald Regan, *For the Rec-*

ord (New York: Harcourt Brace Jovanovich, 1988); Michael Deaver, *Behind the Scenes* (New York: Morrow, 1987); David Stockman, *The Triumph of Politics* (New York: Harper & Row, 1986); Alexander Haig, *Caveat* (New York: Macmillan, 1984); and Peggy Noonan, *What I Saw at the Revolution: A Political Life in the Reagan Era* (New York: Random House, 1990).

Biographies and interpretations, mostly critical, include Betty Glad, "Reagan's Midlife Crisis and the Turn to the Right," *Political Psychology*, 10 (1989), 593–624; Anne Edwards, *Early Reagan* (New York: Morrow, 1987); Bill Boyarsky, *Ronald Reagan: His Life and Rise to the White House* (New York: Random House, 1981); Robert Dallek, *Ronald Reagan: The Politics of Symbolism* (Cambridge: Harvard University Press, 1984); Michael Paul Rogin, *Ronald Reagan the Movie, and Other Episodes of Political Demonology* (Berkeley: University of California Press, 1987); Lou Cannon, *President Reagan: His Greatest Role* (New York: Simon & Schuster, 1991); and Garry Wills, *Reagan's America: Innocents at Home* (Garden City: Doubleday, 1987). Haynes Johnson, *Sleepwalking through History* (New York: Norton, 1991), is a journalistic history of the administration as well as a biographical interpretation.

For the political events and actors between Nixon and Reagan, see, for the Ford interregnum, Gerald Ford, *A Time to Heal* (New York: Harper & Row, 1979); Jerald terHorst, *Gerald Ford and the Future of the Presidency* (New York: Third Press, 1974); and Robert Hartmann, *Palace Politics: An Insider's Account of the Ford Years* (New York: McGraw-Hill, 1980). On Carter, see Carter's own works: *Why Not the Best?* (Nashville: Broadman, 1975), *A Government as Good as Its People* (New York: Simon & Schuster, 1977), and *Keeping Faith: Memoirs of a President* (New York: Bantam, 1982). In addition, consult James Wooten, *Dasher* (New York: Summit, 1978); Betty Glad, *Jimmy Carter: In Search of the Great White House* (New York: Norton, 1980); Erwin C. Hargrove, *Jimmy Carter as President: Leadership and Politics of the Public Good* (Baton Rouge: Louisiana State University Press, 1988); Charles O. Jones, *The Trusteeship Presidency: Jimmy Carter and the United States Congress* (Baton Rouge: Louisiana State University Press, 1988); Gaddis Smith, *Morality, Reason, and Power: American Diplomacy in the Carter Years* (New York: Hill & Wang, 1986).

For the New Right, see Sidney Blumenthal, *The Rise of the Counter-Establishment* (New York: Harper & Row, 1986); David W. Reinhard, *The Republican Right since 1945* (Lexington: University Press of Kentucky, 1983); Alan Crawford, *Thunder on the Right: The "New Right" and the Politics of Resentment* (New York: Pantheon, 1981); Gilliam Peele, *Revival and Reaction: The Right in Contemporary America* (New York: Oxford University Press, 1986); Thomas Ferguson and Joel Rogers, *Right Turn: The Decline of the Democrats and the Future of American Politics* (New York: Hill & Wang, 1986); and Jerome Himmelstein, *To the Right: The Transformation of American Conservatism* (Berkeley: University of California Press, 1989).

Theodore H. White, *America in Search of Itself: The Making of the President, 1956-1980* (New York: Harper & Row, 1982), is a masterful survey of the American social and political scene from Eisenhower through Carter as well as a first-rate survey of the 1980 election. Other works on politics and elections include Everett C. Ladd, "Brittle Mandate: Electoral Dealignment and the 1980 Presidential Election," *Political Science Quarterly*, 116 (Spring, 1981), 1-25. Gerald M. Pomper et al., *The Election of 1980* (Chatham, N.J.: Chatham House, 1981); Pomper et al., *The Election of 1984* (Chatham, N.J.: Chatham House, 1985); Austin Ranney, ed., *The American Elections of 1980* (Washington: American Enterprise Institute, 1981); Ranney, ed., *The American Elections of 1984* (Durham: Duke University Press, 1985); Thomas Ferguson and Joel Rogers, eds., *The Hidden Election: Politics and Economics in the 1980 Presidential Campaign* (New York: Pantheon, 1981); Jack Germond, *Blue Smoke and Mirrors: How Reagan Won and Why Carter Lost the Election of 1980* (New York: Viking, 1981); Germond and Jules Witcover, *Wake Us When It's Over: Presidential Politics of 1984* (New York: Macmillan, 1985); Charles O. Jones, ed., *The Reagan Legacy* (Chatham, N.J.: Chatham House, 1988); Sidney Blumenthal and Thomas Edsall, eds., *The Reagan Legacy* (New York: Pantheon, 1988); Dilys Hill et al., eds., *The Reagan Presidency: An Incomplete Revolution?* (New York: St. Martin's Press, 1990); David Mervin, *Ronald Reagan and the American Presidency* (New York: Longman, 1990); David Boaz, ed., *Assessing the Reagan Years* (Washington: Cato Institute, 1988); Larry M. Schwab, *The Illusion of a Conservative Reagan Revolution* (New Brunswick:

Transaction, 1991); Jane Mayer and Doyle McManus, *Landslide: The Unmaking of the President, 1984–88* (Boston: Houghton Mifflin, 1988); and Sidney Blumenthal, *Our Long National Daydream* (New York: Harper & Row, 1988). My conclusions about Reaganomics rest heavily upon Lowell Gallaway and Richard Vedder, "The Distributional Impact of the Decade of the 1980s," scheduled for publication in *Critical Review*.

On foreign policy, see David E. Kyvig, ed., *Reagan and the World* (Westport, Conn.: Greenwood, 1990); Kenneth Oye et al., eds., *Eagle Defiant* (Boston: Little, Brown, 1983); Oye et al., eds., *Eagle Resurgent?* (Boston: Little, Brown, 1985); Morris H. Morley, ed., *Crisis and Confrontation* (Totowa, N.J.: Rowen Littlefield, 1988); Coral Bell, *The Reagan Paradox* (New Brunswick: Rutgers University Press, 1989). For sharply contrasting viewpoints, see Jonathan Kwitney, *Endless Enemies: The Making of an Unfriendly World* (New York: Congdon & Weed, 1984), and Anthony Dolan, *Undoing the Evil Empire: How Reagan Won the Cold War* (Washington: American Enterprise Institute, 1991). On relations with the USSR, see Strobe Talbott, *The Russians and Reagan* (New York: Vintage, 1984); Talbott, *Deadly Gambits* (New York: Knopf, 1984); and Seweryn Bialer and Michael Mandelbaum, eds., *Gorbachev's Russia and American Foreign Policy* (Boulder: Westview, 1988). Intriguingly, there is a far vaster literature on U.S.–Latin American relations, a representative sampling of which includes Abraham F. Lowenthal, *Partners in Conflict* (Baltimore: Johns Hopkins University Press, 1987); Lars Schoultz, *National Security and United States Policy toward Latin America* (Princeton: Princeton University Press, 1987); and Thomas W. Walker, ed., *Reagan versus the Sandinistas: The Undeclared War on Nicaragua* (Boulder: Westview, 1987).

Epilogue

It is much too early for a substantial scholarly literature on George Bush and his administration. Two early efforts are Gerald Pomper et al., *The Election of 1988* (Chatham, N.J.: Chatham House, 1989), and Colin Campbell and Bert Rockman, eds., *The Bush Presidency: First Appraisals* (Chatham, N.J.: Chatham House, 1991).

Index